WITHDRAWN

The Well Enchanting Skill

Gräfin Vergebliches Müh'n, die beiden zu trennen.
In eins verschmolzen sind Worte und Töne—

F. W. Sternfeld
(*photograph by Françoise Legrand*)

The Well Enchanting Skill

Music, Poetry, and Drama in The Culture of the Renaissance

Essays in Honour of

F. W. STERNFELD

Edited by

John Caldwell, Edward Olleson
and Susan Wollenberg

CLARENDON PRESS · OXFORD
1990

Oxford University Press, Walton Street, Oxford OX2 6DP

Oxford New York Toronto
Delhi Bombay Calcutta Madras Karachi
Petaling Jaya Singapore Hong Kong Tokyo
Nairobi Dar es Salaam Cape Town
Melbourne Auckland

and associated companies in
Berlin Ibadan

Oxford is a trade mark of Oxford University Press

Published in the United States
by Oxford University Press, New York

British Library Cataloguing in Publication Data
The Well enchanting skill: music, poetry, and drama in
the culture of Renaissance: essays in honour of F. W. Sternfeld.
1. Western music, 1400–1750
I. Caldwell, John 1938–   II. Olleson, Edward
III. Wollenberg, Susan   IV. Sternfeld, F. W.
780'.903
ISBN 0-19-316124-9

Library of Congress Cataloging in Publication Data
The Well enchanting skill: music, poetry, and drama in the culture of
the Renaissance: essays in honour of F. W. Sternfeld / edited by
John Caldwell, Edward Olleson, and Susan Wollenberg.
1. Music—17th century—History and criticism.   2. Music—16th
century—History and criticism.   3. Music and literature.
4. Sternfeld, Frederick William, 1914–   .   I. Sternfeld, Frederick
William, 1914–   .   II. Caldwell, John, 1938–   .   III. Olleson,
Edward.   IV. Wollenberg, Susan.
ML55.S832   1989   780'.9'032—dc20   89-16363
ISBN 0-19-316124-9

Photoset by Rowland Phototypesetting Ltd
Bury St Edmunds, Suffolk
Printed in Great Britain by
Bookcraft (Bath) Ltd
Midsomer Norton, Somerset

Foreword

by Sir Michael Tippett

I have known Fred Sternfeld for a long time; indeed, I can't remember precisely when, why or how we first met. I am not a scholar, so it could not have been in relation to anything covered, for instance, by the essays in this symposium.

It must have been due solely to Fred's interest in what living composers were up to: also, to his duties in the Faculty of Music at Oxford. From meeting younger generations of performers and conductors, I've indeed realized what a charismatic figure he was in his university teaching days. There is no doubt that he passed on to all his students a rare erudition, which nevertheless treated the music of all periods as something living and vital.

When I was free, I myself used to go to Oxford, at his request, to attend performances of my music and answer questions from students and others, generally in the Holywell Music Room. I came to know this room very well and feel an affection for it, because of its association with Fred. I developed a great fondness, as well as esteem, for Fred as my guide on these occasions. Generally, we would relax afterwards in the warm hospitality of his home with his wife Sophia, without whose company my visit could not have been complete.

Here I learnt what the three themes were which brought Fred and myself ever closer: opera, Shakespeare and Goethe. Fred seemed to know it all. Even in my own workroom, if I wanted help over something from Goethe, I would receive the answer simply at the touch of the telephone. I have only known now—from Sophia, I think—that Fred has total recall: from a mind stacked with experience and knowledge. Goethe was the subject of his doctoral thesis at Yale University. Much later, in the prime of his scholarship he turned to Shakespeare and music. But the *magnum opus* of his mastery will surely be his book on the origins of opera. It was heartbreaking when eye troubles seemed to make the completion of the book unlikely.

My dear Fred, now that the danger is set aside, at least to some extent, please use all your time and faculties to continue it to the end. This is what all the contributors to this collection of essays in your honour would wish. It is what close friends like myself would wish. It is certainly what Sophia would wish.

To be formal, Frederick W. Sternfeld is honoured through the essays in this book because he has been the contributor in person to so many friends, colleagues and students. Here, we find scholarship herself emulating the achievements of the man.

February 1989   Michael Tippett

Preface

A Festschrift is a slightly un-English phenomenon; and for all Fred Sternfeld's acquired and deeply treasured Englishness it is his cosmopolitan
nature that has enlivened the study of opera, of English music and poetry,
and of much else besides, in the University of Oxford during the past 30 years
and more. Rarely has a candidate for this form of scholarly approbation
been more obviously worthy of it, as the distinction of our contributors
shows. The idea of this collection of essays has been a long time in the
gestation, an inevitable feature of modern academic life. But here it is at last,
and happily coinciding with a new peak in the creativity of its dedicatee.

To cover all of Fred's multifarious interests in a single volume would have
been quite impossible. A glance at Peter Ward Jones's Bibliography will
show how widely they range. Goethe, film music and James Joyce are
amongst those represented in his earlier published work and never finally
relinquished. The connecting threads in a lifetime of musical scholarship are
drama, poetry, England and the Renaissance. They have come together most
impressively in his work on Shakespeare and on opera, and especially in
recent years on early opera and its precursors, the subject of a forthcoming
book. But no catalogue of his scholarly concerns could do justice to the
breadth of his mind, an inspiration to generations of undergraduates,
research students, and fellow teachers. The subject matter of the present
volume has been deliberately limited to the sphere of the Italian Renaissance,
and to English music, poetry, and drama of the late sixteenth and early
seventeenth centuries – two areas in which Fred Sternfeld has left a special
mark. This has meant the inevitable exclusion of many who would have
liked to join us in paying tribute to him now, but without some such
limitation no single publication would have sufficed.

Fred was born in Vienna on 25th September 1914—just after the chain of
events that ushered in the modern world had been set in motion. But his
formative years were spent in the relative stability of the post-War city; he
received a classics-based *Gymnasium* education, and from 1933 he studied
at the University with Robert Lach and Egon Wellesz. He also spent some
time in England, studying with Dent in Cambridge. His recollections of what
must have been increasingly difficult years are recounted without bitterness
—they are of singing under Strauss, of swimming the lakes and climbing the
mountains of his native Austria.

But in 1938 he emigrated to the USA, where he completed his doctorate on
Goethe and Music under Schrade at Yale (1943); he taught at the Wesleyan
University, Middletown (Conn.) from 1940 to 1946 and at Dartmouth

College, Hanover (New Hampshire) from 1946 to 1956. While at Dartmouth he taught not only music but also mathematics (to naval cadets). There he continued to pursue his remarkable range of musical interests, including a lifelong interest in modern music, but there was a decisive turn towards the study of the Renaissance and of music in Shakespearian drama. In 1948 he founded the journal *Renaissance News* which he edited until 1954.

In 1956 Fred came to England with Sophia and took up a University Lecturership at Oxford with, from 1965, a Fellowship at Exeter College; in 1972 he became Reader in the History of Music, from which he retired in 1981. To England he brought not only his wealth of scholarship but also that strong yet subtle English idiom which endeared him to so many and has proved such an effective medium in his teaching. The stream of publications continued unabated and has earned him international respect. As lecturer, tutor and supervisor he is remembered with special affection. Never, it seems, does he forget a pupil; and many who were not, formally, his pupils have been, as it were, adopted and given like support and encouragement. His lecturing, for example on Wagner's *Tristan* or Verdi's *Otello*, frequently attracted outsiders, filling the Music Faculty's lecture-rooms to capacity; and he has always been in demand as a speaker outside the Faculty, not only at international musicological events but at meetings of undergraduate clubs and learned societies to speak on all sorts of aspects of music and German, Italian or English literature. His long-lasting seminar for postgraduate students has introduced many to the disciplines of scholarship and has won him lifelong friendships.

It is difficult to imagine what English musical thinking would have been like during the last 30 years without Fred Sternfeld. Our Foreword illustrates one aspect of his wide-ranging attachments and his unassuming interest in the making of modern opera. He is a superbly knowledgeable connoisseur of that demanding art-form, bringing to bear on it not only his profound musical insight but his imaginative understanding of theatrical craft. He is both a severe critic of professional performances and a sympathetic encourager of student enterprises, knowing instinctively what can legitimately be expected at all levels. It is a rare conversation with him that does not at some point touch on Peri, or Monteverdi, or Gluck, or Mozart, Wagner, Verdi, Stravinsky or Tippett. If not that, then perhaps Ovid, Poliziano, Goethe or Stoppard. All this he has combined with devotion to research and an unfailing willingness to edit, to serve on committees, and generally to oil the wheels of scholarship.

We offer these essays in esteem and affection, wishing their recipient on his 75th birthday many more such productive years as those that have passed.

John Caldwell
Edward Olleson
Susan Wollenberg

Contents

I. MUSIC, THEATRE, AND TEXT IN THE ITALIAN RENAISSANCE

II. MUSIC AND THE THEATRE IN SEVENTEENTH-CENTURY ENGLAND

III. ENGLISH MUSIC AND ENGLISH POETRY

Contents

I
Music, Theatre, and Text in the Italian Renaissance

A Typology of Francesco Corteccia's Madrigals: Notes towards a History of Theatrical Music in Sixteenth-Century Italy

Howard Mayer Brown

IN spite of extensive preliminary studies by scholars such as Alessandro D'Ancona, Angelo Solerti, Federico Ghisi, Wolfgang Osthoff, Nino Pirrotta and, not least, Frederick Sternfeld, the history of music in the Italian theatre of the sixteenth century remains to be written.[1] Such a history will not be easy to write because of the daunting richness and diversity of the material to be studied, and because of the difficult bibliographical problems that need to be faced. In the first place, the historian of the Italian Renaissance theatre must account for differing conventions in a number of written genres: farce, comedy, tragedy, pastoral, sacred plays and so on, and he must in addition attempt the even more difficult task of assessing the role of music in the ephemeral activities of the various sixteenth-century *commedia dell'arte* troupes.[2] Moreover, many of the songs mentioned in the play texts themselves come from a repertory different from that played and sung between

---

[1] Alessandro D'Ancona, *Le origini del teatro italiano*, 2nd edn., Turin, 1891; Angelo Solerti, *Musica, ballo e drammatica alla corte medicea dal 1600 al 1637*, Florence, 1905; Federico Ghisi, *Feste musicali della Firenze medicea (1480–1589)*, Florence, 1939 (repr. 1969); Wolfgang Osthoff, *Theatergesang und darstellende Musik in der italienischen Renaissance (15. und 16. Jahrhundert)*, Tutzing, 1969; Nino Pirrotta & Elena Povoledo, *Li due Orfei. Da Poliziano a Monteverdi*, Turin, 1969 (rev. & trans. Karen Eales as *Music and Theatre from Poliziano to Monteverdi*, Cambridge, 1969); Frederick W. Sternfeld, 'Aspects of Italian Intermedi and Early Operas', *Convivium musicorum: Festschrift Wolfgang Boetticher*, ed. H. Hüschen & D. R. Moser, Berlin, 1974, pp. 367–71; idem, 'The Birth of Opera: Ovid, Poliziano and the *lieto fine*', *Analecta musicologica*, xix (1979), 30 ff.

[2] See Marvin T. Herrick, *Italian Comedy in the Renaissance*, Urbana, 1960; idem, *Comic Theory in the Sixteenth Century*, Urbana, 1964; idem, *Italian Tragedy in the Renaissance*, Urbana, 1965.

the acts as *intermedi*.[3] And the concept of 'theatrical music' must be defined broadly enough to encompass compositions performed at entertainments that took place not within the playhouse (or, more accurately, in rooms turned into theatres), but rather out of doors or in palaces or assembly rooms when plays were not being offered. That is, a history of Italian theatrical music will need to account for compositions commissioned and performed in connection with banquets, processions and mythological tableaux, performed in the streets, in palace courtyards, on rivers and in other outdoor locations, and intended for the entertainment of distinguished guests, the celebration of important events in the history of ruling families and for a variety of other kinds of civic, courtly and state occasions.[4]

The bibliographical difficulties in writing such a history will be immense, if only because the surviving play texts and the accounts of dramatic performances list and describe so much music that no longer exists, and because so much theatrical music hidden among the works of the madrigalists cannot be associated with particular events. The knowledge of so much dramatic music now lost should, of course, be used as evidence in evaluating the past, for we have more information about the proportion of surviving to lost compositions intended for Italian dramatic occasions than for almost any other repertory of the late Middle Ages and the Renaissance. The extant music commissioned for and first performed at unidentified (and probably unidentifiable) theatrical events has hardly been studied at all, perhaps because to do so involves more speculation and hypothesis than scholars feel they should indulge in. The fact remains, however, that we need to sift through the works of all the madrigalists to try to distinguish compositions written for dramatic occasions from the rest before we can begin to assess the character and extent of theatrical music in the Renaissance, a task I wish to begin in this essay by considering the kinds of madrigals Francesco Corteccia wrote and by attempting to identify those most likely to have been composed for dramatic or political occasions.

The secular music of Corteccia forms an ideal repertory for a study of the social uses of the sixteenth-century madrigal, if only because the composer spent his entire life in Florence and seems to have enjoyed particularly close

---

[3] On the music performed in the plays themselves see Pirrotta, *Music and Theatre*, pp. 76–119. On *intermedi* see Nino Pirrotta, 'Intermedium', *MGG*, vi. 1310–26; Elena Polvoledo, 'Intermezzo: Dalle origini al secolo XVIII, Italia', *Enciclopedia dello Spettacolo*, vi. 572–6; and David Nutter, 'Intermedio', *The New Grove*, ix. 258–69.

[4] On Florentine (and other) dramatic entertainments of various kinds, see *Les Fêtes de la Renaissance*, ed. Jean Jacquot, Paris, 1954–75, esp. Michel Plaisance, 'La Politique culturelle de Côme Ier et les fêtes annuelles à Florence de 1541 à 1550', iii. 133–52; A. M. Nagler, *Theatre Festivals of the Medici, 1539–1637*, New Haven, 1964; *Il luogo teatrale a Firenze . . . Firenze, Palazzo Medici Riccardi, Museo Medicea, 31 maggio/31 ottobre 1975* (exhibition catalogue), ed. Mario Fabbri, Elvira Garbero Zorzi & Anna Maria Petrioli Tofani ('Spettacolo e musica nella Firenze Medicea, Documenti e restituzioni', i), Milan, 1975; and *Il potere e lo spazio. La scena del principe: Firenze e la Toscana dei Medici nell'Europa del Cinquecento* (exhibition catalogue), Milan, 1980.

ties with the ruling Medici family, especially Duke Cosimo I.[5] Corteccia seems to have produced compositions regularly for the Florentine State from the 1530s onwards.[6] As a member of the Florentine Academy and the *de facto* official composer to the Medici he is the very model of a musical courtier, and thus more committed than most of his contemporaries to the composition of dramatic and political music, genres more closely related to one another in sixteenth-century Italy than in many other periods. Moreover, there seems no reason to challenge Alfred Einstein's speculation that Corteccia took unusual pains to prepare the publication of his own madrigals.[7] He reissued his first volume of madrigals *a* 4 (published originally in 1544) in 1547, the same year that saw the publication of a second volume along with his only book of madrigals *a* 5 and *a* 6.[8] Although his music was confused with that by Arcadelt in anthologies of the 1530s and 1540s, few of his madrigals not included in the three volumes he edited were ever published.[9] Thus virtually the entire corpus of his surviving secular music appeared in print in 1547, when he was about 45 years old. That fact, too, simplifies the study of the composer's intentions with regard to his music, for it focuses the attention narrowly on a particular time and place: Florence from the restoration of the Medici in 1530—and especially

[5] See Mario Fabbri, 'La vita e l'ignota opera-prima di Francesco Corteccia musicista italiano del Rinascimento', *Chigiana*, n.s. 2, xxii. (1965), 185–217.

[6] See Alfred Einstein, *The Italian Madrigal*, trans. Alexander H. Krappe, Roger H. Sessions & Oliver Strunk, Princeton, 1949, i. 278–88. Einstein surely exaggerates in claiming (p. 283) that the theatrical pieces are altogether different from the madrigals proper, implying that they are all artless, homophonic and cut up by rests in all the voices. For the music of the Florentine courtly *intermedi* of 1539 with music by Corteccia see note 10 below. On the music for the courtly *intermedi* in Florence in 1565, with music by Corteccia which no longer survives, see Pirrotta, *Music and Theatre*, pp. 176–82.

[7] *The Italian Madrigal*, i. 276, 278.

[8] Modern edition in *Music of the Florentine Renaissance*, ed. Frank A. D'Accone ('Corpus mensurabilis musicae', xxxii), viii–x: *Francesco Corteccia: Collected Secular Works*, American Institute of Musicology, 1981. Madrigals are referred to hereafter by volume and by item within the volume: I = First Book *a* 4; II = Second Book *a* 4; III = Third Book *a* 5 & *a* 6.

[9] On the madrigals attributed to Arcadelt and others that Corteccia published in his three volumes see D'Accone in Corteccia, *Secular Works*, I, p. xiii. For madrigals that have at least one attribution to Corteccia but do not appear in any of his three books see *The Anthologies of Black-Note Madrigals*, ed. Don Harrán ('Corpus mensurabilis musicae', lxxiii), American Institute of Musicology, 1978–80: 'Con lei fuss'io', *sestina* plus *envoi* by Petrarch (I/2, No. 36); 'Donna vostra beltà', *ottava rima* (I/2, No. 33); 'Non ved'hoggi', canzone-madrigal, probably by Pietro Bracharaio (I/2, No. 29); 'Perche la vita e breve', incomplete canzone by Petrarch (I/2, No. 31); 'Se per honesti preghi', madrigal (II, No. 9); and 'Vivace fianna che con dubbia speme', ballata-madrigal (I/2, No. 30). 'Alma perche si trist', attributed both to Arcadelt and to Corteccia (but not in any of Corteccia's own volumes) is in Jacques Arcadelt, *Opera omnia*, ed. Albert Seay ('Corpus mensurabilis musicae', xxxi), II (American Institute of Musicology, 1970), No. 3. 'Oyme mort'e il bel viso' is attributed to Corteccia in *RISM* 1541/15, No. 30, but does not appear in any of his three books. I have found no madrigals by Corteccia using musical material from settings of the same texts by other composers, but this is a subject that needs further study.

after Cosimo's accession to power in 1537—to 1547, the year in which Corteccia's madrigals came off the presses in Venice.

Two cycles of theatrical music are well known among Corteccia's works: the seven madrigals on poems by Giovambattista Strozzi used as *intermedi* for a performance of Antonio Landi's *Il Commodo* given as a part of the celebrations in 1539 for the wedding of Cosimo I to Eleonora of Toledo,[10] and the five madrigals on poems by Ugolino Martelli intended for a performance of Francesco d'Ambra's *Il Furto* by the Accademia Fiorentina in 1544.[11] In addition, the booklet issued to commemorate the events of 1539 also includes the compositions by Corteccia and others for the entrance of Eleonora into Florence and for the couple's bridal banquet.[12] The two sets of madrigals for comedies exemplify the two most important kinds of early sixteenth-century *intermedi*: in the first place the aulic or courtly *intermedi* (to borrow Pirrotta's term), presented with elaborate costumes and stage machinery, each tableau sung and played by a different group of often mythological characters, the sort of *intermedi* mounted only for very special occasions of state; and in the second place the simpler *intermedi* performed between the acts of virtually every learned comedy from the 1520s onwards, straightforward cycles of madrigals presumably sung by the same group of musicians at the end of each act.[13] It is altogether characteristic of the two types that for the one a souvenir booklet was issued to describe the events in detail and to give Corteccia's music, and that for the other no evidence at all survives in any of the texts of the plays to indicate that such a performance took place. We know about it only from the madrigal books themselves.

Whereas much attention has been paid to the elaborate courtly *intermedi*, the rather more frequently performed sets of madrigals intended for normal comedies have been relatively neglected in scholarly literature, doubtless at least in part because they are so ephemeral and so difficult to identify. Besides those for *Il Furto*, we know of three incomplete sets of madrigals written for comedies in the first half of the sixteenth century: those composed presumably by Verdelot for two of Machiavelli's plays, *La Clizia* and *La Mandragola* (two of the four surviving madrigals are the same for both plays), and a cycle of four madrigals by Arcadelt identified through the

---

[10] The festivities are discussed in detail and all the music is given in *A Renaissance Entertainment*, ed. Andrew C. Minor & Bonner Mitchell, Columbia, 1968. See also Bonner Mitchell, *Italian Civic Pageantry in the High Renaissance: A Descriptive Bibliography of Triumphal Entries and Selected Other Festivals for State Occasions*, Florence, 1979, pp. 50–54.

[11] The madrigals for *Il Furto* are in Corteccia, *Secular Works*, I, 37–41. On the 1544 performance, see *Il luogo teatrale*, pp. 83–4.

[12] Ed. Minor & Mitchell, *A Renaissance Entertainment*, pp. 97–223.

[13] For a summary of the kinds of *intermedi* presented in the sixteenth century—those in which the music was played out of sight of the audience ('intermedi non apparenti'), those that were staged ('intermedi apparenti'), those that consisted only of instrumental music, those that consisted of *moresche* and *mascherate*, and so on—see Nutter, 'Intermedio'.

nature of their texts as theatrical by Osthoff and Pirrotta, although there is no way of knowing for which comedy the music was originally intended.[14]

The function of the *intermedi* was simply to mark the act breaks, either by suggesting the passage of time or by commenting on the preceding or following action.[15] In this respect Corteccia's music for *Il Furto* is typical. To some extent it comments directly on the play.[16] In the first madrigal, 'Udendo ragionar che qui si denno' (I, 37), sung after the prologue, the singers, who identify themselves as gypsies (presumably the personae they maintained for the other *intermedi* as well), mention 'il furto', and in the last madrigal, 'O come nulla vale' (I, 41), sung after Act IV, they anticipate the happy denouement by announcing that it will come about through the return of a man from Spain (that is, Maestro Cornelio's long lost son Valerio). The remaining three madrigals, although they relate to events in the play, do not allude directly to any of the characters. 'Quanto sia dolce voglia' (I, 38), sung after Act I, on man's desire to propagate himself, clearly refers (though without mentioning him) to the old doctor Cornelio and his wish for a young wife and a new heir; it is obviously theatrical, since it addresses the audience directly. 'Non le parol'o l'herbe' and 'A gran torto si lagna' (I, 39 and 40), sung after Acts II and III, on the parlous state of being in love, are about the young lovers Mario and Camilla, although the poems could be taken as being about love in general; they contain no specific references to the play.

The middle three madrigals for *Il Furto* could be performed as they stand as *intermedi* in any one of a number of comedies, so stereotyped are the dramatic situations in Italian Renaissance comedy, and so general are the words set to Corteccia's music. Indeed, it may be that madrigals used as *intermedi* were to some extent interchangeable; they were not always composed specially for a particular play or for a particular performance. Machiavelli, for example, used some of the same madrigals for both *La Mandragola* and *La Clizia*, and in 1568 Antonfrancesco Grazzini (Il Lasca) wrote in the preface to his new edition of *La gelosia* that he was including for the first time the *intermedi* originally written for the play but not published in

---

[14] On the Verdelot *intermedi* for Machiavelli's plays see Osthoff, *Theatergesang*, i. 213–37, and H. Colin Slim, *A Gift of Madrigals and Motets*, Chicago & London, 1972, i. 85, 92–104; the music given there, ii. 333–5, 347–9, should be emended by the altus parts published in Slim, *Ten Altus Parts at Oscott College Sutton Coldfield*, Santa Ana, 1978. On Arcadelt madrigals presumed to be *intermedi* see Osthoff, *Theatergesang*, i. 270–74, and Pirrotta, *Music and Theatre*, pp. 124–5, 151. The four madrigals are published in Arcadelt, *Opera omnia*, IV, Nos. 6, 8, 14 and 17. Einstein (*The Italian Madrigal*, i. 282) seems to imply that Corteccia set *intermedi* for plays by Giovan Maria Cecchi. Texts for the *intermedi* survive for the following plays by Cecchi: *Il donzello* (Venice, 1585), *L'esaltazione della croce* (Florence, 1589), *Il servigiale* (Florence, 1561) and *Lo spirito* (Venice, 1585), but none includes texts set by Corteccia.

[15] See Pirrotta, *Music and Theatre*, esp. pp. 120–72.

[16] The play is in *Commedie del Cinquecento*, ed. Aldo Borlenghi, ii (Milan, 1959), 7–113.

the first edition of 1551 because they had not been performed at the première.[17] The nature of Corteccia's madrigals for *Il Furto* and of some of the other sets of *intermedi* gives us some confidence, then, to suppose that Corteccia included his cycle in the second edition of his first book of madrigals *a 4* not only against the possibility of revivals of that play, or merely to commemorate a particularly memorable performance. Rather, it seems likely that he wished to have them in his selected secular works to serve as models for other similar cycles, and because they could be used in other plays or simply as madrigals like any others.

If the texts of a set of *intermedi* for a 'normal' comedy need not be unified in subject matter or closely connected with the plot of the play, so likewise the music need not share common elements, to judge from the four surviving sets. If the same group of singers was to perform a whole set, of course, all the madrigals will be notated in the same or similar clefs. Thus, four of the five madrigals for *Il Furto* are in so-called high clefs (G2, C2, C3, F3), implying presumably the collaboration of women as singers (like the group formed by the beautiful Barbera Salutati for the performances of Machiavelli's *La Clizia* and *La Mandragola*). But not even all the clefs need be the same throughout a set of madrigals intended for the same play.[18] That the fifth madrigal for *Il Furto*, 'O come nulla vale' (I, 41), has a set of clefs different from the others (C2, C3, C4, F4) means either that the personnel of the group changed slightly or that the same singers were constrained to display their versatility of vocal range.

Sets of madrigals for normal *intermedi* need not all be in the same mode or tonal type; two of the five madrigals from *Il Furto*, for example, are in D-Dorian with one flat, and the remaining three represent G-Dorian, C and F modes.[19] Such madrigal cycles are not all set to the same verse type. For example, D'Accone describes two of the madrigals in *Il Furto* as madrigals proper, two as ballata-madrigals and one as a canzone-madrigal.[20] Theatrical madrigals, in other words, include all the verse types found in regular madrigal anthologies; there seems not to be a kind of poem specially connected with *intermedi*. And sets of *intermedi* madrigals do not all have

---

[17] 'Perche gli intermedi, che si recitarono nella presente commedia, non furono quello ch'erano ordinati per lei . . . noi nel ristamparla habbiamo dal compositore avuto i propri ed gli abbiamo aggiunti, e cavatone quelli altri' (p. 11).

[18] Since the so-called courtly *intermedi* involve new groups of actors and musicians for each tableau, they do not all have the same clefs throughout. See, for example, those by Corteccia for the *intermedi* of 1539 in Minor & Mitchell, *A Renaissance Entertainment*.

[19] The mode or tonal type with final on D and a signature of one flat is rare in Corteccia's music, but it is clearly to be distinguished from the compositions on D without a signature. Apart from the madrigals in *Il Furto*, there are only two others in Corteccia's three books with a final on D and a signature of one flat: I, 3 (*a voce pari* with clefs C4 C4 C4 F4) and III, 8 (built around a canon, and with so-called high clefs like the madrigals from *Il Furto*).

[20] In the critical notes to Corteccia, *Secular Works*, D'Accone gives the verse type for each madrigal.

the same musical texture. While two of Corteccia's madrigals for *Il Furto*, 'Udendo ragionar' (I, 37) and 'Quanto sia dolce voglia' (I, 38), for example, are entirely homophonic or very nearly so, the other three all include passages in imitative polyphony.

Even more than 'normal' madrigals, those intended for the theatre need to project their words, which is why the madrigals for *Il Furto* are as homophonic as they are, although the presence of so many chordal passages hardly begins to explain how Corteccia conveys the meaning of the words to his listeners across the footlights. The fact that all the madrigals for *Il Furto* are notated in C—they are *note nere* madrigals—contributes more towards an understanding of Corteccia's technique for projecting words, since the *note nere* style was devised in the late 1530s, shortly before these madrigals were composed, presumably to allow composers a greater variety of note values and hence more changes in pace from one phrase to the next, just in order that the words could be more effectively declaimed.[21] In 'Non le parol'o l'herbe' (I, 39), for example, the third madrigal for *Il Furto* (see Ex. 1.1), Corteccia communicates the words of the poem more by changes of pace and texture than simply by writing homophonic passages. The first two lines of the poem, moving largely in crotchets, are each set to a point of imitation. The succeeding antiphonal passage, on 'venenoso liquore' (bar 9), speeds up; it moves in quavers and even semiquavers, and three of the four voices declaim the words together in the same rhythm, which helps to clarify the sense of the rather complicated sentence by placing emphasis on its subject. Moreover, the change of texture marks the important cadence at the end of the first major musical section. The homophony of 'ponno saldar quell' amorosa piaga' (bar 12) brings the listener's attention to the main verb of the whole stanza. Finally, after more declamation in quavers, the pace slows down again, and the melodic line reaches its high point with the long homophonic passage (beginning in bar 17) that marks the rhetorical climax of the poem at the line 'Ma sol animo pronto, aldac'et forte': it is only the ready, courageous and strong soul that can cure love's wound.

The melodic lines of 'Non le parol'o l'herbe' are slightly incoherent considered independently of the words, although not perhaps quite as formulaic as in many of Corteccia's madrigals.[22] Corteccia does not write

---

[21] See James Haar, 'The *Note Nere* Madrigal', *Journal of the American Musicological Society*, xviii (1965), 22–41, and Don Harrán, 'Some Early Examples of the madrigale cromatico', *Acta musicologica*, xli (1969), 240–46. All the compositions in the anthologies devoted to *note nere* madrigals are published in *The Anthologies of Black-Note Madrigals*.

[22] Formulaic in that the melodies go over the same ground repeatedly, as in 'Se ben par dur'et grave' (I, 9), which might be described as a composition in which the superius descends from g' to d' and then makes a cadence formula (complete or incomplete) on g' approached from the $b'b$ above (making the phrase from bar 21 to bar 24, which ascends as high as d'', a striking adventure), or 'Felici et lieti giorni' (II, 41), in which the superius does almost nothing but descend stepwise from c'' either to b', a' or g'.

Ex. 1.1

elegantly balanced phrases that combine to form a beautifully proportioned structure. Instead, he moves his relatively short-breathed phrases now quickly, now slowly, now high and now low to enhance and support the meaning (or perhaps better said the rhetorical flow) of the words, producing what might reasonably be described as the 'contorted rhythms' that Pirrotta complains of.[23] In effect the composer establishes a fixed reading of the poem. In deciding which words and phrases to emphasize, Corteccia all but ignores poetic structure. Lines 4–6 of 'Non le parol'o l'herbe', for example, 'Ch'a tal uso ... nel core' (bb. 11–16), parallel lines 1–3; both tercets alternate lines of seven, eleven and seven syllables, and both have the same rhymes: *abc*. But the musical setting of the two tercets are not related melodically, and Corteccia does not even build the phrases in the two passages in the same way.[24] Each moves at a different pace, and each is shaped in quite a different way, according to which words and phrases Corteccia thought it important to stress (the first tercet as two points of imitation followed by a brief antiphonal closing, the second tercet as three short fast-moving phrases, the second with a homophonic opening, the whole serving as preliminary to the slower-moving homophonic highpoint of the piece at bars 17–22).

It is true but over-simple to say merely that Corteccia closes each line with a cadence. A more acute assessment of his qualities as a composer will note that he groups phrases together, reserving the most striking or most perfect cadences for ends of sections: bars 10, 16 and 22, for example, in 'Non le parol'o l'herbe'.[25] He uses, in other words, a kind of musical enjambment to help clarify the shape and meaning of the words. At the most important cadences the tenor moves from the second to the first degree of the scale, and the superius from the seventh to the eighth.[26] Nevertheless, we cannot speak in Corteccia's music of a 'superius–tenor framework' of the sort so familiar from fifteenth-century music by northern European composers, for in 'Non le parol'o l'herbe', and indeed in all of Corteccia's other madrigals *a 4*, fourths abound between superius and tenor, and the two voices together do

[23] *Music and Theatre*, p. 236.

[24] Corteccia is not inspired to repeat the music even when he repeats the words 'che non teme di morte' in bars 19–22. The superius–bass orientation of these madrigals may well be Corteccia's heritage from the frottolists. On the way that Corteccia all but ignores the form of poetry 'in favor of meaning and impassioned delivery' see Einstein, *the Italian Madrigal*, i. 288.

[25] A more refined sense is needed of how and where cadences occur and how they are correlated with the syntax both of the words and of the music. Cadences do not always take the form the theorists describe. In 'Non le parol'o l'herbe', for example, both the cadence at the end and that in bar 22 are clearly very important (that in bar 22 since all motion stops after it, since it is prepared by repetition of the words, and since it divides the music and the poem into two halves), yet neither follows the paradigm given by most sixteenth-century theorists.

[26] On the cadence formulas appropriate to each voice in sixteenth-century polyphony, see Bernhard Meier, *Die Tonarten der klassischen Vokalpolyphonie*, Utrecht, 1974, pp. 75–86.

not make self-sufficient or satisfactory two-part counterpoint. Instead, the superius and bassus form the contrapuntal framework of the music. It is striking, for example, how often in 'Non le parol'o l'herbe' the bassus (rather than the tenor) has the most exact (or indeed the only) imitation with the superius.[27] Yet it would be true to say that the tenor nevertheless determines the mode, as sixteenth-century theorists say, because of the nature of the most important cadences (except, quite strikingly in 'Non le parol'o l'herbe', at the very last cadence), because the tenor emphasizes modally important notes (g, c' and g', but also d'), and also because of the ranges of each voice and their relationship to one another. That is, in 'Non le parol'o l'herbe' the ranges of the superius and tenor clearly operate within the plagal form of the C mode, the altus and bassus within the authentic.[28] It seems clear that Corteccia himself would have labelled the madrigal a representation of the plagal form of the transposed sixth mode.

The *intermedi* for *Il Furto* (and the theatrical cycles by Arcadelt and Verdelot), in short, do not differ in any way, either prosodically or musically, from any of Corteccia's other madrigals. While they are slightly more homophonic than normal madrigals, they are written in a variety of musical textures. The madrigals for *Il Furto* are all through-composed, but those for the 1539 *intermedi* and the cycles by Arcadelt and Verdelot include some with formally significant repetition. To judge from these cycles, theatrical compositions represent a variety of verse types. All the madrigals for *Il Furto* but only half of those for the 1539 *intermedi* (and none of the theatrical cycles by Arcadelt and Verdelot) were written in *note nere*, so neither the manner of notation nor the style associated with it would appear to be relevant in determining theatrical intention.[29] Within each theatrical cycle the same or similar clefs are used, but they are quite different between one set and the next, so it is clear that there was no fixed convention about the grouping of singers appropriate for theatrical performances; women were included as well as all-male groups. Nor are the theatrical cycles tonally unified, which explains why the 1539 *intermedi* are scattered throughout Corteccia's three volumes, all of which are modally ordered.[30]

[27] Corteccia commonly gives the bass the only imitation or the closest imitation with the superius. In the first book of madrigals *a* 4, for example, the opening point of imitation uses that disposition of voices in the following madrigals: Nos. 4, 5, 8, 11, 14, 17, 24, 28, 29 and 34.

[28] The ranges are superius $g'-f''$ (plagal form); altus $g-c''$ (but g is reached only once, and the voice moves mostly between c' and c'', that is, in the authentic form of the octave); tenor $g-a'$ (plagal form); bassus $c-c'$ (authentic form).

[29] Since Corteccia's *note nere* madrigals are apparently scattered at random throughout his three volumes, it seems clear that he himself did not regard the style as a suitable criterion for ordering his works.

[30] Corteccia follows the principles outlined in Harold S. Powers, 'Tonal Types and Modal Categories', *Journal of the American Musicological Society*, xxxiv (1981), 428–70, and Powers, 'Modal Representation in Polyphonic Offertories', *Early Music History*, ii (1982), 43–86. Corteccia's first book *a* 4 is especially interesting since the reissue of 1547 is in a slightly different order from the original edition of three years before. The principles he followed will

Since there was no special madrigalian type or musical style appropriate only for the theatre, we need to survey all of Corteccia's madrigals before we can attempt to suggest which of them might have been written for some dramatic entertainment, and to do that it is convenient to consider them according to verse type (even though that division is unlikely to be relevant to their theatrical intention) as well as by subject matter. It is clear that the typology by verse type suggested by Don Harrán for Verdelot and for the anthologies of *note nere* madrigals applies to Corteccia as well.[31] Like Verdelot, Corteccia set a few sonnets and stanzas in *ottava rima* and a number of ballate, canzone stanzas, and madrigals proper, as well as poems that rather resemble ballate and canzone (what Harrán and D'Accone call ballata-madrigals and canzone-madrigals) and a single exceptional epitaph in the form of a quatrain.[32]

To get a more sharply focused view of Corteccia's style and of the nature of his madrigals, however, we need to correlate the verse types with musical form.[33] Madrigals that are through-composed—without any formally significant repetition—all reflect the same attitude on the part of the composer towards setting words to music, whether they are ballate, ballata-madrigals, sonnet fragments or whatever. In some madrigals, on the other hand, the composer has repeated sections of music to new lines of text. In these he has taken a more purely formal attitude towards the poem he set, without creating a kind of music in every case appropriate only to one particular set of words. He has made the structure of the music reflect in one way or another the form of the poem.

It is hardly surprising that Corteccia wrote more through-composed madrigals than any other kind, given our assumptions that the whole aesthetic point of the new genre was to cultivate a kind of music without schematic repetition, in which the new poetical content of each strophe is matched by new music.[34] The absence of formally significant repetition, however, does not mean either that the composer never repeated his musical material, or that he failed to shape his musical fabric satisfactorily. In 'Vidi

---

be the subject of another essay. The madrigals for *Il Furto*, an addition to the later reprinting, are an exception to the rule of modal ordering in being grouped together at the end of the volume.

[31] See Don Harrán, 'Verse Types in the Early Madrigal', *Journal of the American Musicological Society*, xxii (1969), 27–53.

[32] 'Se qui non chiusi' (II, 18) sets a quatrain by Michelangelo 'in memory of the fifteen-year old Francesco Bracci, who died in Rome on 8 January 1544' (quoted from D'Accone's edition of the second book *a* 4, p. xviii).

[33] Virtually all of Corteccia's madrigals have end repetition (that is, with the last line or two of text and music repeated to make a formal closure), a feature we can therefore ignore in considering form.

[34] Pirrotta, *Music and Theatre*, p. 145. The following madrigals *a* 4 by Corteccia are through-composed: I, Nos. 1, 3, 5, 6, 7, 8, 10, 15, 16, 18, 27, 28, 30, 32, 36, 37, 38, 39, 40, 41 and 42; II, Nos. 3, 4, 6, 10, 11, 12, 13, 14, 15, 17, 18, 19, 22, 23, 24, 25, 26, 28, 29, 30, 32, 33, 38, 40 and 41.

Ex. 1.2

fra l'herbe verde' (I, 30—see Ex. 1.2), for instance, the music falls clearly into three sections, each consisting of two balanced phrases, the first ending on the fifth degree of the scale, C, and the second on the final, F.[35] The musical form is at odds with the form of the verse. The poem has eight lines rhyming *aabcbcdd* (that is, divided into 2 + 4 + 2 lines); Corteccia, however, divided it as though it consisted of 2 + 3 + 3 lines, with the more important cadences occurring in bars 9 and 18, and musical enjambment joining lines 4 and 5 and lines 6 and 7. The music ignores the rhyme scheme in favour of the flow of ideas.

The first section (bars 1–9), announcing the presence of a white ermine in the grass, consists of a properly formal opening point of imitation followed by antiphonal duets that expand to give emphasis to the words 'bianch' hermellin'. Homophony seems more appropriate for the narrative second section (bars 10–18), in which the poet describes how the ermine ran to hide, although here Corteccia has included a madrigalism for the word (and the idea) 'suavemente', slowing down the motion slightly and offering a suitably suave harmonic progression. In the third section (bar 19 to the end) the poet runs after the ermine, which hides 'where I would lose myself' ('ond'io perdei me stesso'); the music first offers a diminution of the beginning, an obvious madrigalism illustrating 'velocemente' rather than a formal recognition of any element of the poetic structure, and then the madrigal ends with a straightforward declaration of its final line (varied on repetition) in a polyphony (or rather antiphony) characteristically devoid of imitation.[36]

As in many (perhaps most) Corteccia madrigals, the melody of 'Vidi fra l'herbe verde' seems to go over the same confined melodic space again and again, though not perhaps as much as in some madrigals, such as 'Poichè l'empia mia sorte' (II, 23), in which the voice presents virtually every permutation of the fourth between a' and e', so that the great melodic events of the piece are the occasional descents to d' or ascents to c'' (Ex. 1.3). In this madrigal, moreover, a number of phrases begin with a motto anticipation, and some phrases repeat a motif several times, both techniques that are hallmarks of Corteccia's melodic style, in its declamatory nature still palpably grounded in the earlier techniques of the frottola.[37]

Somewhat related in aesthetic outlook to the earlier frottola, too, are those madrigals that hark back to the schematic repetition schemes of the canzone or ballata, that is, those madrigals with formally significant repetition, in which either some part of the opening phrases returns at the end (the ballata

[35] The bass in 'Vidi fra l'herbe verde' does not imitate the superius more exactly than the other voices, as in so many of Corteccia's other madrigals (see note 27).

[36] The poem is presumably a masked love poem: the poet would lose himself in the person of his ermine-clad lady.

[37] Both Einstein (*The Italian Madrigal*, i. 284) and Pirrotta (*Music and Theatre*, p. 167) point out resemblances between some of Corteccia's madrigals and the style of the frottola. Pirrotta comments on the frottolistic harmonic orientation of the 1539 *intermedi* as well as on their formulaic declamation.

Ex. 1.3

scheme), or the second couplet of text is sung to the same music as the first (the canzone scheme). The second largest group of Corteccia's madrigals *a 4* consists of those in which some part of the opening section returns at the end, a group that comprises all the ballate Corteccia set and many of the ballata-madrigals, but includes some madrigals proper as well.[38] In many of them only the third phrase of the opening section serves as a refrain at the end, to give the madrigal a slightly clearer and more sharply profiled musical form. Madrigals in which the second couplet of text is set to the same music as the first make up a much smaller group.[39] These canzone-like madrigals invariably comprise those with opening couplets rhyming *abab* (not always, however, those analysed by D'Accone as canzone or canzone-madrigals).

Among Corteccia's madrigals a few follow other formal principles than those just enumerated. There are two settings of stanzas in *ottava rima*, for example, one of them ('S'io potessi voler'—II, 37) anonymous and the second ('Io dico e dissi'—II, 31) from Ariosto's *Orlando furioso*, in which a reciting formula is repeated in the top voice over and over again. Corteccia has added polyphony beneath the given voice to create sets of variations. The setting of the anonymous stanza offers a melodic line in its top voice that James Haar has identified as a melody known from other similar madrigals.[40] Quite possibly, then, Corteccia made further use of traditional airs which we have not recognized. In several madrigals he acknowledged in his music the stanzaic character of the poem in yet other ways. Both of the quatrains in the sonnet 'Liet'et beati spirti' (I, 11), for example, end with the same music, and the two tercets have their own refrain different from that of the quatrains; clear cadences, with complete stops, mark the ends of each stanza. The internal strophes of 'Non so per qual cagion' (I, 17), on the other hand, are repeated, while the beginning and the end of the madrigal are unrelated to each other. 'Madre de'dolci amori' (II, 13) is through-composed, but each of its stanzas is marked with an unusually clear-cut cadence, with a complete stop afterwards. The musical organization of 'Se vostr'occhi lucenti' (II, 5) involves the repetition over and over again in constantly shifting order of the five notes between c' and g' in the top voice.[41]

No matter how important it is to correlate verse type and musical form in order to understand Corteccia's personal style, however, the verse types do

---

[38] I, Nos. 4, 12, 13, 14, 19, 20, 21, 22, 24, 26, 29, 31, 33, 34 and 35; II, Nos. 1, 2, 7, 8, 9, 16, 27, 34, 35 and 36.

[39] I, Nos. 2, 9 and 23; II, Nos. 20 and 39.

[40] 'Arie per cantar stanze ariostesche', *L'Ariosto: la musica, i musicisti: Quattro studi e sette madrigali ariosteschi*, ed. Maria Antonella Balsano, Florence, 1981, pp. 41–3; also Einstein, *The Italian Madrigal*, i. 285.

[41] D'Accone does not label 'Liet'et beati spirti' a sonnet. Other madrigals with unusually clear recognition of the stanzaic structure include 'Con quel coltel col qual gia t'uccidesti' (II, 21), 'Io vorrei pur fuggir, crudel amor' (I, 25) and 'O begli anni de l'oro' (II, 11). On 'Se vostr'occhi lucenti', see James Haar, 'A Sixteenth-Century Hexachord Composition', *Journal of Music Theory*, xii (1975), 32–45.

not reveal theatrical intention or even the attitude he and his contemporaries in the 1530s and 1540s had towards their texts. Rather, it is the subject matter of the madrigals—quite simply whether or not they deal with love in the first person singular—that will tell us best whether or not a particular madrigal was intended for the theatre. Like his contemporaries, Corteccia mostly set poems that treat of love: happy, unhappy, fulfilled or unfulfilled. Almost all the poets whose works he set remain unidentified, a situation that will surely gradually change as we catalogue and study more of the poetic sources of the sixteenth century. The few poets we know are Florentines (except for Ariosto): Lorenzo Strozzi, Giovambattista Strozzi, Ugolino Martelli and Antonfrancesco Grazzini (Il Lasca).[42] Unlike many of his contemporaries, Corteccia set only a few poems from Petrarch's Canzoniere, and those few he treated as special cases, such as the unusually madrigalistic and modally sophisticated 'Gionto m'ha amor' (I, 15), the gravely animated motet-like 'Quel foco ch'io pensai' (III, 14) and the canonic five-voice 'Perch'io veggio et mi spiace' (III, 12).[43]

As we might expect, the love poems either extol the beloved or complain of her cruelty or indifference. Invariably the poet speaks in the first person: 'I' praise or complain about 'my' lady. In some of the poems, however, love is treated in more joking or ironic terms (a poetic tone not always easy to catch, at least not for us *oltremontani*), as for instance in the madrigal about the high cost of loving, 'Donna fra più bei volti honesti et cari' (I, 34), or that extolling the courtesans of Florence, 'Non so per qual cagion l'alma mia donna' (I, 17). In some the play of words appears to be more important than any expression of emotion, as in Lorenzo Strozzi's debate between hating and loving, 'S'io v'odiasse, madonna' (II, 9), or the anonymous *ottava* 'S'io potessi voler quel ch'io non posso' (II, 37), juxtaposing having ('potere') and wanting ('volere'). A few madrigals, moreover, are clearly dedicatory, at least three of them intended for the first ladies of Florence and doubtless sung from time to time, if not commissioned for and first performed, at official banquets or other festivities. The new Helen who is compared with Helen of Troy in 'Se Grecia si fe'tanto nominare' (I, 21) can only be Cosimo's bride Eleonora of Toledo, and 'Poichè ci siamo affaticati' (II, 33) explicitly praises 'unica Leonora'.[44] Moreover, given that 'margherita' means 'daisy' in Italian, the new flower that adorns the Arno in 'Nuovo fior'e apparso al

[42] For information about the poets of Corteccia's madrigals so far identified see the critical notes in D'Accone's edition.
[43] See also 'A voi rigolgo il mio debile stile' (I, 10), 'Nessun visse gia mai' (III, 17) and 'S'honest'amor' (III, 21). Neither 'A voi' nor 'Perch'io veggio' is identified by D'Accone as by Petrarch; see *Petrarch's Lyric Poems. The Rime sparse and Other Lyrics*, trans. & ed. Robert M. Durling, Cambridge, Mass., 1976, Poems 71 and 72, where they are inner stanzas of canzoni. On 'Quel foco' see Einstein, *The Italian Madrigal*, i. 287–8.
[44] Two other madrigals can be described as dedicatory: 'So ben, lasso, et ogn'hor men dolgo' (II, 40), which pits the low-born 'legno' against the high-born lady 'alloro'; and Ariosto's *ottava* 'Alcun non puo saper da chi sia amato' (II, 16) on friendship in hard times.

'nostro cielo' may well have been Margherita of Austria, the illegitimate daughter of Charles V who arrived in Florence in 1536 as the new bride of Duke Alessandro de' Medici.[45]

Asking which of the madrigals among the 108 in Corteccia's three volumes are theatrical is a question of context and social usage: what were madrigals for, and how and when were they used? Those devoted wholly to personal love are doubtless those intended for the normal occasions when madrigals were sung: informal patrician or aristocratic entertainment, to while away an afternoon or evening, as entertainment after meals, for nocturnal serenades and so on, either performed by the patricians themselves or sung for them by professional musicians or by combinations of professionals and amateurs, with or without instrumental accompaniment. We catch glimpses of everyday musical life in the literature of the period, which allows us to see at least darkly how and in what contexts secular music was normally performed at that time. The opening of *Le cene*, Grazzini's collection of stories in the manner of Boccaccio, for example, introduces us to a group of well-born young men of Florence who spend a winter afternoon singing madrigals (apparently unaccompanied) by Arcadelt and Verdelot.[46] Aretino's scurrilous *Ragionamenti* include a scene where the heroine, making an illicit excursion one night from her temporary home in the convent, attends what seems to be a private social club (for pimps) where a group of four musicians sing a madrigal to the lute.[47] The comedy *Gl'Ingannati* performed for the Accademia degl'Intronati in Siena in 1538 describes a ridiculous love-lorn old gentleman who spends much of his day writing madrigal texts and singing love songs in a cracked voice to an out-of-tune lute.[48]

Those few madrigals written for purposes of State, most of them quite unusually homophonic in texture as befits political songs, may well have been performed either for official occasions or in private for the flattery of the duke. Apart from those already mentioned that are dedicated to Margherita and Eleonora, and Ariosto's more general encomium in praise of rulers, Corteccia, as patriotic citizen and dutiful courtier, wrote several madrigals that quite simply and explicitly praise the duke ('Voi che seguite'l

[45] See, among other places, Eric Cochrane, *Florence in the Forgotten Centuries, 1527–1800*, Chicago & London, 1973, pp. 33–7.

[46] Antonfrancesco Grazzini (Il Lasca), *Le Cene*, ed. Riccardo Bruscagli, Rome, 1976, p. 8.

[47] Pietro Aretino, *I Ragionamenti*, n. p., [1965], p. 45: 'erano quattro, che guardavano sopra un libro, ed uno con un liuto argentino, accordato, con le voci loro, cantava: *Divini occhi sereni*.' François Lesure & Claudio Sartori, *Il nuovo Vogel*, Staderini, 1977, lists two settings of Bonifazio Dragonetto's poem 'Divini occhi sereni', one by Giordano Passetto published in 1541 (*Nuovo Vogel*, 2147) and one by Philippe Verdelot published in a number of editions from 1533 onwards (*Nuovo Vogel*, 2866–7, 2871–81). For the passage in English see Aretino, *The Ragionamenti*, trans. & ed. Peter Stafford, London, 1970, pp. 56–7.

[48] Borlenghi, *Commedie*, i. 186–7; in English translation in *Five Italian Renaissance Comedies*, ed. Bruce Penman, Harmondsworth, 1978, pp. 212–13.

fior'—II, 14) or Florence in the guise of 'Palla', presumably not only Pallas Athene but also a punning reference to the Medici *palle* ('Non già per farvi oltraggio'—II, 17—and 'Non mai più lieta o più felice vita'—II, 30). We shall never know the specific occasion for which these madrigals were composed, if indeed there was one, for the words are so generally laudatory they would be appropriate whenever it was deemed suitable to demonstrate patriotic enthusiasm. Two State madrigals, however, do seem to refer to particular political (or economic) events, and we may well be able to date these more precisely by carefully considering the historical record. In 'Rose, gigli, e viole' (II, 15) the anonymous poet has Lyons (if that is the 'bel paese che la Saone irrora') exult that as it gets richer, Florence gets poorer. And since Florence cries 'Palle, palle' in 'Felici et lieti giorni' (II, 41, in which the poet goes on to say that these happy days will be days of glory and true peace for the city) and seems to taunt Rome, yearning for the sweet yoke of the *palle*, the madrigal may celebrate an event of importance for both cities, perhaps even the election of the Medici Clement VII as Pope in 1523 (when Corteccia was only 21).

But even if we eliminate the State madrigals from consideration as theatrical compositions (although 'Rose gigli e viole' might have been performed at some sort of pageant) and also those many compositions that deal with love as a personal thing, we are still left with as many as 30 madrigals in Corteccia's three books with words that suggest they may have been conceived for dramatic entertainments of one kind or another. Table 1.1 lists them all with a brief summary of their subject matter.

It is difficult to understand with certainty the meaning of many of these texts and therefore to judge accurately whether they were intended for some sort of festivity, and if so which, simply because the poems themselves do not offer enough information. Corteccia's three madrigals about stars or lights that lead mankind from error to salvation illustrate the dilemma perfectly. The beautiful, serene star in 'Vagha stella serena' (I, 5) leads through this valley of shadows on the way of salvation ('camin retto') from earthly to divine concerns. Surely it is the same light born of the sun ('quest'alma luce . . . che nasce dal celest'et divin sole') as that in 'Segua quest'alma luce' (I, 22), which also illuminates the 'camin retto' that leads us to well-being ('salute'); the same, too, as the light of 'Dal più bass'et profondo' (I, 32), which leads out of error and shadows ('che fuor d'error'et tenebre conduce'). On first reading, the imagery of these poems would appear to be Christian. But the poems do not make explicit references to Christian theology, and the anonymous poet has chosen not to explain the exact nature of the light or of the salvation it offers. Just what is the light that leads us to divine concerns? What, in particular, is the light born of the sun?

The importance of the sun, and indeed of all the stars and planets, to man's well-being and the sun's special role in nourishing man's *spiritus* through music were well recognized in the neo-Platonic philosophy of the Florentine

TABLE 1.1. *Corteccia's madrigals most likely to have been written for theatrical use* (excepting those for *Il Furto* and for *intermedi* in 1539)

A che ne stringi (I, 8)	Thirst for gold has taken away the golden age.
A che pianger invano (II, 19)	Since God ('quel Divin Motor') punishes sinners, they should be without hope.
Caso, fortun'et sorte (III, 24)	Fate rules the world, and we must anticipate the bad even in good times.
Chi ne'lacci amorosi (II, 20)	Love favours the fearless and strong, not those who lament.
Chi viver sempre vuol (I, 12)	Whoever wants to be happy should follow Venus and Cupid.
Come divers'et strano (III, 11)	Beauty takes many forms.
Dal più bass'et profondo (I, 32)	A light leads us out of error and shadow.
Devrebbon pur hormai (III, 3)	Concentration only on the acquisition of worldly goods is wrong.
Di strani et varii luoghi (II, 28)	We astrologers have come to celebrate this happy day.
Ecco che pure omai (II, 4)	The return of my beloved from the lands of shadows makes the world rejoice.
Ecco che vi si mostra (II, 32)	We return victorious from our battle against love.
Eccoti Arno beato (III, 16)	Daphne descends from heaven.
Foll'e pur il desio (III, 10)	On the transitory nature of life.
Lasso, dove son io? (II, 2)	Where am I? Others enjoy my desire, while I lament.
Liet'et beati spirti (I, 11)	I give thanks to the celestial spirits who guide the universe, who have given me victory in Florence today.
O fidi parvoletti (III, 5)	Putti, enflame human hearts!
Poscia che'l fier amor (II, 3)	Since Pallas does not wish to concede victory to Venus, we demonstrate that we can conquer love.
Quando prend'il cammino (I, 42)	In praise of autumn.
Quanto puot'il saper (II, 12)	In praise of astrology.
Quanto sicuri et lieti (I, 36)	We live happily in the industrious silver age.
Questo io tesseva et quelle (I, 18)	I made garlands for Daphne, but now, alas, a storm has come up.
Se ben par dur'et grave (I, 9)	The joy of love makes up for its pains.
Segua quest'alma luce (I, 22)	Follow the light born of the sun that leads to salvation.

TABLE I.I. *Continued*

Spiegat'angeli voi (III, 22)	Invocation to angels and others to rejoice.
Stolt'è colui (III, 2)	Astrology is a necessary guide to good works.
Tant' in giovenil petto (II, 39)	Do not follow the false god of love.
Una sola saetta (I, 31)	Cupid's arrow struck two hearts, wounded one, and passed through the other.
Vagha stella serena (I, 5)	A star leads us from earthly to divine things.
Vener del terzo ciel (I, 10)	Venus, come remove the evils from Florence.

Marsilio Ficino, founder of the Platonic Academy (arguably the predecessor of the more official Accademia Fiorentina, of which Corteccia was a member), singer of Orphic hymns to the lyre and a strong believer in astrological music.[49] Corteccia's three madrigals about light must in fact refer to that very serious and characteristically Florentine study of pagan philosophy, a hypothesis that gains credence from the fact that three other madrigals by Corteccia probably also relate to Ficino's views about astrological influences on mankind. In 'Quanto puot'il saper men che la voglia' (II, 12) we are told only that astrology should show how knowledge can help us much more than vain desire, and in 'Stolt'è colui' (III, 2) that without astrology nothing good or beautiful can be accomplished. We do not know whom the followers of astrology address ('hoggi vegnamo . . . a celebrar la bella festa *vostra*') in celebrating the festival that is the subject of 'Di strani et varii luoghi' (II, 28). To suppose, however, that they refer to the neo-Platonic beliefs that the stars and planets influence our lives and our well-being places them squarely within a Florentine intellectual tradition that illuminates their meaning in a significant way.

Two other madrigals by Corteccia may also be connected to Ficino's intellectual interests (and, not incidentally, to Frederick Sternfeld's as well). It is difficult to imagine who can be supposed to sing 'Ecco che pure omai' (II, 4) but Orpheus. Who but he can celebrate a return from the shadows and horrors ('dalle più folte tenebre et horrori')? Who else can rejoice at the return of his beloved (described, perhaps significantly, as 'mio vivo sole') from the dead? The singer may in fact be the Orpheus of Ficino's Orphic hymns, for in the end the point of the madrigal is to give thanks to the 'lume alt'e giocondo', the (doubtless neo-Platonic) light that has the power to make the world either happy or sad. Its presence in Corteccia's madrigal

[49] See D. P. Walker, 'Ficino's *Spiritus* and Music', *Annales musicologiques*, i (1953), 131–50, and Walker, 'Le Chant Orphique de Marsile Ficin', *Musique et poésie au XVIe siècle*, ed. J. Jacquot, Paris, 1954, pp. 17–33.

books is less surprising as a reflection of current Florentine philosophical beliefs than because it is set polyphonically, since Orpheus as a theatrical figure in sixteenth-century Italy almost always improvised his singing to the lyre.[50] Or can it be that the formulaic declamatory top line of 'Ecco che pure omai' gives us Corteccia's version of a traditional improvisatory formula appropriate for the theatrical impersonation of a Greek demi-god, or perhaps even some reflection, however pale, of Ficino's lost manner of Orphic singing to the lyre? Whatever the truth, it is at least a possibility that this madrigal was the companion to 'Lasso, dove io?' (II, 2), set to a poem which simply does not make its subject clear. The singer complains that others enjoy his desire while he laments; he does not know where he is or what his present situation means. He could be Orpheus in the underworld; whether or not he is meant to be, he is surely some theatrical character.

Neither the three madrigals about the light that influences mankind nor the three in praise of astrology appear to be cycles of compositions intended as *intermedi* for a single play, since each uses a different set of clefs. Indeed, they may merely be academic madrigals, intended to be sung at meetings of the Accademia or other reunions of neo-Platonists. Only 'Di strani et varii luoghi' (II, 28) is explicitly theatrical, since the singers describe themselves as 'we who follow astrology', and they explain that they have come together from various places 'today' to celebrate a happy occasion. The Orpheus madrigals are different again, for Orpheus himself is the speaker. At least their existence raises the possibility that in the second quarter of the sixteenth century some sort of entertainment, hitherto unknown, was given in Florence which involved Orpheus as one of the principal characters.

The possibly neo-Platonic madrigals of Corteccia, not all of them assuredly theatrical, form a group that should be studied further for the light they can shine on music's place in the intellectual life of Florence in the sixteenth century. A second group not about love—those with serious, moralizing texts—should also be studied together, at least partly for what their words tell us about the ethical beliefs of sixteenth-century Florentines: that an excessive concentration on the acquisition of worldly goods is wrong ('A che ne stringi'—I, 8—and 'Devrebbon pur homai'—III, 3), that industriousness is virtuous ('Quanto sicuri et lieti'—I, 36), that sinners will not go unpunished ('A che pianger invano'—II, 19), that the joys of life are transitory ('Caso, fortun'et sorte'—III, 24—and 'Foll'è pur il desio'—III, 10) and that beauty takes diverse forms ('Come divers'et strano'—III, 11). They may have been intended only for performances when a particularly serious composition was requested, but we should not rule out the possibility that some or all of them may have been intended as *intermedi* for plays, even though none makes explicit theatrical references. Such texts would

[50] See, among other places, Howard Mayer Brown, 'Lira da braccio', *The New Grove*, xi, 22.

seem to be most appropriate for tragedies, which in sixteenth-century Italy invariably involved a chorus that took limited part in the action and sang (or recited?) long moralizing commentaries at the end of each act.[51] Pirrotta suggests that 'A che ne stringi' might have been performed as a chorus in a tragedy, but so might any of the others.[52] Indeed, 'A che ne stringi', which declares that man's greed for gold has driven away the golden age, could have formed part of a set of choruses for a single play with 'Quanto sicuri et lieti', which praises the industrious silver age of the 'present'. Both are notated in the same clefs, and both can be construed as related in subject matter.

A third group of possible theatrical madrigals by Corteccia is made up of those that deal with mythological figures apart from Orpheus, especially Venus, Cupid and Daphne. In a sense they too, of course, belong among the neo-Platonic madrigals, for Venus has astrological influence over mankind as surely as Apollo or the sun, according to Ficino's beliefs.[53] At least one of them, 'Madre de'dolci amori' (II, 13), is surely theatrical, for the singers, addressing Venus directly, claim to be celebrating 'today' her ancient game. But any of the other Venus or Cupid madrigals may well have been intended for some festivity: 'Vener del terzo ciel' (I, 10), in which she and her son are asked to remove all evil influence from Florence ('Di questa Palla et del bel nostro fiore'); 'Chi viver sempre vuol' (I, 12), in which those who wish to be happy are exhorted to follow the rule of Venus and Cupid; or 'O fidi parvoletti' (III, 5), in which Cupid's putti are encouraged to enflame men's breasts.[54]

While we cannot by any means be certain that some of the serious texts or those about Venus and Cupid were intended for the theatre, there can be little doubt about three poems by Giovambattista Strozzi, two of them about Daphne. 'Eccoti Arno beato' (III, 16) conjures up a theatrical Daphne descending from some theatrical machine to take her part in a dramatic event. 'Questo io tesseva et quelle' (I, 18) laments the fact that the garlands the poet has prepared for Daphne have been rendered useless by the onset of

---

[51] See Herrick, *Italian Tragedy*; and Marzia Pieri, 'La "Rosmunda" del Rucellai e la tragedia fiorentina del primo Cinquecento', *Quaderni di teatro*, ii/7 (March 1980), 96–113. On the few musical compositions associated with tragedies see Einstein, *The Italian Madrigal*, i. 253; Osthoff, *Theatergesang*, i. 180; Pirrotta, *Music and Theatre*, pp. 141, 158; and H. Colin Slim, 'Un coro della "Tullia" di Lodovico Martelli messo in musica e attribuito a Philippe Verdelot', *Firenze e la Toscana dei Medici nell'Europa del '500* ('Biblioteca di storia toscana moderna e contemporanea', xxvi), Florence, 1983, pp. 487–511.

[52] *Music and Theatre*, p. 158. Einstein (*The Italian Madrigal*, i. 283–4) implies that these two madrigals belong together in the same play or other festivity.

[53] See Walker, 'Le Chant Orphique', p. 19.

[54] Einstein (*The Italian Madrigal*, i. 283) writes of 'Vener del terzo ciel' that it 'might have served as a motto for the Florence of the Medici'. 'O fidi parvoletti' might well have been the companion to one of the other Venus madrigals as part of a festivity. One other madrigal, 'Quando prend'il cammino' (I, 42, in praise of autumn), is set to a text which suggests the possibility that it might have served as *intermedio* to a comedy.

a (doubtless theatrical) storm. Just as surely theatrical are two other madrigals among Corteccia's works: Strozzi's 'Spiegat'angeli voi' (III, 22), an invocation to angels and others to bless the entertainment that is implied but not explained, and the rather more serious anonymous sonnet 'Liet'et beati spirti' (I, 11), which thanks the blessed spirits who follow the eternal order of the celestial bodies for the victory they have given the poet that day in Florence.

Finally, there is a group of madrigals by Corteccia that deal with love not in the first person singular but rather, like the *intermedi* for *Il Furto*, in the abstract. These poems, like the serious moralizing texts, would have been equally appropriate for serious social occasions or for dramatic entertainments. They are equally divided between those that praise love—'Se ben par dur'et grave' (I, 9), 'Una sola saetta' (I, 31) and 'Chi ne'lacci amorosi' (II, 20)—and those that condemn it—'Poscia che'l fier amor' (II, 3), 'Ecco che vi si mostra' (II, 32) and 'Tant'in giovenil petto' (II, 39).

Having isolated a substantial number of Corteccia's madrigals that might have been composed for dramatic entertainments, our next step is to identify the plays or other kinds of festivities for which the music was intended. But we may never be able to do that, since few of the printed comedy texts include *intermedi*, and few of the tragedies include choral commentaries set to music that still survives. We should, of course, look especially closely at plays performed in Florence in the 1530s and 1540s.[55] The most likely play given in Florence before 1539 to have been adorned with music by Corteccia was surely Lorenzino de' Medici's *Aridosia*, performed for the wedding of Duke Alessandro de' Medici to Margherita of Austria in 1536. Music is hardly mentioned in the play itself, and none of the manuscript or printed editions includes texts for the *intermedi*.[56] We do not even know if Corteccia was asked to set them. Indeed, we know only indirectly that there were *intermedi*, from Vasari's account of the dispute that arose between the playwright (who Vasari says was also in charge of the music) and the stage architect Bastiano da San Gallo, called Aristotile, over remodelling the Ospedale dei Tessitori to include a gallery for the large instruments that could not be moved in addition to the gallery for singers that already

[55] For a chronology of some of the most important plays presented in Florence in the sixteenth and seventeenth centuries see *Il luogo teatrale*, pp. 167–8. On other kinds of Florentine pageantry between 1494 and 1545 see Mitchell, *Italian Civic Pageantry*, pp. 35–55.

[56] Lorenzino de' Medici, *Aridosia*, ed. Emilio Faccioli, Turin, 1974, lists all known sources for the play. Music is mentioned in passing only twice, in Act II scene 4 (p. 27 in the Faccioli edition), when the servant Lucido tells his miserly master Aridosio that the neighbours have heard ghosts playing and singing at night; and at the very end (p. 80), when Aridosio explains why he cannot have the festivities, including dancing, at his house for the three weddings that have come about. For information about the 1536 celebrations see also Mitchell, *Italian Civic Pageantry*, pp. 46–8.

existed.[57] If Corteccia did compose *intermedi* for *Aridosia*, it is not surprising in any event that attention is not called to them in the composer's collected works, for within a year of the play's performance Lorenzino had assassinated his cousin Alessandro, and not long after Corteccia's three volumes were published Lorenzino himself was struck down by the henchmen of Cosimo I.[58] In short, it was not a wedding anyone in Florence in the 1540s would have wanted to commemorate.

We shall certainly never know the dramatic destination for all of the possibly theatrical madrigals of Corteccia, and it is unlikely that we shall know the dramatic destination of most of them. It is nevertheless important to attempt to differentiate theatrical from non-theatrical madrigals—we ought to make the same attempt with the madrigals of all the major composers of the century—if only because such a hypothetical classification emphasizes how few musical differences there are among madrigals written for different purposes, and because it focuses our attention on the meaning of the poetry and hence helps us to get closer to the sense of the notes, which in turn furthers our aim of understanding the essential character of sixteenth-century music.

---

[57] Giorgio Vasari, *Le vite de' piu eccellenti pittori, scultori e architetti*, ed. Carlo L. Ragghianti, Milan, 1943, iii. 147–9; in English translation, ed. William Gaunt, London, 1927, iii. 296.

[58] For a brief summary of all these events see the introduction to *Aridosia*, ed. Faccioli, pp. xiii–xv.

2

'Glorious Vanities': Reality and Unreality in Seventeenth-Century Venetian Opera

Jane Glover

> Ah! let not Censure term our Fate our Choice,
> The Stage but echoes back the Publick Voice.
> The Drama's Laws the Drama's Patrons give,
> For we that live to please, must please to live.[1]

THIS is the raw truth about theatrical entertainment: more than any other art form it must conform to the wishes of its clientele. Whatever creative urges and artistic aims and endeavours go into the theatre, it is still governed by the necessity to entertain its audience. In a successful theatrical era the process is self-generating and reciprocal. Theatres feed audiences, and audiences feed theatres. Thus it was in seventeenth-century Venice, when, after something of a slump in theatrical activity, the infant art form opera arrived on its doorstep in 1637.

If the Venetians (creators, performers and audiences) had not seized on opera as energetically and enthusiastically as they did, it quite simply might not have survived. Venice transformed opera from being a convenient means of displaying courtly affluence into a vital spectacle of universal appeal, in which reality and unreality were subtly combined in an alluring conglomerate of theatrical magic. It became the most popular art form of the seventeenth century. It captivated the voracious support and enthusiasm of the widest possible public. It drew on the talents of every type of creative artist (writers, composers, architects, painters, singers, actors and dancers). Through the dramatic structures that it imposed, the vocal lines it developed and the instrumental textures that it exploited, it ultimately wrought the

---

[1] From Samuel Johnson, *Prologue (spoken by Mr. Garrick) at the Opening of the Theatre in Drury-Lane*, 1747.

most profound influence on every subsequent genre of musical composition. In short, seventeenth-century Venetian opera changed the course of the history of European music.

For many reasons, Venice was right for opera, and opera was right for Venice. Politically the Republic continued to decline. For over a century repeated losses of territorial, maritime and trading power had caused the gradual disintegration of her world supremacy. The impending wars in Crete were to torture her for the next 30 years. Venice was greatly in need of an escapist diversion, and opera provided it perfectly. Socially, too, Venice was highly appropriate. Unlike other Italian cities, she was not dominated by the single family or potentate, like the Medici in Florence or the Gonzaga in Mantua, but she boasted several wealthy families, noblemen and merchants alike. They possessed the sort of buildings which could house opera, and, more to the point perhaps, they had sufficiently full purses to sponsor it. And artistically there was much in opera to which the Venetians were more than sympathetic. It drew upon their time-honoured love of spectacle and their ability to create it. With this it combined the strong element of music, which so enriched Venetian life on all levels. The sort of stories that it told were mythological and therefore commonly known. Above all, opera made a splendid addition to the Venetian celebrations of the Carnival season, whose atmosphere of enjoyment and frivolity ensured lively and receptive audiences.

But, quite apart from a social context which provided a perfect environment for the development of public opera, another chief factor, which accounts for the astonishing and continued activity in seventeenth-century Venetian opera houses, was the quality of the artistic personnel. Monteverdi, now aged 70, was *maestro di cappella* at St Mark's. Despite his age and the fact that his earlier successes in court opera were many years behind him, he could not resist being drawn into the latest developments. His two masterpieces for the Venetian public opera, *Il ritorno d'Ulisse in patria* and *L'incoronazione di Poppea*, were not cast in the same meticulously mythological mould as his previous triumphs; like everything he wrote at all stages of his life, they were astonishingly and impressively modern. Working alongside Monteverdi in those early years, and continuing for long after his death, was his talented pupil and friend Francesco Cavalli, who was to succeed him as the most prominent and revered Venetian musician of his time, both in church music and, particularly, in the theatre. Not only did he work for all the major opera houses in Venice; he also secured several prestigious engagements elsewhere. Other contemporaries and successors of Cavalli, such as Pietro Andrea Ziani and Marc' Antonio Cesti, began their operatic careers in Venice during the 1640s and 1650s and went on to eminence outside the city, particularly at the Austrian courts of Vienna and Innsbruck. Just as Venice had been richly endowed with painters in the sixteenth century, now in the seventeenth it was richly endowed with musicians; and this musical talent was to bear its fruit particularly in the theatres.

From the first, the differences between Venetian public operas and their courtly predecessors were clearly apparent. Contrary to current practice in Rome and Florence, public opera was not an individual performance for a particular festivity: now operas were shown repeatedly, and consequently with plots unrelated to any specific occasion. The first important difference was in libretto construction. The Roman five-act formula, with its prologue and epilogue saluting its patrons or guests, was invalid in a context where audiences went to the theatre simply for entertainment. Stories began to be told in three acts. Prologues, if they existed at all, were considerably curtailed and bore some relation to the plot without trying to involve any member of the audience. Epilogues vanished completely.

A second important difference was in the subject matter and in the handling of it. Following the trends of their predecessors, the very first Venetian music dramas were based upon mythological themes. *L'Andromeda* of 1637 was followed by such titles as *Le nozze di Teti e di Peleo*, *Adone*, *Arianna*, and *Gli amori di Apollo e di Dafne*. But gradually the strength of this mythological ancestry began to evaporate, as newer dramatic concepts became apparent. With librettos like *La Didone* (for Cavalli) and *L'incoronazione di Poppea* (for Monteverdi) Francesco Busenello introduced classical-historical subjects. He also established a more accentuated division between serious and comic, or principal and subordinate characters. The addition of secondary characters removed the pressure from the main protagonists and allowed them to be seen in a more balanced context. The *valetto* and *damigella* in *Poppea* are among the earliest examples of young servants at the courts of the rich and potentially tragic, and it is they who, for example, provide contrast immediately after the death of Seneca. The three *damigelle* in *Didone*—splendid character sketches of court gossips—do so after the first meeting of Dido and Aeneas.

But the choosing of a classical-historical subject for an opera libretto did not merely mean telling the story: in many cases the librettists rewrote it. It is here that we begin to observe elements of unreality creeping into librettos. Because opera was now public and audiences had to be courted, entertained, and then persuaded to return to the theatre on another night, it was necessary to end the operas happily. At the end of Busenello's *Didone* for Cavalli, for example, Dido does not die but must marry Iarbas. This makes for a quite extraordinary construction. Curiously like Berlioz's later treatment of the same story, Busenello's first act is entirely devoted to the fall of Troy, principally to account for Aeneas's flight from it but also to incorporate the tragedy of Cassandra. This means that Dido herself does not appear until the second act, and that the main story, with Dido, Aeneas (now rather an irrelevant character) and the elevated Iarbas, is confined to the last two acts. In the preface to his published libretto Busenello loosely excused himself for these adjustments by his statement that 'poets are licensed to alter not only Fiction but also History'.[2]

To a certain extent the librettos of this early Venetian period also reflect their very audiences. A colourful, intriguing society such as Venice produced colourful, intriguing librettos, as Busenello's *Poppea* of 1642 clearly demonstrates. The story of the Roman emperor Nero who abandons his wife Ottavia, causes the death of his counsellor Seneca, ruins the lives of Drusilla and Ottone and crowns his mistress as his empress is very far from the supernatural accidents of immortal characters, idealized monarchs or pagan deities, all enacting discreet tragedies where the violent action takes place off-stage. Here we are observing how people treat each other: how real emotions such as ambition, jealousy or passion overcome reason, decorum and even dignity; and how in consequence the happiness and fulfilment of some necessitate the unhappiness and downfall of others. There is a strong parallel here to the great paintings of sixteenth-century Venice. However unreal may be the context of altered history or mythological tradition, the people themselves, and the emotional situations they inhabit, are very real.

Musically, composers responded spontaneously to the new type of libretto and had in their armoury a whole range of musical means with which to express these various emotions. In *Poppea* Monteverdi juxtaposes many such examples. When we meet the rejected Empress Ottavia for the first time, we are eavesdropping on the very private and desolate thoughts of a woman whose husband has deserted her for someone younger; and Monteverdi follows her tortured feelings in a soliloquy of ever-changing ingredients. This speech is set not as an aria but as dramatic and powerful recitative, based on the heritage of Camerata principles. It emphasizes the natural inflections of the text's speech rhythm and moves into melisma and extension, even into measured music, at affective words, phrases or moods. By contrast, the music that Monteverdi supplies for the younger, more straightforward characters such as the page and the maid is altogether lighter, more direct and, coming from a septuagenarian, astonishingly youthful. Even the ending is surprising. After all the dramas of hysteria, banishment and suicide, *Poppea* ends, not at the magnificent coronation ceremony, but with one of the most intimate love duets ever written. 'Pur ti miro' was to set a trend in opera-endings that was followed for several decades.[3] It is this combination of spectacle and intimacy that characterized Venetian opera throughout the seventeenth century.

---

[2] Contrary to current practice, Busenello's libretto was not published at the time of the first performances. A brief *Argomento e scenario della Didone* sufficed for immediate needs, and the complete text, together with this preface, was published in a collection of Busenello's texts in 1656.

[3] Monteverdi's authorship is, however, disputed; see A. Chiarelli, '*L'incoronazione di Poppea o Il Nerone*: problemi di filologia testuale', *Rivista italiana di musicologia*, ix (1974), 117–51.

By the time Monteverdi died in 1643 opera was a firm fixture in Venetian life. The two decades that followed his death show operatic activity at its most ferocious, and operatic achievement at its peak. By 1651 six opera houses were functioning simultaneously. Patterns had been established in the contracting of singers, the building and reuse of sets, the publishing and marketing of librettos and the rehearsal and performance of the works themselves. It was a heady period of activity, precarious in terms of survival (a flop could mean the closure of a theatre, and a singer's whole career could likewise be ruined) but always buzzing with intrigue and glamour. The dazzling, brittle and brutal commercial management was a far cry from the operatic ventures mounted in the courts.

In order to retain the faithful curiosity of audiences, librettists and composers were constantly seeking variety and novelty. Giovanni Faustini, whose texts dominate this central peak period of Venetian operatic activity, might be termed the first professional librettist, for he lived entirely by his writing for the theatre; and it is a sign of the times that he could do so, albeit with difficulty. Unlike his predecessors, Faustini did not base his plots on mythological or even historical sources. He preferred instead to invent them himself. His librettos are more or less all in the same mould, centring on two or three pairs of princely lovers, who are variously coupled and uncoupled throughout the opera. The actions of these main characters are always love-motivated, and the situations in which they find themselves usually highly bizarre. They are supported by their servants: generally two or three to one of the main characters, and with a pair of young lovers (*valletto*- and *damigella*-like) among them. They often include a Leporello-type comic manservant and other stock characters of a distinct *commedia dell'arte* derivation, such as elderly fathers and aged nurses. Finally there are the gods. It was a pattern that rarely altered and never failed. The differences between librettos are in situation and event, not in outline or principle.

As the demand for complexity and novelty in dramatic plot increased, so the librettist had to discover the means of supplying it. Chief among the methods used by Giovanni Faustini was disguise. The element of disguise, which appeared in Faustini's first libretto, *La virtù degli strali d'Amore* of 1642, persisted strongly throughout the 1650s, when indeed it was one of the decade's most characteristic features. The first works by both Nicolo Minato and Aurelio Aureli, the most notable and successful of the next generation of librettists, each include disguise. *Il Ciro*, an opera by Sorrentino and Cavalli of 1654, has no fewer than four characters in disguise for part or all of the opera. And, as a short cut to an immediately complex situation, there was of course magic, in the shape of enchantresses, furies, spells and love potions.

Faustini's plots were thus becoming much more geared to the dramatic, the theatrical, the complex and, most of all, the unreal. Such indeed was the unreality which confronted the audiences in the theatre that the librettists felt it necessary to preface their published texts with elaborate forewords outlining, often in several pages, the events which have brought about the situations of the protagonists. But it must be remembered that, however complex and unfathomable some of these librettos may appear to the twentieth-century historian, seventeenth-century audiences had been conditioned to them by over a decade's experience. It was a self-generating process: the more complex and unreal the plots, the more the audiences were intrigued. Once they had mastered a plot with perhaps two disguises, it was necessary to add a third lest they became too familiar with, and therefore bored by, the present format. The primary function of opera was still to entertain the audience, with whatever device that might be needed.

Musically these devices were the same as they had been in the earlier, formative years: dramatic recitative on the one hand and self-contained arias on the other. Both these were retained, interspersed with occasional string ritornellos for aural contrast and sometimes with added string accompaniment in arias for colour. Choruses and big ensemble effects were not important. With the new type of Faustini libretto, emphasis was entirely on a handful of individual characters and the interplay between them, so comment or even participation by larger groups was simply not relevant. Indeed, the most impressive musical feature of this peak period is the complete parity and balance between recitative and aria, and the fact that the one flowed into the other with natural and easy malleability. There are very few hard lines in these operas: no heavy double bars followed by extended ritornellos introducing static and protracted arias. Nothing felt contrived; everything felt spontaneous. Contrast there certainly was, for, more than any other composer before Mozart, Cavalli and his contemporaries were instinctively aware that contrast is the essence of drama. But that contrast was always achieved in a spectacularly fluent manner.

This fluency is mirrored in the precious surviving autograph scores of Cavalli, which show exactly how he composed. He seems to have worked straight through a libretto from beginning to end, writing rapidly and fluently according to the requirements of the text. He then went back and altered various passages, filling in the string parts and perhaps rewriting complete sections. But the spontaneity and immediacy of his initial reaction to the libretto still survive the various layers of correction and alteration. So Cavalli's music is always inspired by text and by situation. He would often cheerfully ignore the metrical indications supplied by the librettist, whereby seven-syllable lines implied aria and eleven-syllable lines recitative. If the situation, or even a passing mood, suggested it, he would write measured music, perhaps only for a few bars, and then slip back easily into unmeasured music. There are countless examples in his scores where arias, or micro-arias, have been written on recitative texts, and vice versa.

But it must not be thought that Venetian librettists and composers were incapable of writing longer arias of purely musical delight, for these were becoming increasingly important as the century progressed. Individual singers were becoming favourite stars with their audiences, who (then as now) were often drawn to opera performances by the calibre and reputation of a particular artist. So there began to be incorporated into the dramatic scheme deliberate areas where an individual could express in soliloquy his particular state of mind, be it delight, anxiety, rage, jealousy or despair. A particularly popular aria type was the lament, usually in triple time, often with string accompaniment and frequently over a ground bass. This was often the musical highlight of a whole work, with the most organized formal structure and the most sensuous vocal line. These mid-century laments had a distinguished ancestry, bearing in mind Monteverdi's *Lamento d'Arianna* of 1608 or his *Lamento della ninfa* of 1638. But what is again impressive about the incorporation of arias and laments into the operas of this peak period is that they were never irrelevant or disproportionate to that important dramatic flow. A distinguished example can be found in Cavalli's *Eritrea*, where Theramene, who loved the now disguised princess Eritrea before her supposed death, has become insane with grief. When we first meet him, he sings a lament which has all the popular requirements: ground bass, gentle vocal line, added string parts. But with brilliant theatricality Cavalli and Faustini inform us of Theramene's agitated mental state by making him incapable of sustaining his lament. After only a couple of sentences, the ground bass formula is interrupted, and he moves into less stable musical material (Ex. 2.1).

Such musical and dramatic sophistication was alas not to survive in the third period of opera performance in seventeenth-century Venice. From around 1665 onwards there was an increase in unreality of situation and characterization, and a simultaneous decline in any sort of theatrical or emotional reality. Indeed, the general impression is of everything becoming wildly out of control, just as Venice's political situation was. One operatic consequence of her continuing military misfortunes was a curious recourse to classical-historical librettos based on military heroes. Nicolo Minato, for example, produced three such works in the mid 1660s: *Scipione Affricano*, *Muzio Scevola* and *Pompeo Magno*; and there were often desperate prefaces in which librettists tried to draw impertinent parallels between the glories of ancient Rome and the supposed glories of contemporary Venice. But, as before, using a classical subject for a libretto did not merely mean telling the story. It had to be adapted to current Venetian tastes and moulded to fit the pattern that continued to draw in the audiences. Not only historical endings but entire motivations were changed, so events of vast historical significance were made completely subordinate to the amorous entanglements of the principals. In *Pompeo Magno*, for example, the formation of the first Roman triumvirate, between Caesar, Pompey and Crassus, is dismissed in a few bars of recitative. The *argomenti* in Minato's librettos consist of two sections. The first is entitled 'Di quello, che si ha dall'historia' and often even cites the

Ex. 2.1

THERAMENE

Vol-to a - ma - to, sos - pi - ra - to, la - - - gri - ma - - - - - - - - - - - - - - to mio ri - sor - to bel, bel _____ con - for - - - - - - - - - - - to. _____ Se già mor - to t'ar- - si in - cen - si e as - se - si fac - i, hor che spir - ti hai vi- -va - ci, dal tuo spo - so ac - cog - li, ac - cog - li, ac - cog - li i ba - ci. Che par - lo? Ov - e tras - cor - ro? Del no - to scon - so- -la - to il va - neg - gian - te ar - di - re. Scu - sa, Per - do - na, ò si - re.

classical source, for instance Plutarch for *Scipione Affricano*. This is immediately followed by 'Di quello, che si finge', in which characters and events, and the motivations behind them, are jumbled and reconstructed. There was also an increase in sensation and violence for their own sake. In *Scipione Affricano* a corpse is dressed up as one of the main characters and casually abandoned on stage; in *Muzio Scevola* the captured queen cuts off the head of a guard who has tried to rape her and appears triumphantly with it; and in *Pompeo Magno* there is even a murder on stage. On these terms, even *Poppea* seems civilized and restrained.

By now librettists were fighting what was to be a losing battle against the formidable opposition of singers and audiences. As Italy's most celebrated singers became popular to the point of idolization, they and their audiences demanded more and more opportunities for the display of their purely technical and virtuoso talents. This meant that composers too were under pressure in meeting demands for extra arias. These were added even during the course of the rehearsal period immediately before production, and many librettos of the 1660s onwards have *addenda* giving the texts of last-minute insertions. A hilarious and quite early example of arias thus disrupting dramatic coherence is found in Busenello's libretto for *Giulio Cesare* of 1656. After Caesar is stabbed by the conspirators, he utters his celebrated line 'Et tu, Brute?'; but he then sings a three-stanza aria before he dies. The librettist Aureli complained bitterly of this practice, which so much distorted the dramatic flow of an opera, in the disconsolate preface to his *Claudio Cesare* of 1673:[4]

I present you with my Claudio, more endowed with arias than with incidents. What can I do? If this is the way Venice now wants it, I must try and provide it.

This move towards the aria's monopoly of opera inevitably led to the breakdown of dramatic fluency. Plots merely staggered from one aria opportunity to another, and all the librettist could do was supply a framework which would incorporate this jerky procedure. Aureli was not reticent about expressing his frustration and dissatisfaction in print. He blamed not only the audiences but also the singers (referring to their extravagant temperaments: 'gl'humori stravaganti de' Signori Musici recitanti'). He also went so far as to admit that his only motive for continuing to write operas was financial gain. Clearly, opera was no longer the carefully integrated efforts of librettist and composer that it had been barely a decade earlier.

Musically there were two obvious consequences of this aesthetic shift. The first was that arias became increasingly sophisticated in structure, taxing in vocal expertise and altogether longer and more frequent. Certainly all the opera scores from the latter part of the century abound in arias of all types,

---

[4] Performed at the Teatro S. Salvatore; music by Boretti.

albeit presenting only superficial emotions, and they show how much better the composers were getting at composing, and how much better the singers were getting at singing. But this concentration on arias took its toll in the quality of recitative for powerful expression. In earlier years aria and recitative were used in alternation at moments of intense passion and feeling; and this accounts for the tremendous energy, spontaneity and variety of the operas as a whole. Once the aria began to dominate, balance was distorted. Recitative was relegated to a position of a mere link between closed forms; the significance of the drama itself was reduced, and the whole operative focus shifted. This distorted dramatic pattern laid a solid foundation for the type of structure that persisted for almost a century. The inexorable succession of da capo arias linked by recitative could only be transcended by a composer of the stature of Handel, who alone achieved operatic immortality through the drama inherent in his music. While there is no doubt that the works of the 1660s and later decades continued to provide individual arias of outstanding beauty and merit, they were never able to achieve the dramatic equilibrium and fluency that the works of earlier decades had provided.

But by the end of the seventeenth century operatic prominence had slipped away from Venice. Through the very excellence of its mid-century products, opera had been taken to other cities and even to other countries; and enthusiasm for the art form and new energy for creating it began to emerge in other centres. Naples, Vienna, Paris, and in the early eighteenth century London all nurtured thriving operatic establishments, and all produced or attracted the artistic talent to continue the development of the form. But Venice's operatic legacy must not be underestimated. Quite apart from its influence on other genres (oratorio, cantata, even instrumental music), there are hundreds of surviving operatic scores from the seventeenth century, of constant allure to scholars, performers and, of course, audiences. For however much we may evaluate the parts of an opera by dissection and scrutiny, it is ultimately in the theatre that a work as a whole succeeds or fails. The seventeenth-century librettists themselves, whose printed texts were available to the public without their musical and theatrical contexts, were often anxious to stress this point. Aureli concluded the preface to his *Perseo* of 1665 with the plea: 'Do not judge this work by its shadow on the printed page, until you have seen it in the theatre'.[5] The ultimate testimony of an opera's worth must come from the audience. The final word is therefore given to a seventeenth-century English traveller, Robert Bargrave, who concluded a seven-year Grand Tour of Europe with a visit to Venice in the carnival season of 1655. His enthusiasm was boundless:

The Varieties of Carnival entertainments are as unconfin'd, as are men's fancies, every minute and every place affording new. But above all, surpassing whatsoever

[5] Performed at the Teatro SS. Giovanni e Paolo; music by Mattioli.

their Inventions can else stretch to, are their Operas (or Playes) represented in rare Musick from beginning to end, by select Eunuchs and women, sought out through all Italy on Purpose.[6]

He went on to conclude that the operas he had witnessed had given him much more pleasure than had all his previous European experiences:

Nay I must needs confess that all the pleasant things I have yet heard or seen, are inexpressibly short of the delight I had in seeing this Venetian Opera; and as Venice in many things surpasses all places else where I have been, so are these operas the most excellent of all its glorious Vanities.

An illustrated version of this paper was originally given as the Henry Rowatt Bickley Memorial Lecture at St Hugh's College, Oxford, on 27 May 1982.

[6] 'Account of a Grand Tour, 1648–55', Oxford, Bodleian Library, MS Rawlinson C. 799, ff. 173–4.

3

The Italian Seventeenth-Century Cantata: A Textual Approach

Carolyn Gianturco

ONE of the earliest studies of the Italian seventeenth-century cantata was written by Henri Prunières in 1926.[1] For the first time a serious attempt was made to define the genre and to describe the contributions to it by several composers in order to determine the various stages of its definition. Much of what Prunières had to say was and still is useful; he was a discerning scholar who was truly attracted to the aesthetic values of music, and who at the same time realized that documents were an essential aid in forming rational musicological opinions. But one of the main theses of his study should perhaps be reconsidered, especially since it seems to have become an accepted tenet in the evaluation of the seventeenth-century cantata.

After recalling that Renaissance madrigal poetry, though usually of good literary quality, was only the handmaid of the music, Prunières went on to speak of the reversal of the roles of poetry and music that occurred at the beginning of the seventeenth century, when 'music had now to be [poetry's] very humble servant convicted at last of destroying the poetry'. He was delighted to be able to add, however, that 'music was not to wait long for her revenge'. He argued that it was the cantata 'which enabled music to recover from the blow struck at it by the Florentines',[2] implying consistently that its music was composed without regard to the text.

Prunières would certainly have agreed that, in general, any discussion of vocal music should not ignore the text on which it is based. It is only reasonable to suppose that the poetic text which the composer set to music could be an aid to understanding his response and particular creative musical process. Furthermore, one could suspect that in seventeenth-century Italy, a period of great and relatively widespread interest in literature, when it sometimes seems as though all who could write were writing poetry, the composer would indeed take note of the text before him and perhaps be

---

[1] 'The Italian Cantata of the XVII Century', *Music & Letters*, vii (1926), 38–48, 120–32.
[2] Ibid., p. 39.

influenced by it. Prunières, instead, came to a different conclusion with regard to the cantata. In his judgement, poetry played a subordinate, if not non-existent, role in determining musical form and style in the Italian seventeenth-century cantata. What is more, either explicitly or implicitly this same attitude has continued to colour successive considerations both of the cantata in general and of the works of individual composers.[3]

It is the intent of the present study to offer another evaluation of the relationship between music and poetry in the cantata. In the past it would have been difficult to examine enough works by a sufficient number of Italian composers to come to any valid conclusions about the genre, since the enormous corpus of cantatas was available only in scattered manuscript and early printed sources. However, the recent publication of sixteen volumes of cantatas—over 400 pieces by 26 composers working in various centres within and outside Italy—makes such a task more possible.[4] Naturally, a comprehensive history of the cantata cannot be written on the basis of this selection alone. At the same time, given the number of cantatas presented, plus the fact that the texts are offered separately in poetic layout, valid considerations on the relationship between text and music can be made.

Such an investigation obviously requires a knowledge of Italian

---

[3] Among those who make no connection between cantata text and music are, for example, Manfred Bukofzer, *Music in the Baroque Era*, New York, 1947; Eugen Schmitz, *Geschichte der weltlichen Solokantate*, rev. edn., Leipzig, 1955; Helmut Hucke, 'Kantate', *MGG*, vii. 563–75; Hanns-Bertold Dietz, 'Musikalische Struktur und Architektur im Werke Alessandro Stradellas', *Analecta musicologica*, ix (1970), 78–93; Lino Bianchi, 'Cantata', *Dizionario enciclopedico universale della musica e dei musicisti: Il lessico*, i (Turin, 1983), 465–72. Among those who suggest that a connection exists but yet analyse works without either revealing what this might be or taking it into consideration are, for example, Alberto Ghislanzoni, *Luigi Rossi: Biografia e analisi delle opere*, Rome & Milan, 1954; Helmut Haack, 'Kantate', *Riemann Musik Lexikon: Sachteil*, Mainz, 1967, 438–41; Nigel Fortune & Colin Timms, 'Cantata', *The New Grove*, iii. 694–8. Among those who have attempted to come to grips with the problem are Gloria Rose, 'The Cantatas of Giacomo Carissimi', *The Musical Quarterly*, xlviii (1962), 204–15; Cecilia Kathryn Van de Kamp Freund, 'Alessando Scarlatti's Duet Cantatas and Solo Cantatas with Obbligato Instruments' (dissertation), Northwestern University, 1979, 88–95; Lawrence Edward Bennett, 'The Italian Cantata in Vienna, c.1700–c.1711' (dissertation), New York University, 1980, 509–45.

[4] *The Italian Cantata in the Seventeenth Century*, general ed. Carolyn Gianturco, New York, 1985–7: i: Luigi Rossi, ed. Francesco Luisi; ii: Giacomo Carissimi, ed. Günther Massenkeil; iii: Marc'Antonio Pasqualini, ed. Margaret Murata; iv: Marco Marazzoli, ed. Wolfgang Witzenmann; v: Barbara Strozzi, ed. Ellen Rosand; vi: Antonio Cesti, ed. David Burrows, & Giovanni Legrenzi, ed. Stephen Bonta; vii· Francesco Gasparini, ed. Gabriella Biagi-Ravenni; viii: Maurizio Cazzati, ed. Anne Schnoebelen; ix: Alessandro Stradella, ed. Carolyn Gianturco; x: Giovanni Bononcini, ed. Lowell Lindgren; xi: Alessandro & Atto Melani, ed. Robert L. Weaver; xii: Pietro Simone Agostini & Mario Savioni, ed. Irving Isley; xiii: Alessandro Scarlatti, ed. Malcolm Boyd; xiv: Giovanni Maria Bononcini, Giuseppe Colombi, Domenico Gabrielli & Giovanni Maria (Angelo) Bononcini, ed. Alessandra Chiarelli; xv: Agostino Steffani, ed. Colin Timms; xvi: Carlo Capellini, Giovanni Battista Pederzuoli, Antonio Draghi, Filippo Vismarri & Carlo Agostino Badia, ed. Lawrence E. Bennett. All subsequent musical references are to this series.

seventeenth-century poetry and an awareness of what the poet might have considered his particular aims and problems. Unfortunately, Italian literary scholars offer almost no reliable information on the subject. Benedetto Croce's harsh dismissal of seicento poetry, and his equally low regard for music and for texts set to music, did much to inhibit others from considering seventeenth-century poetic literature seriously.[5] While present-day Italian scholarship aims at freeing itself in general from his imposing dogmas, this has not yet been accomplished as far as the seventeenth century is concerned. Among the best studies on this period are those by the German, W. Theodor Elwert, whose books on style and versification are the ones the Italians themselves frequently turn to.[6] For the most part, however, one must examine the literature itself, rather than critical evaluations of it, if one hopes to regard it objectively.

A necessary starting-point is an awareness of Italian poetry in terms of form: the genres in use before the seventeenth century and how they were internally structured, and the structural novelties introduced in poetry written for music both before and during the period under consideration. Then the musical cantatas may be examined to determine the presence of traditional and newer poetic structures, and also to notice whether these structures provoked any set response on the part of composers.[7]

Angelo Poliziano's *Orfeo* (1480), though based on earlier *sacre rappresentazioni*, was the first play in Italian on a non-religious subject. One sees here characteristics which were to remain constant for more than a century. The prologue is entirely in lines of eleven syllables, the length considered to be the most dignified and most perfect. Thereafter, apart from two pieces in Latin which were sung by Orpheus, the drama proceeds in sections of either all hendecasyllabic lines or mixed hendecasyllabic and heptasyllabic lines. Poliziano makes much use also of strophic forms associated with popular or improvised literature, the straightforward *canzonetta* and the *canzonetta a ballo* or *ballata* which employed a refrain, adopting them for a solo song and for the chorus pieces, all of which were set to music; stanzas are of eight lines (*ottave*) or six lines (*sestine*). Typical rhyme schemes throughout the play are either alternating (abab etc.) or interlocking (aba bcb etc.). Poliziano composed other *canzoni a ballo* and *canzonette* along the same lines as those in *Orfeo*; as one would expect, the formal difference between *canzone* and *canzonetta* is mainly one of length.

It is interesting to note that the verse plays of Ludovico Ariosto, which were not intended to have music, are entirely in eleven-syllable lines. His *Satire*, long dialogues of continuous *terzine* of interlocking rhymes, are also

[5] See W. Theodor Elwert, *La poesia lirica italiana del Seicento*, Florence, 1968, 2 ff.
[6] Ibid.; also *Versificazione italiana dalle origini ai giorni nostri*, Florence, 1976.
[7] See Carolyn Gianturco, 'Cantate dello Stradella in possesso di Andrea Adami', *Atti del Convegno Internazionale Alessandro Stradella, Siena 1982*, forthcoming in *Chigiana*.

written in this manner. For his epic poem *Gerusalemme liberata* (published 1581) Torquato Tasso also employed only hendecasyllabic lines, and with great skill and variety. Narration, description, indirect and direct discourse are carried forth in the twenty chapters, or *canti*, only in octaves of such lines (with the customary rhyme scheme of abababcc etc.). But Tasso, like others, also experimented with blank verse, the so-called *versi sciolti*. Several of his dialogues and eclogues, filled with the pastoral characters who were to continue to populate Italian literature, are composed to such seven- and eleven-syllable lines. His most famous play, *L'Aminta* (1573), called by Tasso a '*favola boschereccia*', is made up almost completely of *versi sciolti*; exceptions are the rhymed madrigals (seven- and eleven-syllable lines) for the chorus.

Another pastoral play, and an exceedingly popular one, was Giambattista Guarini's *Il Pastor fido* (1584).[8] Once again blank verse reigns supreme, even the *coro* occasionally having lines of this type. In addition, however, the chorus has rhyming, strophic canzonas (heptasyllabic and hendecasyllabic lines), such as that at the end of Act IV, 'Oh bella età de l'oro'. One rhymed piece for the chorus, 'Cieco Amor, non ti cred'io, is unusual in having lines of five, seven, eight and eleven syllables; Guarini explained that here the chorus was to dance, and so the music was composed first to accommodate their steps, then the poetry. It is clear that it was exceptional both to have lines of these lengths and for the music to have been written before the poetry.

Thus far Italian serious poetry could have been composed entirely of lines of odd numbers of syllables, either in rhymed poetry or in blank verse. In plays, traditional or popular closed forms were inserted into this format. These were generally strophic (*canzone, canzonetta*) but not necessarily so (*madrigale*). They, too, were of lines of an odd number of syllables. Clearly it was the uncommon change from one poetic rhythm to another and the passage from one form to another which distinguished the dramatic genre.

Part I of Giambattista Marino's *Rime* (1602) consists of sonnets, each constructed of fourteen hendecasyllabic lines; Part II contains (single-stanza) madrigals and (strophic) canzonas of varying length and of a mixture of heptasyllabic and hendecasyllabic lines. For example the *canzone* 'O baci avventurosi' has seven fourteen-line strophes with a four-line concluding strophe, but 'Filli, cor del mio core' has fourteen strophes of five lines each. Marino's collection contained all sorts of poems—'amorose, marittime, boscherecce, heroiche, lugubri, morali, sacre, & varie'—and had 25 printings in the seventeenth century alone. His was not an introvert expression of personal feelings in the sensual manner of Tasso, but rather an objective style which directed itself to the intellect through all the techniques rhetoric had to

---

[8] For a discussion of music associated with the play see Arnold Hartmann, Jr., 'Battista Guarini and *Il Pastor fido*', *The Musical Quarterly*, xxxix (1953), 415–25.

offer, resulting in poetry which was unusual, vivid, exaggerated and complicated. As poetry which strove to avoid the expected and which therefore intended to be difficult and cause surprise, it became the model for
seventeenth-century poets who together with its inventor created a golden
age: 'Marinismo'.[9]

While Marino liberated the content and style of Italian poetry, Gabriello
Chiabrera must be accredited with removing its formal barriers. Through
contact with Marc'Antonio Muret, the friend of Ronsard, Chiabrera took
up the ideas of the Pléiade and began to crusade for the suitability and
acceptance of a variety of versification in serious Italian poetry. For example,
he suggested that now blank verse should be used for heroic poems. He also
gave examples of lines that contained between four and twelve syllables,
praising the wonderful variety of rhythm that the resulting different accen-
tuations would offer poets. Moreover, composers had told him that such a
variety, and certainly the shorter lines, were better for music. Chiabrera
indeed wrote much poetry to be set to music, and composers often made use
of his two books of *Canzonette* (1591), his *Scherzi e canzonette morali* and
Maniere de' versi toscani (1599).[10]

It was logical then, given the literary scene at the turn of the seventeenth
century, that Ottavio Rinuccini should have chosen a *favola pastorale* as the
sort of play to write for setting entirely to music.[11] In the main he was
conservative in his choice of poetic metres. Most of *Dafne* employs a mixture
of heptasyllabic and hendecasyllabic lines which rhyme. In addition, and as
was to be expected, he used several strophic structures too: the prologue by
Ovidio is in traditional eleven-syllable rhyming lines, but more modern lines
of even numbers of syllables are used in the pieces for the *coro*. Rinuccini's
other operas, *Euridice*, *L'Arianna* and *Narciso*, follow the same pattern. At
first only Chiabrera embraced his own suggestion about the merits of *versi
sciolti* and adopted them in *Il rapimento di Cefalo*. But then Alessandro
Striggio also found them to be suitable for his *Orfeo*, set by Monteverdi
(1607). Moreover, while the prologue and many *canzoni* are still in lines of
an odd number of syllables, Orpheus' solo songs 'Ecco pur ch'a voi ritorno'
and 'Vi ricorda, o boschi ombrosi' use lines of eight syllables. Rinuccini's
Tirsi e Clori of 1615 also adheres to the newer tendency by having the two
protagonists alternate hexasyllabic octaves and then giving Tirsi seven
strophes of varying length but again all of hexasyllabic lines. Stefano Landi
took Chiabrera's lesson even more to heart: his *La morte d'Orfeo* of 1619

[9] For an excellent discussion of Marino's style and place in history see Elwert, *La poesia
lirica*, 1–141.
[10] Chiabrera apparently invented the genre of *scherzi* and wrote 21 such poems, all brief
rhyming mixtures of seven- and eleven-syllable lines. The term recurs most notably in the
music of Monteverdi and in the poetry of Giovan Filippo Apolloni.
[11] See F. W. Sternfeld, 'The First Printed Opera Libretto', *Music & Letters*, lix (1978),
121–38.

not only employs blank verse; in addition, the solo songs and choruses have lines of many different lengths (generally although not exclusively of an odd number of syllables), either mixed or not, such as: 4, 5, 7; 6; 7, 11; 7, 11, 5; 9. In all cases the new *favola in musica* saw the translation of the closed poetic forms into closed musical forms, that is into arias, duets, trios, choruses and so forth; such text as was not thus organized was allowed to proceed with the drama as quickly and 'naturally' as possible in *stile recitativo*.

It is not surprising that genres which were offshoots of the poetic-musical drama, oratorio and cantata, followed along the same lines. Alessandro Grandi distinguished in his collections of 1620 and 1626 between arias, or more traditional solo songs, and the newer cantata in just this way.[12] His strophic canzona and *balletto*, single-strophe madrigal and fourteen-line sonnet, in short the closed forms, do not have the poetic and musical variety of his cantatas. The secretary of Arcadia and an important early historian of Italian literature, Giovanni Mario Crescimbeni, wrote a definition of the seventeenth-century cantata which supports this observation. Describing various sorts of poetry, he stated that 'for music certain other kinds of poetry were introduced, which today one commonly calls cantatas, which are composed of verses and short verses rhymed without rule, with a mingling of arias, sometimes for one voice, sometimes for more; and they were and are made with dramatic and narrative [elements] mixed therein'.[13] He also clarified that *arie* and *ariette* were 'those small groups of rhymed lines' which one finds here and there in larger dramatic works intended for music.[14] This applied to poems which were short dramatic episodes of either direct discourse (told directly by the person or persons involved), indirect discourse (related through a narrator, since cantatas were not meant to be acted) or a mixture of both. Such poems were written with the express intention of being set to music.[15]

The seventeenth-century Italian cantata would normally have had a continuous and not traditionally structured text of generally heptasyllabic and hendecasyllabic lines (either freely rhymed or unrhymed) interrupted from time to time by some closed poetic form, strophic or not, of any number

---

[12] *Cantade ed arie*, Venice, 1620 (only the second edition exists, and that only in a transcription by Alfred Einstein now in the Smith College Archives; my thanks are due to John Whenham for letting me see his microfilm of the transcription); *Cantade ed arie . . . Libro terzo*, Venice, 1626 (the only copy is in the British Library).

[13] *Commentarj intorno alla sua volgar poesia*, i (Rome, 1702), 240; his *L'istoria della volgar poesia* (Rome, 1698) does not mention the cantata.

[14] *Commentarj*, i. 68.

[15] Other contemporary writers on Italian literature are less helpful. Francesco Saverio Quadrio (*Della storia e della ragione d'ogni poesia*, Bologna, 1739–49) merely repeats Crescimbeni or else discusses only the later, eighteenth-century cantata; Ludovico Antonio Muratori (*Della perfetta poesia italiana*, Modena, 1706) does not discuss the cantata, and in his sections on opera he reveals himself to be ignorant about music and moreover not attracted to it.

of lines of any length but which always rhymed. Generally the former style was employed for description and narration, the latter for expressing an emotional state. Over the seventeenth century as a whole, the tendency in the unstructured text was initially to have the lines rhyme, whereas by the end of the century *versi sciolti* predominated (as in the works set by Gasparini and Alessandro Scarlatti); closed forms demonstrate an increasing preference for lines of an even number of syllables (mainly eight and four) over odd numbers.

A similar understanding of what the genre 'cantata' meant may be gained from study of the many literary works called cantatas by such prolific poets as Giovan Filippo Apolloni and Sebastiano Baldini,[16] and from the compositions entitled cantatas by several composers, beginning with Barbara Strozzi and Giacomo Carissimi and continuing throughout the century.[17] Most of the poetry, in the style of Marino, deals with the subject of love, and both the poet and composer expected their work to be performed as a piece of chamber music for a few nobles. Mention is also made in the literature of 'cantate morali'; these again are chamber cantatas of like format but with a principally didactic or moralistic text. In a parallel category are the sacred texts written for cantatas to 'be performed either as chamber music or in some oratory. 'Cantata per fare una serenata', or simply 'serenata', is a title often found on cantatas which were intended for a larger, more public audience. These works, although again of the same general type as the chamber cantata, were often longer and for more than one singer, and they were sometimes divided in two parts; as serenatas were intended as entertainments for a particular guest or occasion, there may be a topical allusion in the course of the work.

Given the interest in Italian poetry in general and the obvious novelty of dramatic literature in particular, demonstrated by the stream of intellectual essays that argued for or against the new trends and by the numerous academies founded especially to present new works, is it reasonable to suppose that composers could have ignored the poetry they were setting? Occasionally a composer set an old poem, but normally he set one given to him by the poet, which had been requested by a patron: would the poet, after his effort to master the new style, have allowed the composer to proceed

---

[16] I am grateful to Giorgio Morelli for letting me see the catalogues he is preparing of the poetry for music of these poets, which enabled me to examine the literary sources directly.
[17] I cannot agree with Alberto Ghislanzoni (*Problemi della storia musicale. Mitologia e Fandorie. Genesi della cantata*, Rome, 1979) or with Ellen Rosand and Colin Timms (*The Italian Cantata*, v & xv resp.), who suggest that one might apply the term 'cantata' to all vocal chamber music. In the seventeenth century closed forms would not have been called cantatas but simply arias for one or more voices. It is therefore best not to consider the following works in *The Italian Cantata* as cantatas proper: Carissimi, Nos. 13, 15, 20, 21, 23; Strozzi, Nos. 2–13, 19–21, 24–39, 41–3, 50–51, 55–6; Legrenzi, No. 20; Savioni, Nos. 1, 3, 7, 8; Agostini, No. 16; Alessandro Melani, Nos. 3–4; Steffani, Nos. 7, 11, 16, 20–24; Vismari, No. 6.

without regard for his text? Would the patron and his friends, most of whom considered themselves *cognoscenti*, have enjoyed a composite art form in which the art that they undoubtedly understood best—the poetry—was glossed over?

The musical cantata proves that the answer to all these questions is no. On the contrary, the composer created with regard for and with an understanding of the text before him. It was clearly the poet who determined the mood and how many solo singers (or characters) were needed. But a number of other, more subtle aspects of the music may also be attributed not to an arbitrary aesthetic consideration on the part of the composer, but simply to his decision to implement the dictates of the text.

RECITATIVE AND ARIA

The poet determined how many closed forms there were to be in his cantata and where to place them. The composer generally followed his outline by setting the closed poetic forms as closed musical forms (aria, duet etc.) and the rest of the text as recitative. If the poet decided to have no, few or many closed forms, the composer generally complied. A clear, albeit exaggerated, example of this is Luigi Rossi's long comic Cantata No. 19, 'Sotto l'ombra d'un pino', which is written entirely in recitative text and set in such music; his sacred Cantata No. 21, 'Nel dì ch'al Padre eterno' offers the same situation. The text of Alessandro Stradella's Cantata No. 5, 'L'avete fatta a me', instead abounds in closed forms and has only four lines of recitative, and so does the musical setting. Most cantata texts, however, alternated recitative and aria more frequently; the music did the same.

If one does not realize the dominant role the poet played in this regard, one is apt to affirm incorrectly that certain composers preferred more (or fewer) arias in their works, thus attributing to them formal and stylistic characteristics for which they were not responsible. How much recitative or aria was in a cantata depended on the poet.

STROPHIC ARIAS

Poets often wrote closed forms in two or more symmetrical stophes; composers accordingly wrote music which was repeated for each strophe of text. This procedure was followed by every composer throughout the century. Most often there are two poetic-musical strophes (such as 'Vi sono pochi affé' in Draghi's Cantata No. 12 and 'Povero core' in Giovanni Bononcini's No. 2), but occasionally there are three (such as 'Amanti, fuggite' in Marazzoli's two-voice Cantata No. 12 and 'Di quattr'aquile gonzaghe' in Strozzi, No. 1) or four ('Il viver amante' in Cazzati, No. 21).

If one sees in the presence of strophic forms a preference for them on the part of the composer, or in an absence of them a reluctance on his part to write them, one could falsely conclude that strophic forms illustrate either a 'modern' or a 'conventional' attitude on the part of a composer.

NON-STROPHIC ARIAS

When the poet has written a closed form which does not exhibit strophic structure, the composer will not write a strophic closed form. If the poetry is of more than one strophe or stanza but these are not symmetrical (that is, they exhibit differences of number of lines, number of syllables per line or rhyme scheme), the composer will write a non-strophic, sectional form which adheres to the poetic divisions. Most bipartite (AB) pieces result from this situation, that is, they are settings of two non-symmetrical stanzas of poetry: for example, see 'Amo Filli e tanto basta' in Rossi's Cantata No. 2, 'Dammi pace, o gelosia' in Marazzoli, No. 2, 'Deh, chi misera t'addita' in Carissimi, No. 7, 'Quant'io viva infelice' in Legrenzi, No. 23, 'Astri rigidi, se collassù' in Stradella, No. 14, 'Gelosia, deh dillo tu' in Agostini, No. 15, 'Fugga pur l'impero' in Steffani, No. 3. Although tripartite ABC forms resulting from three non-symmetrical poetic strophes are not to be found in the cantatas in question, there are quadripartite ones (see 'Quando avran fine' in Savioni, No. 5, and 'S'altra donna pari a te' in Colombi, No. 2). Continuous, or single-section, musical forms are settings of continuous texts (see 'Pianga il rio al pianto mio' in Scarlatti, No. 1).

To credit a composer with writing continuous or sectional pieces as a personal aesthetic choice, and therein to see a musical preference for one form over another (AB over strophic, for example), would be to misread his intentions and most likely misrepresent his real contributions to the genre and its closed forms.

ARIOSO

At certain points in a section of recitative a composer may decide to set the text in aria style (not form). The text may be repeated, even several times; the vocal line will be given curving phrases of melody (as opposed to the more static, repeated-note idiom of recitative); and the continuo will assume a quicker and more regular rhythm. The text at these moments will always be either a single hendecasyllabic line or a hendecasyllabic line with one or more other lines of similar or different lengths. It was common for a poet to write an eleven-syllable line at the end of a recitative just before a closed form as a final and often summing-up line, which also might serve to introduce the aria, duet, etc.; and it was common for composers to highlight the importance of this text by musical means. It was also common for a poet to write a provocative or weighty hendecasyllabic line in the course of a recitative, and once again a composer could reinforce his intention. Such musical sections may be called *ariosi*, a term used by Vismarri in his Cantata No. 1, *Scioglieasi baldanzoso*.

It is important to recognize that the text for the arioso is recitative text, often not even a complete sentence or idea; otherwise these sections may be mistaken for arias and other closed forms (which were always textually complete in themselves) and the wrong conclusions drawn as to seventeenth-century form (including statements which affirm, for example, that certain 'arias' are quite short or begin in one key and end in another).[18] Moreover, if arioso is confused with aria, then when it is accompanied by instruments other than the continuo (as in Stradella's Cantatas Nos. 13 and 14) it will not be recognized for the accompanied recitative that it is, and thus the history of that technique will be obscured.

REFRAIN/RITORNELLO/INTERCALARE

Poets may organize a cantata in such a way that some text will be repeated in the course of the work as a refrain: its repetition is part of the poetic structure. This is demonstrated both by literary sources, where such repetitions are clearly indicated, and, when these are lacking, by the texts as transcribed from the scores.[19] Such a refrain (called then an *intercalare* and today sometimes a ritornello) could be part of a recitative or part or all of a closed form; the composer responded as expected and set the recitative as such (see Rossi's Cantatas Nos. 19 and 21) or as arioso (Cesti, No. 3, and Scarlatti, No. 10), and the closed form as such (Marazzoli, No. 15, and Stradella, No. 2).

If one wrongly believes that a refrain cantata has been so organized on the composer's initiative, then the poet's determining role in formulating refrain structures (with all that this implies for the history of the da capo aria) will not be realized.

WORD SETTING

All the composers under consideration were concerned to convey to the listeners the meaning of the texts. This is evident from the attention they paid to poetic structure and from their habit of using pauses and cadences to coincide with punctuation. It is also clear from the stress through repetition, *fioriture* and word-painting that they gave to key words in either recitative or closed forms, and from the atmosphere (comic, playful, serious, dramatic) that they tried to create according to the text to be sung. In addition, however, some composers seem to have been influenced more than others by the text even in their shaping of a vocal line. Composers such as Carissimi and Stradella make the notes and rhythms perfectly suit the subtle rise, fall and stress inherent in the language; others, such as Pasqualini, Rossi and Strozzi, are careful of the text but prefer to let the voice exhibit its capabilities; still others, such as Alessandro Melani, Gasparini and Scarlatti, tend to sacrifice the text for interesting and effective musical motifs.

If the role words played in suggesting motifs or themes to a particular

[18] For an example of the sort of errors that can result from mistaking arioso for aria see Kathleen Chaikin, 'The Solo Soprano Cantatas of Alessandro Stradella' (dissertation), Stanford University, 1975.

[19] In *The Italian Cantata* only those textual repetitions which have been deemed necessary to the sense or structure of the poem have been included in the poetic layouts.

composer is not realized, one could incorrectly believe that certain stylistic musical characteristics were, in general and through arbitrary choice alone, typical either of a composer or of a period. One would then not recognize the poet's contribution in the creation of the so-called 'motoric rhythm' and 'instrumental vocal line' of the seventeenth century.[20]

There are of course examples of composers who occasionally did not follow the indications for form or style in a cantata text. They may not have changed from recitative to aria as stipulated but, as Vismarri in his Cantata No. 5, beginning with 'Care selve frondose', set recitative as aria;[21] they may not have repeated the music to a strophic text, as Cazzati in 'Oh misera sorte' of No. 14; or they could have set non-symmetrical strophes to repeated music, as one finds in Stradella's 'Alma che tenere' of No. 12. These were the exceptions, however, not the rule. What is more, unless the rule is understood, the exception will never be appreciated.

It must not be concluded from the above discussion that it was only the poet who made decisions which had musical consequences; the patron certainly had his say, at least in deciding on the performers (which may mean that even the poet had to comply with the number or types of actor-singers to be involved in his cantata) and the location of the performance. Nor must it be concluded that composers added nothing to the cantata apart from what may be seen as exceptions or as disobedience to the poet's dictates. In fairness to the poet, however, the composer must not be given credit for what he did not create; moreover only a textual approach to the Italian seventeenth-century cantata will spotlight his own unique contribution. Such an approach will also reveal the inner workings of a collaboration between two artists in what is truly a poetic-musical genre.[22]

[20] Gary Tomlinson, ('Music and the Claims of Text: Monteverdi, Rinuccini, and Marino', *Critical Inquiry*, viii (1981–2), 565–89), though he does not discuss poetic structure either alone or in connection with music, finds that Monteverdi's music was better, more interesting and more dramatic when the poet's text was of better quality; when the poetry was less good, then the composer had more difficulty, and his effort was less successful.

[21] As early as 1691 Giuseppe Gaetano Salvadori, in his *Poetica toscana all'uso* (published in Naples), distinguished between 'natural' arias, which set poetic closed forms, and 'arie cavate', which are 'extracted' from text normally adopted for recitative (pp. 74–6).

[22] I should like to thank Howard Smither and Francesco Giuntini for their constructive criticism of the first draft of this paper.

4

'Two Practices, Three Styles': Reflections on Sacred Music and the Seconda Prattica

Eleanor Selfridge-Field

THERE are two possible histories of Western music: one is of the music as notated, and the other is of the music as performed (or heard). In twentieth-century musicology it has been common to approach the second line of history through the writings of 'music theorists'. Some key theorists of the sixteenth and seventeenth centuries (e.g. Zarlino, Kircher) were astute intellectuals whose respect for music as notated dominated their sense of music as heard. Others, whose numbers increased in the seventeenth century, were practising musicians who wrote manuals on some aspect of performance. A third, more distant, stream of writers on music, whose labours began in the later half of the seventeenth century, were those we might call critics. Predominantly drawn (in Italy, at least) from the ranks of the practising clergy, they created an enlightening but neglected body of information on performance from the perspective of listeners. For some historical purposes the differences between the views of speculative theorists, practical musicians and embryonic critics may seem unimportant, but they prove to be helpful in reaching a fuller understanding not only of the changes that occurred in Italian music between roughly 1580 and 1700 but also of later interpretations of them.

Monteverdi has long been acknowledged as the first to distinguish between the 'two practices', and recently Palisca has also identified him as the first to distinguish 'three styles', theatre, chamber and dance, as concomitants of three methods of performance—respectively the 'oratorical', the 'harmonic', and the 'rhythmic'.[1] Because Monteverdi was unsystematic, it is important to bear in mind that the 'two practices' concept, first

---

[1] Claude V. Palisca, 'The Genesis of Mattheson's Style Classification', *New Mattheson Studies*, ed. George J. Buelow & Hans Joachim Marx, Cambridge, 1983, pp. 415 f. The attribution is a slight misrepresentation, since Monteverdi placed these particular styles under the rubric of music that was suited to courts; he was addressing the Emperor Ferdinand III and the general needs of '*gran prencipi*'. The 'three styles' of Monteverdi's contemporary Marco

mentioned in the preface to the Fifth Book of Madrigals (1605) and expanded on Monteverdi's behalf by his brother Giulio Cesare in the preface to the Scherzi musicali (1607), preceded by more than three decades the exposition of the 'three styles' in the preface to the Eighth Book of Madrigals (1638).

Monteverdi's original point of departure, in calling attention to the existence of two practices, was *harmony*. A list of composers whose work was considered illustrative of the practice 'that turns on the perfection of harmony' included the names of many of the giants of Renaissance sacred music—Ockeghem, Josquin, Mouton, Clemens non Papa, Gombert, Willaert and Zarlino. The champions of the newer emphasis on sensitivity to textual meaning ('that turns on the perfection of melody') are, correspondingly, champions of madrigal and monody—Marenzio, Luzzaschi, Peri, Caccini and, above all, Cipriano de Rore. What was thought to be particularly 'expressive' among the madrigalists was dissonance. To formal theorists concerned with adherence to rules dissonance was permissible only in prescribed circumstances, while to composers concerned with suiting the music to its text it was welcomed as a means of intensifying expression. What attracted Monteverdi to the music of Rore might have repelled more formal theorists: this was the licence to subordinate rational considerations to expressive needs, and it was shortly to be extended to the licence to refine interpretations in the actuality of performance.

This divergence of opinion about licence is fundamental to the metamorphosis of the Italian Renaissance into the Italian Baroque. The reason it is fundamental is that it signals an important differentiation between music as a context for intellectual exercise and music as an aural experience. What exposes the shift of emphasis in Monteverdi's time (and indeed in his midst) is something palpable—the rise of a generation of composers who lacked a grounding in the teachings of Willaert and Zarlino, who were not trained in the rules of counterpoint, who did not depend, in fact, on music as written down or published, and who thrived on the experience of spontaneous interpretation at the moment of performance. This group included the early sonata composers Marini and Castello, who never sang as choirboys or trained to be church organists (thus avoiding the formalities of music education of those who did) but who played string or wind instruments according to principles they seem to have developed for themselves along the

---

Scacchi formed the more familiar triad of church, chamber and theatre taken over by Mattheson in 1739 and taken as gospel by Manfred Bukofzer (*Music in the Baroque Era*, New York, 1947, p. 16 & *passim*). Palisca's study is valuable, however, in showing (p. 422) that in devising classifications Mattheson was influenced by Monteverdi in the *Neu-eröffnetes Orchestre* (1713) and *Kern melodischer Wissenschaft* (1737), while in the expanded scheme in the *Vollkommener Capellmeister* (1739) he seems to have been influenced by Kircher (as distilled through a host of intervening writers).

way. They represented a second stream of composers who, for much of the seventeenth century, coexisted with composers of more traditional demeanour. The sonata was a predilection of these composers in an era in which traditionalists still adhered to the canzona.[2] The vocal analogue of this orientation, which posits more value in the performance than in the composition, was of course the cantata.

If harmonic licence was the measure of 'practice' as described in the Fifth Book, then the level of rhythmic intensity was the measure of 'style' as described in the Eighth. In the preface to the Eighth Book of Madrigals (1638) Monteverdi, paying lip service to Plato, defines what he considers to be the most important *passioni* or *affettioni*—those of ire (*concitato*), of serenity (*molle*) and of the intermediate (some would say Aristotelian) temper, moderation (*temperato*).[3] Monteverdi's terminology is more innovative than the music to which it relates. The melodically stationary semiquavers of the *stile concitato*, for example, abounded in battle madrigals of the later sixteenth century; the languid minims of the *stile molle* occurred in many contrasting passages of the sacred vocal, as well as the secular vocal, repertory of the early seventeenth. What is perhaps most noteworthy is Monteverdi's sensitivity to mood as an abstract quality to which a graduated response is possible: now long passages of unrelieved semiquavers, for example, may replace the setting of individual words in the manner of 'madrigalisms'. This objective has an apt equivalent in the concurrent introduction of character designations ('allegro', 'adagio') in collections of instrumental music by Monteverdi's contemporaries in Venice. For

[2] Eleanor Selfridge-Field, 'The Canzona and Sonata: Some Differences of Social Identity', *International Review of the Aesthetics and Sociology of Music*, ix (1978), 111–20.

[3] What is usually called the *prima prattica* accords well with the Platonic view of the purpose of music, while the *seconda prattica* is aligned more with the Aristotelian. Platonic rationalism concentrated on abstract concepts—'harmony', numerical relationships and other features that could be explained systematically. Aristotelians favoured the view that music should stimulate the passions, because ultimately such release should promote the catharsis that was otherwise sought in tragedy. Aristotelians thus looked beyond the work of art to the response of its beholders. Formal theorists were predominantly of a Platonic turn of mind, while the early Italian critics seem to have been more Aristotelian in their underlying orientation. Varying descriptions of the nature and meaning of the modes have tended somewhat to blend these otherwise disparate points of view. While in a great many accounts numerical relationships dominate the underlying theory, in others affective associations are linked with specific modes (or intervals). That is, a fixed relationship between the rational and expressive qualities of music is assumed. It was on the basis of such relations that Platonists advocated the avoidance of improperly disposed modes, while Aristotelians accepted their use for emotive ends. In Platonic thought, these 'affective' associations have less to do with states of the soul than with ethics. What is *affected* is more behavioural than sentimental. Plato commented on the moral force of melody, and Plato as paraphrased by Zarlino was held to maintain that harmony without a text of moral import was of little consequence. Ethical implications, as distinct from expressive effects, suggest analogies with oratory, as distinct from poetics. Here an important divergence in implication occurs between persuasion and expression.

example, in Castello's First Book of Sonatas (1621) lingering prolation signs preclude the possibility that such words referred to tempo.

Since discussions of 'two practices' and 'three styles' both originate purely in association with Monteverdi's madrigals, sacred music seems by default to be irrelevant to the mood of innovation that the *seconda prattica* is taken to have represented, but this cannot have been the case. The most cursory examination of the newly composed works of the time reveals that while the contrapuntal style was not prominent in the secular repertory, the monodic style to which the *seconda prattica* was linked made itself very much at home in the sacred repertory. If, in Monteverdi's view, opera was in the 'oratorical' style, then by extension the motet and the oratorio (as well as the cantata) should have been also.

The persuasive power promised by a study of rhetoric was singularly well suited to the purposes of the Counter-Reformation. By 1600 the music of Palestrina was seen as the embodiment of the guidelines of the Council of Trent for works that exhibited clarity in style and language, and which evoked personal pietism. The pietist movement of the early seventeenth century, however, brought a complete realignment of artistic and philo-sophical values, for the style of composition that best accommodated the introspective, personal reflections of pietism was monody. Some excellent and very moving examples of pietistic monody are found in the anthology *Ghirlanda sacra* (1625), to which numerous chapel singers who worked under Monteverdi (Grandi, Rovetta, the young Cavalli and others) contributed.

The motet was an increasingly important genre of sacred music in Italy as the seventeenth century progressed, and it is not surprising that stylistically it was frequently equivalent to the chamber cantata. The motet well suited the movement toward personalization of worship because, not being an element of the liturgy, it did not derive its text from a fixed menu. Motets were commonly interchanged with instrumental pieces, such as sonatas, between the Psalms of Vespers services in Venetian churches over much of the seventeenth century. Motet texts could be (and frequently were) devised to reflect (often allegorically) on worldly events; their effect was, to *cognoscenti*, to temporalize the timeless. This temporalization was intended to be conducive to a spontaneous regard for the text.

In the more philosophical thought of the seventeenth century the glory of the universe comprised the infinite variety and novelty of the visible world as well as the direction of all wills toward a common good in the invisible realms of the spirit. Particularly in the later seventeenth century, these lofty realms were not infrequently indistinguishable from the paradises created on earth by temporal rulers. Details of history and mythology were disarmingly interposed to suit particular occasions. The myth of Orpheus could be extended to confirm the value of Christianity, as allegory intertwined fable and history. Orpheus' harp was suggestive to the facile Baroque mind of

King David's harp.[4] In keeping with such an orientation, the presumed divinity of music made the presence of musicians desirable in palaces and princely estates.[5] Hierarchies of angels had long populated the celestial spheres of both theologians and astronomers. Gaffurio had claimed in the 1490s that the Muses had been deprived of their rightful place by the angels of Revelation,[6] but by the seventeenth century a unified identity was at times almost imaginable. In Catholic realms the sacred and the secular were blended into a mesmerizing whole.

Nowhere was the blending of sacred and secular more evident than on the Venetian opera stage of the seventeenth century. Here men and gods met and conversed. The interaction of the earthly king, Ulysses, and the heavenly king, Zeus, in Monteverdi's *Il ritorno d'Ulisse in patria* (1640) is reminiscent of the meeting of *musica humana* and *musica mundana* in the 1581 *Balet comique de la reine*.[7] Even as the motet that celebrated today's rite of passage temporalized the timeless, so opera realized abstractions of space. An invisible Heaven might be represented by a visible Zeus. Oratorio, which was not staged, did not require realization in the same way, but there is growing evidence that many oratorio librettos of the later seventeenth and early eighteenth centuries were allegories in which real people of the time were disguised as religious heroes of the past.[8]

In Stefani's phrase, what may have differentiated the allegories of oratorio from the allegories of opera was that the former 'had a real foundation in aesthetic experience'.[9] In the view of the time, it was only through sound that access to the higher orders of the universe was available. Certainly, but ironically, it was the degree of importance attached to sound itself that seems most greatly to have differentiated opera from oratorio by the end of the seventeenth century. This is not said to denigrate the quality of opera performances but only to note the extent to which they were diminished by visual and social distractions. Audiences looked to the theatre as the perfect venue for social and political intercourse. It is difficult to know now whether the chief value of elaborate sets, machines and costumes was artistic enhancement or visual distraction. The lack of visual interest in the oratorio

---

[4] Gino Stefani, *Musica barocca: poetica e ideologia*, Milan, 1974, p. 136.

[5] Ibid., p. 193.

[6] Claude V. Palisca, *Humanism in Italian Renaissance Musical Thought*, New Haven, 1985, p. 18.

[7] As pointed out by F. W. Sternfeld in his Oxford lectures on the origins of opera. For this earlier festivity the harmony of the supernatural spheres, or *musica mundana*, emanated from a decorated cage on the king's left, the harmony of human activity, or *musica humana*, from the stage opposite the king, and music of the ethical realm, or *musica instrumentalis* (offered by Pan), from a box on the king's right. Thus arrayed, Boethius's divisions of music, like the divisions of an army, converged on the imagined enemies of the State.

[8] Discussed in Eleanor Selfridge-Field, *Pallade Veneta: Writings on Music in Venetian Society, 1650–1750*, Venice, 1985, *passim*.

[9] *Musica barocca*, p. 137

must inevitably have forced much greater concentration on the music itself. It now seems reasonably likely that between 1675 and 1725 the development of idiomatic writing for individual instruments was fostered far more in Venice in oratorio than in opera.[10]

The universality of purpose that Catholicism proclaimed was counterbalanced in a sense by the growing emphasis on differentiation in performance. *Affetti* could be built into the composition through harmonic, melodic or rhythmic considerations. *Accenti*, the specific devices of ornamentation to which so many practical manuals of the seventeenth century devoted themselves, were left to the discretion of the performer.[11] Viewed philosophically, *affetti* were emotive ends and *accenti* the musical means to them.

The development of an entire vocabulary of musical devices for ornamentation and elaboration seems to have been fostered, at least in Venice, by the motet. Stefani has called attention to the alliance, by that time, of music and nature, which accounts for the frequency with which 'birds' and 'flowers' come to represent the persuasive powers of music.[12] *Fioritura* is thus well named, and collections of sacred music with titles referring to a *giardino* or a *ghirlanda* (e.g. the Venetian motet anthology *Ghirlanda sacra*) are very much in character with the intellectual climate.

The Counter-Reformation was a prime source of early music criticism for reasons that are slightly convoluted. Cultural achievement was viewed as a recommendation for the Church, and commentaries about that achievement were therefore energetic in their praise. But the praise could not be hollow, because there had to be a perceived religious function for the arts. In the case of music ('*la scienza di Paradiso*') that purpose was to open the conduits of communication with the divine. The role of ornamentation (*accenti*) was seen to be that of evoking an appropriate state of mind (*affetto*) to initiate the process of such apprehension. Music offered a unique path to celestial truth.

Some appreciation of this orientation is essential to an understanding of the many informative writings about both sacred and secular music that occur in a monthly journal of the late seventeenth century entitled *Pallade*

---

[10] Eleanor Selfridge-Field, 'Music at the Pietà before Vivaldi', *Early Music*, xiv (1986), 382.

[11] There seems little reason to doubt that what the word '*affetto*' originally intended was simple quivering emotion, suggestive of active rather than passive response to a message, and thus rhetorical in function. The term '*affetto*' was commonly used in the titles of published collections of secular music in Monteverdi's time. There were madrigals and sonatas in the *Affetti amorosi* (1611) of Marc'Antonio Negri and instrumental pieces of sundry kinds in Marini's first opus, the *Affetti musicali* (1617). Besides being used in commentaries and titles, however, the term '*affetto*' was also used as a performance instruction. To '*cantare con affetto*', according to Francesco Rognoni (writing in the *Selva di varii passaggi*, Milan, 1620; facs. edn. Bologna, 1970), required the execution of *maniere*, or ornaments thought to add 'grace and expressiveness'. *Tremoli, groppi, trilli* and *esclamazioni* were among the *accenti* that Rognoni offered to aid the cause of singing '*con gratia e maniera*'. Rognoni also spoke of '*il lireggiare affettuoso*'; Marini (Op. 8, 1626) and Scarani (1630) offered passages to be played '*con affetti*' (apparently meaning with a bowed tremolo).

[12] Op. cit., pp. 98–101.

Veneta. The journal was initiated in 1687 by Francesco Coli, a Lucchese book censor for the Inquisition who was resident in Venice, where his tasks seem to have included the approval of texts for sacred vocal music, and his inclination seems to have led him to attend performances tirelessly. In contrast to Renaissance thinkers, Coli did not perceive the scientific essence of music to consist in numerical relationships but rather in those conduits to the perception of divine purpose and order that are, in numerous specific passages, equated with what earlier writers would have called the affections. *Affetti* helped to put the listener in the right frame of mind to perceive celestial truths and were available only through the medium of music. Coli was equally verbose about oratorios and motets.

Coli concentrates heavily on the matter of audience response to music. What the audiences of his experience responded to were *trilli, gorgie* and other *maniere*. Some motets sung at San Marco for the Feast of St Joseph (19 March) in 1688 were performed 'with *affetto* so devotional that that sacred habitation seemed like a Paradise in tears'.[13] Such performances seem to have incorporated not the terraced emotional dynamics of the *seconda prattica* but moments of crystallized (usually pietistic) feeling. This may seem a curious rotation of the concept of affections, since it focuses not on what was composed but on those details of performance that began, in a sense, where the composition ended. This reorientation is very much apiece with the emphasis on individualization that distinguished both the oratorians' quest for direct communication and the Baroque performer's quest for particularization. It is no small irony, however, that by the end of the seventeenth century the 'clutter' that the Counter-Reformation had once sought to strip away had become newly symbolic of reverence.

Many performances were evaluated on the basis of whether they succeeded in moving their hearers. The role of ornamentation in achieving this end is cited again and again. For example, Angela Vicentina of the Ospedaletto (elsewhere described by Misson as 'une petite créature qui enchante') sang a solo motet before the Elector Maximilian Emanuel of Bavaria in February 1687 that caused Coli to comment, 'If she were not so young, one might wonder whether it was she who taught the nightingales about song, *il trillo, le gorgie,* and *il batter* when the world was in its infancy.'[14] Five months later this 'little spirit of Paradise' sang a motet ('Quando videbo te' by Carlo Grossi) in which she 'explained with song her desire to depart from this lachrymose sea of the world and to throw open to all the listeners a paradise of joy'.[15] It was said that the world had not heard a 'voice more sweet, a manner more open, a throat more mellow, a chest less

---

[13] Selfridge-Field, *Pallade Veneta*, p. 214.
[14] Ibid., p. 155.
[15] Ibid., p. 177.

restrained, nor even a tongue more ready for the *passaggi*, the *fughe*, the leaps [and] the trills from the time of Orpheus until now'.[16]

Coli was gratified by a performance of Spada's now lost oratorio *Santa Maria Egizziaca* at the Pietà in September of the same year. In the role of Zosima, the singer Francesca offered a song of penitence (which in the context of the libretto signified heathen acceptance of Christianity) that brought tears of happiness to the singer's eyes. The 'little instruments of gold on which Apollo has turned upside down all the highest prerogatives of music' appealed again to mythological authority, as of course did the title of the journal itself. Lucrezia, Barbara and Francesca were praised for the expressiveness of their '*passaggi, trilli, gorgie, gratie* and *dolci maniere*'.[17] Repeat performances for cardinals and bishops were arranged. Francesca, who 'possesses a superhuman quality in playing the theorbo', had an additional role in an August performance of the same work: she 'carried the entire audience into ecstasies of admiration with the galant *ricercate* that she improvised [*tentò*] on the lute' during the interval.[18]

Coli did not ignore the virtues of composition *per se*. In reporting on the performance of a Grossi motet, 'Omnis spiritus laudet Dominum', he asserted that in composing the most superb fugues that art can invent 'Signor Grossi must have tipped over the musical urn in which *le crome* and the well-tuned *biscrome* conceal themselves'.[19] Yet it was in the performance that the work's true worth was realized:

> O what sweet *passaggi*, O what rare *gratie* that little Angel of paradise made us hear, in particular in that 'Maiora sperate pareva', like a seraphim who, with the lighted coals of those notes, touched our silent lips because she created an echo of that prophecy that God wills through angelic hosts to subdue the Unfaithful.[20]

To Coli the subdued sounds of the Venetian night were especially entrancing. In the calm of evening the lingering echoes of the day revealed Paradise on Earth. In the last of the writings about music that can be verifiably attributed to Coli (one which concerns the celebration of the Feast of Ascension in 1688) the interests of the gods of the Greeks and the Holy Redeemer are intertwined with the glorious destiny of the Most Serene Republic. Coli concludes his account:

---

[16] Ibid., p. 175. The acceptance of *passaggi* as appropriate devices in a sacred setting was apparently gained slowly over the seventeenth century, for Cavalieri, in the preface to his *Rappresentazione di anima e di corpo* (Rome, 1600), considered *passaggi* to violate the mandates of the Counter-Reformation. *Passaggi* similarly filtered into German teachings on musical rhetoric at a relatively late date; references to them can be found in Bernhard's undated *Tractatus* (late seventeenth century) and J. G. Walther's manuscript 'Praecepta' (1708).

[17] Ibid., p. 188.

[18] Ibid., p. 184.

[19] Ibid., p. 194.

[20] Ibid.

This affair lasted until two in the night [i.e. two hours after sunset]; and . . . Apollo
. . . granted liberty to the Muses to enjoy the sound of the harmony . . . After the
lamps were lighted in the boats and the instruments picked up, one heard, variously
by one voice and by more, songs so suave and full of sweetness that, the silence on
these banks dispersed, nothing else seemed to exist except our ears. The breezes
themselves were tuned to our dearest satisfactions, which also carried with them the
syllables, the accents, and the fugues of those further away who thought they were
singing to themselves. [The goddess] Echo . . . a lover of these Orpheuses, restated
entire verses, repeated the trills, hushed the rests, and replicated the *passaggi* with
such content to our ears that they wanted to be petrified in order to relay the sounds
to those voices of Paradise, since it seemed that on the same route along which the
Redeemer had passed that very day to glory, the angels had descended to sing of their
triumphs on these seas.[21]

Our perceptions of the *seconda prattica* are bound up with a large
spectrum of otherwise quite diverse bodies of thought. To start with, there is
all the Italian speculative thought of the Renaissance, which is itself bound
up with the pronouncements of antiquity. Renaissance Italians were very
much absorbed by questions of poetics, and of the relationship between
poetry and music.[22] Kirkendale claims that this rapture with the tenets
of antiquity extended even to instrumental music.[23] To the extent that
sixteenth-century Italian theorists were intellectuals, formal music theory
was greatly contaminated with convoluted rationalizations that portrayed
the musical needs of a polyphonic era as being compatible with statements of
philosophical purpose devised in a much earlier era in which polyphonic
music was, as best we know, unknown. It is probably the word *affetto*,
which was in common use in the writings of the sixteenth century,[24] that has
caused commentators on the *seconda prattica* to link Monteverdi's pronouncements with this earlier body of writings. Monteverdi himself, to the
extent that he was at heart a practical musician, may mislead us into thinking

[21] Ibid., p. 226.
[22] In particular, the interrelationships between poetry, oratory and music were extensively
debated. For Marsilio Ficino (a fifteenth-century translator of Plato) the musician was a model
for both the poet and the orator. Zarlino insisted (in his *Sopplimenti* of 1588) on a basic
methodological distinction between the poet and the orator, who relied on separate modes of
imitation. The *seconda prattica* represented one definition of the relationship between poetry
and music. Palisca's recent monograph, *Humanism in Italian Renaissance Musical Thought*,
provides an illuminating commentary on heavily debated issues regarding analogies between
the function of poetry and the function of music. Was music addressed to intellect or to
imagination? Was it mimetic? Was it fundamentally idealistic? Was its purpose essentially
ethical or affective? Did it, in the end, comprise all these ends to varying degrees? See especially
Palisca's chapter 'The Poetics of Music' (pp. 369–407).
[23] The ricercar as it was developed in the 1530s and 1540s was a response, he claims, to the
elevated position of self-imitation associated with Cicero's concept of 'thematic' coherence.
See Warren Kirkendale, 'Ciceronians versus Aristotelians on the Ricercar as Exordium',
Journal of the American Musicological Society, xxxii (1979), 31 & *passim*.
[24] Vincenzo Galilei had written in *Il Fronimo* (1568), for example, that only notes in long
values were suited to expressing 'affections'.

that he too was motivated mainly by an interest in upholding the dictates of antiquity.

Then there is all the German music theory of the seventeenth and eighteenth centuries in which rhetoric, as distinct from poetics (but again on the pretext of classical superiority), was a dominant preoccupation.[25] Among German music theorists of the seventeenth century, who were particularly indebted to Quintilian,[26] an interest in rhetoric led to efforts to identify and recommend musical equivalents for figures of speech. Where the Italians (even in their high regard for rhetoric) were motivated to search for generality, the Germans by and large sought definition and specificity. The musical equivalents (*figurae*) of specific rhetorical devices could involve various schemes of melodic repetition and manipulation, specific harmonic and rhythmic traits, and occasionally slightly abstract characteristics, such as the compass of parts. Whereas, therefore, Monteverdi's three '*affettioni*' were broadly extrapolated from texts, the *figurae* catalogued by German theorists were finely tuned to specific text elements of a few words, finite in their associations and in a sense re-rationalized from the liberated state of musical expression as it was conceived in the early seventeenth century.

Among German theorists a familiarity with the broad practice of sacred vocal music in Italy seems to have been limited to certain works known better by notation than by sound. Excepting Athanasius Kircher (1601–80), a Jesuit theologian and mathematician who spent most of his adult life in Vienna and Rome, the German theorists who wrote on musical rhetoric in the seventeenth century (Burmeister, Herbst, and Bernhard) were practical musicians with positions in Lutheran churches in northerly areas of Germany. The ramifications of cultural pluralism between Italian composers as they understood themselves and as they were understood by later German theorists are ignored often enough, but at the price of equating things that are not equal: the concept of *Affektenlehre*, generally attributed to Mattheson but lately held to be more an invention of twentieth-century musicology,[27] has little enough to do with the general concept of *affetti* or with Monteverdi's pronouncements in his Eighth Book. The confidence we place in any effort at classification (whether Kircher's subdivisions of the 'church style' or Mattheson's subcategories of the 'three styles') is misplaced

---

[25] The very valid distinction between ideas inspired by the study of rhetoric and those inspired by the study of poetics seems often enough to be ignored when music of Monteverdi's time is seen through the filter of eighteenth-century German music theory and twentieth-century American musicology. Thus, to cite but one recent instance, Gary Tomlinson refers to 'poetical and/or rhetorical' expression in Monteverdi's music and to 'the expressive rhetoric' of Rinuccini somewhat to the detriment of his argument that Ariadne lamented without the distraction of madrigalisms ('Monteverdi's "Via Naturale alla Immitatione"', *Journal of the American Musicological Society*, xxxiv (1981), 95, 101).

[26] George J. Buelow, 'Johann Mattheson and the Invention of the *Affektenlehre*', *New Mattheson Studies*, p. 395.

[27] Ibid., pp. 394–404.

in one sense: the German search for an optimum classification scheme ran counter to the universalist world view of the Counter-Reformation.

It was not until the middle of the eighteenth century, when genealogies tracing the origin of an idea to Plato or Aristotle or Cicero or Quintilian (it really no longer mattered) were subsumed by the single notion of 'antiquity', on which what is sometimes called the 'new paganism' was founded, that the notions of classification and unification could coexist peacefully. By that time the sounds of the *seconda prattica* were gone.

5

Curtio Precipitato—Claudio Parodiato

Silke Leopold

COMPOSERS have always responded creatively to the works of other composers, whether challenged by unusual thematic material, by new technical ideas or by a certain unmistakably personal idiom. Ravel's piano compositions 'A la manière de Borodin' (and Chabrier) belong to this sphere of activity, as do, for example, Clementi's *Musical Characteristics*, Op. 19;[1] also part of the same phenomenon, however, are Mozart's 'Haydn' Quartets and the Guarini madrigals of Monteverdi written in response to the music of Marenzio.[2] The further we go back in history, the harder it becomes to perceive connections of this kind between individual works—not only because the musical repertory has come down to us in such a fragmentary fashion that the tracking down of direct references is, if anything, governed by chance, but also because the detection of such interactions becomes the more difficult, the less we are able to say about the typical musical idioms of one particular composer in relation to those in generally common usage. To take one example: in the 'Aria a imitazione del Radesca alla piamontese nel liuto' from Adriano Banchieri's *Barca di Venetia per Padova*, what is it that is specifically typical of Radesca?—what distinguishes this composition from countless other chamber duets of this period which to our ears sound similar? The answer to such a question evades us not least because we do not know sufficient compositions by either Enrico Radesca or by his contemporaries to be able to denominate Radesca's own individual style.

Moreover, the boundaries between stylistic copy and parody (in the modern sense) are altogether fluid. That the 'Aria ad imitazione del Radesca' belongs to the realm of parody is made clear by the lute imitation 'trenc ten ten ten, tronc ton ton toro tronc' with which the middle voices accompany Horatio (bass) and Rizzolina (soprano). However, are the two madrigals 'alla Venosa', the 'Madrigale. Stile del Marenzio Romano' and the 'Madrigale a imitazione del Spano napolitano' from the *Barca di Venetia per*

---

[1] The compositions of the *Musical Characteristics* dedicated to Mozart are dealt with by Volker Scherliess in 'Clementis Komposition "alla Mozart"', *Colloquium 'Mozart und Italien' (Rome 1974)*, ed. Friedrich Lippmann, ('Analecta musicologica', xviii), Cologne, 1978, pp. 308–18.

[2] See Alfred Einstein, *The Italian Madrigal*, Princeton, 1949 (repr. 1970), ii. 678 ff.

Padova intended as parodies or as stylistic copies? We cannot answer conclusively either way, especially since what we today regard as perhaps the single most characteristic feature of a composer like Gesualdo, namely expressive harmony, does not once appear in the two madrigals 'alla Venosa'.[3]

In the 1720s and '30s a large number of vocal works were produced in Venice of such a similar conception that Wolfgang Osthoff has spoken in this connection of 'a Venetian school of Monteverdi'.[4] It is doubtful whether Monteverdi actually stood at the head of a school that was the starting-point and focus for these multifarious musical exchanges and cross-references —the unclear chronology of the works warns us to be cautious in the face of such assertions. Moreover, Monteverdi not only provided ideas by which others then felt themselves challenged to produce their own compositions, but also took up in turn the stimuli of other composers in his own music: 'Ohimè ch'io cado ohimè', for example, was written in response to Carlo Milanuzzi's 'O come vezzosetta' rather than the reverse.[5] One thing, however, may be stated with certainty about all of these pieces which resemble one another: they are not parodies but stylistic copies. They are the fruits of a serious occupation with the ideas of another composer, works to be viewed seriously, with lofty artistic claims.

A different case is respresented by Tarquinio Merula's extended composition for bass that gave name to his collection *Curtio precipitato*, published in 1638. Denis Arnold has already pointed out that this work bears a relationship to Monteverdi,[6] and in particular to the *Combattimento di Tancredi e Clorinda*. Arnold cites a passage from 'Curtio precipitato' in which the 'Sinfonia ad immitatione d'un cavallo' and a piece in 'genere guerriero' (which he incorrectly describes as 'stile concitato') refer directly to Monteverdi's *Combattimento*. In fact the 'Sinfonia ad immitatione d'un cavallo', which is heard three times in the course of the composition, is modelled on Monteverdi's 'Trotto del cavallo'. It is precisely the nature of this imitation, however, which indicates that Merula was scarcely concerned with producing a stylistic copy, or responding seriously to Monteverdi's scenic idea: rather, it seems that 'Curtio precipitato' is intended as a

---

[3] On parody in the madrigal comedies of Orazio Vecchi and Adriano Banchieri see Andreas Wernli, *Studien zum literarischen und musikalischen Werk Adriani Banchieris (1568–1634)*, Berne & Stuttgart, 1981, esp. pp. 151 ff. Wernli claims to be able to recognize parody in the madrigal 'alla Marenzio', but he does not make it clear in so doing whether he is using parody in the sense of stylistic copy or in the sense of caricature.

[4] Wolfgang Osthoff, *Das dramatische Spätwerk Claudio Monteverdis*, Tutzing, 1960, p. 78 n. 29.

[5] This is shown by a musical and literary comparison: for example, Monteverdi's opening verse takes up an identical verse in Milanuzzi's composition; see Silke Leopold, *Dichtung und Musik im italienischen Sologesang des frühen 17. Jahrhunderts* (in the press).

[6] 'Some Colleagues and Pupils', *The New Monteverdi Companion*, ed. Denis Arnold & Nigel Fortune, London 1985, pp. 120 f.

parody—a parody not only of the *Combattimento* but equally of several other specific characteristics of Monteverdi's style.

Merula's collection, the full title of which reads CURTIO PRECIPITATO *Et altri Capricij Composti in diversi modi vaghi e leggiadri à voce sola*, is a curious conglomeration of serious and parodic pieces, of popular melodies and texts spiced with dialect. The collection ends with the canzonetta 'Sentirete una canzonetta' on the well-known 'Girometta' melody, with a drone-like instrumental accompaniment;[7] from the world of popular music for entertainment are derived likewise two pieces in Venetian dialect, 'Conza lavez e colder' and 'Non ha'l regno d'amor'. Alongside them, however, are found the two serious pieces described as 'Canzonetta spirituale', 'Hor ch'è tempo di dormire', a sad lullaby of Mary for the baby Jesus over the 'Ninna-Nanna' bass, and 'Chi vuol ch'io m'innamori', a text taken up by Monteverdi in his *Selve morale e spirituale*. Unequivocally parodic, on the other hand, is the 'Canzonetta in sdrucciolo', 'Quando gli ucelli porteranno i Zoccoli', in which the match between content and form is deliberately less apt. The verse is couched in the august metre of epic poetry, though slightly distorted, of course, by the *sdrucciolo*-endings, and the music is in the style of epic recitation over a long-held bass chord; the text enumerates an interminable series of abstruse expostulations of the kind, for example, that a camel would more easily go through the eye of a needle than the singer forget his adored one. Last but not least among the unimaginable events thus presented is the notion that the Germans could forget drinking:

> Quando li muti canteranno favole
> e gli tedeschi non sapran più bevere,
> li sorci piglieran le gatte gnavole
> e fuggiranno i cani da le lievere,
> amaro sarà il zuccaro e dolce i pevere,
> il mar di piante, i monti d'acqua carichi,
> allora finiranno i miei rammarichi.

The multi-sectional 'Fiori fiori o quanti fiori', with its consistently false musical accents and incessant parallel stresses, is also a musical parody, on the 'new simplicity' of the ariette.[8]

The mere fact that it was published together with pieces of this kind should make us suspicious of the seriousness of 'Curtio precipitato', as well as the description 'Capricio', which Merula accords to this piece too by his observation 'altri Capricij' in the title of the collection. Text and music bear out this suspicion, for the heroic story that underlies the work is presented here in a kind of plebeian running commentary as far removed from Tasso's epic poetry as John Gay is from Metastasio. The text is concerned with

---

[7] Pr. Osthoff, op.cit., pp. 37 f., where its 'Girometta' origin is also mentioned.
[8] See Leopold, *Dichtung und Musik*.

Marcus Curtius, a figure of Roman popular legend; in the fourth century BC a wide crevasse had opened up in the forum, and the oracle signified that it would close up only after the sacrifice of Rome's most prized possession. As a good Roman Marcus Curtius took this oracle to refer to the courage of the warrior and, seated on his horse in full military apparel, he plunged himself into the deep fissure. His sacrifice was accepted, and the crevasse closed up.

The poet of 'Curtio precipitato' is not known. Two sonnets addressed to Merula precede the printed music; possibly one of the two authors, Claudio Sacchelli or Roberto Poggiolini, is also the author of the 'Curtio' text. Unlike Tasso's account of the fight between Tancredi and Clorinda, which describes the event with the detachment of reportage, so to speak, behind the 'Curtio' text there stands a narrator who speaks in the first person, who sees the hero ride up to the crevasse and attempts to hold him back:

> Curtio ove vai? Non far questa pazzia,
> fermati col malan che dio ti dia,
> ché se tu salti te ne pentirai.

In this tone—that is, in highly flavoured colloquial speech—the poem continues, interspersed with more or less coarse oaths (as for example 'quel matto cornuto'), until at the end of the first quarter of the text Curtius plunges into the crevasse. From here on the narrator indulges in reflections on the sense and nonsense of such an action: whether for the sake of posthumous fame it is worth giving one's life, since dead one can no longer profit from posthumous fame anyhow; in any case, he, the narrator, would have behaved differently:

> S'io fossi stato all'hora,
> vi dico il mio pensiero,
> non gl'havrei fatto affé da cavagliero.
> E fosse andato pur Roma in malora,
> so ch'il medesmo ancora
> fatto alcun altro havria
> e prima di cadere
> saria stato a vedere
> come quel capitombo
> lo riusciva, e d'imitarlo invece
> havrebbe riso poi di chi lo fece.

This is, in all conscience, scarcely a heroic approach—trivializing the valiant sacrificial leap into a somersault, breaking out into laughter rather than lapsing into reverential emotion, and politely giving precedence to a braver man rather than making a heroic sacrifice oneself. In the whole undertaking the narrator can discern nothing more than an act of stupidity, and the text ends with an appeal to the listeners:

Hor voi ch'havete inteso
la pazzia di costui:
Eccì alcun che sia pazzo al par di lui?
Ditemi pur fra voi chi sarà quello
di sì poco cervello
che per lasciar che dire
a la plebe ignorante
si contenta morire.
Vadasi ad impiccar pur chi n'ha voglia,
che morirà giocondo
e darà dopo se che dire al mondo.

It is conceivable that 'Curtio precipitato' owes its origin to topical motive: who would be so stupid as to sacrifice his life for posthumous fame? Merula dedicated the collection to Giovanni Battista Barbo, 'Marchese di Soresina & Maestro di Campo della Militia nel Cremonese per sua M.ᵗᵃ Cattolica'. As a dedicatory work to a military leader this text could not be described as anything other than a piece of impudence, if the dedicatee did not himself cherish such unheroic thoughts. At a time when the great powers France and Spain, on the fringes of the Thirty Years War so to speak, were haggling over the estates of Lombardy and engaging in skirmish upon skirmish in the Duchy of Milan, the supreme commander of the Cremonese troops could in fact have felt little desire to sacrifice his life for the cause of the Spanish occupiers.[9] The narrator can in truth only imagine one reason alone why Curtio could have thrown himself into the crevasse:

convien che l'habbi fatto
non per altro se non perch'eri un matto.

No less grotesque than the text, couched in rhyming *versi toscani*, is Merula's setting. At first glance 'Curtio precipitato' appears like one of those countless *versi toscani* declamations which appear from about 1615 in the prints of solo song—dramatic scenes, for the most part with a plaintive content, laments and *lettere*. Merula avails himself of all the means of vocal chamber music of his day, including recitative passages, virtuoso cadenzas, sections in triple time, dance-like rhythms and ostinato basses. This supposedly serious music, however, is interspersed with places in which the coloratura at the cadence is a little too long or expansive, the exclamations just a fraction too emphatic, and the meaning of the words interpreted just a little too precisely to do justice to the gravity of the situation. Perhaps the coloratura of 'circa al gettari in basso', which plunges downwards over a span of more than two octaves, may still be accepted as normal word-painting coloratura (Ex. 5.1). The setting of 'difficil passo' (Ex. 5.2),

[9] See Domenico Sella & Carlo Capra, 'Il Ducato di Milano dal 1535–1796', *Storia d'Italia*, xi (Milan, 1984), 13 ff.

Ex. 5.1

cir - ca_al get-tar-ti a bas - - - - - - - - - - - - - - - - - so

Ex. 5.2

sa - rà un dif - fi - cil pas -

- so

however, exceeds the customary amount of musical word-painting, as does the almost onomatopoeic coloratura towards the end of 'ti rompi il collo' (Ex. 5.3). The 'passi così brutti' are in a sense 'brutti', but 'horrid' in a way that provokes laughter, not horror (Ex. 5.4). And with its doleful sounds of 'ai, ai, ai', which ought strictly speaking to be a kind of cadential ornamentation of the word 'pentirai', the setting of the admonition 'te ne pentirai' is more reminiscent of a thrashing in the tradition of the *commedia dell'arte* than of epic recitation (Ex. 5.5).

Alongside these grotesquely caricatured formulas of the declamatory style, such as were universally in use at this time, concealed in the triple-time sections there is a series of idioms which both verbally and musically refer to Monteverdi. At first glance it may appear much too far-fetched to connect the saraband-type rhythms in the first large triple-metre section of 'Curtio precipitato' with Monteverdi (Ex. 5.6). This saraband rhythm, as Monteverdi uses it in 'Non voglio amare' is indeed extremely rare in the Italian repertory,[10] but the similarities between the rhythmic features of 'con

---

[10] The rhythm later typical of the saraband first appeared in the fourth decade of the seventeenth century in France: see Richard Hudson, 'Sarabande', *The New Grove*, xvi. 489 ff. & bibliography.

Ex. 5.3

ti | rom - pi il col - lo

Ex. 5.4

in pas - si co - sì brut - ti

Ex. 5.5

te ne pen - ti - rai ai ai ai

Ex. 5.6

a

Con vo - ler rad - driz - zar con vo - ler rad - driz - zar

b

no no no no non gli ha - ver non gli ha - ver no no no no no

voler raddrizzar' and 'Non voglio amare', and between 'no no non gl'haver'
in Merula and the 'no no' in Monteverdi (Ex. 5.7) would nevertheless be
much too vague to serve as exclusive proof of Merula's parodic intent. Two
other passages in the same triple-metre section refer so unequivocally to
Monteverdi, however, that these similarities too appear in a different light.
Merula's text reads:

> che quel matto cornuto
> insomm'è risoluto
> saltando voler dar gusto alla gente;
> non gl'haver compassione
> anzi se vuol cader dagli un urtone.

Ex. 5.7

Ex. 5.8

The words 'saltando voler' are set by Merula to a triadic idea, which
musically interprets the leaps by its rise and fall (Ex. 5.8). In the third part of
Monteverdi's *Madrigale amoroso* 'Ninfa che scalza il piede' a shepherd
invites a nymph to dance to the sound of his instrument:

> Dell'usate mie corde al suon potrai
> sotto l'ombra di quest'orno
> a tempo il passo
> muover d'intorno

and at the words 'a tempo il passo', that is to say, at the invitation to dance,
the same triadic sequence is to be found as in Merula, though here on the
downbeat rather than the anacrusis (Ex. 5.9). And at the end of this section
Merula repeats the triadic sequence in the bass, while the voice gives

Ex. 5.9

Ex. 5.10

Ex. 5.11

prominence to the word 'dagli' in a manner that is suited to neither the meaning nor the sound of the word (Ex. 5.10)—especially since the word 'urtone', which is really the main word of the text, thus disappears inconspicuously in the cadence.

A glance at Monteverdi's madrigal 'Augellin che la voce al canto spieghi' provides the answer to the question of where Merula found the idea for this 'dagli, dagli', for in Monteverdi's madrigal the little bird is bidden to hurry to the narrator's beloved and tell her that he is unhappy:

> e con dogliosi accenti
> dille queste parole

Although written in a different time signature, Monteverdi's setting is identical to that of Merula (Ex. 5.11).

In the second large triple-metre section, in which Curtio's plunge is described, Merula conveys even to those less intimately acquainted with Monteverdi's music the secret of who is peeping from behind his musical ideas in this piece. This section, to the words

> Da capo a piedi armato
> a guisa d'un Ruggiero
> con gale e con pennacchi in su'l destriero
> s'è nell'alta voragine gettato

constitutes a self-contained structural unit, with an instrumental interlude over the Ruggiero bass in accordance with the phrase 'a guisa d'un Ruggiero'. Twice in the course of this section, in each case before the opening words 'Da capo a piedi armato', the equine sinfonia is heard, whose

Ex. 5.12

Ex. 5.13

prototype must have been known to even the least educated music lover. The beginning of the voice part, however, is a direct quotation from Monteverdi's 'Se vittorie si belle' (Ex. 5.12). This style of composition, with a drone-like bass and triadic arpeggiation in the vocal part in triple metre, if indeed no invention of Monteverdi's, is nonetheless defined by him in the preface to the Eighth Madrigal Book as 'genere guerriero', and in the *Madrigali guerrieri* it is raised for the first time to a principle of composition and presented systematically. Just how closely this 'genere guerriero' was bound up with the name of Monte erdi is also shown by Heinrich Schütz, whose 'Es steht Gott auf' begins with a similar quotation from 'Armato il cor'.

Whether the last triple-metre section also relates directly to Monteverdi or comically parodies a universally fashionable style cannot be determined, for the stepwise descending ostinato bass that Merula fixed on here as his target appears not only in Monteverdi's 'Lamento della Ninfa' but also in so many compositions by other musicians that a direct connection cannot be proved. Since, however, the Monteverdian 'no no' from 'Non voglio amare' is heard once again in this section, there is an obvious suspicion that Monteverdi is also intended in this instance (Ex. 5.13*a*). Merula begins this last triple-metre section with an apparently endlessly falling bass line, which after one and a half octaves becomes aware of ending up much too far down in the depths and then, by means of an upward leap of a seventh, makes a twist out of the straight line. The ostinato bass produced in this fashion is, as it were, one note too short: it consists of seven notes, and the upper part becomes displaced against the ostinato, so that the caesuras do not always coincide (Ex. 5.13*b*). That Merula's incomplete ostinato scale is intended as a caricature is shown by a look at other basses of this kind; for whenever at this time scalic ostinatos were used, the scales are always heard in their entirety, that is to say, with a repetition of the keynote at both the upper and lower octave; occasionally this keynote was even reinforced at the end of the ostinato statement with a cadence.

None of these hints of Monteverdi would alone be adequate proof of Merula's parodic intentions. Taken together, however, they show clearly that the great old Venetian master represented a challenge of a special kind—especially since Merula, who worked as *maestro di cappella* in Monteverdi's native Cremona, must constantly have had to come to terms with working in the shadow of Monteverdi. 'Curtio precipitato' appeared in print in the same year as Monteverdi's Eighth Book of Madrigals—and with the same publisher, Bartolomeo Magni. We know from the preface that the Eighth Book was ready for printing in 1637 and that only the death of the dedicatee Emperor Ferdinand II delayed it. With the exception of the madrigal 'Augellin che la voce al canto spieghi', which had already been published in 1619 in the Seventh Book of Madrigals, and 'Non voglio amare', which appeared in print only after Monteverdi's death, the works to which Merula makes reference in 'Curtio precipitato' all come from this Eighth Book of Madrigals, which he may have seen long before it appeared in print. 'Curtio precipitato' is thus a winking obeisance by Merula before this highly exacting publication, which both through its preface and through the works themselves burst the boundaries of contemporary vocal chamber music—and 'Curtio precipitato', with its clear yet never malicious innuendo, is at one and the same time both irreverent and respectful.

Translated by Ewan West

II
Music and the Theatre in Seventeenth-Century England

6

Shakespeare's Provoking Music

David Lindley

As Act IV of *Measure for Measure* opens, a boy is singing to Mariana the song 'Take, O, take those lips away'. Upon the entrance of the duke, however, Mariana embarrassedly despatches the singer and excuses herself:

> I cry you mercy, sir, and well could wish
> You had not found me here so musical.
> Let me excuse me, and believe me so,
> My mirth it much displeas'd but pleas'd my woe.

The duke replies:

> 'Tis good; though music oft hath such a charm
> To make bad good and good provoke to harm.

This brief episode, seemingly detachable from the action of the play,[1] nevertheless encapsulates a number of characteristic features of Shakespeare's deployment of song in his plays and, in the ambiguities of response it demands, serves as an appropriate point of departure for more general consideration of the functions of music in his work.

At the simplest dramatic level it creates a mood of wistful melancholy, marking out the difference of the isolated world of Mariana of the moated grange from the urban world of Vienna. As a contrast, the song comes initially as a relief, something to be savoured by Mariana and the audience with uncomplicated pleasure. But song has a further effect: once its stasis and unity between the audience and characters are dispelled as the play returns to its dramatic action, so it invites interpretation as a fixed picture or emblem. This potential of dramatic music is exploited by Shakespeare most notably in Richard II's meditation in his cell, but scarcely a song passes without some kind of reflection upon it, whether it is the 'blank' song that Brutus's page sings to him or Feste's song to the drunken Toby Belch and Andrew Aguecheek. In this case Mariana's apologetic confusion at being

---

[1] Peter J. Seng (*The Vocal Songs in the Plays of Shakespeare*, Cambridge, Mass., 1967, p. 184) goes so far as to suggest that 'it seems possible that the song may be a Jacobean interpolation into Shakespeare's text'.

caught out in the indulgence of her pleasure jolts the audience too from their
easy complicity. But the ambiguity of the duke's response is also typical of
the way Shakespeare rarely allows his audience to leave a song or a musical
moment without some undercutting of a simple response. The most famous
invocation of music's power, in Act v of *The Merchant of Venice*, for
example, is followed by Portia's wry comment:

> The crow doth sing as sweetly as the lark
> When neither is attended; and I think
> The nightingale, if she should sing by day,
> When every goose is cackling, would be thought
> No better a musician than the wren.
>
> (v. i. 102–6)

Portia, like the duke, insists on the way in which it is the listener who
conspires to create music's effect—a view to be explored more fully later, but
one which perhaps justifies concentrating attention upon the ways in which
song characterizes singer or audience. As far as Mariana is concerned, as
F. W. Sternfeld suggests, the duke's comments indicate that

Mariana's purpose is 'to make bad good' as the boy's song of deserted love consoles
her. . . . But to give oneself up to this melancholy stanza . . . is also an act of
self-indulgence and therefore likely to provoke good to harm.[2]

The significance of songs, however, extends beyond their particular
moment, and the duke's comment serves the vital function of placing the
episode within the main thematic preoccupations of the play. Music 'provokes' by working directly upon the feelings and passions. It is precisely
these faculties which in more violent and destructive form are aroused in
Angelo and exhibited in the sensual environment of the brothel. The duke's
paradoxical formulation of the powers of music, indeed, links with Angelo's
tortured meditation on the attraction Isabella exerts over him, as he demands 'Dost thou desire her foully for those things / That make her good?'
(II. ii. 174–5). The analogy is of considerable significance, not only for this
play but especially for the way it is more generally revealing of Renaissance
attitudes towards music. At first sight the introduction of Mariana surrounded by melancholy and potentially self-indulgent music seems to set her
apart not merely from the earlier, unmusical action but also from Isabella,
whom we first encountered seeking admission to a nunnery and complaining
that the restrictions on the sisterhood were not sufficiently harsh. But the link
that is made between the provocative effects of womanly beauty and of
music serves to define the disturbing way in which the two female characters,
apparently at conventionally opposite ends of the Renaissance spectrum of
womankind, are yet united (and potentially interchangeable) in their effect
upon the male.

---

[2] *Music in Shakespearean Tragedy*, London, 1963, p. 88.

At the same time the link testifies to the analogous ambiguity of music itself in Renaissance thinking. For, as has often enough been observed, music and love go together.[3] Both love and music are at once supra-rational, symbolic of the divine, and sub-rational, sensual and disorderly. So too, womankind is assumed to be irrational and yet may stand as an ideal. The potency of this identification emerges most clearly in the attacks on music (especially theatrical music) made by Northbrooke, Gosson, Stubbes and Prynne.[4] All of them see music as potentially dangerous because it solicits appetite and renders men open to all kinds of temptation. Especially significant in the present context is the way in which the term 'effeminate' is repeatedly employed. Stubbes's warning is typical:

Wherefore, if you wold haue your sonne softe, womanish, vncleane, smoth mouthed, affected to bawdrie, scurrilitie, filthie rimes, and vnsemely talking, brifly, if you wold haue him, as it weare, transnatured into a woman, or worse, and inclyned to all kinds of whordome and abhomination, set him to dauncing school, and to learn musicke, and than shall you not faile of your purpose.[5]

It is this nexus of attitudes, bringing together music, love and effeminacy, that is exploited in *Troilus and Cressida*. It, like *Measure for Measure*, has only one song, 'Love, love, nothing but love', sung by Pandarus in Act III scene 1. Pandarus is said by Helen to be 'full of harmony' (III. i. 50), though we have seen quite enough of his conduct and characteristic speech to recognize the moral inappropriateness of this designation, however accurately it may represent his performing skill. The audience consists of Paris, already introduced as 'one besotted' on 'sweet delights' (II. ii. 142), and Helen, insistently addressed as 'sweet queen' by Pandarus. The self-evident function of the song is to characterize and feed the lustful pair. It is precisely a song of this sort which might have spurred Prynne to complain:

such songs ... depraue the manners of those that heare or sing them, exciting, enticing them to lust; to whoredome, adultery, prophanes, wantonnesse, scurrility, luxury, drunkennesse, excesse, alienating their mindes from God, from grace and heauenly things.[6]

While it is easy to dismiss the excesses of this complaint, it would be foolish to deny that this song must briefly persuade the audience to suspend moral judgement as they take pleasure in Pandarus's performance. It would be wrong for a producer to cast the role with an actor who could not sing well,

---

[3] See Gretchen Ludke Finney, *Musical Backgrounds for English Literature 1580–1650*, New Brunswick, 1962, Ch. IV.

[4] John Northbrooke, *A Treatise Against Dicing, Dancing, Plays and Interludes* (1577), ed. J. Payne Collier, London, 1843; Stephen Gosson, *The Schoole of Abuse* (1579), ed. Edward Arber, London, 1869; Phillip Stubbes, *Anatomy of Abuses* (1583), ed. Frederick J. Furnivall, London, 1877–9; William Prynne, *Histriomastix* (1633).

[5] Ed. Furnivall, p. 171.

[6] *Histriomastix*, p. 267.

or to divert attention from the song by extraneous business. The effect of the song must be to involve us in the sensual world, to make us experience its seductiveness. Shakespeare, like Puritan opponents of the theatre, clearly accepted that the provocative power of music is exerted on the audience of the play as well as on the characters within it.

Music in itself cannot tell lies; it can only be accepted or ignored. A singer cannot seem not to mean what he or she sings. It is context and reflection that can qualify our response to a song, and they are only possible when we are released from the song's spell. The context of Pandarus's song is clear, and its significance is amplified in the larger context of the play. Troilus at the beginning of the play complains that love has made him womanish— 'weaker than a woman's tear' (I. i. 9). But later, as Cressida prepares to depart, he tells her that he fears what will happen, since he 'cannot sing, / Nor heel the high lavolt' (IV, iv. 84–5) as can the youth of Greece. He seems to want to reassert his manhood and valour by disclaiming competence in these effeminate arts. At a simple level his fears are shown to be justified when Cressida is seduced by Diomed in a scene that has no music, but which in its cloying repetition of the word 'sweet' links directly back to the scene of Pandarus's song, with its similar repetitive insistence upon sweetness. Troilus has spoken of the 'sweet music' of Cressida's voice—but that siren sweetness diverts him from manly chivalry as surely as Pandarus's sweet song exemplifies the sensual effeminacy of Paris and Helen. The identification of music and lust, and of both with the dangerous enticement of the female, is thus intensified.

The full force of the ambiguity that attends music in *Troilus and Cressida* is revealed in the use made of the martial trumpet. Traditionally the Lydian mode was conducive of love and sensuousness, but the Dorian roused men to valorous action. Indeed, when Gosson complained of the state of music in his time he specifically singled out the abandonment of 'those warlike tunes which were used in auncient times, to stirre up in us a manly motion' in favour of the 'new descant with the daunces of *Sybaris* to rocke us asleepe in all ungodlinesse'.[7] When Ajax enters to challenge Hercules, Agamemnon instructs him:

> Give with thy trumpet a loud note to Troy,
> Thou dreadfull Ajax, that the appalled air
> May pierce the head of the great combatant,
> And hale him hither.
>
> (IV. v. 3–6)

One might expect this sound to stand in clear distinction to the 'Lydian' music of Pandarus, but this 'manly' trumpet heralds not Hector but Cressida, who arrives at the Greek tents in the company of Diomed. In a

---

[7] *The School of Abuse*, p. 69.

simple but dramatically forceful manner the opposition between the manly music of war and the effeminate music of the chamber is blurred, imaging the play's sceptical consideration of the ways in which battle and lust both issue from the disordered motions of human passions.

Where, then, does this leave the celebrated invocation of symbolic music spoken by Ulysses? 'Take but degree away, untune that string, / And hark what discord follows', he says (1. iii. 109–10). It is of course possible to preserve the authority of the image by seeing the music of the play as an abuse and distortion of that potency, as the music that provokes the good to harm especially by its blurring of gender roles in the way Puritans feared. One might use the argument employed by John Case in defending music against its detractors:

those which are glad to take any occasion to speak against musicke, will . . . affirme that it maketh men effeminate, and too much subiect vnto pleasure. But whom, I praie you, doth it make effeminate? Surely none but such as without it would bee wanton: . . . the same musicke which mollifieth some men, moueth some other nothing at all: so that the fault is not in musicke, which of it selfe is good: but in the corrupt nature, & euill disposition of light persons, which of themselues are prone to wantonnes.[8]

This might seem securely to contain the problematic aspects of the music of *Troilus and Cressida*, but it does not really serve, for example, to distinguish safely the healing music with which Cerimon awakes Thaisa in Act III scene 2 of *Pericles* from the perverted music that surrounds the presentation of the Daughter of Antiochus in Act I scene 1 and helps to deceive Pericles as to her virtuous attractiveness. He is emphatically not 'prone to wantonness'.

Case's argument rests upon the assertion that music is 'of it selfe good', an assertion that could only be validated if music was referred out of the chances of human agency to the divine of which it was claimed to be a mirror. That music was so regarded in the Renaissance is now a common-place, but this musical symbolism brings problems with it. Just as music's authority could be derived from its presumed reflection of celestial harmony, so the power of rulers is sanctioned by reference to a 'natural' and God-given order. It is no coincidence that Case celebrates in his treatise the possibility of co-opting music in the service of the State, for whose harmonious hierarchy it could be made to stand as an image and in whose interests its practice might be controlled. It is indicative of the strains involved in this ideological capture of music that the duke in *Measure for Measure*, whose anxiety about rule and control is the spring of the plot, should register nervousness about the dangerous provocation of Mariana's music, and it is revealing that cosmic harmony should be invoked by Ulysses in a speech whose pious

[8] *The Praise of Musicke* (1586), p. 58. On the question of Case's authorship of this treatise as well as *Apologia musices* (1588) see Howard Barnett, 'John Case—An Elizabethan Music Scholar', *Music and Letters*, l (1969), 252–66.

certainties are undermined at every level by the characters and action of
Troilus and Cressida.

It is this anxiety that is the fuel for Puritan diatribes. They too assert that
'true music' is expressed in the harmonious relationship of master and
servant,[9] but, less convinced of the symbolic identity of music than Case (or
Lorenzo in *The Merchant of Venice*), they try to contain the dangerous
potential which they recognize in music by attempting to demarcate its
world and by banishing that which is dangerous to the realm of the female
'other'. For the Puritans music needs controlling, and the control is expressed by an effort to delimit the contexts within which it is permissible and
by allowing only music whose words are unexceptionable. Their attitudes,
as Gretchen Finney has remarked, are surprisingly close to those of the
musical humanists of the sixteenth century, who also expressed contempt
for instrumental music, which 'can do no more than tickle the ear', and
sought therefore to promote the words of songs over the music. She cites
Bardi's comment, 'just as the soul is nobler than the body, so the words are
nobler than the counterpoint', as characteristic of the shift from a symbolic
to a fundamentally rhetorical view of the sources of music's power.[10] Taken
together, the efforts of Puritan opponents and humanist theorists alike
testify to the shaking of the certainties of the symbolically conceived
universe.

In Shakespeare's dramatic world it was still possible to employ music as an
image of divine harmony, for example in the music that cures Lear, raises
Thaisa, accompanies the bringing to life of Hermione's statue or charms the
nobles in *The Tempest*. But in dramatic terms this symbolic possibility is not
so much a secure guide for discriminating between proper and improper uses
of music in every circumstance as one aspect of a diverse nexus of attitudes
which inform Shakespeare's uses of music.

In Spenser's *The Faerie Queene* the same birds sing in the corrupted Bower
of Bliss as accompany the harmonious vision of the Garden of Adonis. Music
is morally neutral until invested with significance by its auditors. This,
indeed, is the real significance of Portia's comment quoted earlier. Juxta-
posed with Lorenzo's celebration of heavenly harmony it raises questions of
fundamental importance. Earlier in *The Merchant of Venice* the song 'Tell
me where is fancy bred?', sung over the caskets as Bassanio prepares to make
his choice, has a double effect. It colours the scene with its harmonious glow,
and it symbolizes the opposition of the world of Belmont to the unmusical
world of Venice. But at the same time the song is working in Portia's interest
in its heavy rhyming hints to the lover she wishes to accept as to the casket
he should choose. It is employed deliberately to subvert the patriarchal
authority which puts Portia's marriage to the chance of the choice of caskets,

[9] See Finney, *Musical Backgrounds*, p. 77, where she quotes Gosson: 'The love of the King
and his subjects, the Father and his childe, the Lord and his Slave . . . this is right Musicke'.
[10] Ibid., pp. 128–9.

and it speaks, however benignly, of her 'feminine' deviousness and the exercise of her powers of persuasion.

If music is from one point of view a branch of rhetoric, then it is not only the character of the listener which is placed in question but also the motivation of the initiator of the song. So Prospero's music, however heavenly, is ultimately a rhetorical instrument of his power and subject, therefore, not to the heavens but to the will of its user.[11] Prospero is prepared to tell lies (in 'Full fathom five') or to mislead the conspirators; and at the climax of the work it is his enchanting music which puts his enemies in his power. *The Tempest* is a play concerned with power, as much recent criticism has argued, and music plays a significant part in articulating the problematic aspects of its exercise.

Two songs very similar in dramatic function explore further the ways in which music's effect is conditional on the motivation of the singer as much as on the moral quality of the recipient. In *Two Gentlemen of Verona* 'Who is Silvia' is sung beneath Silvia's window ostensibly to advance the suit of Thurio. In *Cymbeline* Cloten orders a song, 'Hark, hark! the lark at heaven's gate sings', to attempt to influence Imogen in his favour. Both suitors have been instructed in the unexceptionable doctrine that women are especially likely to respond to music's insinuating powers. Both songs, we must assume, are well performed and will therefore charm the audience. As Auden observes, both are examples of 'music being used with conscious evil intent'.[12] But the most interesting aspect of these two songs is their total failure to work their end upon their intended recipients. Imogen simply fails to appear, and Cloten's debased, bawdy understanding of music's power to 'penetrate' is thereby justly rebuked. Silvia acknowledges the 'sweetness' of the song but immediately sees through the motives of Proteus (who might have been the singer) and dismisses him abruptly. Shakespearean comedy characteristically permits the triumph of the feminine, and here that triumph is characterized by the women's resistance to the complacent male assumption of the power of their music.

Even more emphatic is the way in which the triumph of the ladies in *The Merry Wives of Windsor* is enacted in the entirely virtuous song 'Fie on sinful fantasy' with which they torment Falstaff in Act v scene v. The contrast between this song and the garbled mishmash of the erotic and the religious in Sir Hugh Evans's 'To shallow rivers, to whose falls' (III. i), sung as he admits his womanish 'great dispositions to cry', is obvious. There is further irony in that the ladies' musical tormenting of Falstaff also enables the deception of Doctor Caius and Slender and the successful thwarting of patriarchal authority in securing the match of Fenton and Anne Page. No doubt this

---

[11] Further see my 'Music, Masque and Meaning in *The Tempest*', *The Court Masque*, ed. David Lindley, Manchester, 1984, pp. 47–59.

[12] 'Music in Shakespeare', *The Dyer's Hand*, London, 1963, p. 515.

outcome would have reduced William Prynne to apoplectic fury, since for him the effeminacy of song is inextricably linked to the dangers of cross-dressing on the contemporary stage, which threatened both the stability of gender distinction and hierarchy. Once again a modern audience would do well to recognize the added force that each of these musical episodes acquires when read against the context of received attitude. These women employ the most moral of musics to effect a just censure of male appetites and prohibitions.

If in comedies such as these the conventional association of song and 'effeminacy' is subverted, in *Hamlet*, Act IV scene v, the singing of Ophelia raises questions of much greater complexity. As Winifred Maynard observes:

> The scene of Ophelia's madness shows more powerfully than perhaps any other scene of Shakespeare's his genius in the usage of song, in his choice of kind in respect both of its emotional effects and its appropriateness to the dramatic texture.[13]

Much has been written on the pathos of the scene, much has been suggested about its characterization of Ophelia, about the double reference of her songs to her dead father and to Hamlet,[14] but for this essay the most instructive comment is offered by the anonymous Gentleman who pleads for Ophelia's admission:

> Her speech is nothing,
> Yet the unshaped use of it doth move
> The hearers to collection. They aim at it,
> And botch the words up fit to their own thoughts
> (IV. v. 7–10)

The dramatic power of this scene (and the critical industry it has supported) derive essentially from this fact. Ophelia's mad music provokes reaction, but that reaction is directed only by the audience who seek to make it render sense. Horatio agrees to her being admitted because he fears that 'she may strew / Dangerous conjectures in ill-breeding minds'. How this might happen is immediately and graphically illustrated as her first song, 'How should I your true love know', seems to the queen to be alluding uncomfortably to her own situation. To her fevered imagination it might seem like Ophelia's version of Hamlet's 'Mousetrap', making what should be concealed dangerously public.

Ophelia's singing is music loosed from its moorings, from any anchor in the rational control of its performer. It offers, therefore, a dramatic threat of disorientation, which the listeners on stage, and the audience as a whole, must struggle to contain. When the queen describes the death of Ophelia she declares 'she chanted snatches of old lauds, As one incapable of her own

---

[13] *Elizabethan Lyric Poetry and its Music*, Oxford, 1986, p. 161.
[14] See Seng, *The Vocal Songs*, pp. 131–4.

distress' (IV. vii. 178). The queen's account is a rhetorical set piece which romanticizes Ophelia's death and thereby confines its effect to one of pathos. The real threat that Ophelia had briefly seemed to offer at the beginning is safely defused by attributing her words only to her own madness.

But the effect of the scene cannot so securely be contained. Once again it is important to place the musical episode in the play's wider context if we are to sense its full significance. It is revealing that Ophelia should be searching particularly for the queen as she first enters, and that it is the queen who delivers her epitaph. Throughout the first part of the play Ophelia's dutiful obedience to her father represented the ideal purity of womankind in contrast to the wantonness of the queen. But her madness allows her to speak freely of buried desires and appetites which neither her stage audience nor many subsequent critics seem ready to allow as her real feelings. It is typical of the need to circumscribe the implication of Ophelia's songs that the only source of her derangement that her on-stage audience will allow is grief for her father. But if music by its passionate nature is 'feminine', and in madness explicitly sub-rational, then her songs assert her kinship with the queen, even as they expose the difference between Gertrude's enslavement by passion and her own subjection to her father and sometime lover. At one level, indeed, the scene endorses Hamlet's view of the essential frailty of women, even as it raises disquieting questions about the effect of such assumptions on the much-coerced Ophelia.

The force of the anxieties this scene registers is enhanced by its parallel to Hamlet's own adoption of an 'antic disposition'. The revenger's madness results from his being trapped in a position where the desire for revenge cannot be satisfied within an acceptable social framework of justice. Ophelia, in so far as her madness arises, like Hamlet's, out of the killing of a father, is similarly but more comprehensively trapped—by her femininity. The fact that she sings makes the audience experience the pressure of her feeling, but the absence of rational control, the very fact that it is in music that she speaks, testifies to the impossibility of her finding a means of action. Furthermore, the very way in which this scene presents her as a spectacle of suffering enables her distress to become no more than the cause of action in the male characters. By a terrible and disturbing irony the passive Ophelia's eruption into self-speaking is destined to be marginalized into a pretext for others' actions. While this speaks something of Renaissance attitudes to women, it is in no small part possible because of contemporaneous assumptions about music. The scene is powerful precisely because the capacity of music to provoke response in an audience threatens to rupture those systems which confine Ophelia.

By contrast the companion piece, Desdemona's 'Willow Song', for all its undoubted efficacy in heightening the pathos of the climax of *Othello*, seems simple, even tendentious, as it conspires in the reduction of the character of Desdemona from the wilful opponent of her father to the passive victim in

virginal white.[15] Sternfeld is right to contrast the indecorum of Ophelia's
musical performance with Desdemona's private singing.[16] But the indecorum of Ophelia's scene is more than social and witnesses to more stresses
within the play as a whole than merely those that afflict her character. Here is
'provoking music' indeed.

It is no small part of the effect of the songs both of Desdemona and
Ophelia that their words either are, or are like, the words of popular,
traditional song. Generally in Shakespeare's plays such songs, often no more
than odd snatches, are 'impromptu' songs, quite different from the 'performed' songs with which this essay began. As Auden says, 'an impromptu
song is not art but a form of personal behaviour. It reveals, as the called-for
song cannot, something about the singer'.[17] Such is indeed the case in
Ophelia's singing, or in the sad recollections of the humorously named
Silence in 2 *Henry IV*. But popular song, like any other kind of music, existed
in a context of attitudes which enabled it to be used in a play for purposes
beyond those of simple character depiction. For Puritans it was the association of popular song with carnival and drunken festivity that made it
dangerous, and it was the socially menacing vagabondage of the minstrels
who disseminated it that they wished most earnestly to control. The attacks
on music and the attacks on the theatre both issued out of a fear of the threat
to harmonious and godly society that each of them seemed to pose. Even
John Case, intent upon saving music from Puritan attacks, found it necessary
to confess: 'I dare not speake of dauncing or theatrall spectacles, least I pull
whole swarmes of enimies upon me'.[18]

In many ways it would seem that Shakespeare was content to permit these
associations to work in the most obvious fashion. Iago incites Cassio's
drunkenness with 'And let me the Cannikin clink'; Toby Belch, Andrew
Aguecheek and Feste, having rejected songs of 'good life', cement their
disrespect for authority in the catch 'Hold thy piece'; Stephano, Trinculo
and Caliban celebrate their design against Prospero with 'Flout 'em and
scout 'em', which asserts menacingly 'Thought is free'.[19]

But in at least two plays popular song is used with much greater subtlety.
Autolycus enters *The Winter's Tale* after the leap of time has first landed us
in the worried exchange of Polixenes and Camillo, dispelling the gloom with
'When daffodils begin to peer'. Critics in general have assented in the 'joyous

[15] But for a more positive reading of the uses of music in the play, see Lawrence J. Ross,
'Shakespeare's "Dull Clown" and Symbolic Music', *Shakespeare Quarterly*, xvii (1966),
107–28.
[16] *Music in Shakespearean Tragedy*, pp. 54 ff. Seng dissents (*The Vocal Songs*, p. 133).
[17] *The Dyer's Hand*, p. 522.
[18] *The Praise of Musicke*, p. 79. See also *Apologia musices*, p. 37: 'Nihil hic dicam de
theatricis et bacchanalibus tibijs quae tedas furiasque libidinis, insania et amoris excitant'.
[19] In the slightly more exalted 'Come, thou monarch of the vine', in *Antony and Cleopatra*,
though the aristocratic characters do not actually sing, the same association of music with
drunken danger to social stability is made.

roguery' of Autolycus and his songs. His singing, it has been claimed, is the reason why this 'rascal' is sympathetic. As John H. Long puts it: 'That such a character can immediately enlist the sympathy of the spectator is due, in large measure, to the fact that he is singing a lilting song.'[20] But while it is undoubtedly true that the effect of Autolycus's songs on the audience is to persuade them to suspend moral judgement on him, and to enter into the freshness of a pastoral world, his singing raises some awkward questions in the thematic structure of the work as a whole.

In *As You Like It* the courtly songs of Amiens had formed an important element in the effort of the banished duke and his associates to 'translate' into a 'sweet style' their adversity and the real conditions of life in the forest. Jacques punctures the complacency of the idealizing pastoral as he parodies 'Under the greenwood tree' with the verse of his own making, 'If it do come to pass'. He can not only 'suck melancholy' out of a song but can comment bitterly upon the jolly refrain 'Come hither' with his 'Greek invocation to call fools into a circle'. In the later play Autolycus seems to combine in himself both of these possibilities. He 'translates' the audience into another world, but at the same time his presence guards against too simple an idealization of the pastoral environment.

He is introduced as a masterless servant—that bogey of Elizabethan and Jacobean society—and while his songs indeed characterize the holiday atmosphere of the countryside, they are also the typical stock of the balladeer. He is an interloper into the pastoral world even as he apparently typifies it. He sings for money, and Perdita is worried at the potential scurrility of the matter of his songs. Later he is to appear as a counterfeit courtier, articulating the unease that attends Perdita's dialogue with Polixenes about social class. In many ways, then, Autolycus's function is to bring to the surface the tensions that underly the romance of the shepherdess who is really a princess in disguise. She can be permitted to derive her innocence from the idealized surroundings of the pastoral, but we cannot be permitted to interpret this as a blueprint for social revolution. Autolycus's ambiguity ensures that we recognize the essentials of social hierarchy. He is carnivalesque, but we are never in doubt that he, like the riotous figure of Toby Belch, will be put in his proper place as his mercenary music and all it stands for is superseded by the heavenly charm that restores Hermione to her husband. Autolycus enacts, perhaps, the essential conservatism of allowed carnival, which may turn the world upside-down for a season but will thereby make the necessity of order more self-evident.

The case of the Fool in *King Lear* is very different. He articulates his despair at the conduct of his master in songs and snatches which in their riddling wisdom prefigure the lesson the deluded king must learn as he opens himself 'to feel what wretches feel'. It is, of course, too facile to see the lessons

---

[20] Quoted in Seng, *The Vocal Songs*, p. 227.

in human sympathy and contempt for the trappings of authority which both Lear and Gloucester learn as some kind of revolutionary philosophy. Nevertheless it is not the least striking feature of the play that the popular music which elsewhere carries with it suggestions of subversion should here be an image of truthful perception (though even here the Fool's songs must be replaced by the healing music for which Cordelia calls in the later stages of the play).

The differences in thematic function between the songs of Autolycus and the songs of the Fool attest to the complexity of Shakespeare's dramatic dealings with music. Received wisdom, whether of Puritan opponents or courtly supporters, relied on the possibility of distinguishing clearly between proper and improper music, between the heavenly and earthly, manly and effeminate. In the world of the theatre, itself precariously poised in Renaissance society on the edges of legitimacy, alternately attacked and defended, such polarities are threatened. Caliban and Ariel sing in different vocabularies, but the sentiments of 'No more dams I'll make for fish' and 'Where the bee sucks, there suck I' are identical. Peter J. Seng may wish that Caliban's song 'illustrates his inferior nature' while 'there could hardly be a better hymn of praise' than Ariel's,[21] but the simple opposition is in important respects an illusion, born of the desire of auditors to contain and direct the stimulus that song offers. Music may be an emblem of order and an instrument of power, but the individual expression it allows and the unspecificity of its effects mean that the dramatist, like Prospero, can only watch in disappointment as Ariel eludes command. Therein lies the potency of Shakespeare's provoking music.

[21] Op. cit., pp. 263, 272.

7

Some Musico-Poetic Aspects of Campion's Masques

Christopher R. Wilson

CAMPION's position as a masque writer is put succinctly by F. W. Sternfeld:

That curious and fascinating structure, the Jacobean masque, boasted several begetters, notably Ben Jonson, Campion, Daniel, Beaumont and Chapman. In collaboration with Inigo Jones, Jonson eventually became its unchallenged master. Indeed, his spectacular achievements have tended to obscure the unique contribution of Campion who, in fact, was the only one of these five poets to master the craft of music as well. Certainly, up to and through the year 1613 Campion occupied a rôle second only to Jonson in importance, so that the latter's comment to Drummond that, next to himself, only Chapman and Beaumont knew how to write a masque, was quite unjust to Campion and merely revealed his own prejudices in the matter.[1]

Sternfeld goes on to reflect on the relative importance of Campion as a composer of masques, intimating that we assess him not only according to the artistic quality of the masques themselves but also within the historical context in which Campion wrote. He states that 'the year 1613 represents the summit of Campion's achievement in masque composition, with the production of three works in this genre';[2] and yet 1613 was also the last year in which Campion contributed (substantially) to the genre.

This seeming paradox might be explained in two ways. First, the un-savoury social and political circumstances surrounding the marriage of Frances Howard and Robert Carr, (newly created) Earl of Somerset, for which Campion's last masque was written, and their destructive conse-quences meant that Campion lost favour at court, certainly in 1615 if not earlier. Secondly, the early years of the seventeenth century saw radical changes in the arts, emanating mainly from Italy. As David Lindley eloquently reports:

---

[1] 'A Song from Campion's *Lord's Masque*', *Journal of the Warburg and Courtauld Institutes*, xx (1957), 373.
[2] Ibid.

[the] change of direction exhibited in this [Somerset] masque is a symptom of the shift from a Renaissance to a Baroque art, from an art which draws its strength from the system of correspondence in the divinely ordered universe, to one whose main effort is focused on the attempt to astonish and thereby to move an audience.[3]

Campion, experimenting in *Somerset*, was not given another chance. As Lindley concludes in his discussion of *Somerset*:

Perhaps the least satisfying of Campion's works in the genre, its imperfections can be seen to arise from the conjunction of changing taste and changing artistic philosophy with the particular and peculiarly disabling circumstances of the marriage it celebrated.[4]

Any discussion of Jacobean masques must embrace both the social and political events which a masque is celebrating and the artistic means by which an author may construct his work. The interpretation of Campion's masques in the light of their social and political backgrounds has until very recently been sadly neglected. Happily, we now have David Lindley's expert and clear account.[5] This paper is concerned more with certain artistic aspects of Campion's masques operating as it were on a different, but not separate, level from what lies behind the content of a masque.

The change from Renaissance to (quasi-)Baroque in the masque was hastened, even determined, by Ben Jonson and his team. Campion's demise as a masque writer, leaving aside political considerations, has to do with his apparent inability to cope with or adapt to the poetico-philosophical slant that Jonson gave the masque. Campion was no dramatist like Jonson, Beaumont or Chapman. There are no plays from his pen. Rather, his was the lyric voice of the intuitive Renaissance musical poet. As Jonson sought to increase the poetical meaning and dramatic effect of the masque, displacing both architect and musician,[6] so Campion (and Daniel) were eclipsed.

At the start of his masque career Jonson probably aimed to fulfil 'the Renaissance Platonist ideal of a perfect composite art form, giving equal importance to all the arts',[7] and in so doing not only affect the spectators —to move them to greater virtue and wisdom—but also involve them in the very process of art's creation. This artistic ideal Jonson derived from French and Italian theory and, to a lesser extent, practice.[8] The interrelationship of

---

[3] *Thomas Campion*, Leiden, 1986, p. 233.

[4] Ibid., pp. 233–4.

[5] *Campion*, pp. 174–234: 'The Masques'.

[6] See further D. J. Gordon, 'Poet and Architect: The Intellectual Setting of the Quarrel between Ben Jonson and Inigo Jones', *Journal of the Warburg and Courtauld Institutes*, xii (1949), 152–78.

[7] Mary Chan, *Music in the Theatre of Ben Jonson*, Oxford, 1980, p. 141.

[8] See further Frances Yates, *The French Academies of the Sixteenth Century*, London, 1947; D. P. Walker, 'The Aims of Baïf's *Académie de poésie et de musique*', *Journal of Renaissance and Baroque Music*, i (1946), 91–100; and one of the best studies of Renaissance neo-Platonism, D. P. Walker, *Spiritual and Demonic Magic from Ficino to Campanella* ('Warburg Institute Studies', xxii), London, 1958.

art forms was commonplace in Renaissance thinking, in turn prompted by the philosophies and poetry of Classical antiquity: Plato, notably transmitted through various sources; Virgil, Catullus, Ovid, Propertius, Claudian —much more widely read in the Renaissance than he is today—and others. The coincidence of dance, music, spectacle and poetry, however, was not an aesthetic parallelism but a correspondence of symbolic meaning: divine art imitating, even descended from, the cosmic order of things,[9] so that there was a perfect harmony at all levels within a masque. This would be made possible, as it was in the influential *Balet comique de la reine* (1581),[10] not only by the happy collaboration of the various artists involved but also by the 'restraint' shown by the author in not favouring one art form at the expense of the others.

That this was Jonson's attitude to the masque, even from the outset, has been questioned, since he often appears to give pre-eminence to the position of the poet.[11] Jonson's developing and destructive quarrel with Inigo Jones is well known and has already been mentioned. His attitude towards music and musicians is clearly less arrogant but no less equivocal. It seems likely, for example, that Jonson quarrelled with Ferrabosco after *Love Freed from Ignorance and Folly* (1611).[12] It is equally conjecturable that relations with his other major collaborators, Robert Johnson and Thomas Giles, became no less strained. The important, structural position that music occupied in the early masques was certainly diminished by 1612; it hardly became simply an accessory or ornament for dance and song,[13] but its role changed from a literal to a philosophical one enhancing a (Renaissance) neo-Platonist ideal of separate arts, music, poetry and dance exerting a conjoint, and at the most sophisticated level complementary, existence.[14] Moreover, the type of music (for song) increasingly preferred by Jonson was that of Nicholas Lanier—a more declamatory type, 'stylo recitativo', more easily and usefully integrated into the dramatic flow,[15] and epitomizing the shift from Renaissance rhetoric to Baroque 'affection'.

[9] See Margaret M. McGowan, *L'Art du Ballet de Cour en France (1581–1643)*, Paris, 1963, pp. 13–24.

[10] Paris, 1582; facs. ed. Giacomo Alessandro Caula, Turin, 1965; facs. ed. Margaret M. McGowan ('Medieval & Renaissance Texts & Studies', vi), Binghampton, NY, 1982; trans. & ed. C. & L. MacClintock ('Musicological Studies and Documents', xxv), American Institute of Musicology, 1971. See McGowan, *L'Art du Ballet de Cour*, pp. 42–7.

[11] See further *The Works of Ben Jonson*, ed. C. H. Herford and others, Oxford, 1925–52, viii. 402–6.

[12] See Chan, *Music in the Theatre*, p. 272.

[13] See J. P. Cutts, 'La Rôle de la musique dans les masques de Ben Jonson', *Les Fêtes de la Renaissance*, ed. Jean Jacquot, Paris, 1956, pp. 285–303.

[14] A point made by Jean Jacquot to Cutts at the end of his paper. See also Chan, *Music in the Theatre*, p. 142 n. 11.

[15] See further MacDonald Emslie, 'Nicholas Lanier's Innovations in English Song', *Music & Letters*, xli (1960), 13–27, and Peter Walls, 'The Origins of English Recitative', *Proceedings of the Royal Musical Association*, cx (1983–4), 25–40.

The development of the Jonsonian masque in the decade after 1604 is gradual but clearly defined, both self-generated and externally influenced, notably it might be argued by Campion. In Jonson's first, *The Masque of Blackness* (6 January 1605), music assumes a non-dramatic, emblematic role of equal importance with poetry, speech and spectacle. The masque opens with a song of welcome and celebration, performed by a Triton and two sea-maidens or 'sirens', whose presence Jonson most likely owed to the example of the *Balet comique*.[16] In his description of the masque Jonson is as it were manifestly more concerned with the significance of a song than with its type or manner of performance. No mention is made of how the music was performed. This is especially true of the dances. Jonson is at pains to describe the movement of the dances, so that we may be aware of their symbolic meaning,[17] but, as Mary Chan points out, 'the music . . . was regarded philosophically as inseparable from the meaning of the dance itself'—an obvious Platonic unity. 'This means that aesthetically it needed to provide little more than a rhythmic emphasis.'[18] The song 'Come away, we grow jealous of your stay'[19] separates the masque dances and the revels. Jonson provides an instructional rather than a lyric song, to whose dramatic content Ferrabosco is quick to respond with an elementary declamatory setting. (The words 'Come away', 'Bring away', 'We shall have' etc. generally signified a declamatory setting in Jacobean masque songs.) The dramatic content is as yet not predominant in such songs. As Chan points out:

Ferrabosco's settings of the songs in Jonson's early masques strike a nice balance between the ideal of heightened speech and a musical shape which complements the poetic structure. Ferrabosco's masque songs support the philosophic basis of the masque: for the poetry is not to be regarded as dramatic or narrative but as an aspect of an emblem created by several art forms equally.[20]

In his next masque, *Hymenaei* (5 January 1606), Jonson is similarly more concerned with the philosophical meaning and function of music than with its actual content or structural placing in the masque.

Against this Jonsonian background the music and poetry of Campion's

[16] Jonson owned a copy of the *Balet* description; see Chan, *Music in the Theatre*, p. 141 n. 8. The music in Jonson's masque is less elaborate than that of the *Balet*. The opening number of the latter, for example, is a five-part chorus with instrumental accompaniment; Jonson has a simple three-part song.
[17] See D. J. Gordon, 'The Imagery in Ben Jonson's *Masque of Blacknesse* and *Masque of Beautie*', *Journal of the Warburg and Courtauld Institutes*, vi (1943), 125 ff.
[18] *Music in the Theatre*, pp. 150–51, esp. n. 39. A. J. Sabol, *Four Hundred Songs and Dances from the Stuart Masque*, Providence, Rhode Island, 1978, suggests Nos. 52, 53, 54 and 225–7, though with serious doubts.
[19] Ferrabosco, *Ayres*, 1609, No. 3; Sabol, *Four Hundred Songs*, No. 1. Compare Oxford, Christ Church, MS Mus. 439, p. 31.
[20] *Music in the Theatre*, p. 156.

first masque, *Lord Hays* (6 January 1607), by way of contrast is less emblematic and more functionally integrated. While striving to preserve a balance, Campion has allowed music to gain the upper hand.[21] The whole patterning and movement of the masque is guided by its music, following a tripartite structure of discovery of the scene, masque dances, and revels. Moreover, more than any other writer, Campion is careful to describe how the music was performed. Following theatrical convention, he provides two groups of musicians: actors playing and singing, and musicians separate from the actors. In *Lord Hays*, the musician actors are six Silvans (four players plus two singers), an Howre, Silvanus and Zephyrus. The musicians are a 'consort of ten' (playing 'basse and meane' lutes—five bass and tenor lutes—a bandora, a double 'sackbott', a harpsichord and two treble violins), a 'consort of twelve' (nine violins and three lutes), a consort of six cornetts, an ensemble of six voices (drawn from the choir of the Chapel Royal) and a consort of 'hoboyes'. The musical scheme of the masque, with its structural divisions not separate in performance, is represented in Table 7.1.

The 'loud' music 'hoboy' entry for the king and his party is conventional, though Campion attaches no theatrical significance to the use of the

TABLE 7.1

(first section)	1 Entry of the king: 'hoboyes'
	2 Discovery of the scene: 'consort of ten'
	3 Descent: 4 Silvans, playing lutes
	Song 'Now hath Flora': Zephyrus and 2 Silvans (bass; tenor, treble)
	4 Dialogue song 'Who is the happier': 2 Silvans
(second section)	5 Dance song 'Move now': 4 Silvans
	6 Song of Transformation 'Night and Diana': 4 Silvans et al.
	7 Chorus (+echo) and instrumental consorts: climactic middle tutti, 42 musicians
	8 Dance: instrumental
	9 Procession of Night: cornett consort and voices performing a 'motet', 'With spotles mindes'
	10 Dance: 'consort of twelve'
	11 Dialogue song 'Of all the starres': 2 basses and 2 trebles
(third section)	12 Dance: revels
	13 Dialogue song 'Tell me gentle houre of night' followed by farewell chorus (+echo)

[21] How much this had to do with Lord Hay is not clear, but his love of music almost certainly influenced the amount in *Lovers Made Men* (22 February 1617).

'hoboy',[22] knowing that it will 'rival the trumpet for his sound'. No music can be confidently assigned to this entry, although Thurston Dart suggested some in Cambridge, Fitzwilliam Museum, MS 734.[23] The masque itself begins, rather 'operatically', with the consort of ten playing an instrumental version of the song 'Now hath Flora' that follows.[24] As the song begins, the instrumental colour changes from the mixed consort to four lutes accompanying treble, tenor and bass voices.[25] Campion's ayre is typically and unpretentiously 'light' and purely lyrical. It is related to Watson's 'With fragrant flowers', performed at *The Entertainment of Elvetham* (1591) set by Pilkington (1605, No. 20), and comparable to 'Zephyrus brings the time that sweetly scenteth', set by Yonge (1588, Nos. 52–3) and Cavendish (1598, No. 22).

Less conventional, indeed a noticeable innovation, is Campion's introduction of the dialogue song into a masque.[26] That this was historically significant is further attested by Jonson's use of the type in his song of two 'fays', 'Seek you majesty, to strike?', and 'Nor yet, o you in this night blessed' (*Oberon*), which follow Campion's format in a slightly simplified manner.[27] Partly by their novelty and partly by their enhanced dramatic quality, Campion effectively employs the dialogue songs, with punctuating choruses, to conclude each section of the masque. 'Who is the happier' is in fact a poem of four quatrains: an opening, trochaic, ABCB rhyme followed by three iambic AABB quatrains and a single line refrain. (Jonson has three trochaic quatrains AABB, which include a couplet refrain.) The song is shared by three solo voices, treble, tenor and bass (probably two Silvans and Zephyrus), and a final chorus. Campion's song is not exceptional out of context. It is often compared with John Davies's 'A Contention betwixt a Wife, a Widow, and a Maide' (*Poetical Rapsody*, 1611 edn., p. 7). Though no music survives, it was probably performed in a manner similar to the dialogues in Thomas Ford, *Musicke of Sundrie Kindes* (1607, No. 11), and Ferrabosco, *Ayres* (1609, Nos. 26–8).

During the next song, 'Moue now with measured sound',[28] performed

---

[22] On its symbolic use see F. W. Sternfeld, *Music in Shakespearean Tragedy*, rev. edn., London, 1967, pp. 217–22.

[23] 'The Repertory of the Royal Wind Music', *Galpin Society Journal*, xi (1958), 74.

[24] The consort would almost certainly have been drawn from the King's Private Musick, which included Lupo playing the violin and Robert Johnson the lute.

[25] Song printed at the end of the *Discription* (1607), sigs. D2^b–D3 and E3^b; ed. David Greer, *Twenty Songs from Printed Sources*, London, 1969, No. 1.

[26] See Ian Spink, 'English Seventeenth Century Dialogues', *Music & Letters*, xxxviii (1957), 155–63.

[27] See further Cutts, 'La Rôle de la musique', p. 290.

[28] Campion reset this ayre to 'The Peacefull Westerne winde', *Two Bookes*, II, No. 12); except for one rhythmical alteration, the music is identical. Contrary to Sabol (*Songs and Dances for the Stuart Masque*, Providence, Rhode Island, 1959, p. 163) and W. R. Davis (*The Works of Thomas Campion*, London, 1969, p. 100 n. 27 and p. 221 n. 41), Campion's tune is not a 'musical allusion' to the popular 'Westron wynd' tune—London, British Library, MS

first by lutes and then by voices and lutes, trees of gold 'dance according to the measure of the time which the musitians kept in singing, and the nature of the wordes which they deliuered'. The 'measure' is a typical duple-time almain. Two parts, corresponding to the stanzaic form, divide A.A 4 + 4 bars, B.B 8 + 8 bars. Each A section divides internally 2 + 2 bars, and each B section 4 + 4 bars, characterized by key. The poem, effectively two stanzas, comprises two lines of 6 + 6 syllables each, and four lines of 14 syllables each. The setting is insistently accentual because no syllable receives more than the basic unit pulse, here a crotchet. Campion's song interprets the dance it accompanies. Certain lines refer to the characteristics of the dance itself:

> Moue now with measured sound,
>> You charmed groue of gould,
> Trace forth the sacred ground
>> That shall your formes unfold. . . .

> Yet neerer *Phoebus* throne
>> Mete on your winding waies, . . .

> Let Hymen lead your sliding rounds, . . .
> Ioyne three by three . . .

Others refer to its signification, for example 'Much ioy must needs the place betide where trees for gladness moue'. In other masques Campion employs interpretative dance songs: 'Dance now and sing, the ioy and loue we owe' (*Caversham Entertainment*); 'Aduance your Chorall motions now' (*Lords*). Similar songs are found elsewhere. In *Hymenaei* Jonson writes:

> Now, now, beginne to set
>> Your spirits in actiue heat,
> And since your hands are met,
>> Instruct your nimble feete.
> In motions swift and meete,
> The happy ground to beate
>> (ll. 300–305)

—to which was danced 'a most neate and curious measure, full of *Subtilty* and *Deuice*'. In *Hymenaei* Thomas Giles arranged the dances; in *Lord Hays* he composed the dance set to the song 'Triumph now with Ioy and mirth',

---

Royal App. 58, No. 346 (John Stevens, *Music and Poetry of the Early Tudor Court*, London, 1961, p. 130)—nor does it have anything to do with Taverner's tune in the 'Western Wynd' Mass—which, in any case, does not appear to be a variation of the popular tune. Nor does the subject matter of Campion's lyric link up with the context of and allusion to Zephyrus in the masque. There is an incomplete arrangement of the song for viols, flute, lute, cittern and bandora in Rosseter, *Lessons for Consort*, 1609, No. 20.

and he presumably acted as dancing master for this masque as he did in
Beauty, Haddington, Queens, Oberon and *Lords*.

Shortly afterwards there follows the song of transformation, 'Night and
Diana charge', sung and played by the Silvans three times in all, as the trees
of gold change into the Knight Maskers,[29] and concluded by the chorus
'Againe this song reuiue'. This chorus is immediately repeated 'in manner of
an Eccho' by the various instrumental ensembles accompanying ten voices
split into two groups. This music forms the first main dance, played as
Campion states by 42 musicians. In fact, Campion's list here amounts to 38,
so we must assume that the four Silvan lutenists took part (no music
survives). The music for the second main dance, which immediately followed the first, was composed by Lupo. It was begun by the violins and
continued, 'in forme of an Eccho', by the other instrumental ensembles.[30]
During the procession of Night, six cornetts and six voices performed a
'sollemne motet',[31] 'With spotles mindes', being a commentary on the
significance of the procession:

> We this graue procession make
> Chast eies and eares, pure heartes, and voices
> Are graces wherein *Phoebe* most reioyces.

Immediately the motet finished the violins began the third masque dance.
This was Thomas Giles's piece printed as 'Triumph now with ioy' at the end
of the Description, and performed most probably like the second dance.
Then follow the 'measures', which were probably a pavan and galliard,
possibly using a pre-existing piece and perhaps arranged by Giles.[32] Another
dialogue song follows shortly, 'Of all the starres', sung by two basses and
two trebles. The song, for which no music is extant, is a farewell to Hesperus
and concludes with a chorus repeated as he departs, which is a signal for the
revels to begin. These are described by Campion as 'Currantoes, Levaltas

---

[29] On the significance of this see Lindley, *Campion*, pp. 181–3, 201.

[30] Printed in the *Discription*, 1607, sigs. D4^b–E, to the words 'Shewes and nightly reuels'.
A version appears in Rosseter, *Lessons*, No. 8, and British Library Add. MS 10444, No. 54,
No. 80, Nos. 95–7, 'The Lord Hay his Masque'; Sabol, *Four Hundred Songs*, No. 4.

[31] Dart ('The Repertory of the Royal Wind Music', p. 74) suggests Alfonso Ferrabosco's
'Exaudi Deus' (Cambridge, Fitzwilliam Museum, MS 734, f. 22). This may well be incorrect,
since Dart based his assumption on a perhaps over hasty interpretation of this manuscript. He
divided the manuscript(s) into three sections: unworded chordal pieces, and two sets of
instrumental pieces. It is on these two instrumental sections, presumably, that Dart assigned
the provenance and probable significance of the partbooks. The second section comprises 23
pieces, 20 being almandes; the third, in a different but consistent hand, is a variety of dances
headed '5 part things for the cornetts' (six of the thirteen are printed in *Suite from the Royal
Brass Music of King James I*, ed. Dart, London, 1959). He is mistaken to include 'Exaudi
Deus'–'Quoniam' and Bassano's 'Oy me dolente' in the second section, since that begins,
according to the original numbering, with an almande. This motet, therefore, need have
nothing to do with the King's Musick or Campion's masque.

[32] On the hitherto confused subject of 'measures' see John M. Ward, 'The English
Measure', *Early Music*, xiv (1986), 15–21.

and galliards' and are the conventional brisk triple-time dances.[33] A short interjection by Night heralds the end of the revels. Now follows, somewhat unconventionally, a fourth main dance, composed by Lupo, played by the violins, and printed at the end of the Description with the words 'Time that leads the fatall round . . .'.[34] The last music in the masque is the third dialogue song 'Tell me gentle howre' sung by a tenor and a bass, concluded by a chorus which is repeated 'with seuerall Ecchoes' in the manner of the great chorus earlier. Thus it forms a grand vocal and instrumental finale for which, unfortunately, no music survives.

Six years were to elapse before Campion's next masque. During this time Jonson's masques developed significantly. The masque immediately following *Lord Hays*, Jonson's *Masque of Beauty* (10 January 1608) is clearly influenced by Campion and at the same time still artistically related to *Blackness*. As in *Blackness*, the musicians in *Beauty* are an integral part of the masque and help to discover some of its mysteries and fiction. *Beauty*, however, is simpler in that it operates on a more straightforward emblematic level, especially in its spectacle, dance and songs. Each stage of the masque is punctuated by music, following the convention set by *Lord Hays*. The opening song, 'So beautie on the waters stood', is both a celebratory and uncomplicated dance-song, performed while the sixteen masquers come ashore and dance the first masque dance. Ferrabosco's setting is the faithful servant of the text and musically quite simple.[35] Similarly, the songs which interrupt the revels, 'to give them [the dancers] respite',[36] are restrained according to the nature of their texts, at the same time punctuating the progress of the masque. Jonson is unusually careful to describe their manner of performance, so acknowledging in addition to their contribution to the emblem of the masque their separate musical identity—*musica instrumentalis*.

In the *Masque of Queens* (2 February 1609) Jonson introduced for the first time—though possibly related to the Dance of Humours and Affections in

---

[33] Otto Gombosi, 'Some Musical Aspects of the English Court Masque', *Journal of the American Musicological Society*, i (1948), 3–19; see also Sternfeld, *Music in Shakespearean Tragedy*, pp. 250–56.

[34] As Peter Holman points out (*Campion, The Discription of a Maske*, facs. edn., Menston, 1973, 'Introductory Note'), Campion mentions that the dance finished with 'a light change of musick and measure' which is not to be found in the version printed with the Description. Holman suggests adding an anonymous lute piece in British Library Add. MS 38539, f. 2^v—here compare 'Lord Hayes Corant' in the Tollemache Manuscript and Edinburgh, National Library of Scotland, Adv. MS 5.2.15, p. 119 for bandora—to satisfy Campion's detail. This, according to Holman, would make a perfectly acceptable 'masque alman', characteristic of Lupo. The 'incomplete' piece is also present in Rosseter, *Lessons*, No. 22. A two-part version exists in British Library Add. MS 10444, No. 54, 'A Masque'; Sabol, *Four Hundred Songs*, No. 79.

[35] Ferrabosco, *Ayres*, 1609, No. 21.

[36] Compare 'Nay, you must not stay' (*Oberon*); 'O what fault' (*Love Freed*).

Hymenaei and the 'capriccious Daunce' of the 'twelve boys' in the *Hadding-ton Masque*[37]—an antimasque as an integral (first) section of the masque. In so doing he greatly extended the emblematic and dramatic possibilities of the masque, a problem that occupied him continuously. In *Oberon* (1 January 1611), for example, he first addressed the task of unifying antimasque and main masque. In addition to novel and effective scenic devices which enabled the antimasque to grow into, rather than be dissolved by, the main masque,[38] Jonson transformed his *personae* from (antimasque) fictional characters to symbolic persons actually present at the masque, a procedure which he found difficult enough to handle and yet one which Campion boldly attempted to follow in his *Somerset* masque. *Oberon* is further distinguished by the increased functional or dramatic nature of its songs, in contrast to the philosophical lyrics of the earlier masques, whose more insistent declamation reflects their flattened tone and structural literary formalism in the context of the masque plot. In the artistic companion to *Oberon*, *Love Freed from Ignorance and Folly* (3 February 1611), Jonson overcame many of the transition problems by concentrating more on the poetry and less on the scene. The antimasque, for example, is developed as a miniature drama in itself so that the transformation to 'realism' may be more apparent. The songs maintain their functional position, although those for the revels are more emblematic.

When compared with *Lord Hays*, Campion's *Lords* masque exhibits two distinct Jonsonian developments, an antimasque and a plot. Much has been written about the nature of this masque, often from opposing standpoints. Enid Welsford was not impressed by its philosophical content and refused to allow that its construction was other than 'confused and poor'.[39] More recently, A. Leigh DeNeef attempted to counter Welsford and others by explaining the philosophical levels and equivocal symbolism in *Lords*: 'much of the difficulty readers have had with it results from a confusing of literal and figurative levels of meaning'.[40]

A (Jacobean) masque written for a specific occasion, in this case the marriage of the Princess Elisabeth and Frederic, Count Palatine, generally in its emblem celebrated that occasion and little else. There would normally be little philosophical intricacy or hidden symbolic reference. Yet in *Lords* Campion seems to be evolving an emblem far more complicated than the occasion demanded. To what extent does Campion simply celebrate the marriage and its circumstances; or how far is he, in Jonsonian fashion, trying

[37] See further Chan, *Music in the Theatre*, pp. 190, 196.
[38] Described in detail in Stephen Orgel, *The Jonsonian Masque*, Cambridge, Mass., 1965, pp. 82–91. See also Chan, *Music in the Theatre*, pp. 232–4.
[39] *The Court Masque*, Cambridge, 1927, p. 192.
[40] 'Structure and Theme in Campion's *The Lords Maske*', *Studies in English Literature, 1500–1900*, xvii (1977), 95–103.

to say through music and poetry something more lasting in the medium of the masque?

That Campion was attempting something more than a simple, allegorical masque is suggested by the mixed and often confused reactions of its contemporary audience. No matter how sophisticated the emblem or deep the level of meaning, the court audience, providing it understood English and could see properly, would not find the intent or immediate symbolism of a masque hard to follow. (The Description could supply the hidden meanings and inner subtlety later, much as a printed score might complement a first performance today.) John Chamberlain, probably on hearsay, wrote that the *Lords* masque was 'very rich and sumptuous, yet it was very long and tedious, and with many devices, more like a play than a masque'.[41] Sir John Finett said that 'it was the richest show but showde not the rychest that I haue seene, [which] seemed to be a singularity of some of the affectio[n] (though perhaps unseasonable) [of] concealed brauery'.[42] Jones's scenic devices impressed wonderfully; Campion's literary emblem mystified, so it would seem.

The problem revolves around the functional identity of the central figures, Orpheus and his perhaps unlikely companions, Entheus and Prometheus. What character does Orpheus represent? That he is a musician, as would be expected, is most probable. Much of his behaviour is conventional, as for example when at the instigation of Entheus he is asked to 'giue a call' with his 'charm'd musicke' to discover a scene of the main masque. But elsewhere Campion endows in him greater, unusual powers. Why, at Jove's command, does Orpheus and not Mercury release Entheus from Mania's cave? Is it because, as Shapiro has suggested,[43] only the music of Orpheus can 'tame the wild beasts'; or is Campion expecting too much? Indeed, it is Orpheus who banishes, in an outmoded Jonsonian manner, the antimasque before the main masque, creating harmony out of disorder, having managed to secure the release of Entheus, the 'Poeticke furie', without setting 'chaos' and 'disorder' free:

> Let Musicke put on *Protean* changes now,
> Wilde beasts it once tam'd, now let Franticks bow.

That Campion expects much of Orpheus's harmonizing powers is explicit throughout the masque. This may be why author and designer collaboratively gave Orpheus more than simply musical symbolism, represented in part by his costume:

[he] was attired after the old Greeke manner, his haire curled and long; a lawrell wreath on his head, and in his hand hee bare a siluer bird.

[41] *The Letters of John Chamberlain*, ed. N. E. McClure, Philadelphia, 1939, i. 428.
[42] London, Public Record Office, State Papers Domestic, xiv, Vol. 72, f. 64ʳ.
[43] I. A. Shapiro, *A Book of Masques: In Honour of Allardyce Nicoll*, Cambridge, 1967, pp. 98–9.

No mention here of harps or the conventional lyra da braccio. The silver bird is probably the silver or white swan emblem, representing 'Poesie'. Furthermore, the laurel wreath may connect Orpheus with Entheus, who also wore a laurel wreath—laurel being the symbol of poetry[44]—and who unmistakably represents poetry. Campion therefore seems to be emphasizing the union of music and poetry, their harmonizing power and their adornment of love. With the introduction of Prometheus and, later, Sybilla he adds two further characteristics, creativity and memorability. In other words, if we accept an interpretation of Campion's symbolic persons as outlined above, then it would appear that in addition to celebrating the marriage, at one level, at another Campion is celebrating the special qualities of music and poetry interacting with the scenic design. Moreover, in the figure of Prometheus Campion seems to be celebrating not only the creativity but also the artistic ingenuity of the scenic devices and changes. Is not Campion's allegory also, retrospectively lest it intrude upon the marriage celebration, a self-conscious reference to the creators of the masque, in Orpheus/Entheus to the musician–poet Campion himself and in Prometheus to the designer, Inigo Jones?

Music plays a more dramatically integrated part in *Lords* than it did in *Lord Hays*. The Description does not make it clear who the musicians are or what they play. The only specific reference is to a 'double consort'; we may surmise, quite happily, that Orpheus was the main actor-musician and that he sang and played several songs. But there are no attendant actor-musicians of the *Lord Hays* 'silvan' kind. Most of the music must have been performed off-stage. The opening scene is discovered while the double consort plays. Two consorts, probably similar to those in *Lord Hays*, were separately placed at each side of the lower stage. After a short speech by Orpheus, the consorts announce the first appearance of Mania, who describes this music as a 'powerfull noise'. This would imply 'hoboyes', similar to the 'contentious Musique' of *Hymenaei*. An exchange between Orpheus and Mania precedes the next antimasque entry: 'at the sound of a strange musicke twelue Franticks enter'. This is reminiscent of *Love Freed*: 'there was heard a strange Musique of wilde Instruments'. A dance of 'Lunatickes' immediately follows 'fitted to a loud phantasticke tune'.[45] The mad dance subsides and a 'very solemne ayre' is played softly during Orpheus's speech. This seems to be the first instance of a musical recitation in a masque, and it is an

---

[44] See Cesare Ripa, *Iconologia* (Rome, 1603), Padua, 1618, p. 212.

[45] J. P. Cutts ('Robert Johnson and the Court Masque', *Music & Letters*, xli (1960), 111–26) sees a link between the mad scene in Webster's *Duchess of Malfi* and *Lords*, conjecturing that Johnson supplied the (same) music for both. This, however, does not accord with the extant bill of account, in which Johnson is shown as having received £10—for setting songs, with Lupo(?) (Exchequer of Receipt, Pell Order Books, XII, f. 183ᵛ; printed in Paul Reyher, *Les Masques anglais*, Paris, 1909, pp. 508–9, and less precisely in Stephen Orgel & Roy Strong, *Inigo Jones: The Theatre of the Stuart Court*, London, 1973, pp. 241–2). Sabol's theory that Coprario supplied (or arranged) this music is more tenable.

extraordinary example of music theatre. The declamatory song 'Come away, bring thy golden theft' is the next musical incident.[46] Its similarity to the Jonson–Ferrabosco type is unmistakable. Then follows a conventional dance song, celebrating the marriage, during which 'according to the humour of this Song, the [eight] Starres [of extraordinaire bignesss] mooued in an exceeding strange manner', for which, according to Campion, Jones excelled. After the transformation scene and the Pages' dance[47] comes 'Wooe her, and win her', a stereotyped Renaissance courtship song, invoking theories on 'love' and musical effects working on that subject.[48] Then come the masquers' main dances, which are interrupted by dialogue songs included to give the dancers time to 'breathe' or rest, as in the revels in *Beauty*.[49] A song, 'Come triumphing', another dancing song, 'Dance, and visit now the shadowes of our joy', a farewell song, 'No longer wrong the night', and a final dance conclude the musical element of the masque.

The musical content of *Lords* is both successful and stylistically up to date, reflecting the happy musico-poetic relationship climaxing in 1613 between Campion and the masque's chief composer, John Coprario. That the masque's philosophical and dramatic coherence is less successful might be explained by Campion's unsuitable attempt to emulate the Jonsonian masque, whose artistic development after 1607 had been rapid and extensive, and more specifically by Campion's inability to control Inigo Jones's imaginative flair. Campion may well have had the double problem of having to fit an increased philosophical and dramatic masque concept—his own intent—around rich and extravagant scenic devices thought up before the emblem had been properly or fully worked out. That this was a major problem in Jonsonian dramatic masques is well documented in the quarrel between Jonson and Jones. But Campion may already be hinting with gentle irony at this difficulty in his statement following the description of the moving stars:

I suppose fewe haue euer seene more neate artifice, then Master *Innigoe Iones* shewed in contriuing their Motion, who in all the rest of the workmanship which belong'd to the whole inuention shewed extraordinarie industrie and skill, which if it be not as liuely exprest in writing as it appeared in view, robbe not him of his due, but lay the blame on my want of right apprehending his instructions for the adoring [*sic*] of his Arte.[50]

Campion's last masque did not benefit from the expert contribution of Inigo Jones, who was in Italy at the time, but suffered, it would seem, because

---

[46] Frequently compared with 'Come away, arm'd with loues delight' (*Two Bookes*, II, No. 17), which may be an arrangement.

[47] Sabol suggests 'The Pages Masque' music (*Four Hundred Songs*, No. 109).

[48] See further Sternfeld, 'A Song from Campion's *Lord's Masque*', p. 373, and Lindley, *Campion*, p. 233.

[49] Sabol suggests three dances by Coprario (*Four Hundred Songs*, Nos. 73–75).

[50] *Campion's Works*, ed. P. Vivian, Oxford, 1909, p. 93.

of an incompetent Florentine architect, Constantine de Servi, who was reluctant 'to impart his intentions'. In order to bypass this lack of collaboration, after his less severe experience in *Lords*, Campion eschewed any real attempt at dramatic flow and coherence, preferring instead to base his 'whole Inuention upon Inchauntments and seuerall transformations'. This, in addition to poor designs, as Jonson was quick to point out snipingly through his *Irish Masque*, was not a successful formula.

The music in *Somerset* is as interesting and varied as in any Jacobean masque. In addition, more survives for this masque than for any other. All the types of masque songs are present except dance songs. Descriptions of how the music was performed are, significantly for Campion, lacking. This is particularly frustrating in the antimasque dance section, which is of special interest. It appears to be in the form of a dumb-show interlude, similar to the *ballet de cour* kind, often used in the opening sections and very much in vogue in English drama at the time.[51] Campion's interlude begins with the entry of four Enchanterers who, 'when they had whispered a while as if they had reioyced at the wrongs which they had done to the knights', began their dance. Then, in turn, four Winds, Elements and Continents enter. After having danced together 'in a strange kinde of confusion', they move away four by four. Campion, however, does not furnish any musical details, so that the sort of instrumental symbolism of, say, *Gorboduc*, Act I scene I, or *Hamlet*, Act III scene ii, line 145, can only be conjectured (without too much difficulty), signifying Campion's apparent lack of interest in music theatre, in the shift away from descriptive or functional (instrumental) music in his masques. A chorus, not uncommon in dumb shows, punctuates the end of the interlude and the beginning of the next, dramatically scarcely related scene. The chorus is on-stage, comprising Harmony and nine musicians who either sing or play. The chorus has a mainly functional role, particularly in the central portion of the masque from the departure of the Enchanterers to the entry of the Skippers. The only other information on how the music was performed may be gleaned from the songs printed at the end of the description, which inform us that Lanier and John Allen sang.[52] It seems likely they performed off-stage: it is just possible that Lanier also played the on-stage part of Eternity. The presence of Lanier as composer and singer heralds the beginning of a new era in masque composition in which Campion took little or no further part.

The unique contribution Campion made to the Jacobean masque, as F. W. Sternfeld intimated, lies in the function he gave, as poet, to music. Without Campion, Jonson would almost certainly have continued to see music as an

[51] See further Sternfeld, *Music in Shakespearean Tragedy*, esp. pp. 214–19.

[52] John Allen was praised by Jonson in *Queens*: 'that most excellent *tenor* voyce, and exact Singer'.

adornment of the masque emblem. Campion gave music a theatrical function in addition to its philosophical which, had he possessed the musical language, might have led on to opera and the new Baroque style. Instead he fell victim to what was to become the masque's own undoing, its over-emphasis on lavish scenic design and conflicting artistic aims.

8

'Comus': The Court Masque Questioned

Peter Walls

THE debate on the genre of *Comus* has been going on for at least two centuries. Dr Johnson, while admitting that 'a work more truly poetical is rarely found', declared that 'as a drama it is deficient. The action is not probable'.[1] Thomas Warton expressed similar views, although he at least made some attempt to put aside inappropriate expectations:

We must not read Comus with an eye to the stage, or with the expectation of dramatic propriety ... Comus is a suite of speeches, not interesting by discrimination of character; not conveying a variety of incidents, not gradually exciting curiosity: but perpetually attracting attention by sublime sentiment, by fanciful imagery of the richest vein, by an exuberance of picturesque description, poetical allusion, and ornamental expression. This is the first time the old English Mask was in some degree reduced to the principles and form of rational composition.[2]

Although Warton responded to one element in *Comus*, his view of it as a compendium of incidental literary delights ignores any sense of progression through the work, and his lack of sympathy with the workings of the 'old English Mask' suggests an incapacity to view *Comus* in terms of that genre.

Haunting nearly every critical discussion of *Comus* is the question, 'Is *A Maske Presented at Ludlow Castle* really a masque?' Describing the court masque as a dramatized dance, Enid Welsford concluded that *Comus* is a dramatized debate in which dance is quite inessential.[3] Some very different ideas have been proposed: Gretchen L. Finney postulated that 'Milton was writing a musical drama in the Italian Style',[4] while Don Cameron Allen concluded that 'in its external structure "Comus" is a melange of various tendencies and styles that never merge into anything intensely organic'.[5] Stephen Orgel expresses the conviction that Milton's *Maske Presented at Ludlow Castle* is unequivocally a masque:

---

[1] *Lives of the English Poets* (1779–81), ed. G. B. Hill, Oxford, 1905, i. 168.

[2] John Milton, *Poems upon Several Occasions*, ed. Thomas Warton, London, 1785, p. 262.

[3] *The Court Masque*, Cambridge, 1927 (reprinted New York, 1962), p. 314.

[4] 'Comus: Dramma per Musica' in *Musical Backgrounds for English Literature, 1580–1650*, New Brunswick, 1962, p. 194.

[5] 'Milton's Comus as a Failure in Artistic Compromise', *English Literary History*, xvi (1949), 112.

That Milton was constantly aware of his work as a real masque—as a symbolic representation of the milieu in and for which it was created, as a production wherein, when the lords and ladies became masquers, the real world became indistinguishable from the world of the masque—is obvious from the frequency and complexity with which references to the audience, the Earl of Bridgewater and his family and court, are woven into the fabric of the piece.[6]

Orgel is absolutely right, but the debate makes it clear that *Comus* has some features which obscure its identity as a masque. Those features, in fact, make it structurally fascinating, since the masque-like and un-masque-like elements stand in a critical relationship to each other. Milton's purposes can be seen more clearly by closely examining the structure of *Comus*.

The masque-like elements in *Comus* stand out from the rest with striking clarity. A perfectly regular courtly masque could be extracted from *Comus*. This 'regular' masque—adapted by its avoidance of spectacular transformations and by its very modest musical requirements to the conditions at Ludlow Castle—would follow the usual progression from antimasque to main masque. The antimasque would begin at line 93 with the entry of Comus and his 'rout of monsters, headed like sundry sorts of wild beasts . . . making a riotous and unruly noise'. It would continue without a break until line 147, thus including Comus's initiation of the 'midnight shout and revelry' and the climax of these rites in the rout's 'measure (in a wild rude & wanton antick)'.[7] This antimasque section would conclude with Comus's exclamation:

> Break off, break off, I feel the different pace,
> Of som chast footing near about this ground.
>   (lines 145–6)

Then by jumping to line 958 the main masque could begin. There the 'Scene changes, presenting *Ludlow* Town and the Presidents Castle; then com in Country-Dancers, after them the attendant Spirit, with the two Brothers and the Lady'. Then would follow the songs and dances of the main masque and the Attendant Spirit's epilogue.

Such a masque would be very like a domesticated *Pleasure Reconciled to Virtue*. The Egerton children would not have had speaking parts, but courtly masquers never did anyway. The Attendant Spirit's songs in this part of *Comus*, like the songs of many masque presenters, underline the emblematic significance of the set dances. After the simple, innocent and joyous country dancing, he sings:

[6] *The Jonsonian Masque*, Cambridge, Mass., 1967, p. 102. Orgel goes on to discuss in some detail the identification of Henry Lawes with the swain 'who with his soft pipe and smooth dittied song / Well knows to still the wild winds when they roar / And hush the waving woods'.

[7] This reading is from Milton's autograph manuscript of *Comus* (the Trinity College, Cambridge manuscript); see *The Works of John Milton*, ed. F. A. Patterson, New York, 1931–8, i. 493, note to stage direction following line 144. All Milton quotations are from this volume.

> Back Shepherds, back, anough your play,
> Till next Sun-shine holiday,
> Here be without duck or nod
> Other trippings to be trod
> Of lighter toes, and such Court guise
> As *Mercury* did first devise
> With the mincing *Dryades*
> On the Lawns and on the Leas.
>
> (lines 957–64)

The song makes a distinction between the kind of dancing country dancers perform (with 'ducks and nods') and the more courtly steps of the three masquers. The Attendant Spirit's next song presents the masquers and establishes the conventional contrast between the main masque dances (which illustrate the virtue of the dancers) and the disorder of the antimasque:

> Noble Lord, and Lady bright,
> I have brought ye new delight,
> Here behold so goodly grown
> Three fair branches of your own
> Heav'n hath timely tri'd their youth,
> Their faith, their patience, and their truth,
> And sent them here through hard assays
> With a crown of deathless Praise
> To triumph in victorious dance
> O're sensual Folly, and Intemperance.
>
> (lines 965–74)

The Attendant Spirit's final speech is, like Daedalus's final song in Jonson's *Pleasure Reconciled to Virtue*, an exhortation to pursue the virtue that has been vindicated in the masque:

> Mortals that would follow me,
> Love vertue, she alone is free,
> She can teach ye how to clime
> Higher than the Spheary chime;
> Or if Vertue feeble were,
> Heav'n it self would stoop to her.
>
> (lines 1017–22)

In these sections of *Comus* music and dance are used in a way which is thoroughly typical of the courtly masque. The antimasque dances and masque dances are sharply contrasted, and the virtuous nature of the masque dances is emphasized by the masque songs. Hence we are dealing with a miniature but complete courtly masque.

All this, however, accounts for only about one eighth of the total text of

Comus. If we disregard the Attendant Spirit's prologue,[8] then the excluded part of the text all takes place between the antimasque and the main masque sections of the 'regular' masque outlined above. None of this central section is particularly masque-like (although Sabrina's intervention to free the Lady from Comus's spell has a precedent in Johnson's *Love Freed from Ignorance and Folly*, where the Muse's Priests intervene to free Love from the Sphynx).

Given that the 120-odd lines discussed above form a short but perfectly regular masque, Milton's procedure could be described as follows: he has replaced the transformation scene (normally of cardinal importance) by an extended dramatic sequence which takes place in the antimasque world. This long section is fundamentally un-masque-like, although it has a few masque elements. It is framed by a real antimasque and a real main masque.

The transformation scene in a 'normal' masque separates the antimasque from the main masque: it is the key moment when, as if by natural necessity, virtue overcomes vice, or wisdom and sophistication displace folly and vulgarity. In the regular masque extracted from *Comus* this relationship between masque and antimasque and the dramatized assertion that virtue must overcome vice would be preserved; but the extended middle section of Milton's text calls these fundamental structural and thematic rules into question. The Elder Brother describes the significance of Minerva's emblems in a way which is thoroughly in accord with the iconography of the courtly masque:

> What was that snaky-headed *Gorgon* sheild
> That wise *Minerva* wore, unconquer'd Virgin,
> Wherewith she freez'd her foes to congeal'd stone?
> But rigid looks of Chast austerity,
> And noble grace that dash't brute violence
> With sudden adoration, and blank aw.
>
> (lines 446–51)

Noble grace dashing brute violence with sudden adoration and blank awe is an almost perfect description of what happens at the transformation scene in the typical Jonsonian masque. But it does not happen quite so readily in *Comus*. The Elder Brother's confidence, if not entirely misplaced, is at least not completely endorsed by Milton. The whole middle section of *Comus* works partly by setting up emblematic expectations in a context where, for most of the time at least, realistic conditions prevail. In other words, we expect to watch an allegorical presentation of moral victory, but instead we are faced with a dramatization of the kind of moral uncertainty and danger that is often encountered in real life.

[8] A prologue preceding the antimasque and presented by characters who belong primarily in the world of the main masque was not unknown in the masques at court; see, for example, Ben Jonson's last masque, *Chloridia* (1631), and Aurelian Townshend's *Albion's Triumph* (1623).

Dramatic tension is created by the possibility that virtue will not automatically overcome vice, and much of the action depends upon the inability of a virtuous but frail human to recognize vice for what it is. The Lady addresses Comus as 'gentle shepherd' (line 270) and 'gentle villager' (line 303); does he look obviously different from the Attendant Spirit 'habited like a shepherd' (line 489)? She tells Comus,

> Shepherd I take thy word,
> And trust thy honest offer'd courtesie,
> Which oft is sooner found in lowly sheds
> With smoaky rafters, than in tapstry Halls
> And Courts of Princes, where it first was nam'd,
> And yet is most pretended
>
> (lines 320–25)

This might seem a rather unusual comment to find in a masque (from which the possibility of a wicked prince was usually excluded), but perhaps more significant is the fact that the Lady is substituting for a normal masque assumption based on an emblematic mode of thought an equally conventional emblem; her mistake is to accept any kind of emblematic mode or, in other words, to accept any appearances as an indication of the reality. Stephen Orgel, discussing Jonson's depiction of Comus in *Pleasure Reconciled*, makes in passing a nice comparison with Milton's work:

The audience at Ludlow Castle was being taught to mistrust appearances. In contrast, the spectators at Whitehall in 1618 had more faith that the aesthetic judgement was the right one. Merely by looking at Jonson's Comus, they knew who and what he was.[9]

Milton's Comus boasts of the power 'to cheat the eye with blear illusion / And give it false presentements' (lines 155–6); Inigo Jones might have made the same claim—but Jonson always made sure that the illusions in his masques expressed a higher reality or moral truth.

There are yet more surprising reversals of normal masque assumptions. Comus's banquet, for which 'The Scene changes to a stately Palace, set out with all manner of deliciousness' (following line 657), is a main masque tableau which could have come from Jonson's *Oberon* where we find: 'There the whole *Scene* opened, and within was dicouer'd the *Frontispice* of a bright and glorious *Palace*, whose gates and walls were transparent' (lines 138–40).[10] In Milton's masque, however, this tableau has been usurped by

---

[9] *The Jonsonian Masque*, p. 153. A related point is made by C. C. Brown in *John Milton's Aristocratic Entertainments*, Cambridge, 1985, p. 88: 'Here the audience is being invited to a mixture of reactions unusual in the self-conscious devices of comedy or masque, for Milton's technique with the masque has a way of reasserting a realism, a moral realism, through the celebratory gestures'.

[10] This and other Jonson references are from *Ben Jonson*, ed. C. H. Herford & Percy & Evelyn Simpson, Oxford, 1925–52, Vol. 7.

the forces of the antimasque. Moreover, in this scene Comus puts forward a traditional masque argument:

> Wherefore did Nature powre her bounties forth,
> With such a full and unwithdrawing hand,
> Covering the earth with odours, fruits and flocks,
> Thronging the Seas with spawn innumerable,
> But all to please and sate the curious taste?
> And set to work millions of spinning Worms,
> That in their green shops weave the smooth-haired silk
> To deck her Sons . . .
> Beauty is natures brag, and must be shown
> In courts, at feasts, and high solemnities
> Where most may wonder at the workmanship
> (lines 709–16, 744–46)

Words like 'sate' and 'brag' undermine his point of view, but apart from these indications of a different authorial attitude the speech seems fit for a main masque. It is, after all, a point of view which is implied by titles such as *The Masque of Beauty*, and the speech itself comes close in content to one of the masque songs in *Neptune's Triumph*:

> Why doe you weare the Silkwormes toyles;
> Or glory in the Shellfish spoyles?
> Why do you smell of Amber-gris,
> Of which was formed *Neptunes* Neice
> The Queene of Loue; vnlesse you can,
> Like Sea-borne *Venus*, loue a man?
> Your lookes, your smiles, and thoughts that meete,
> *Ambrosian* hands, and silver feete,
> Doe promise you will do't.
> (lines 484–5, 494–7, 501–3)

The key phrase in the Jonson song is 'and thoughts that meete', since it points to the masque's dependence on emblem: fair must be good, and ugly must be foul, and there can be no disparity between the ladies' physical beauty and their inner dispositions. The Elder Brother's statement that 'he that hides a dark soul, and foul thoughts / Benighted walks under the mid-day Sun' (lines 382–3) could have no place in one of Jonson's masques. In *Comus* the traditional masque pattern is established and in some measure preserved, but its structural and thematic identity as an animated emblem is exposed to alien pressures. While Milton preserves the basic movement from disorder and intemperance to the virtuous pleasures of the main masque, his treatment of the genre makes the point that this progress is far from automatic.

In the long middle section of *Comus* music sometimes participates in the untrustworthiness of appearances—soft music complements the other seemingly main-masque features of Comus's banquet, for example. But by and large the use of music and dance corresponds to normal masque usage. Comus and his retinue are associated with 'barbarous dissonance' (line 550) and the sounds of 'riot and ill manag'd Merriment' (line 171). The anti-masque contains a 'wild, rude, and wanton antick', while the main masque dances are described by the songs which introduce them as dignified and courtly. Most importantly, nobody of Comus's party ever sings. Song has a power and dignity above that of ordinary speech—the Attendant Spirit 'with his soft Pipe and smooth dittied Song / Well knows to still the wilde winds when they roar, / And hush the waving Woods' (lines 84–8). Song is reserved for the Lady and the Attendant Spirit to seek help ('Sweet Echo' and 'Sabrina Fair'), for Sabrina, the goddess of the river, to introduce herself ('By the rushy-fringèd bank') and for introducing the main masque dances. The lady's song is described as 'a fort and solemn breathing sound' (line 555). The Attendant Spirit's songs at the end of the masque emphasize that he has more than mortal vision and that he resides above the confusion of this world. All the songs move beyond the human uncertainties which inform so much of the spoken verse, and they are all either sung by or addressed to an immortal being.

Milton was quick to acknowledge that in Henry Lawes he had a musician whose worth and skill as a composer and—in *Comus*—as a performer could help establish these aesthetic/moral distinctions in his work. But any appreciation of the relationship between musical expression and moral authority had been well lost by the time Dr Johnson and Thomas Warton mused on the nature of *Comus*.[11]

POSTSCRIPT

Since writing this essay I have read Maryann Cale McGuire's excellent book *Milton's Puritan Masque* (Athens, Ga., 1983). McGuire argues as I do that *Comus* makes a moral point by refusing to adopt the normal assumptions of the form in which it is so explicitly cast.

[11] John Dalton's eighteenth-century version of *Comus*—set as an 'opera' in 1738 by Thomas Arne (ed. Julian Herbage ('Musica Britannica', iii), London, 1951)—allots airs indiscriminately to good and bad characters; indeed, the devil has many of the best tunes.

9

Milton's Opera?

Elizabeth Mackenzie

DRYDEN'S *The State of Innocence* has not had a good press. It was odd enough, as Dryden said in 1677, to 'publish an opera which was never acted'; odder is the misconception which has persisted, even among some scholars, that it is simply a version of *Paradise Lost* in heroic couplets. Milton himself may be responsible for this misunderstanding—albeit unintentionally—in the notorious remark about 'tagging' his verses.

There are three early sources for the story of Dryden's visit to Milton 'to have leave to put his *Paradise Lost* into a drama in rhyme. Mr. Milton received him civilly, and told him he would give him leave to tag his verses.' This is Aubrey, possibly direct from Dryden himself but not published until 1813, although Malone refers to it in 1800. *The Monitor* for April 1713 repeats a story which goes back to Dryden 'almost forty years' before, quotes Milton and adds that Waller accompanied Dryden. Jonathan Richardson, the only early biographer of Milton to refer to Dryden's visit, writing in 1734 thinks it necessary to explain the 'tag' joke, again attributing it to Milton. There is also Marvell's poem printed with the second edition of *Paradise Lost*, advertised for sale in July 1674. If we persist with A. W. Verrall in believing that the visit did not take place,[1] then Marvell is the origin of the tagging joke. If, as seems likely, Marvell took over the joke, we may assume that Milton was pleased enough with it to repeat it to him, though not necessarily because of a triumph over Dryden. I believe that Milton knew perfectly well what Dryden intended, but before discussing the common ground between the two poets we must ask whether Dryden was merely proposing to bring the verse of *Paradise Lost* up to date by putting it into couplets.

The *Monitor* account might seem to support this view. It reports that Milton advised Dryden that some of his 'points' were 'so awkward & old fashioned' that he might as well leave them as he found them. ('Point' has the sense of 'phrase', often a musical phrase, as well as the pinched-in or tagged ribbon or cord.) The presence of Waller could have encouraged this remark;

---

[1] *Lectures on Dryden*, Cambridge, 1914, p. 220.

116   *Elizabeth Mackenzie*

even more than Dryden he must have seemed the epitome of the new, smooth poetry. Dryden traced the invention of the heroic couplet to him, and the changing taste is illustrated by the fortunes of the volumes of poems which Milton and Waller brought out in 1645. Milton's took to 1660 to sell out, Waller's needed three editions within a year. There is a sense of different poetic generations also in the remark about *Paradise Lost* reported by Richardson:[2] 'This man (says Dryden) Cuts us All Out and the Ancients too.' But Dryden rejects the praise of Nat Lee, in the poem prefaced to *The State of Innocence*, 1677, that Dryden had refined the 'old fashion'd' gold of Milton as rather 'the effect of his love to me, than of his deliberate and sober judgement'. *Paradise Lost* is 'undoubtedly one of the greatest, most noble, and sublime Poems, which either this Age or Nation has produced'. When for the fourth issue of *Paradise Lost* Milton's printer asked him to provide a note on the verse, 'a reason of that which stumbled many . . . why the Poem Rimes not', Milton defended his practice as the recovery of 'ancient liberty . . . from the troublesome and modern bondage of Rimeing'. Dismissing the current controversies about rhyme in the phrase 'famous modern poets carried away by custom'—and presumably dismissing too the practice of Tasso and Spenser, as he had rejected their subject matters (*Paradise Lost*, ix. 30 ff.)—he locates himself firmly in an older argument in which the linking of rhyme with the barbarians was a commonplace. He is not crass enough to plead for an English hexameter, tacitly accepting, it would seem, the English blank verse line in its place, and he takes his stand with the vernacular against Latin, with Ariosto against Bembo, as he had put it.[3] But the liberty he claims is ancient; against the moderns. The rather odd reference to Spanish and Italian poets as well as to barbarism and the orators suggests that he may have Ascham's *Scholemaster* in mind.[4]

Dryden's proposal may perhaps have influenced the decision to produce a second edition of *Paradise Lost*, either to protect the poem or to take advantage of renewed interest in it. His visit to Milton probably took place in February; *The State of Innocence* was registered in April, and Dryden tells us that he took a month to write it. No one could have imagined that it would not be printed until 1677. Marvell's poem is in a sense defensive, explanatory as well as commendatory. One phrase only is necessarily directed against Dryden, who had proposed to 'change in scenes, and show it in a play'. It praises Milton for scorning to pander to current taste by writing in rhyme, but the decision to do so and the defence were made long before Dryden's visit. It is possible to argue that the 'Town-Bayes' is a reference to the fashionable poets who wrote in rhyme rather than specifically to

---

[2] *The Early Lives of Milton*, ed. Helen Darbishire, London, 1932, p. 296.
[3] *Reason of Church Government: Complete Prose Works of John Milton*, New Haven & London, 1943–82, i. 811.
[4] Ed. L. V. Ryan, Ithaca, NY, 1967, pp. 145 ff.

Dryden.[5] Already in *The Rehearsal* (1672) the Bayes figure is a composite attack on the authors of the heroic play; more immediately Davenant than anyone else. When Marvell borrows Bayes from Buckingham to use as a comic figure in his attack on Samuel Parker in *The Rehearsal Transpros'd* (1672), the figure is almost completely separated from its source and used simply as a type of inspired and extravagant folly to belabour his target. It is ironic that Milton was thought to have had a hand in this attack on Popery, a charge which is strenuously denied by Marvell in the second part of *The Rehearsal Transpros'd* (1673). But all this takes us back before Dryden's visit. There is some reason, then, to believe that *Paradise Lost* seemed old-fashioned in its metre, even to its friends. Is there any reason to suppose that Dryden meant to bring it up to date? It is only necessary to look at *The State of Innocence* to see that his aim was quite different.

Aristotle was claimed as authority for the belief that the heroic poem had two manifestations, epic and tragedy. Dryden often discusses them as the two aspects of the same kind: 'A heroic play ought to be an imitation in little of an heroic poem.'[6] Quite apart from what we might deduce from the poems themselves, there is every reason to believe that Milton shared this view. He weighs the claims of epic and tragedy and sees them both as governed by the same moral decorum, able to 'imbreed and cherish . . . the seeds of virtu, and publick civility'. He recommends such critics as Aristotle, Horace, Castelvetro and Tasso because they teach 'what the laws are of a true Epic Poem . . . what decorum is, which is the grand masterpiece to observe'.[7] His first objection to contemporary tragedy is the mixing of kinds.[8] More important is the evidence, in the Trinity Manuscript, of his own drafts for dramas on historical and on sacred subjects. He seemed, in the 1640s at any rate, to share the prevailing belief that historical subjects were of themselves suitable for heroic treatment, close to the views expressed by Davenant in his preface to *Gondibert* and to the practice of Dryden in *Annus Mirabilis*, though in concentrating on British history Milton is harking back to Spenser. His plans for sacred history, in theory at least, would automatically merit heroic status. One might ask whether, unlike *Samson Agonistes*, Milton ever had performance in mind. In the case of the plans on the theme of the Fall we may conclude that he did. In the draft entitled 'Adam unparadiz'd' the movements of Gabriel are carefully noted; he is either 'descending or entering', and on stage he 'passes by the chorus'. In three out of the four versions of the Fall story mutes are included; they could have no

[5] See for example J. A. Wittreich, Jr., 'Perplexing the Explanation: Marvell's "On Mr. Milton's *Paradise Lost*"', *Approaches to Marvell*, ed. C. A. Patrides, London, 1978, pp. 280 ff.

[6] 'Of Heroic Plays' (prefaced to *The Conquest of Granada*, 1672): *Essays of John Dryden*, ed. W. P. Ker, Oxford, 1926, p. 150.

[7] *Reason of Church Government*, p. 816; *Of Education: Complete Prose*, ii. 404–5.

[8] 'Of that sort of Dramatic Poem which is called Tragedy' (preface to *Samson Agonistes*).

conceivable part to play except to the eye. In the fourth version they are acknowledged to be masque figures. In all four versions mention is made of a chorus that sings; in three of them the choruses are of angels. Among his authorities for a sacred tragedy in the preface to *Samson Agonistes* Milton cites Paraeus, who 'commenting on the *Revelation*, divides the whole book as a Tragedy, into Acts distinguisht each by a Chorus of Heavenly Harpings and Song between'. In *The Reason of Church Government* Paraeus had provided him with 'the majestic image of a high and stately Tragedy, shutting up and intermingling her solemn Scenes and Acts with a sevenfold *Chorus* of hallelujahs and harping symphonies'.[9] He also associates his chorus in the *Samson* preface with contemporary Italian practice, which has suggested to some critics Tasso's *Aminta* or Guarini's *Pastor fido*, but the references to Paraeus make it possible at least that he is thinking of sung choruses where he might be inclined to associate ancient and contemporary Italian practice. We do not know what he saw or heard in Italy, but it is safe to assume from his contact with the Florentine Academies and particularly with Giovanni Batista Doni that he was aware of the work of the Florentine *camerata* of an earlier generation—Giovanni de' Bardi and Vincenzo Galilei among them—who sought to recreate the musical performance of ancient tragedy or indeed of epic. As Tasso says, 'heroic poems can be sung to the most perfect kind of music, as Homer's were'.[10] In a letter to Doni in 1634 Pietro de' Bardi sums up the experiments of his father, 'designed to extract the essence of the Greek, the Latin and the more modern writers'; Vincenzo Galilei had been even more specific in claiming that the importance of music lay in the contribution it made to 'the expression of the concepts of the mind by means of words'; monody, he maintained, provided the moral and emotional influence which counterpoint prevented. We may be reasonably sure that Milton was aware of the theoretical beginnings of what was to turn out to be opera. We can only wonder whether any of the music he brought back with him from Italy was in the new expressive style. All six composers are madrigalists, but at least one of them, Cifra, had set some 30 of Tasso's *rime* as strophic songs; and another of them was Monteverdi.

Milton's memory of Florence starts off the whole autobiographical passage of *The Second Defence*, but the only suggestion that he might have seen an opera comes from a letter of 1639/40 to Holstenius, and that refers to Rome.[11] He thanks Holstenius for the introduction to Cardinal Francesco Barberini, who had welcomed him to what he describes as a magnificent public musical performance. It probably took place in the theatre of the Barberini Palace; there is a fair chance that Bernini staged it. It is not possible to discover which opera—if opera it was—Milton could have seen; it almost

---

[9] *Reason of Church Government*, p. 815.
[10] *Discourses on the Heroic Poem*, Book 6, trans. Mariella Cavalchini & Irene Samuel, Oxford, 1973, p. 204.
[11] *Complete Prose*, i. 334.

certainly involved recitative and chorus. It is not surprising in any case that he should not have called it an opera. Evelyn, in his diary entry for 19 November 1644,[12] reports that he had just missed seeing in Rome 'a publique opera', explaining 'for so they call shews of that kind', which suggests that the word in that sense was new to him; his is indeed the first use of the word recorded in the Oxford English Dictionary. This had been written and staged by Bernini, whose productions were famous for their magnificence. It was not until Evelyn actually saw opera in Venice (probably among others Monteverdi's *Incoronazione di Poppea* and Cavalli's *Giulio Cesare*)[13] that he understood what was really new, the fact that the story was sung throughout:

represented in Recitative music . . . with variety of Sceanes painted & contrived with no lesse art of Perspective, and Machines, for flying in the aire, & other wonderfull motions . . . it is doubtlesse one of the most magnificent and expensful diversions the wit of man can invent.[14]

When in London in 1659 he saw 'a new opera after the Italian way' the definition is the same, 'in Recitative Music and Sceanes'.[15] It is interesting that both Milton and Evelyn comment on the public performance, unlike the private performance of masques in England. Normally, the story of the masque would not be sung, though as Jonson tells us in his *Lovers Made Men* (1617) 'the whole Maske was sung (after the Italian manner) *stylo recitativo*'.

It is perhaps because Samuel Johnson knew opera after the development of the aria that he insists that *The State of Innocence* is not an opera but 'rather a tragedy in heroick rhyme'. Dryden would not agree. What can claim to be the first English opera, Davenant's *The Siege of Rhodes* (1656) exactly meets Evelyn's definition—'A Representation by the Art of Perspective in Scenes, and the story sung in Recitative Musick', as Davenant describes it. Dryden follows him in explaining that 'in the rebellious times' Davenant was forced 'to introduce the examples of moral virtue writ in verse, and performed in recitative music. The original of the music, and of the scenes which adorned his work, he had from the Italian operas.' Dryden is prepared to include opera under the heroic poem here; he describes *The Siege of Rhodes* as the first English heroic play, but he is critical of what he feels is Davenant's confusion of poem and play. Political necessity might have dictated the musical form of *The Siege of Rhodes*, but he fears that it is for musical reasons that the poem *Gondibert* imitates the structure of stage poetry (the drama), with five books equivalent to five acts and cantos equivalent to scenes.[16] This was two years before we know that *The State of Innocence*

[12] *The Diary of John Evelyn*, ed. E. S. De Beer, Oxford, 1955, ii. 261.
[13] Ibid., ii. 474 n. 6.   [14] Ibid., ii. 449–50.
[15] Ibid., iii. 229.
[16] 'Of Heroic Plays', pp. 149–50.

was in Dryden's mind. Davenant admits, at any rate, that his stanza in
Gondibert was chosen for musical reasons:

Nor does alternate Rime by any lowlinesse of cadence make the sound less Heroick,
but rather adapt it to a plaine and stately composing of Musick; and the brevity of
the Stanza renders it lesse subtle [tricky] to the Composer, and more easy to the
Singer; which in *stilo recitativo*, when the story is long, is chiefly requisite.

But he is genuinely devoted to the union of words and music; he seems to
look back to Tasso when he hopes that, as the works of Homer once were,
his cantos might be sung at village feasts; 'For so . . . did Homer's spirit, long
after his body's rest, wander in Music about Greece.'[17] Incidentally, *The
Rehearsal*, mocking the heroic play, finds it relevant to laugh at a battle in
recitativo (at this date surely a joke against Davenant?) and at machines.
As Bayes sagely remarks, 'did you ever hear any people in Clouds speak
plain? . . . when once you tye up spirits, and people in Clouds speak plain,
you spoil all.'

When Davenant defends his alternately rhyming verses as the most
suitable for recitative, he may be arguing against the more common couplet;
there can never be any reason to challenge rhyme as proper for words that
were to be sung. Milton's own practice shows this, not only in *Comus* and
Arcades (though if we are to trust the printed text, the couplets in the latter
are spoken and not sung) but also of course in the psalm paraphrases and the
hymn *On the Morning of Christ's Nativity* and *Samson Agonistes*. He is
aware of the influence of the music on the form of the Greek chorus, 'a kind
of stanzas framed only for the music, then used with that chorus that sung',[18]
and defines *Samson Agonistes* again as a poem, not a play for performance,
in which such stanzas are 'not essential', as though to claim that the
employment of the chorus has musical precedent but that to follow it in
details of metre would be inappropriate. Even those Italian critics most
eloquent against rhyme for the larger genres allowed it for the smaller. If
Trissino is included among the other commentators whom Milton praises,[19]
Milton would have authority for the use of rhyme for choruses of tragedy in
the vernacular, as well as for other lyric poetry.

Milton died early in November 1674, and we do not know whether he
realized what Dryden had made of *Paradise Lost*—or indeed whether
Marvell knew when he wrote his poem. If Milton was expecting something
like an opera, *The State of Innocence* would not have surprised him. The
story certainly is sung throughout, if we can trust Dryden's description of the
work. Only twice does he abandon his heroic couplets and occasional
triplets: for the song and dance of Eve's dream in Act III, though this of

---

[17] Author's preface to *Gondibert* (ed. D. F. Gladish, Oxford, 1971, p. 17).
[18] Preface to *Samson Agonistes*.
[19] *Of Education*, pp. 404–5.

course is rhymed, and for the whole of the second scene in Act II, where Lucifer appears in a whirling black cloud. The reader supposes at first that this is enacting Lucifer's opening words, 'Am I become so monstrous? so disfigur'd', but when Uriel appears and restores the sunlight the blank verse continues, and rhyme is resumed only for the final couplet of the scene. As for the hymns and choruses, the opera was to open with 'A symphony of warlike music', and when the defeated angels have fallen out of sight 'Tunes of Victory are play'd and an Hymn sung'; when we are shown the angels prostrate on the lake 'a Tune of Horror and Lamentation is heard'. Music is intended between Acts I and II: 'a Song expressing the change of their Condition; what they enjoy'd before; and how they fell bravely in Battle, having deserved Victory by their Valour; and what they would have done if they had conquer'd.' At the end of Act II scene i Adam and Raphael 'ascend to soft Musick, and a song is sung'. Shortly before the end of Act v angels and blessed spirits descend 'with soft Musick; a Song and Chorus', but though the singing and harping of the angels haunts Eve's recollections of paradise, the opera does not provide a final chorus. It is remarkable that Dryden does not give us the words for any of these hymns and songs; the work of the librettist is really incomplete. But it is the only evidence we have; it seems that the words were never set to music.

Milton makes provision for machines in the Trinity Manuscript drafts, so we must suppose that Dryden's use of them would seem natural. The war in heaven with which the opera opens takes place out of sight during the prolonged symphony of warlike music. The stage is almost wholly dark, and the scene 'represents a Chaos, or a confused Mass of Matter'. But the rebellious angels are seen to fall from the heavens which open, 'wheeling in the Air, and seeming transfix'd with thunderbolts', and they fall through the bottom of the stage. The victorious angels are 'discover'd . . . brandishing their swords'. Then the music ceases, and there is a shift of scene to the lake of brimstone, with the fallen angels appearing on the lake and the 'Tune of Horror and Lamentation'. This parallels lines 36–81 of the first book of *Paradise Lost*, though of course the events of the war in Heaven are shown again in Book 5 (ll. 654–912). Later in the scene Lucifer and Asmodeus and later the rest of the devils fly to land. In response to Lucifer's command

> A Golden Palace let be rais'd on high;
> To imitate? No, to out-shine the Skie!
> All Mines are ours, and Gold above the rest:
> Let this be done, and quick as 'twas exprest

a palace rises. Dryden does not describe it, as though the recollection of Milton's Pandemonium was enough. Between Acts I and II, as well as the song, Dryden provides for 'the Sports of the Devils; as Flights and Dancing in Grotesque Figures'. More detailed account is given of the arrival of Lucifer and of Uriel in Act II scene i.

The scene changes; and represents above, a Sun gloriously rising, and moving orbicularly: at a distance, below, is the Moon; the part next the Sun enlightened, the other dark. A black cloud comes whirling from the adverse part of the Heavens, bearing Lucifer in it; at his nearer approach, the body of the Sun is dark'ned.

This promises a spectacular effect but one which, through the reliable symbolism of light and darkness, makes its moral point. Lucifer announces: 'I see a Chariot driv'n, Flaming with beams, and in it Uriel'. Dryden's note is more detailed:

From that part of the Heavens, whence the Sun appears, a Chariot is discovered, drawn with white Horses; and in it Uriel, the Regent of the Sun. The Chariot moves swiftly, towards Lucifer; and at Uriel's approach, the Sun recovers his Light.

Later Lucifer flies downwards out of sight, and Uriel drives forward in his chariot. There are no supernatural characters in the next scene, only Adam and Eve, so no machines are envisaged, though Dryden describes the scene with its trees on either side with fruits on them, the fountain in the middle for Eve to look into and the prospect terminating in walks at the end. Machines are used in the next scene for the descent of Gabriel and Ithuriel, who, 'carried on bright Clouds; and flying cross each other, then light on the ground', and for Uriel, who flies down from the sun and departs by flying. But the most careful attention is given to description of the following scene, the 'Night-piece of a pleasant Bower' in which Lucifer substantiates Eve's dream:

> The weaker she, and made my easier prey;
> Vain Shows and Pomp the softer Sex betray.

This we are shown in a combination of dance and song, elucidating each other. It uses some material from the real temptation in *Paradise Lost* and operates as a kind of mock temptation in which moral considerations are translated into spectacle; the actual temptation comes later. With Adam and Eve asleep on the stage, a vision is presented where

a Tree rises loaden with Fruit; four Spirits rise with it, and draw a Canopy out of the Tree; other Spirits dance about the Tree in deform'd shapes; after the Dance an Angel enters with a Woman, habited like Eve.

The Angel encourages the false Eve to taste the fruit and, when she refuses, picks the fruit and gives it to the deformed spirits who instantly appear like angels:

> From Spirits deform'd they are Deities made,
> Their Pinions, at pleasure, the Clouds can invade.

She is convinced and eats:

> Ah! now I believe; such a pleasure I find
> As enlightens my Eyes, and enlivens my Mind.

This provides a text for the reaction of the audience. The transformed angels fly upwards, and then two descend to take the woman by the hand and fly upwards with her. 'The Angel who sung, and the Spirits who held the canopy, at the same instant sink down with the Tree.' Gabriel and Ithuriel, who then enter to Lucifer, do so, it seems, on foot. But the appearance of angels to Adam and Eve in the next scene (Act IV scene 1) is more elaborate:

The Cloud descends with six Angels in it; and when it's near the ground, breaks; and on each side, discovers six more: they descend out of the Cloud. Raphael and Gabriel discourse with Adam, the rest stand at distance.

Eve has already described a 'breaking cloud' full of winged warriors and has fled from the brightness of the light, which neatly removes her from the scene. Milton's Eve is of course distracted by domestic duties. Only Raphael and Gabriel depart by cloud; the others simply go off. There is only one more elaborate descent, but Dryden makes use of visual effects in the description of the middle part of the garden, with the four rivers and the two crucial trees of Life and Knowledge, and before the words of temptation from Lucifer Eve sees a serpent which 'makes directly to the Tree of Knowledge, on which winding himself, he plucks an Apple; then descends, and carries it away.' This enables Dryden to have his Lucifer in human form. Divine anger against Lucifer is signalled by claps of thunder. Instead of the many visions which Milton's Adam is shown in order to demonstrate the future effects of the fall, only one is possible here. 'The scene shifts, and discovers Death of several sorts: A Battle at Land, and a Naval Fight.' The immortality of the blest is also shown visually, though with provision for music: 'a Heaven descends, full of Angels and blessed Spirits, with soft Musick; a Song and Chorus.' At the final departure from Eden the angels are present only through description in the verse, and though Raphael's voice is heard last there is no triumphant chorus, only the metrical virtuosity of the concluding couplet, entirely faithful to the spirit of Dryden's original:

> But part you hence in peace, and having mourn'd your Sin,
> For outward Eden lost, find Paradise within.

Johnson observed that the personages of *The State of Innocence* are 'such as cannot decently be exhibited on the stage'. Milton's Trinity Manuscript drafts show the extent to which that action was earthbound, and Dryden's version of the story of the fall is necessarily the same. In fact the more the supernatural figures arrive by air, the more one is aware of this. So Adam's complaints seem to have more force ('Why am I not ty'd up from doing ill?'); judgement as well as explanation is delivered by Raphael; there is no explanation from God of Adam's position or of the human predicament as a whole. Inevitably the expansiveness and complexity of the epic is sacrificed; even more significantly, so is its moral significance. Milton must have anticipated this in deliberately choosing the epic not the play. However,

Dryden has deployed Milton's material with all the wit proper to a heroic poem, showing moreover a profound understanding of what Milton was about; the change of focus was forced on him by his choice of form. Marvell's poem had hinted—whether or not he knew what Dryden's opera was like—that in such taking over of the material plagiarism might be involved:

> So that no room is here for Writers left,
> But to detect their ignorance or Theft.

This is the kind of charge that Dryden deliberately meets in acknowledging his debt to Milton: 'this poem has receiv'd its entire Foundation, part of the Design, and many of the ornaments from him.' The idea or invention, which could issue as poem or play, is wholly Milton's—and to that extent *The State of Innocence* can be seen as Milton's opera. The design or disposition retains much that Milton had conceived but is necessarily changed, to turn poem into drama. Of the ornaments—the 'clothing in apt, significant and sounding words'[20]—much of Milton remains.

If we can only guess what Milton might have thought of *The State of Innocence*, we can perhaps discover what difference the writing of it made to Dryden's ideas about opera. The preface to *Albion and Albanius* (1685) contains his most fully developed views. His definition remains the same except that he has added dancing to the scenes and machines, and he specifies vocal and instrumental music to represent 'the poetical tale or fiction'. He still insists that to be an opera, the story must be sung. He may be following St Evremond (*Sur les opéra*, 1677) in acknowledging that opera 'admits of that sort of marvellous and surprising conduct, which is rejected in other plays' and in restricting his discussion of the supernatural to pagan figures. And he still sees opera as a heroic kind—as indeed St Evremond had done, in claiming Ariosto as a precedent. But Dryden feels some conflict between the decorum of the heroic play and the decorum of opera.

If the persons represented were to speak upon the stage . . . the expressions should be lofty, figurative and majestical; but the nature of an opera denies the frequent use of these poetical ornaments; for vocal music, though it often admits a loftiness of sound, yet always exacts an harmonious sweetness.

Though he claims the authority of the originators of opera, the Italians, whoever writes being obliged to follow their design, he is clearly now uneasy with a form that seems to demand want of thought and lowness of fancy. Particularly what he calls 'the songish part', as distinct from the recitative, aims 'to please hearing rather than to gratify the understanding. It appears, indeed, preposterous at first sight, that rhyme, on any consideration, should

---

[20] Preface to *Annus Mirabilis: Essays*, i. 14–15.

take place of reason'.[21] He is playing with a proverb here, rather than giving the game away, but there are still some grounds to believe that he had second thoughts about rhyme. He had abandoned it for the heroic play in *All for Love* (1678). In the poem to the Earl of Roscommon (1684) rhyme, even improved by Petrarch, is 'At best a pleasing Sound, and fair barbarity'. And there is Jonathan Richardson's anecdote, that Dryden amazed one Sir W. L. by speaking so loftily of *Paradise Lost*:

Why Mr. Dryden, says he . . . 'tis not in Rime. No. nor would I have done my Virgil in Rime if I was to begin it again . . . and yet Dryden had some Years before Rim'd Milton in his State of Innocence.[22]

[21] Preface to *Albion and Albanius*: ibid., i. 271.
[22] *Early Lives of Milton*, p. 296.

10

'Valentinian', *Rochester and Louis Grabu*

Peter Holman

In the summer of 1683 Charles II, ever on the look-out for novel entertainment, sent the actor Thomas Betterton to Paris to recruit an opera company. The Newdigate newsletter for 14 August 1683 reported that 'The Manager of ye Kings Theatre intend wthin short time to pforme an Opera in like manner of y^t of ffrance. Mr Betterton wth other Act^{rs} are gone ov^{er} to fetch ye designe'.[1] To judge from letters sent to the Duke of York from Richard Graham, Lord Preston, the English Envoy Extraordinary to the French court, Betterton's journey was something of a disappointment:

I should not have presumed to give your Highnesse the trouble of this, if something of Charity had not induced me to it. I do it at the instance of a poor servant of his Majestyes who sometimes since was obliged by a misfortune to leave England. It is Mr Grabue, S[i]r, whom perhaps y[ou]r highness may remember.

Mr Betterton coming hither some Weeks since by his Majestyes command to endeavour to carry over the opera, & finding that impracticable, did treat with Mons[ieu]r Grabue to go over with him to endeavour to represent something at least like an Opera in England for his Majestyes diversion. He hath also assured him of a pension from the House, & finds him very willing and ready to go over. He only desireth his Majestys protection when he is there, and what encouragement his majestye shall be pleased to give him if he finds th[a]t he deserves it. I take the confidence therefore on his behalfe humbly to beseech y[ou]r Highnesse to speake a good word for him to the King, whose protection he only desireth whilst he is in England, and I doubt not but he will performe something to his Majestyes, & your Highness's satisfaction.[2]

Louis Grabu, the French or possibly Spanish violinist, first came to England around 1665 and quickly rose to be Master of the King's Musick.[3] His misfortune was to be dismissed from his court post in 1674, to be owed a

[1] *The London Stage 1600–1800*, Part 1: *1660–1700*, ed. William van Lennep, Carbondale, 1965, p. 320. I should like to thank Basil Greenslade, Robert D. Hume, Keith Walker, Harold Love and Curtis Price for reading this paper and for offering expert advice.

[2] 22 September 1683: London, British Library, Add. Ms 63759, p. 91.

[3] The best biography of Grabu is in *A Biographical Dictionary of Actors, Actresses, Musicians, Dancers, Managers and other Stage Personnel in London, 1660–1800*, ed. Philip H. Highfill and others, Carbondale & Edwardsville, 1973–, vi. 290–94.

large amount in arrears of pay for several years—a total of £627. 9s. 6d. is mentioned in one document—and to be hounded out of England along with a number of his Catholic colleagues during the Popish Plot of 1679; a passport allowing him to return to France was issued on 31 March of that year.[4] Grabu's second career in England is, of course, remembered for his collaboration with Dryden in *Albion and Albanius*, the patriotic allegorical opera that was disastrously produced in the period of upheaval following the death of Charles II and the Monmouth revolt in the spring and early summer of 1685.[5] This was, presumably, the 'something at least like an Opera' referred to in Lord Preston's letter. Grabu's return to the English theatre began, however, not with *Albion and Albanius* but with an important play production whose music, remarkably, has mostly remained unrecognized.

Valentinian, Fletcher's bloodthirsty tragedy about a Roman emperor's rape of his general's wife, was not one of the more popular Jacobean plays during the Restoration period, at least not at first. Although it was one of the plays from the pre-Civil War repertory of the Blackfriars Theatre that was assigned to the King's Company at the beginning of 1669, no performance of it is recorded until almost the end of Charles's reign, when it achieved a measure of popularity in an adaptation by John Wilmot, Earl of Rochester.[6] Rochester's *Valentinian* is conventionally placed at the end of his career. Graham Greene, for instance, assumes that he worked on it in the spring and summer of 1679, only to lay it aside in the autumn of that year at the time of his celebrated conversion to religion.[7] Although it was never finished—his admirer Robert Wolseley wrote in the preface to his 1685 edition of the play that 'Lord Rochester intended to have alter'd and corrected this Play much more than it is, before it had come abroad'[8]—there is evidence that an early version existed more or less ready for performance as early as 1675 or 1676, though it is likely that Rochester continued to tinker with the play until his death in July 1680. A manuscript version entitled 'Lucina's Rape or the Tragedy of Valentinian' exists with a cast-list that coincides exactly with the known membership of the King's Company for the 1675–6 season. Rebecca Marshall, for instance, who is given in the manuscript as playing the heroine, Lucina, left the stage around March 1677.[9] We do not know whether the

---

[4] *Records of English Court Music*, ed. Andrew Ashbee, i: *1660–1685*, Snodland, 1986, p. 172; *Calendar of State Papers, Domestic, 1679–1680*, London, 1915, p. 338.

[5] For the background to *Albion and Albanius* see *The Works of John Dryden*, xv (ed. Earl Milner & George R. Guffey, Berkeley, 1976), 323–55, and Paul Hammond, 'Dryden's *Albion and Albanius*: the Apotheosis of Charles II', *The Court Masque*, ed. David Lindley, Manchester, 1984, pp. 169–83.

[6] *The London Stage: 1660–1700*, p. 152.

[7] Graham Greene, *Lord Rochester's Monkey*, London, 1974, p. 204.

[8] Quoted in Arthur Colby Sprague, *Beaumont and Fletcher on the Restoration Stage*, Cambridge, Mass., 1926, pp. 165–6.

[9] London, British Library, Add. MS 28692 (title-page reproduced in Greene, op. cit., p. 186). See *The London Stage: 1660–1700*, p. 238; also, on Rebecca Marshall, Highfill, *Biographical Dictionary*, x. 108.

King's Company performed *Lucina's Rape* at that time; the fact that no music survives for it in contemporary manuscripts and printed song books may indicate that, for some reason, its production never reached the stage.

The first recorded performance of Rochester's *Valentinian* was given in the Hall Theatre at Whitehall by the United Company on 11 February 1683/4, more than three years after its author's death.[10] It was evidently a success, since it seems to have been repeated there in 1686 and 1687, and a copy of Wolseley's edition now in Claremont College Library has two manuscript cast-lists that are compatible with the composition of the United Company for the seasons 1688–9 and 1691–2 respectively, though no record survives of performances then.[11] Historians have always presumed that the Whitehall performances of *Valentinian* were preceded by a run in the commercial theatre, since it was unusual at this time for an ordinary spoken play to be given its première at court. Productions at the Hall Theatre fell mostly into three groups: revivals of popular plays from the commercial repertory, visits of foreign companies (such as the French opera group that Betterton tried to arrange in the summer of 1683) and special productions of masques or masque-like plays given in the pre-war manner with lavish music and with courtiers in the cast—the outstanding example is Crowne's *Calisto*, given in the Hall Theatre in February 1675.[12] Although *Valentinian* is a play rather than a masque, as we shall see, it was produced with masque-like music using court musicians, which suggests that its production was planned from the outset for the Hall Theatre at Whitehall. Furthermore, to judge from Wolseley's 1685 text, it was organized by a group of literary courtiers as a tribute to its author; the prologue for the first performance, for instance, was written by one of Rochester's closest friends, the playwright Aphra Behn.[13] Certainly, its audience can hardly have failed to see in the figure of Valentinian, consumed by lust and surrounded by sycophants, an uncomfortable parallel with Charles and his court.[14]

It is strange that Grabu's music for *Valentinian* has almost escaped notice, since scholars could easily have been led to it through the invaluable bibliography *English Song Books 1651–1702* published in 1940 by Cyrus Day and Eleanore Boswell Murrie. Their index of literary sources reveals that the three songs from the 1685 text of the play, 'Injurious charmer of my vanquished heart', 'Kindness hath resistless charms' and 'Where would coy Aminta run', appear with musical settings in contemporary song books. The first appears anonymously in the fifth book of John Playford's *Choice Ayres*

---

[10] *The London Stage: 1660–1700*, pp. 325–6.

[11] Ibid., pp. 369, 375–6.

[12] See Eleanore Boswell, *The Restoration Court Stage*, Cambridge, Mass., 1932, pp. 177–227.

[13] For Behn's friendship with Rochester see Maureen Duffy, *The Passionate Shepherdess*, London, 1977, esp. pp. 189–98.

[14] See J. Harold Wilson, 'Satiric Elements in Rochester's *Valentinian*', *Philological Quarterly*, xvi (1937), 41–8.

and Songs, announced in the *London Gazette* for 10 April 1684, while the other two are found in Grabu's *Pastoralle*, advertised in the same newspaper just over two months later on 23 June 1684.[15]

Pastoralle—or to give it its full title, *Pastoralle / A Pastoral in French beginning with / an Overture & some Aires for Violins adorn'd / with several Retornels in Three Parts for / Violins & several Chorus's for Voices / in Four Parts & Five Parts for Violins, besides / other Aires & some English Songs; all lately / Compos'd by Lewis Grabue Gentleman / late Master of his* MAJESTIES MUSICK—survives apparently in only a single copy, now in the Pepys Library at Magdalene College, Cambridge. It contains, on folio 2, a dedication in French to Louise de Keroualle, Duchess of Portsmouth and Charles II's unpopular Breton mistress:

To Madam, the Duchess of Portsmouth,
Madam, the regard with which you have honoured me is so precious that I would be insensitive to my good fortune if I did not strive to keep a gift that is so dear to me. Your generosity and the help of the Muses have obtained it for me, and with their help I hope to retain it. If, in this offering, they [the Muses] have inspired something pleasing to you, then I would happily and humbly ask you to permit me, Madam, the honour of the style of your humble and obedient servant,

L. Grabu[16]

Clearly, Grabu was in the Duchess of Portsmouth's favour at the time, if not under her formal patronage. *Pastoralle* is unusual in that it has no indication of publisher or printer, although it is a finely engraved folio volume; presumably it was a private product intended for the duchess and her immediate circle, though how or why Pepys acquired the unique copy is not known. Grabu was certainly under Portsmouth's patronage to some extent early the next year, for Edward Bedingfield wrote to the Countess of Rutland on 1 January 1684/5 that:

Wee are in expectation of an opera composed by Mr Dryden, and set by Grabuche, and so well performed at the repetition that has been made before his Majesty at the Duchess of Portsmouth's, pleaseth mightily . . .[17]

As the leader of the French interest at court, the duchess was the obvious person to patronize the French-style *Albion and Albanius* and, perhaps, to sponsor a publication containing a French pastoral.

The wording of the title-page of *Pastoralle* suggests that it contains the music for more than one work, though it is not immediately clear where the 'Pastoral in French' ends and the 'other Aires & some English Songs' begin

---

[15] Michael Tilmouth, 'A Calendar of References to Music in Newspapers Published in London and the Provinces (1660–1719)', *R. M. A. Research Chronicle*, i (1961), 6; Day & Murrie give the first advertisement for *Pastoralle* wrongly as 17 July 1684.

[16] Translation mine (I have simplified Grabu's convoluted language a little). Robert Latham, formerly librarian of the Pepys Library, kindly allowed me to examine the print.

[17] *The London Stage: 1660–1700*, p. 334.

(see Table 10.1). Obviously, if the volume's contents are in any sort of order, then the 'Pastoral in French' begins on page 1 and ends at latest before the first of the *Valentinian* songs on page 41. But since all the movements up to page 36 are in G major, it looks as if Grabu's pastoral actually finishes at the end of the chorus on that page. Thus the ten movements beginning on page 37 with the 'Air pour les haubois' come into the category of 'other Aires & some English Songs'. We know that two of them, the English songs, are from *Valentinian*; there are good reasons for thinking that the other eight are also from Rochester's play, and that *Pastoralle* is not the miscellaneous collection that it appears to be.

By and large *Valentinian* is a fairly typical Restoration adaptation of a Jacobean play. Rochester made Fletcher's plot shorter, simpler, more logical and more focused on the three principal characters: Valentinian, the lustful tyrant, Lucina, the virtuous wife, and Maximus, the wronged husband. Vivian de Sola Pinto suggests that they represented to Rochester three aspects of his own complex character.[18] But to the musician the most interesting effect of these changes is that the new *Valentinian* uses music not only to adorn the play but also to carry forward the action at several points; music in Restoration drama is frequently lavish, but it is rarely as necessary to the plot as it is in the masque. The two songs from *Valentinian* that are found in *Pastoralle* both develop situations that already existed in Fletcher's version of the play. The pastoral dialogue between a nymph and a shepherd 'Injurious charmer of my vanquished heart' in Act IV scene ii is used by Valentinian's courtiers to prepare Lucina for her seduction as they lure her into the emperor's apartment:

> *Enter* Lycinius, Proculus, *and* Balbus. *Musick.*
>
> LYCIN. She's coming up the Stairs: now the Musick,
>   And as that softens—her love will grow warm,
>   Till she melts down. Then *Caesar* lays his Stamp.
>   Burn these Perfumes there.
> PROC. Peace, no noise without.

Evidently Grabu's music had no effect, for when Chylax asks Lucina 'How do you like the Song?' she replies, 'Sir, I am no Judge / Of Musick, and the words, I thank my Gods, / I did not understand'. Like much of the vocal music in *Albion and Albanius*, the dialogue is an attempt to apply the French type of recitative—an arioso-like melody with constantly shifting accents encompassed by frequent changes of metre—to the setting of English words.

The other *Valentinian* song in *Pastoralle*, 'Kindness hath resistless charms', comes at the beginning of the play's final scene; it is a replacement for Fletcher's famous 'Care-charming sleep', set so memorably by Robert

---

[18] *Enthusiast in Wit: a Portrait of John Wilmot Earl of Rochester 1647–1680*, London, 1962, pp. 159–60.

Ex. 10.1

Johnson.[19] In Rochester's version the song illustrates the emperor's seduction of his eunuch (it is a moment of repose before the violent denouement), while in Fletcher's original 'Care-charming sleep' (which comes earlier in the play) lulls Valentinian as he lies dying of poison. Grabu's setting of 'Kindness hath resistless charms' has charming music in the rhythm of a gavotte, though its word-setting is almost comically bad (Ex. 10.1). Grabu was certainly not an incompetent composer in the sense that he was unable to produce acceptable part-writing—as was, for instance, John Banister or Francis Forcer. His bad setting of English is more easily explained by his role as a representative of French culture in England; he doubtless felt it unnecessary and demeaning to study what he probably considered an inferior language. We know from the dedication of *Albion and Albanius* to Charles II that he looked down on English singers: he refers to 'the scarcity of Singers in this Island' as the only defect of his opera's 'full perfection'. It was presumably the combination of Grabu's personal arrogance and the absurdity of his settings of English words that infuriated English musicians from Pelham Humfrey ('he understands nothing, nor can play on any instrument, and so cannot compose') to Edward Dent ('indescribably dull'). Samuel Pepys, too, criticized Grabu's 'manner of setting of words and repeating them out of order', but he recognized with characteristic acumen 'the instrumental musick he had brought by practice to play very just'.[20] Grabu was an excellent exponent of the French orchestral style.

The most original musical episode in *Valentinian* straddles Act III scenes ii and iii. Lucina, sadly wandering in the 'Dear solitary Groves where Peace does dwell', calls for her absent husband's favourite song:

> Go *Marcellina*, fetch your Lute, and sing that Song
> My Lord calls his: I'l try to wear away
> The Melancholy Thoughts his Absence breeds!

---

[19] Robert Johnson, *Ayres, Songs and Dialogues*, ed. Ian Spink ('The English Lute-Songs', 2nd ser., xvii), London, 1961, pp. 34–6.
[20] *The Diary of Samuel Pepys*, ed. R. Latham & W. Matthews, viii (London, 1974), 530, 458; Edward J. Dent, *Foundations of English Opera*, Cambridge, 1928, p. 167.

> Come gentle Slumbers[,] in your flattering Arms
> I'l bury these Disquiets of my Mind
> Till *Maximus* returns—for when he's here
> My heart is rais'd above the reach of Fear.

The words of Marcellina's song 'Where would coy Aminta run' are apparently not by Rochester, since in the 1685 edition it is headed 'By Mr W'—presumably the Robert Wolseley who prepared the edition. Nor is the music by Grabu. It is not in *Pastoralle*, and although it appears anonymously in *Choice Ayres* it is attributed to Robert King in a single-sheet edition of the words in the Luttrell collection of broadsides, now at the William Andrews Clark Library in the University of California; the song has better word-setting than Grabu's English songs as well as a few characteristically English turns of harmony.[21] The single-sheet edition can be dated by its place in the Luttrell collection to between 10 and 21 March 1683/4, so the song was possibly added to the court production at the second performance. The 1685 text contains three prologues, the first 'spoken by Mrs Cook, the first Day, Written by Mrs Behn', the second 'spoken by Mrs Cook, the second Day' and the third 'intended for *Valentinian*, to be spoken by Mrs Barrey', which suggests that three performances were planned but only two were given.

After Marcellina's song, which sends Lucina to sleep, Rochester apparently planned some sort of dumb show to represent the content of her dreams. *Lucina's Rape* at this point has the stage direction 'Here begins the Masque which is to represent a frightfull dreame to Lucina', while the 1685 edition has the direction 'The Song ended, Exeunt Claudia and Marcellina before the Dance' followed by the heading 'SCENE 3. Dance of Satyrs'. A further complication is the existence in Nahum Tate's *Poems by Several Hands and on Several Occasions* (London, 1685) of a '*Mask* made at the request of the late Earl of *Rochester*, for the Tragedy of *Valentinian*'; it has been traditionally ascribed to Sir Francis Fane and is aptly described by Arthur Sprague as a 'tasteless and sometimes ludicrous performance'.[22] It may be that Rochester did ask Fane to write a masque of some sort for this scene, but it is unlikely that the result was what he intended or what was used in the court production, as most scholars have assumed, if only because the piece, with its irrelevant introduction of such characters as Zephyrus, the Moon, Mercury and Venus, has nothing to do with the account of the dream that Lucina describes to her maids a little later:

> In what Fantastique new world have I been?
> What Horrors past? what threatning Visions seen?
> Wrapt as I lay in my amazing Trance,

---

[21] Ken Robinson, 'A New Text of the First Song in Rochester's *Valentinian*', *Papers of the Bibliographical Society of America*, lxxv (1981), 311–12. Ian Spink, *English Song: Dowland to Purcell*, London, 1974, p. 191, assumes that the song is by Grabu.

[22] *Beaumont and Fletcher*, p. 174.

The Host of Heav'n and Hell did round me Dance:
Debates arose betwixt the Pow'rs above
And those below: Methoughts they talkt of Love
And nam'd me often; but it could not be
Of any Love that had to do with me.
For all the while they talk'd and argu'd thus,
I never heard one word of *Maximus* . . .
Mishapen Monsters round in Measures went
Horrid in Form with Gestures insolent;
Grinning throu' Goatish Beards with half clos'd Eyes,
They look'd me in the face . . .

From Lucina's description of her dream it appears that the masque or dumb show consisted of a number of dances designed to express, presumably in choreography rather than words, a 'debate' about Love between what she calls the 'Host of Heav'n and Hell' and 'the Pow'rs above / And those below'. The host of Hell was represented, at least in part, by 'Mishapen Monsters . . . Horrid in Form with Gestures insolent; / Grinning throu' Goatish Beards with half clos'd Eyes'; they are surely the *Comus*-like satyrs referred to in the 1685 text.

A look at the titles of the dances at the end of *Pastoralle* is enough to encourage the suspicion that together they make up the music for the masque that represented Lucina's dream. The 'Air pour Jupiter' and the connected 'Air pour les suiuans de Jupiter' could represent the host of Heaven, while the 'Air pour les songes affreux' and the 'Air pour les satires' suggest the opposing forces of Hell. Suspicion hardens into virtual certainty when the music is examined more closely. The four dances form part of a six-movement suite in G major laid out for five-part strings. It opens with a single-section prelude with tranquil rising and falling scales (Ex. 10.2)—a classic seventeenth-century way of illustrating sleep. This is followed by a stately duple-time dance in dotted rhythms for Jupiter and a livelier triple-time one for his followers. They correspond exactly to the first two movements of the contemporary suite of court branles and with good reason, for in England and France the king always opened the branles, to be followed by his courtiers.[23] The dances for the forces of Hell begin with one for 'frightening dreams' ('songes affreux') full of the rushing scales that were associated with demons in contemporary French operas (Ex. 10.3). (There is a similar though less effective example of the genre in Act II of *Albion and Albanius*.) It is followed by a splendid and suitably rustic loure for the satyrs. The suite ends with a courtly minuet that could have been used to accompany an ensemble dance at the end of the masque (perhaps to illustrate a resolution of the 'love debate'?); alternatively, it could have been used as a postlude to represent Lucina's awakening.

[23] See Matthew Locke, *The Rare Theatrical: New York Public Library Drexel MS 3976*, ed. Peter Holman ('Music in London Entertainment 1660–1800', Air), London, 1989, xvi–xvii.

Ex10.2

Ex. 10.3

The other masque-like episode in *Valentinian* comes in Act IV, scenes ii and iii, shortly after the dialogue 'Injurious charmer of my vanquished heart' described above. As part of his plan to seduce Lucina, Valentinian instructs the eunuch Lycinius to arrange a rehearsal of a masque in order to distract attention from his designs on the heroine. The setting, however, appears to be Whitehall rather than ancient Rome:

> EMP[EROR]. Where are the Masquers that should dance to night?
> LYCIN. In the old Hall, Sir, going now to practise.
> EMP. About it strait. 'Twill serve to draw away
>   Those listning Fools, who trace it in the Gallery;
>   And if by chance odd noises should be heard,
>   As Womens Shrieks, or so, say, 'tis a Play
>   Is practising within.
> LYCIN. The Rape of *Lucrece*,
>   Or some such merry Prank—It shall be done Sir.

The scene that follows is a comic vignette that has no parallel in Fletcher's play, though it is obviously indebted to the dancing lesson in *Le Bourgeois gentilhomme*:

[Scene] Opens and discovers 5 or 6 Dancing-masters practising.

1 DAN[CER]. That is the damn'st shuffling Step, Pox on't.

2 DAN. I shall never hit it.
Thou hast naturally
All the neat Motions of a merry Tailor,
Ten thousand Riggles with thy Toes inward,
Cut clear and strong: let thy Limbs play about thee;
Keep time, and hold thy Back upright and firm:
It may prefer thee to a waiting Woman.

1 DAN. Or to her Lady, which is worse.

Enter Lycinius.   *[Ten dance.*

LYCIN. Bless me, the loud Shrieks and horrid Outcries
Of the poor Lady! Ravishing d'ye call it?
She roars as if she were upon the Rack:
'Tis strange there should be such a difference
Betwixt half-ravishing, which most Women love,
And thor[o]ugh force, which takes away all Blame,
And should be therefore welcome to the vertuous.
These tumbling Rogues, I fear, have overheard 'em;
But their Ears with their Brains are in their Heels.
Good morrow Gentlemen:
What is all perfect? I have taken care
Your Habits shall be rich and glorious.

3 DAN. That will set off. Pray sit down and see,
How the last Entry I have made will please you.

Second Dance.

LYCIN. 'Tis very fine indeed.

2 DAN. I hope so Sir—
                               [Ex. Dancers.

It is hard to resist the conclusion that the pair of movements still unaccounted for in *Pastoralle*, the 'air pour les haubois' and the 'air pour les flutes', are the ones that were used in this remarkable scene of black humour.[24] The first, an unusual rondeau with a gavotte-like main theme contrasted with triple-time episodes, would be a perfect vehicle for the 'shuffling Step' of the dancing masters, while the second, an elegant saraband, would serve well as their second dance. Incidentally, the titles of these two dances were added by a contemporary hand—perhaps that of the composer—to the unique copy of *Pastoralle*.

If my analysis of *Valentinian* is correct, then Grabu's *Pastoralle* contains all the music needed for a performance of Rochester's text, with two exceptions. The first, Robert King's song 'Where would coy Aminta run',

---

[24] Lucyle Hook claims that Motteux's and Eccles's masque *The Rape of Europa by Jupiter* was used instead of this scene for a 1694 revival of *Valentinian*; see 'Motteux and the Classical Masque', *British Theatre and the other Arts 1660–1800*, ed. Shirley Strum Kenny, Washington, 1984, pp. 105–15, and her introduction to the Augustan Reprint Society's facsimile edition of Motteux's text (Los Angeles, 1981).

has been dealt with already, and the second, the 'Musick of Trumpets and Kettle-Drums' called for at the opening of the play, would almost certainly have been improvised on stage by royal trumpeters in the characters of members of Valentinian's retinue. There is no sign that a suite of incidental music (an overture with a suite of dances that were played before the play began and between the acts) was ever written for *Valentinian* by Grabu or anyone else; indeed, the trumpet fanfare specified by Rochester probably made such an overture unnecessary.[25]

Grabu's orchestral writing in *Valentinian* is best understood in the context of the French orchestral tradition. It is in five parts using a single violin part (the *dessus*, written in the French violin clef), three viola parts played by instruments of different sizes tuned in unison (the *haute-contre, taille* and *quinte*, written in the soprano, mezzo-soprano and alto clefs respectively) and a *basse de violon* part played by large bass violins tuned a tone lower than the modern cello. The double bass was not used in French orchestras until well into the eighteenth century, and there is no evidence that it was used in England at least until the 1690s. Orchestras in France also played frequently without continuo instruments, particularly in dance music. The printed scores of French stage works often have separate lines for *basse de violon* and *basse continue*; the former appears only when the upper strings play, while the latter stops for the dances—a feature that is also found in the scores of *Pastoralle* and *Albion and Albanius*.[26] The interest of French orchestral music was concentrated in the treble and bass, partly because the outer parts dominated the texture (the 24 *violons du roi* were theoretically laid out in the proportion 6/4/4/4/6, with oboes and bassoons reinforcing the violins and bass violins), and partly because the three inner parts or *parties de remplissage* were often composed by assistants (which enabled composers to write long stage works quite quickly) and were thus of lesser importance. If Grabu's dances for *Valentinian* sound bland compared to, say, Matthew Locke's incidental music for *The Tempest*, it is because Grabu worked in a tradition that valued elegant melody above other elements of the music. Locke's magnificently angular, dissonant and contrapuntal part-writing appeals to the modern ear, but Grabu and his French contemporaries would doubtless have thought it barbarous and old-fashioned, and in an

[25] The anonymous single treble part entitled 'Dance for Valentinian' that survives in London, Royal College of Music, MS 1172, f. 34ᵛ, has no connection with the music in *Pastoralle* and may have been used in one of the revivals of the play in the 1690s. See *Instrumental Music for London Theatres, 1690–1699: Royal College of Music, London, MS 1172*, ed. Curtis Price ('Music in London Entertainment 1660–1800', A iii), Withyham, 1987.

[26] For the French orchestral style see James Anthony, *French Baroque Music from Beaujoyeulx to Rameau*, London, 1973, pp. 8–10, 90–92; Caroline Wood, 'Orchestra and Spectacle in the *tragédie en musique* 1673–1715: Oracle, *sommeil* and *tempête, Proceedings of the Royal Musical Association*, cviii (1981–2), 25–46; Graham Sadler, 'The Role of the Keyboard Continuo in French Opera 1673–1776', *Early Music*, viii (1980), 148 ff.; Peter Holman, 'An Orchestral Suite by François Couperin?', *Early Music*, xiv (1986), 71–6.

unsuitable idiom for dance music. On the other hand, Grabu's music is certainly not 'indescribably dull', as Dent maintained; it is just different from the theatre music of his English contemporaries.

Although Grabu wrote his music for *Valentinian* in the French orchestral style, there is little doubt that it was played in 1684 by all or part of the English court orchestra, the 24 Violins. The band was not, as is often said, founded in 1660. It was a revival of the pre-Civil War court violin band, but it was reorganized at the Restoration along the lines of the 24 *violons du roi*.[27] It is therefore surprising that more of its surviving repertory is not laid out, like the *Valentinian* dances, in the French five-part orchestral pattern. English composers apparently preferred to write in four parts, with one violin and two viola parts or, after about 1680, with the more modern layout of two violins and one viola part. The only other surviving five-part orchestral music from this period is in *Albion and Albanius*, in Locke's 1666 anthem 'Be Thou exalted Lord' and in some odes of the 1680s by G. B. Draghi and Purcell, though more examples may be hidden in dance suites by court composers such as John Banister and Nicholas Staggins that only survive in two-, three- or four-part manuscripts.[28] It seems that the 24 Violins rarely played as a single ensemble: they were regularly divided into two groups of twelve to serve in the two London commercial theatres, and even in a lavish court production such as the 1676 *Calisto* an augmented 24 Violins was divided into two groups, one placed in front of the stage, the other apparently seated in an elevated position at the back of the scenery.[29] We do not know whether the orchestra for *Valentinian* was organized in the same way, but the handwritten indications 'air pour les haubois' and 'air pour les flutes' (i.e. recorders) for two of its dances suggest that James Paisible and some or all of his French oboe and recorder playing colleagues who appear in the *Calisto* documents also played in *Valentinian*, probably doubling all or some of the violin part. In 1684 they were still probably the only oboe players in England.[30]

Why did Grabu publish *Pastoralle* without any indication that it contained his music for *Valentinian*? After all, Rochester was an admired poet at the time, and his play had been given a prestigious and apparently successful court production. Furthermore, Grabu's music assumes an importance in

---

[27] See Peter Holman, 'The English Royal Violin Consort in the Sixteenth Century', *Proceedings of the Royal Musical Association*, cix (1982–3), 58–9; id., '*Four and Twenty Fiddlers': The Violin at the English Court 1540–1690*, Oxford, forthcoming.

[28] See, for example, Oxford, Christ Church, MS Mus. 1183, and New York Public Library, MS Drexel 3849; a more extended discussion of this point appears in my introduction to *The Rare Theatrical*.

[29] The surviving documents relating to *Calisto* are printed and discussed in Boswell, *The Restoration Court Stage*; my interpretation of their musical aspects will appear in '*Four and Twenty Fiddlers*'.

[30] David Lasocki, 'Professional Recorder Playing in England 1500–1740', *Early Music*, x (1982), 183–4.

TABLE 10.1. *The Contents of* Pastoralle

Page	Title	Key	Scoring
1–2	Pastoralle/ouuerture	G	strings *a5*, *basse continue*
3	Air des amours	G	strings *a5*
4	Menuet	G	strings *a5*
5–6	Ritournelle [and recitative] 'Si tu scauois Jeune bergere'	G	bass, 2 violins (?), *basse continue*
7–10	[Chorus] 'Vive lamour et ses plaisirs'	G	SATB, strings *a5*, *basse continue*
11–12	Ritournelle [and air] 'Ne pretens pas que Je mengage'	G	soprano, 2 violins (?), continuo
12–22	[Dialogue] 'Iris dont les divins attrais'	G	soprano, bass, 2 violins (?), *basse continue*
23–27	Choeur 'Aymons bergere'	G	SATB, strings *a5*, continuo
27	Ritournelle	G	2 violins(?), *basse continue*
28	Bouree	G	strings *a5*
29	Menuet	G	strings *a5*
30–36	[Duet and chorus] 'Aymons berger'	G	soprano, bass, SATB, strings *a5*, continuo
37–39	Air pour les haubois	C	oboes, strings *a5*
39–40	Air pour les flutes	c	recorders, strings *a5*
41	[Song] 'Kindness hath resistless charms'	G	soprano, *basse continue*
42–45	Dialogue 'Injurious charmes [*sic*] of my Vanquisht heart'	g	soprano, bass, *bass continue* (with an instrumental passage *a2*)
46–47	Prelude	G	strings *a5*
47–48	Air pour Jupiter	G	strings *a5*
48–49	Air pour les suivans de Jupiter	G	strings *a5*
49–51	Air pour les songes affreux	G	strings *a5*
51–52	Air pour les satires	G	strings *a5*
52	Menuet	G	strings *a5*

the work that is unusual in a spoken play at the time. It is possible that the composer was concerned not to offend the Duchess of Portsmouth, the dedicatee of *Pastoralle*. Rochester attacked her several times in his satirical writings during his last years, and a number of other satires circulated at the time under Rochester's name, though they are now thought to be spurious. One of these, the famous 'Rochester's Farewell', summed up the relationship between Charles and his Breton mistress in the words: 'But what must we expect, who daily see / Unthinking *Charles*, Rul'd by Unthinking thee?'.[31]

[31] De Sola Pinto, *Enthusiast in Wit*, p. 214.

No wonder Grabu preferred not to tell the duchess exactly what was in his *Pastoralle*.

Finally, a small addition can be made to the known facts of Grabu's life. Hitherto the latest reference to him has been an advertisement for a public concert on 15 November 1694, after which he disappears from the records of England's musical life.[32] We now know why, for on 4 December 1694 a passport was issued to 'Mr Lewis Grabu, a master of music, with his wife and two children, to go to Harwich or Gravesend for Holland or Flanders'.[33]

[32] Tilmouth, 'Calendar', p. 15.
[33] *Calendar of State Papers, Domestic, 1694–1695*, London, 1906, p. 349.

III
English Music and English Poetry

Robert Henryson's Harp of Eloquence

John Caldwell

THE myth of Orpheus occupies the attention of the musical historian on three counts: first, it is the subject-matter of some of the earliest operas and of several later ones; second, it was a potent image in medieval and Renaissance musical thought; and finally, it offers a profound insight into the concept of music in the ancient world itself. It is the second of these aspects that concerns us here, but it should be emphasized how closely connected are all three. Not to dwell on the obvious link between Classical and Renaissance thought, it is the centrality of the myth in the latter that made its use in opera inevitable. An opera is in many ways an enactment of the philosophical tenet that the soul is a kind of harmony. The Orpheus myth is particularly susceptible to such an interpretation, and to illustration from the parallel notions of *musica mundana* (the music of the spheres) and *musica instrumentalis* (the music that we sing or play). It is not only in opera but also in poetry and philosophy that the interplay between all three might be exemplified by this legend.

The Renaissance view of the Orpheus myth was of course refined by its rediscovery of ancient Greek literature; but this did not lessen its fundamental reliance on the Classical Latin sources that had ensured the unbroken knowledge of the legend in Western late antiquity and in the Middle Ages. In Latin the primary sources for the story are the accounts by Virgil (*Georgics*, iv. 453 ff.), by Ovid (*Metamorphoses*, x, and xi. 1–99) and—in a brief but extraordinarily concentrated poem—by Boethius in *The Consolation of Philosophy*, III, Metrum xii 'Felix qui potuit'. Of these, Ovid's version was the most widely drawn upon in later literature, partly because of the popularity of the *Metamorphoses* as a whole, and partly because its treatment is by and large the most developed. It was only rarely, however, that a single source was used by medieval and Renaissance writers: as usually with myths, each relation was based upon an ever-expanding tradition, the result of literary exploration and of personal inventiveness alike.

Widespread though the use of the Orpheus legend is in European literature, it is somewhat surprising to find it as the subject of a major poem by a fifteenth-century Scottish writer. But Robert Henryson is himself a surprising phenomenon, a technically accomplished and subtly ironic poet working within a tradition of schoolmasterly learning that was firmly anchored in the Middle Ages. It is this conflict between the old and the new that makes Henryson so fascinating a poet; and in his *Orpheus and Eurydice* we can observe it more sharply, perhaps, than elsewhere in his output.[1]

The pedantic streak is revealed, in each of Henryson's major extant poems, by his candid admission of reliance on a primary source: 'Aesop' (in the Latin verse translation of Gualterius Anglicus) for the *Fables*, Chaucer for *The Testament of Cresseid*, and Boethius, with the commentary by Nicholas Trivet, for *Orpheus and Eurydice*.[2] Each of them moreover is validated by the device of the *moralitas*, though in the *Testament* this is limited to the final stanza and is not so headed. But there is in any case a strong vein of moral purpose running through all three. The question is to what extent this is compatible with a deeper poetic meaning.

We need not attempt to answer this question in relation to the *Fables* or the *Testament*, though it is tempting to assert an inverse ratio between poetry and morality. But in *Orpheus* the question poses itself in an extreme form, since the *moralitas* is so strongly marked off, by versification and level of discourse, from the fable proper. How important is it to the appreciation of the poem as a whole, and could it even be omitted without serious loss?

It is in the section headed 'Moralitas fabule sequitur' that Henryson reveals his source as Boethius's *Consolation* and Nicholas Trivet's commentary upon it. Up to that point we should hardly have guessed as much, so circumstantially is the tale told. On inspection it does indeed transpire that some of the details not in Boethius (such as the pursuit of Eurydice by Aristeus) could have been derived from Trivet; but there is much else that can be found only in other sources of the fable, and much (of whatever provenance) that is not normally associated with it at all. But the *moralitas* itself is firmly based on Trivet. (The notion of a 'moral', of course, is not Trivet's: the term as used here and in the *Fables* embraces an allegorical explanation of the myth as well as the derivation from it of standards of behaviour.)

Henryson's poem, which has received extensive exegesis,[3] is curiously mixed in tone. Side by side with the unaffected poetry of the tragic narrative

---

[1] *The Poems of Robert Henryson*, ed. Denton L. Fox, Oxford, 1981 (henceforth *Poems*). This edition, with its copious notes, supersedes all previous ones; a reprint of the text with shorter notes was published in 1987.

[2] For this literary device see Chaucer himself in *The Parlement of Foules*, where the source is Cicero's *Somnium Scipionis* and in which for that reason the music of the spheres is discussed, ll. 57–63. Trivet's commentary is given in *Poems*, pp. 384–91; it is much indebted to that of William of Conches: see Charles Jourdain, 'Des commentaires inédites de Guillaume de Conches et de Nicolas Triveth sur La Consolation de philosophie de Boèce', *Notices et extraits*, xx/2 (1862), 40–82.

[3] See esp. *Poems*, pp. cv–cx, 391–425. I owe much to Fox's notes, as will be evident from the following pages.

lie extensive passages of academic and musical learning. The effect of the latter is quickly torpedoed by an ingenuous disclaimer (ll. 240–42):

> Off sik musik to wryte I do bot dote,
> Thar-for at this mater a stra I lay,
> For in my lyf I coud newir syng a note.

Is the sheer pointlessness of the excuse intentional? Henryson has just been enumerating the simple ratios from which the musical consonances are derived. Boethius, in the *De institutione musica*, and the large number of medieval writers who followed him are at pains to emphasize the distinction between the *musicus*, the expert in just such matters, and the man whose skill is purely practical. Is it, perhaps, a survival of the comic Chaucerian notion of Boethius as a singer?

> But trewely, the cause of my cominge
> Was only for to herkne how that ye singe.
> For trewely ye have as mery a stevene
> As eny aungel hath, that is in hevene;
> Therwith ye han in musik more felinge
> Than hadde Boece, or any that can singe.[4]

It is difficult to know whether Chaucer himself in this passage is knowingly and humorously offering a distorted perception of Boethius; but in any case, and whatever the probability of a Chaucerian echo in Henryson just here, it is certain that Henryson's poem as a whole is deeply ironical. This is partly a question of 'structural' irony: for example Eurydice, who in the legend is a good wife to Orpheus, becomes in Trivet and Henryson a symbol for earthly passion, and Aristeus, the lustful shepherd who indirectly causes her death, becomes 'gude vertewe, / Quhilk besy is ay to kepe oure myndis clene'. In addition, the whole poem is permeated by innumerable minor ironies that leaven its 'seriositee' with bathos and litotes.

In Henryson's poem Orpheus, after the death of Eurydice, goes on a journey through the heavens to look for her; and as he descends to earth by way of the planets

> He herd a hevynly melody and sound,
> Passing all instrumentis musicall,
> Causid be rollyng of the speris round

—in other words *musica mundana* (ll. 220–22). It seems to have been Henryson himself who lit on this pleasant conceit, thus bringing to bear on the legend the missing term in the series *musica mundana, musica humana* (as exemplified in the person of Orpheus) and *musica instrumentalis*, the music actually sung and played by him.

This is followed by four stanzas in which the six 'tonys proportionate' are

---

[4] *The Canterbury Tales*, B, ll. 4479–84 ('The Nonne Preestes Tale').

listed together with the 'five hevynly symphonyis' derived from them.[5] The scribes here have played havoc with the terminology to such an extent that it is impossible to know how much of its quaintness (in its Scots dress) is due to Henryson himself. But the meaning is clear enough; and, the virtuoso display of learning over, the poet can confirm (ll. 237–9):

> This mery musik and mellifluate,
> Complete and full wyth nowmeris od and evyn,
> Is causit be the moving of the hevyn.

The ironic disclaimer noted above immediately follows.

The celestial journey having been unsuccessful, Orpheus undertakes his voyage to Hades, vanquishing by his music the power of Cerberus and of the Furies and relieving in turn the punishments of Ixion, Tantalus and Ticius. The vivid description of Hell (there is a particularly venomous attack on prelates and religious) is another individual digression. Then after moving his audience to tears Orpheus regains Eurydice only to lose her in accordance with the familiar legend.

The description of Orpheus playing to Pluto and Proserpina is particularly interesting (ll. 366–70):[6]

> Than Orpheus before Pluto sat doun,
> And in his handis quhite his harp can ta,
> And playit mony suete proporcion,
> With base tonys in ypodorica,
> With gemilling in ypolerica.

Commentators have grasped the broad significance of 'ypodorica' and 'gemilling', but it is possible to refine one's appreciation of the exact image intended. 'Gemilling' does, in a general way, imply music in two parts; but in the late fifteenth century gimel meant more specifically the division of a voice part (usually the treble or mean) into two lines in the context of elaborate choral polyphony. Both treble and mean are high voice parts, and the combination of a gimel in one or both of these with a single low (bass) part was not uncommon in music of the period. It is clear that the significance of 'ypodorica' is that the hypodorian is the lowest of the *toni* according to one standard enumeration; and it would seem likely that 'ypolerica' is intended to refer to the highest.

But 'ypolerica' as it stands is nonsense. It is agreed that the so-called 'locrian' or 'hypolocrian' modes are not in question here. In the system of fifteen in which the hypodorian is the lowest, the highest *tonus* is the hyperlydian. Fox thinks this unlikely to have been the intended meaning,

---

[5] The 'proportions' are 2:1, 3:1, 4:3, 3:2, 4:1 and 9:8; the 'symphonies' or consonances are (in the order given in the poem) the fourth, the octave, the fifteenth, the fifth and the twelfth. The interval of a tone, 9:8, was not regarded as a consonance. See *Poems*, pp. 400–402, where the confusions are satisfactorily unravelled.

[6] See *Poems*, pp. 410–12 (but some of the references there given are now outdated).

pointing out that 'it would be impossible to "gemil" in two unrelated modes'. But the 'gemilling' only applies to the high notes, and we are not in any event to look for a technical description of tonal (or modal) procedures. We simply require a word to signify the high-pitched gemilling as opposed to the deep tones that underpin it. 'Yperlydica' would fit the bill exactly, and it is not too difficult to imagine scribes who were capable of such things as 'emetricus' for 'epitritus' (or for that matter Pluto for Plato) writing 'ypolerica' for 'yperlydica', if indeed that is a fair shot at Henryson's own preferred orthography.

Lines 366–70 thus offer a precise musical image, that of the choral polyphony familiar to the educated city-dweller of the period. That the terminology of the *toni* is used non-technically is no obstacle, any more than it is that Orpheus is playing the music on his harp. His skill was doubtless such as to suggest a range of musical expression far beyond that of which an ordinary mortal or his instrument would have been capable.

This rather sophisticated image widens considerably the range of reference of the poem. It also contrasts strongly—humorously, one might say—with the down-to-earth character of lines such as 'Than Orpheus playit a ioly spryng' or 'Tuke out his harp and fast on it can clink'.[7] Such contrasts are part and parcel of the tissue of irony threaded through the whole poem, though we could also explain the more elevated tone of the ecclesiastical metaphor as being especially appropriate (again ironically) to Pluto's court, and perhaps too as a reference back to the animadversions on popes, cardinals and archbishops heard a few stanzas earlier.

The idea of Orpheus as a personification of *musica humana* or the music of the human soul is not expressly mentioned in Classical sources. It should also be remembered that Plato had argued strongly against the Pythagorean notion that the soul is a harmony because (if one were to accept his not very well defended premises) this would be to deny its immortality.[8] It was moreover comprehensively rejected by Aristotle,[9] but it held sway in the Middle Ages if only because of the currency given to it by Boethius.[10] It cannot be proved that Boethius had it in mind when writing 'Felix qui potuit', but its context in Book III of the *Consolation* renders it probable. Earlier, in the crucial *Metrum* ix, he had recalled the Platonic philosophy of the soul of the universe: 'You, binding soul together in its threefold nature's midst, Soul that moves all things, then divide it into harmonious parts'; and he had gone on to describe the lesser souls of men in terms that suggest a close analogy.[11]

---

[7] ll. 268, 287. [8] *Phaedo*, 91 ff. [9] *De anima*, 407^b–408^a.

[10] *De institutione musica*, I. ii (ed. G. Friedlein, Leipzig, 1867 (Teubner edn.), p. 188).

[11] *Consolation of Philosophy*, ed. & trans. S. J. Tester (Loeb Classical Library), London, 1973, p. 273. Cf. *Timaeus*, 88 B, and Henryson's 'Quhilk armony . . . of this warld, Plato the saul can call' (ll. 223–5)—the sense here, however, is somewhat obscure.

Trivet in his commentary on 'Felix qui potuit' (following William of Conches) calls Orpheus the 'intellectual part [of man] informed by wisdom and eloquence' and Eurydice 'the affective part of man which he desires to join with himself'. In Henryson:

> Faire Phebus is the god of sapience;
> Caliopee, his wyf, is eloquence;
> Thir twa maryit gat Orpheus belyve,
> Quhilk callit is the part intellectiue
> Of mannis saule and vnder-standing, free
> And separate fra sensualitee.
> Euridices is oure affection
> Be fantasy oft movit vp and doun;
> Quhile to reson it castis the delyte,
> Quhile to the flesch settis the appetite.
> Arestyus, this hird that coud persewe
> Euridices, is noucht bot gude vertewe . . .[12]

It would be reasonable to think of Orpheus and Eurydice, seen thus, as a kind of discord, to be resolved only when the affective part had been discarded. But this would be incompatible with Boethius's own moral, whereby to glance back to Hell is to *lose* 'whatever excellence he takes with him' (i.e. Eurydice). Trivet resolves this dilemma by transforming the object of Orpheus's desire into a 'companion of the mind informed by wisdom',[13] and by interpreting the backward glance as a yielding to earthly things.[14]

Whatever we may think of this allegory and the inconsistencies it imposes, there can be no mistaking Henryson's equation of the 'reasonable' part of man's nature with the music of Orpheus. More specifically, his skill upon the harp is an allegory of man's wisdom or 'sapience' in the form of 'eloquence' (ll. 469–74):

> Bot quhen our mynd is myngyt with sapience,
> And plais apon the harp of eloquence;
> That is to say, makis persuasioun
> To draw oure will and oure affection,
> In ewery elde, fra syn and foule delyte,
> This dog [Cerberus] oure saule has no power to byte.

---

[12] ll. 425–36; cf. Trivet, ll. 36 ff.; 'Per Orpheum intelligitur pars intellectiua instructa sapientia et elloquentia. Vnde dicitur filius Phebi et Caliope . . . Iste autem Orpheus per suauitatem cythare, id est elloquentie, homines brutales et siluestres reduxit ad normam rationis . . . Cuius uxor dicitur Euridices scilicet pars hominis affectiua, quam sibi copulare cupit Aristeus qui interpretatur uirtus'.

[13] Trivet, l. 261: '*Donemus uiro comitem*, id est non detineamus eius affectum sed permittamus comitem intellectum sapientia informatum'; Henryson, ll. 616–17: 'Than Orpheus has won Euridices / Quhen oure desire wyth reson makis pes'. Boethius's own line (italicized) echoes Genesis 2: 18: 'faciamus ei adiutorium'.

[14] Trivet, l. 292: '*Quicquid precipuum trahit*, id est quicquid boni laborando acquisiuit per sapientiam et elloquentiam, *perdit dum uidet* inferos, id est dum intentus est istis terrenis et temporalibus que sunt infima'.

The words recur like a refrain:

> Bot quhen reson and perfyte sapience
> Playis apon the harp of eloquence . . .[15]

> Bot quhen that reson and intelligence
> Playis apon the harp of eloquence . . .[16]

And also:

> Quhen Orpheus vpoun his harp can play
> That is, our vndirstanding, for to say . . .[17]

> Than Orpheus, our ressoun, is full wo
> And twichis on his harp and biddis ho
> Till our desyre and fulich appetyte,
> Bidis leif this warldis full delyte.[18]

The concept of the 'harp of eloquence' is derived from Trivet's earlier phrase 'per suauitatem cythare, id est elloquentie'; and it effectively gets rid of the difficulty that the soul as harmony is dependent on the 'instrument' of the body and therefore could not survive it after death (which was Plato's argument). Rather, the rational soul itself is an instrument with its own inbuilt harmony, and its music issues forth as 'eloquence'. Each of the three musics thus has its sonorous counterpart: that of the spheres cannot be heard because it is continuous and ubiquitous, and that of 'instruments' is what we normally describe as music; but *musica humana*, far from being buttoned up in the mind, manifests itself in rational, and more specifically 'rhetorical', discourse.

Henryson's poem is thus a subtle disquisition on the three levels of musical utterance, and it is *musica humana* to which pride of place is given. The *moralitas*, far from being a tiresome appendage, contains the essential point of the poem—and not just because it is the kind of moral allegory that so many medieval authors felt was needed to justify their flights of fancy.[19] The *musica mundana* and the *musica instrumentalis* in the main part of the poem are, by comparison, cursorily treated. The function of the *moralitas* is to validate what might otherwise seem like superficial glosses on the legend.

Henryson's *Orpheus and Eurydice* has been linked, not unnaturally, with two other famous medieval poems: the English fourteenth-century *Sir Orfeo* and Politian's *Favola d'Orfeo*. The former was certainly known in Scotland, but its general tone could hardly be more different: it is a joyous celebration of practical music in all its guises, and it has no deeper philosophical content.

[15] ll. 507–8, of Ixion; Trivet, ll. 207–8: 'Vnde dicit *uelox rota non precipitat caput Yssionis*, scilicit Orpheo canente'.   [16] ll. 545–6, of Tantalus.
[17] ll. 577–8, of Ticius; Trivet, ll. 237–8: 'Vnde dicit *uultur dum satur est modis*, id est modulationibus'.   [18] ll. 610–13.
[19] The most blatant example of this is perhaps the Archpriest of Hita's *Libro de buen amor* (fourteenth century).

Politian's celebrated piece is closely contemporary with Henryson's, but the idea that Henryson could have been influenced by Politian seems absurd. Politian's dramatic fable is truly humanistic, leaving the audience to draw its own conclusions from the tale. It has long been recognized as a precursor of opera, looking forward towards the day when the story of the musician *par excellence* could be told entirely in music.[20]

Henryson on the other hand is scarcely a humanist at all, or if so a half-hearted one at most. His reading was wide and could have made him a humanist had the temper of the time and place been such as to permit it. The musical knowledge he displays would have come from his university arts course: Boethius's *De musica* and Macrobius's commentary on Cicero's *Somnium Scipionis*, from either of which his description of musical proportions could have been drawn, would have been familiar textbooks. The fifteen-mode system in which hypodorian is the lowest and hyperlydian the highest is described in Cassiodorus's *Institutiones*: Henryson could have found it there or in a number of intermediary sources. His knowledge of musical practice was, by his own admission, at second hand. But more impressive than his musical learning is the imagination that enabled him to gloss the legend so effectively and to tell it so circumstantially. It may be possible to pin down particular passages to rather down-to-earth sources (such as the description of the Muses to Eberhard of Béthune's *Graecismus*), but the selection and arrangement of the materials, and above all the playfulness with which the underlying seriousness is kept at bay, are Henryson's own.

Medieval poems are apt to attract scholarly attention for reasons that have to do with anything but poetry. But it is perhaps unrealistic to expect the literature of a distant period to strike the modern reader with the effect originally intended. Who, in any case, were the 'worthy folk' to whom this poem is addressed? Was it read aloud to an audience in the first instance, as the tone so often suggests, or was it intended for silent perusal? Such uncertainties make an absolute critical evaluation unattainable. This is usually thought to be the least successful of Henryson's major poems; but it is one that cannot be read casually, and properly understood it is consistently interesting, diverting and elevating. If it all has to be taken with a pinch of salt, so be it. If Henryson is not a humanist he is perhaps a humorist, but in the oldest and best sense of the word. He is there to be enjoyed, and we shall enjoy him best by first trying to understand him and then reading him with a mind open to every nuance that we have been able to discover.

[20] See R. Rolland, 'L'Opéra avant l'Opéra' in his *Musiciens d'autrefois*, Paris, 1908; N. Pirrotta, *Li due Orfei: da Poliziano a Monteverdi*, Turin, 1969 (2nd edn. 1975; trans. Karen Eales as *Music and Theatre from Poliziano to Monteverdi*, Cambridge, 1982); and F. W. Sternfeld, 'The Birth of Opera: Ovid, Poliziano, and the *lieto fine*', *Analecta musicologica*, xix (1980), 30–51. I should like to record here the pleasure given me by the many conversations I have had with Dr Sternfeld on the subject of the Orpheus myth.

12

Sir Philip Sidney and 'Versified Music': Melodies for Courtly Songs

John Stevens

IN one of the many memorable passages of his *Apology for Poetry* Sidney writes:

Now therin of all sciences (I speak still of human, and according to the human conceits) is our poet the monarch. For he doth not only show the way, but giveth so sweet a prospect into the way, as will entice any man to enter into it . . . he cometh to you with words set in delightful proportion, either accompanied with, or prepared for, the well enchanting skill of music.[1]

Sidney does not spell out precisely what he means in each case, but he clearly raises three practical issues of words and music: (i) the words of a good poem are 'set in delightful proportion', that is, they have in themselves certain 'musical' qualities; (ii) they can be 'accompanied with' music, the exact kind or kinds not being specified; (iii) they can be 'prepared for' music, again in ways that are left unclear, at least in this passage. Sidney cared and had thought a great deal about music in its relations to poetry. This makes it all the more surprising that there is not to my knowledge any up-to-date, published study of the topic.[2]

'WORDS SET IN DELIGHTFUL PROPORTION'
It used to be assumed until fairly recently, and still is in some quarters, that the primary bond between music and poetry in Elizabethan times was an emotional one and that certain deficiencies felt to exist in verse were

---

[1] *An Apology for Poetry*, ed. G. Shepherd, London, 1965 (repr. Manchester, 1973), p. 113.
[2] Until recently the only studies were by B. Pattison: 'Sir Philip Sidney and Music', *Music & Letters*, xv (1934), 75–81; and *Music and Poetry in the English Renaissance*, London, 1948, Ch. IV & *passim*. In 1970 F. J. Fabry brought to light new material: 'Sidney's Verse Adaptations to two 16th-Century Italian Songs', *Renaissance Quarterly*, xxiii (1970), 237–55. Winifred Maynard, *Elizabethan Lyric Poetry and its Music*, Oxford, 1986, pp. 77–89; Edward Doughtie, *English Renaissance Song*, Boston, 1986, pp. 81–6; and Louise Schleiner, *The Living Lyre in English Verse from Elizabeth through the Restoration*, Columbia, Mo., 1984, esp. pp. 11–45.

somehow to be supplied by musical setting.[3] This conception is now frequently challenged. The starting-point of all serious Elizabethan verse-making is well stated by George Puttenham in *The Arte of Englishe Poesie*: 'Poesie is a skille to speake and write harmonically and verses or rime be a kind of Musicall utterance'; or, again, 'our maker by his measures and concordes of sundry proportions doth counterfait the harmonicall tunes of the vocall and instrumentall Musickes'.[4] The point is not that poetry needs music but that it is music. It is complete in itself. It can be complemented; but it does not need completion.

This is not an Elizabethan but a thoroughly traditional, medieval idea. References to *musica* in medieval theory are often misunderstood as referring to music as we understand it, whereas the whole art of making rhythmic constructions in sound, whether with words, voices or instruments, is meant. There is very little discussion of the relationship between words and music as a special dimension in medieval writings because they are in theory at least essentially the same thing. The common three-fold distinction within the 'music', *musica*, that we actually hear (I leave the Boethian metaphysical and philosophical meanings out of account) is between: *musica harmonica*, the music of pitched sounds; *musica metrica*, music or poetry with precisely measured longs and shorts; and *musica rhythmica*, music or poetry with numbered units and, later, rhyme (i.e. syllabic verse and song).[5] Sidney and others (Gabriel Harvey, Spenser, Stanyhurst, Campion) do not seem to have been aware of these medieval categories which were dominant from at least the sixth to the fourteenth centuries. But the main problem they faced could easily have been formulated in these terms.

Their problem was to devise a suitable 'music' for English, to make 'our Mother tongue', as E. K. put it, 'stately enough for verse'.[6] In doing so they naturally turned to classical models. Thanks to Derek Attridge's judicious survey of Elizabethan quantitative verse, *Well-weighed Syllables* (1974), it is no longer necessary to apologize for what used to seem a pedantic aberration of a few rather donnish Elizabethans. The practical results gave little satisfaction, but the endeavour was a highly serious one: to raise English to the level of art. In the following hexameters from the anonymous *Preservation of King Henry VII* the ambitious metrical sentiments are more deserving of attention than is their creaking realization:

[3] 'The words seem to beg to be set to music', J. G. Nichols, *The Poetry of Sir Philip Sidney*, Liverpool, 1974, p. 1.
[4] *The Arte of English Poesie*, ed. G. D. Willcock & A. Walker, Cambridge, 1936, pp. 64, 84.
[5] See further J. Stevens, *Words and Music in the Middle Ages*, Cambridge, 1986, pp. 416–23: 'Theory of *ritmus* and *metrum*'.
[6] From the introductory epistle to *The Shepheardes Calender* (*Spenser's Minor Poems*, ed. E. de Selincourt, Oxford, 1910, p. 5).

You fine metricians, that verses skilfully compile,
(As fine artificers hard iron do refile on an anvil)
This verse irregular, this rustic rhythmery bannish,
Which doth abuse poetry; such verse, such meter abolish . . .[7]

It is in this context that we can best understand what was engaging Sidney's attention in the extensive Eclogues of the *Old Arcadia*. He was contributing his bit to the search for a proper voice for English poetry, which meant most importantly, though not exclusively, a proper 'music', i.e. a proper speech-melody for it. The *Old Arcadia* poems present a bewildering variety of metrical forms, amongst which the classical are included, such as Cleophila's song in sapphics, 'If mine eyes can speake to doo harty errande'.[8] The fourth stanza is about music and also itself creates a distinctive 'music'.

If the sencelesse spheares doo yet hold a musique,
If the Swanne's sweet voice be not heard, but at death,
If the mute timber when it hath the life lost,
    Yeldeth a lute's tune, . . .

A more conventional kind of 'Musicall utterance' can be represented by Cleophila's 'Beautie hath force to catche the humane sight' which 'she' sings to her two unwanted lovers:[9]

Beautie hath force to catche the humane sight.
Sight doth bewitch, the fancie evill awaked.
Fancie we feel, encludes all passion's mighte,
Passion rebelde, oft reason's strength has shaked.

Here the decasyllabic quatrain is patterned not only by cross-rhyme but by a concatenation of repeated nouns. The narrator calls the poem 'an Ambassade in versifyed Musick'.

'Versified music' is a telling phrase. In a metaphorical reading it exactly sums up what I have been trying to say: poetry for Sidney is an art of ordered sound, 'words set in delightful proportion', self-sufficient and satisfying, a 'music' in itself. There is, however, another way of taking the phrase 'versifyed Musick', and one which equally well fits the context. The full text reads: '. . . at the earnest intreaty of Basilius, Cleophila (*first saluting the Muses with a Base vyoll honge hard by her*) sent this Ambassade in versifyed Musick'. (There is always a bass viol or a lute handy in Arcadia). So it is possible that in this fictional setting an actual song was meant—music to which verses had been applied.

---

[7] Cit. D. Attridge, *Well-Weighed Syllables*, Cambridge, 1974, pp. 103–4. It should be noted that the anonymous versifier makes a point of observing the rules of classical 'position'.
[8] Song 12 (*The Poems of Sir Philip Sidney*, ed. W. A. Ringler, Oxford, 1962, p. 30). See also Attridge, op. cit., p. 185.
[9] Song 57 (*Poems*, p. 82); for the context see *The Countess of Pembroke's Arcadia: Being the Original Version* [*Old Arcadia*] (*Complete Works*, iv), ed. A. Feuillerat, Cambridge, 1926, pp. 205–6.

This will bring us to consider in a moment the two main categories under which I shall discuss contemporary Elizabethan and foreign music to which the Sidney poems were related. But first I have to modify the conclusion just reached about the 'music' of poetry as a self-sufficient art. The combined forces of Reformation and humanism (in its narrower sense as the redis-covery of antique, classical ideals) were bringing about a revolution in the way people saw the relation of words and music—a revolution which encouraged the subservience of music to words ('servant' is a dominant image). This led in due course to music being regarded as a 'language', rather than language (poetic language especially) being regarded as a 'music'. One of Sidney's learned Arcadian shepherds observes that his comrade

did much abuse the dignitie of poetry to apply it to musicke, since rather musicke is a servaunt to poetry, for by [the one] the eare only, by the other the minde was pleased.[10]

In this dismissal of music's high purpose (it only pleases the ear) we have moved a long way from the medieval certitude that number is fundamental reality and music one of the means whereby man's highest function, Reason, can find touch with it. The final imaginative failure will be to regard it with Dr Johnson nearly two centuries later as 'an innocent luxury'.

But, to get to practicalities, whatever Sidney's theory may have been, and despite the fact that the 'classical' verses in the *Arcadia* are described as being sung (hexameters, asclepiads, phaleuciacs and the rest), only one such metre can be connected with a surviving piece of music, and that somewhat later. It is the asclepiadic 'O sweet woods the delight of solitariness'.[11] John Dowland took the first two lines only of Sidney's poem and used them as a sort of burden (external refrain) for a lute-song (Ex. 12.1).[12] His setting of the asclepiads disregards the classical metre entirely; and the rest of his song is completely different.

Ex. 12.1

This single example raises a fundamental issue in the handling of the musical evidence. When talking of the twenty or so Sidney settings we have

[10] This well-known deleted passage from the *Old Arcadia* is conveniently available in *Poems*, pp. 389–90.

[11] *Old Arcadia*, Song 34 (*Poems*, p. 68); ed. Feuillerat, p. 157.

[12] *The Second Book of Songs* (1600), No. 10; ed. E. H. Fellowes, rev. Thurston Dart ('The English Lute-Songs', ser. 1, v & vi), London, 1969, pp. 22–3. The couplet appears to serve as an initial refrain.

to distinguish two quite different kinds. The first consists of settings which have come into being through the 'applying' of words to pre-existent music, the second of settings composed by a musician *post factum*, after the poem had been written. The two operations are very different. It follows that 'composed songs', as we may call them, may tell us nothing significant about Sidney and music. Dowland's setting of 'O sweet woods' is a good instance of such non-information.

'WORDS . . . ACCOMPANIED WITH . . . THE WELL ENCHANTING
SKILL OF MUSIC'

First, then, the writing of poems to tunes. The most obvious examples come from *Certain Sonnets*, which Ringler dates as having been written 'in 1581 or earlier' except for the first two poems. Two poems are named 'To the tune of *Non credo già che più infelice amante*', one to a well known Italian song, 'Basciami vita mia', one to a Spanish song, 'Se tu, señora non dueles de mi', one to 'Wilhelmus van Nassaw' (the Dutch national anthem), one 'to the tune of *The smokes of Melancholy*', etc. Some of these are in very simple metres: 'Who hath his fancie pleased', for instance (Ex. 12.2).[13] This 1581

Ex. 12.2

Who hath his fan - cie plea - sed With fruits of hap - pie sight,_____
Let here his eyes___ be___ rai - sed On na - ture's swee - test light._____

A ___ light which doth dis - se - ver, And yet u - nite the eyes,_____ A

light which ___ dy - ing ne - ver, Is cause the loo - ker dyes._____

version of the song of the House of Orange Sidney could have heard, as Ringler suggests, on his visit to the Prince of Orange in 1577.[14] The melody is saved from set-squareness by the rather fetching way in which each odd line is run on into the next. The general procedure is precisely that of hundreds of poems of the broadside ballad and metrical psalm type printed from the mid-sixteenth century onwards. But it would be wrong to think that the two kinds of musical activity I have distinguished revolve round a simple distinction between a professional art of musical composition and a popular or mock-popular kind of balladry. We have to envisage a third domain, one in which courtly lyric is written to sophisticated melody.

One of Sidney's most beautiful courtly lyrics is metrically quite complicated:

[13] *Certain Sonnets*, No. 23 (*Poems*, pp. 151–2). *The New Grove*, xiii. 64, states that the words date from *c*.1568 and that the tune is older.
[14] *Poems*, p. 431.

The Nightingale, as soone as Aprill bringeth
Unto her rested sense a perfect waking,
While late bare earth, proud of new clothing springeth,
Sings out her woes, a thorne her song-booke making:
   And mournfully bewailing,
   Her throate in tunes expresseth
   What griefe her breast oppresseth,
For Thereus' force on her chaste will prevailing.
     O Philomela faire, o take some gladnesse,
     That here is juster cause of plaintfull sadnesse:
     Thine earth now springs, mine fadeth,
     Thy thorne without, my thorne my heart invadeth.

Alas she hath no other cause of anguish
But Thereus' love, on her by strong hand wrokne,
Wherein she suffring all her spirits' languish,
Full womanlike complaines her will was brokne.
   But I who dayly craving,
   Cannot have to content me,
   Have more cause to lament me,
Since wanting is more woe then too much having.
     O Philomela faire, o take some gladnesse,
     That here is juster cause of plaintfull sadnesse:
     Thine earth now springs, mine fadeth:
     Thy thorne without, my thorne my heart invadeth.[15]

The heading of the poem is 'To the same tune', i.e. as the previous poem 'The fire to see my wrongs for anger burneth' sung to the Italian song 'Non credo già che più infelice amante'. When Ringler prepared his authoritative edition of Sidney's poems the song had still not been traced. Thanks, however, to the vigilance of Frank Fabry a version of the song was unearthed and published in 1970.[16] It appears in a set of Winchester partbooks long known to musicologists;[17] they were compiled in the mid 1560s, i.e. some 25 years before the publishing vogue of the English madrigal. The songs are in a Flemish hand, and the pink sheepskin binding is also Flemish. Each volume bears the Tudor royal arms. It is tempting to think that this indicates a close connection with Queen Elizabeth herself or at least with her court, but experts point out that this bookbinder's device was widely used. All that can safely be deduced is that the volumes were prepared and bound in the Netherlands for presentation to a person of some standing and culture in this country.

    The song 'Non credo già che più infelice amante' is for four voices (cantus,

---

[15] *Certain Sonnets*, No. 4 (*Poems*, p. 137).

[16] 'Sidney's Verse Adaptations' (see note 1 above); see also Fabry's 'Sidney's Poetry and Italian Song-Form', *English Literary Renaissance*, iii (1973), 232–48.

[17] Winchester College, Fellows' Library, MS 153. I am grateful to the librarian, Paul Yeats-Edwards, for allowing me to consult the manuscript and for advice.

contratenor, tenor and bassus): they move together chordally; the song is homophonic, governed by a single rhythm. This feature links the song not with the Italian madrigal properly so called (those of Luca Marenzio were the best known to Englishmen in the 1580s) but to the tradition of the villanella, a mock-popular type of song of a kind that was first published in the 1540s in Italy. The disingenuousness has to be insisted on. As Morley observed, the villanella composers deliberately wrote a 'clownish music to a clownish matter' for the sake of 'keeping decorum'.[18]

Assuming that the Winchester partbooks transmit the song Sidney knew (which cannot be proved), the question arises whether the poem was to be sung to the part-song or to its 'tune'. The latter is more likely, the former not impossible. The 'tune' is probably in the treble (though this was by no means universal practice even in the middle of the century); the villanella is the harmonization of a melody. The fit between words and music is a good one (Ex. 12.3), if not perfect in every detail (especially not in the first line with its tense argumentative stresses). It could not conceivably be accidental in the case of so complex a stanza, with twelve lines of two different lengths and elaborate weak endings. But what has to be observed is that, as in the case of much simpler words-to-tune exercises, it does not require of the poet any great musical skill. The exercise is one of syllable counting, metrical organization and rhythmic shaping. No account has been taken or needed to be taken of the melody as such. The latter is not, in this case, of any great merit; the interest of the original, as of Sidney's *contrafactum*, is in its rhythmic interplay, fours, threes, twos, with some characteristic light syncopations.

The tradition of 'courtly' (perhaps one should say 'cultured') melody with which Sidney was most in touch during the time he was writing *Certain Sonnets* was apparently that of Italy. The villanella style originated in Naples (the *villanella alla napoletana*), a fact which Sidney acknowledges in *Certain Sonnets*, No. 27, 'All my sense thy sweetnesse gained'—'*To the tune of a* Neapolitan Villanell'.[19] The tune has not been traced, though the distinctive refrain, 'Fa la la leridan, dan dan dan deridan / Dan dan dan deridan deridan dei', makes it look an eventual possibility. Some 30 years later Robert Jones in *The Muses Gardin for Delights* set Sidney's lyric as a lute-song.[20] If one

[18] Thomas Morley, *A Plain and Easy Introduction to Practical Music*, ed. R. A. Harman, London, 1952, p. 295.
[19] *Poems*, p. 156; Ringler says (p. 432) that 'this is the first appearance of the word and the form in English'. Thomas Whythorne, it is worth noting, refers to the 'Napolitane' as a 'prety mery one' in the verse preface to his *Songes to three, fowre and five voyces* (1571) and exemplifies it. The villanella succeeds the frottola as a generic name for a number of types of light, popular Italian song from *c.*1530.
[20] *The Muses Gardin for Delights* (1610), No. 17; ed. E. H. Fellowes ('The English Lute-Songs', ser. 2, xv), London, 1927, pp. 36–9. Text pr. Edward Doughtie, *Lyrics from English Airs 1596–1622*, Cambridge, Mass., 1970, p. 374; Doughtie observes (p. 595) that Jones's text is 'corrupt in spots'. Jones dedicated this book, incidentally, to Philip Sidney's niece Mary (daughter of Robert), having previously dedicated his *First Book* (1600) to Robert himself.

Ex. 12.3

1. The Night - in - gale, as soone as Ap - rill brin - geth
3. While late bare earth, proud of new clo - thing sprin - geth

2. Un - to her res - ted sense a per - fect wa - king,
4. Sings out her woes, a thorn her song - book ma - king:

5. And mourn - ful - ly be - wai - ling,

6. Her throat in tunes ex - pres - seth

7. What grief her breast op - pres - seth,

8.* For The - reus force on her chaste_____ will pre - vai - ling

9. O Phi-lo - me - na faire, ô take some glad - - - - - - ness,

10. That here is jus - ter cause of plaint - ful sad - - - - - ness:

11. Thin earth now springs, mine fa - deth,

12. Thy thorn with - out, my thorne my heart in - va - deth.

* Line 8, bar 2: original has minim B minim A

abstracts Jones's melody from the accompaniment for lute and bass viol, one is left with an unusual and attractive single-voice song (Ex. 12.4). It could be, of course, that the verbal rhythms of the villanella pattern suggested the tune to Jones. But it is not out of the question that he picked up with the words a tune associated with them. It has the precise rhythmic repetitions, the contrasting triple sections, the syllabic word-setting and the total absence of any 'commentary' by the music on the text that characterized the known villanella. This hypothesis is fraught with historical and logical perils, and I rest nothing substantial on it. I shall return later to the possibility that other

Ex. 12.4

All my sense thy sweet-ness gain-ĕd,   Thy fair hair my heart en - chain-ĕd;

My poor rea - son thy words mo-vĕd   So that thee like heaven I lov-ĕd:

Fa la la le - ri-de-ri-dan fa la la le - ri-dan Fa la la le - ri-de-ri-dan fa la la

le - ri-de-ri-dan Fa la la le - ri-de-ri-dan le - ri-de-ri-dan le - ri-dan dey

While to my mind the out - side stood For mes - sen-ger of in - side good.

composed settings may embody pre-existent tunes to which Sidney's poems were sung.

The other named tune rediscovered by Frank Fabry in the Winchester part-books is attached to *Certain Sonnets*, No. 26, where it is described as '*a* Neapolitan *song, which beginneth*: No, no, no, no'; this presumably belonged to the villanella repertory.[21] It is rather more complex. Sidney's text opens as follows:

> No, no, no, no, I cannot hate my foe
> Although with cruell fire,
> First throwne on my desire,
> She sackes my rendred sprite.

These first four lines are a burden (i.e. an external refrain unit separable and complete in itself); the musical model makes it clear that the 'No no no no' given at the end of each stanza is not a part of the stanza itself but an indication that the burden should be repeated entire: Ringler's text requires some emendation. The anonymous Winchester villanella-type song, 'No no no no, giàmmai non cangerò', sets the burden in an ornamented chordal style, often florid in the treble; the verse section (lines 5–11: Ex 12.5) is in characteristic chordal style with repeated notes, basic harmonies and cross-rhythms. The extreme melodic dullness of this, even more marked than in the case of 'The Nightingale, as soone as Aprill', suggests again the sort of interest Sidney may have been taking in this 'courtly-popular' Italian tradition. The villanella (like, perhaps, the later balletto) provided not

[21] *Poems*, p. 155. Fabry transcribes the whole song ('Sidney's Verse Adaptations', pp. 250–53); there seems to be no warrant in the manuscript for his change of metre in p. 251, bars 1–2.

Ex. 12.5

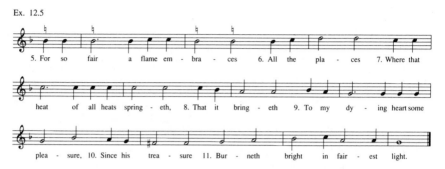

melodies but rather (a newish thing in Western music) harmonized rhythms. It provided thus a stock of interesting new patterns, metrical patterns, to which interesting poetic stanzas could be devised. It was another way of searching for the new voice of Elizabethan poetry.[22]

Other traditions of melody were available to Sidney, including that of the contemporary French chanson, though the evidence is scantier here. The Eighth Song of *Astrophil and Stella*, 'In a grove most rich of shade', was published by Robert Dowland in his varied collection *A Musicall Banquet* (1610), attributed to Tessier.[23] As Doughtie has shown, this is Guillaume Tessier, who first published the music in his *Primo libro dell'arie* (Paris, 1582) 'as a setting for Ronsard's "Le petit enfant amour" (*Odes* 1555, IV, xx)'.[24] Doughtie supposes that Robert Dowland discovered that the tune fitted Sidney's lyric and gave it an accompaniment. It seems possible and perhaps more likely that the tune was already, 30 years earlier, associated with Sidney's poem (*Astrophil and Stella* was being put together 1581–3) and that Sidney indeed wrote for this tune (Ex. 12.6). The style is much more tuneful than that of the villanella; the melody is saved from rhythmic four-squareness only by the slight variation in the length of the lines. The poem has 26 stanzas in Sidney's version, 18 in Downland's book; and it was used, 'imitated'(?), by Fulke Greville in an even longer poem (*Caelica*, No. 75) of 57 stanzas.

The evidence that this melody in Robert Dowland's collection was contemporary with Sidney's poem is incontrovertible. The same cannot be said of the anonymous melody which Dowland provides for 'O dear life,

---

[22] Fabry's rewarding article 'Sidney's Poetry and Italian Song-Form' (see note 16 above) illustrates in detail the way in which two specific traits of Elizabethan poetry owe their predominance to musical contacts—trochaic rhythms and feminine endings.

[23] *Poems*, p. 217. *A Musicall Banquet*, No. 7; ed. Peter Stroud ('The English Lute-Songs', ser. 2, xx), London, 1968, pp. 12–13. Robert Dowland's songbook is dedicated to Robert Sidney, his godfather and brother to Sir Philip. On Robert Sidney and music see *The Poems of Robert Sidney*, ed. P. J. Croft, Oxford, 1984, pp. 48–54.

[24] Doughtie, *Lyrics*, pp. 586–7; for further details see Doughtie's note in *Renaissance News*, xviii (1965), 124–6.

Ex. 12.6

1. In a grace ___ most rich ___ of ___ shade Where birds wan - ton ___
2. As - tro - phel ___ with Stel - la ___ sweet Did for mu - tual ___

mu - sic made, 1. May, then young, his pied ___ weeds
com - fort meet, 2. Both with - in them - selves ___ op -

show - ing New per - fum'd with flow'rs ___ fresh ___ grow - - - ing.
pres - sed But each in the o - ther ___ bles - - - sed.

when shall it be?' (*Astrophil and Stella*, Song 10), a regular, balanced and unremarkable melody without rhythmic interest.[25] However, there is another clue to a possible original tune for this lyric:

> O Deare life, when shall it be,
> That mine eyes thine eyes may see?
> And in them thy mind discover,
> Whether absence have had force
> Thy remembrance to divorce
> From the image of thy lover?

Just after Sidney's death William Byrd published a setting in his *Songs of sundrie natures . . . lately made and composed into Musicke of 3. 4. 5. and 6. parts* (1589).[26] The five-part piece, like most of Byrd's secular songs, is not a madrigal but a consort song in the native English tradition, i.e. an accompanied solo song for voice (treble) and four viols.[27] In the 1589 publication words were fitted to the lower parts 'to serve for all companies and voices', but this does not disguise the basic structure. Only the 'first singing part' sings the tune right through without repeating the words. In the composition as printed in 1589 the phrases of the melody are introduced by, and individually separated by, flowing polyphony in the lower parts. But reconstructed and closed up, as it were, it runs as a continuous tune (Ex. 12.7). There is nothing in the musical shape, the flow of the melody or the tonality to prevent one regarding it as a pre-existent melody associated with Sidney's poem, which Byrd had taken over *in toto*. (Byrd was born in 1543 and had begun his association with the Chapel Royal in 1570; he was well

[25] *Poems*, p. 225; Robert Dowland's text (which omits stanzas 5–7 of Sidney's poem) pr. Doughtie, *Lyrics*, p. 347. *Musicall Banquet*, No. 5; ed. Stroud, p. 9.

[26] No. 33; ed. Fellowes, rev. Dart ('The English Madrigalists', xv), London, 1962, p. 208. In stanza 1 line 3 Byrd's text reads 'my' for 'thy'.

[27] See *The Byrd Edition*, xv: *Consort Songs*, ed. P. Brett, London, 1970.

placed to know the repertoire of tunes at court.) The tune is generously 'imitated' in the lower voice; the contratenor is particularly worth noting as having the whole tune, much of it in approximate canon with the treble (superius). None of this amounts to proof, even given Byrd's known skill and experience in reworking older melodies—in viol fantasies, virginal pieces and so on. But the possibility may be borne in mind. John Ward's madrigal setting (1613) of the last stanza only, 'O my thoughts, my thoughts, surcease', could not possibly be 'deconstructed' in this way.

The consort song with viol accompaniment had flourished at court at least from the 1560s when Richards Edwards, Master of the Children of the Chapel Royal, composer, poet and dramatist, assembled *The Paradise of*

Ex. 12.7

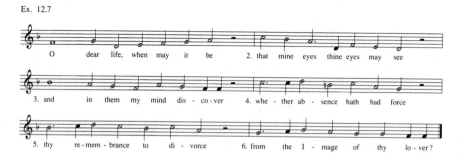

Daintie Devices. It may have provided 'frames', or patterns, for the writing of poems for singing: two of Thomas Lord Vaux's poems are found in such strophic settings.[28] Poems—new poems—were also certainly written at this time to fit already existing compositions; this was possible because the metres were stereotyped (the poulter's measure, for instance: 3 + 3 stresses rhyming with 4 + 3). So there is certainly a *prima facie* case for thinking that Sidney might have written lyrics to be sung in this style or to the separable tunes associated with it. This brings us to the poem 'Who hath ever felt the change of love' (*Certain Sonnets*, No. 24), directed to be sung to the tune of 'The smokes of Melancholy'.[29] It has been suggested that this may have been a consort song; but there seems to be no evidence for it and little probability. Consort songs do not have titles of this kind and, even more telling, they are not in such strange metres.

> Who hath ever felt the change of love,
> And known those pangs that the losers prove,
>   May paint my face without seeing me,
>   And write the state how my fancies bee,
>   The loathsome buds grown on sorrowe's tree.

---

[28] *Consort Songs*, ed. P. Brett ('Musica Britannica', xxii), London, 1967, Nos. 17 & 19.
[29] *Poems*, p. 153.

But who by hearesay speakes, and hath not fully felt
What kind of fires they be in which those spirits melt,
Shall gesse, and faile, what doth displease,
Feeling my pulse, misse my disease.

The metrical problem is epitomized if we juxtapose the third lines of each stanza:

(i) May paint my face without seeing me
(ii) Where former blisse present evils do staine
(iii) Nor breake my word though reward come late

If the last five syllables of each line are to be read accentually, then the pattern must be ◡–◡–◡◡–◡–. Ringler indeed may be right in supposing this unusual pattern to underlie lines 1–4 of each stanza—though it is hard to see how, for instance, the opening line of the poem could possibly fit it. What sort of melody could 'The smokes of Melancholy' have been? It is not easy to imagine. The title suggests a popular song; but it could perhaps have been a song of more complex structure like Dowland's pavan, *Lachrimae*, to which was fitted the lyric 'Flow my teares, fall from your springs'.[30] The tune must at least have had a complex rhythm, not a tum-ti-tum one. Maybe it was this kind of metrical structure which the shepherd Lalus had in mind, in the well-known debate from *Arcadia* (see p. 156 above), when he argued that 'since musike brought a measured quantity with it, therfor the words less needed it'. It would be of extreme interest to recover the tune.

Certain conclusions are beginning to emerge. First, that 'words set in delightful proportion' look for musical notes 'set in delightful proportion' —simply that and nothing more, at least around the year 1580. Secondly, that Sidney could, and did, draw on various traditions of European song and more especially on the 'mock-popular', or 'courtly-popular', traditions of the Italian villanella and Spanish villancico (one example untraced).[31] Putting these together with evidence of native-grown song we can see that the courtly poet, exercised as Sidney was with the problems of the proper verbal 'music' *of* poetry and the proper music *for* poetry, had a wide and diverse repertoire of melody to draw upon. And, thirdly, that the simple distinction one might expect to hold, between tunes which pre-date and settings which post-date the poems, is not always valid: some tunes are little more than rhythms, but these rhythms are shaped and vitalized by harmonic setting in parts; other tunes are so easily detachable from their setting (consort song, metrical psalm) that they could either have preceded them in time or have been taken

[30] John Dowland, *The Second Booke of Songs or Ayres* (1600), No. 2; see Doughtie, *Lyrics*, pp. 101, 475–6.
[31] *Certain Sonnets*, No. 7: 'To the tune of the Spanish song, *Se tu señora no dueles de mi*'; *Poems*, p. 139.

out and used separately. In any case, it was possible to write poems to pre-existent part-music, not simply to monophonic melodies.[32]

'WORDS . . . PREPARED FOR THE WELL ENCHANTING SKILL OF MUSIC'
I should like now to take up again the question of later settings. There are some easy and some very difficult judgments to make. Since what we are interested in is musical evidence which will illuminate Sidney's intentions or unconscious attitudes, then later settings such as John Ward's madrigal 'How long shall I with mournful music stain?', adapted from *Old Arcadia*, Song 30, or Thomas Vautor's imaginative 'Lock up, fair lids, the treasures of my heart' (Song 51) are not relevant to the enquiry.[33] Ward's text is an inaccurate and garbled version of five lines from the dialogue poem between Plangus and Bowlon in the Second Eclogues, a mere excuse for a 'passionate' madrigal. Vautor is completely faithful to Sidney's sonnet; but his moving madrigalian calculations—such as the sudden modulation at the line 'And while, O sleep, thou closest up her sight'—could not conceivably have been envisaged by Sidney. The madrigal settings provide no clue as to what Sidney might have meant by the phrase 'prepared for . . . the well enchanting skill of musick'. It is in the repertoire of lute songs that we have to look for the appropriate sort of music.

The publishing vogue for lute songs began with John Dowland's *First Booke of Songes or Ayres* (1597). But the genre was established well before that time. An interesting manuscript collection in the British Library (Add. MS 15117), described in detail by Mary Chan, contains items which date back to the 1560s and '70s—Richard Edwards' 'Awake ye wofull weights' from *Damon and Pithias*, for example.[34] Among the lute songs are two with words by Philip Sidney, 'My true-love hath my heart and I have his' and 'Have I caught my heavenly jewel?'

Settings of sonnets are rare in the English books of this period, but 'My true-love hath my heart' achieved two, a madrigal setting by Ward (1613) as well as this lute song (Ex. 12.8).[35] The melody as it stands is clearly an art-song. The angular repetition in lines 3, 7, 11 is enough of itself to establish this, not to mention the way the sonnet form is handled (three

---

[32] This is the evident explanation of the sentence in *The Paradise of Dainty Devises* (1576): 'the ditties both pithy and pleasant, as well for inuention as meter, and wyll yeilde a farre greater delight, being as they are so aptly made as to be set to any song in -5- partes, or song to instrument' (ed. H. E. Rollins, Cambridge, Mass., 1927, p. 4).

[33] Ward, *The First Set of English Madrigals to 3. 4. 5. and 6. parts* (1613), No. 12; Vautor, *The First Set: Beeing Songs of divers Ayres and Natures, of Five and Sixe parts* (1619), Nos. 8–9.

[34] Mary Joiner (now Chan), 'British Museum Add. MS 15117: A Commentary, Index and Bibliography', *RMA Research Chronicle*, vii (1970), 51–109.

[35] Add. MS 15117, f. 18ᵛ. Ward, *First Set*, Nos. 1–2; ed. Fellowes, rev. Dart ('The English Madrigalists', xix), London, 1968, pp. 1–11.

Ex. 12.8

quatrains to the same melody followed by the concluding couplet). Never-theless, there is some evidence which supports the notion that behind the sonnet and its art-song setting there may lie a courtly-popular song with a simpler tune. As others have pointed out, there is an earlier form of the lyric attributed to 'the noble knight Sir Philip Sidney' by Puttenham (*Arte of English Poesie*, published 1589, but mostly written earlier).[36] It consists of two four-line verses, a b a b, with the first line repeated as the refrain 'My true love hath my heart'. (Puttenham, incidentally, introduces the lyric in a paragraph about refrain song, which he claims was practised by the Greek poets 'who make musicall ditties to be song to the lute or harpe'.) Such a form is consistent with a less complex version of the tune in which the first phrase of the lute song may have been joined by a simplified form of the last (Ex. 12.9). This is made the more likely by the fact that John Ward's canzonet-like setting begins with a similar phrase and repeats it at the end (Ex. 12.10). It is, of course, logically quite possible that John Ward got this snatch of melody from the voice-and-lute setting in Add. MS 15117.

'Have I caught my heav'nly jewell' is the last song for discussion. The first line came in handy for Falstaff as he greeted Mistress Quickly in *The Merry*

[36] Ed. Willcock & Walker, p. 225.

Ex. 12.9

My true love hath my heart and I have his...

My true love hath my heart and I have his...

Ex. 12.10

My true love hath my heart...

My true love hath my heart...

Wives of Windsor (III. iii. 36). Perhaps it was already by that time in circulation as a popular song. The melody (Ex. 12.11) survives in the same British Library manuscript as 'My true love hath my heart' and again may, like other songs in the manuscript, be of some antiquity.[37] There is nothing particularly 'popular' about the text, which belongs to the favourite Renaiss-

Ex. 12.11

Have I caught my heav'n-ly je-wel Tea-ching sleep most fair to be? Now will

I, now will I teach her that she _____ When she wakes is - - - too too cru-el

ance genre of *basia, baisers,* kissing poems. The melody is interesting for its rhythmic patterns, which are quite unlike anything in English popular song as normally encountered or, for that matter, in English lute song. Again, might it relate to Italian traditions? At any rate the identical rhythmic patterns occur, for example, in Monteverdi's *Orfeo.* If the song 'Have I caught' is not anterior to Sidney (with different words or in an instrumental version)—and only the discovery of a villanella or related type could prove this—it is at least the sort of melody to which Sidney himself wrote songs.

In an earlier paragraph I drew some fairly obvious conclusions about

[37] Add. MS 15117, f. 19. The song is published in *Songs from Manuscript Sources,* ed. D. Greer, London, 1979, No. 3. As Greer rightly observes, the voice part has to be transposed up a minor third; the earlier transcription by J. P. Cutts (*Shakespeare Quarterly,* xi (1960), 89) did not contain this adjustment. I give the voice part from Greer's edition.

Sidney's melodic repertoire. I did not attempt an answer to the question as to what Sidney thought he was doing in having his poems sung. The way he refers to the practices in a letter to his friend Edward Denny suggests normal expectation: 'remember with yowr good voyce, to singe my songes, for they will one well become an other'.[38] I suspect far more were in fact sung than we know about.

Sidney's motives and assumptions were perhaps mixed. He may have regarded himself as heir to a continuing tradition of simple monophonic court-song, for which there is a certain amount of evidence in the early Tudor songbooks, especially in the so-called Henry VIII Manuscript.[39] Alongside this, and occasionally touching it, there was, of course, a flourishing tradition of popular singing—of broadside ballad (and metrical psalm, too). An anthology such as *A Handful of Pleasant Delights* (1584) witnesses to its popularity. Sidney was moved by ballad singing and alludes to it in *The Apology*, but he can hardly have wished to imitate 'the ragged rout of rakehellye rhymers'. More interestingly, Sidney's conscious share in the great enterprise of finding a 'proper voice' for English poetry had led him into endless experimentation with metre and rhythm. Besides the classical experiment, the 'well-weighed syllables' of 'O sweet woods the delight of solitariness', it seems he may well have been interested professionally in the diverse possibilities, the potentialities, of a rhythmically more sophisticated type of melody than English sources provided—hence the use of, especially, Italian models. Finally, there must always have been in Sidney's mind, as a good humanist and man of his age, a desire to realize the ennobling ideal of antiquity of a close union of music and poetry, a union which had been inconceivable in these terms to the barbarous age just past.

[38] J. M. Osborn, *Young Philip Sidney*, New Haven & London, 1972, p. 540.
[39] See J. Stevens, *Music and Poetry in the Early Tudor Court*, London, 1961 (repr. Cambridge, 1978), Ch. 7.

13

'Melancholie Times':
Musical Recollections of Sidney by
William Byrd and Thomas Watson

Katherine Duncan-Jones

IN an often quoted letter to his younger brother, written in October 1580, Philip Sidney advised Robert:

sweete brother take a delight to keepe and increase your musick, you will not beleive what a want I finde of it in my melancholie times.[1]

The word 'want' may suggest that Sidney himself was no performer or singer, though he certainly encouraged those who were. Earlier in the same year he had exhorted Edward Denny to 'remember with yowr good voyce, to singe my songes, for they will one well become an other'.[2] We shall probably never know exactly what Fulke Greville was referring to when he described Sidney calling on his death-bed

for music, especially that song which himself had entitled *La cuisse rompue*; partly (as I conceive by the name) to show that the glory of mortal flesh was shaken in him, and, by the music itself, to fashion and enfranchise his heavenly soul into that everlasting harmony of angels whereof these concords were a kind of terrestrial echo.[3]

But there seems little doubt that Sidney regularly used music in a practical and personal way, to gloss and harmonize particular phases of his life. Greville recorded also that 'there was not . . . an excellent musician . . . that made not himself known to this famous spirit and found him his true friend without hire'.[4] Independent evidence confirms this. For instance, in 1577 Sidney importuned his uncle, the Earl of Leicester, 'in the cace of the poore stranger musicien'.[5] The catholicity of his musical tastes is suggested by his

---

[1] *Prose Works of Sir Philip Sidney* (*Complete Works*, iii), ed. A. Feuillerat, Cambridge, 1923, p. 133.
[2] J. M. Osborn, *Young Philip Sidney*, New Haven & London, 1972, p. 540.
[3] *The Prose Works of Fulke Greville*, ed. John Gouws, Oxford, 1986, p. 82.
[4] Ibid., p. 21.　　　　　　　　　　　　　　　[5] Sidney, *Prose Works*, p. 119.

affectionate account, in A *Defence of Poesy*, of 'some blind crowder, with no rougher voice than rude style', singing the ballad of 'Chevy Chase'.[6]

After his death on 17 October 1586 'melancholie times' of a different kind ensued, but these too were punctuated by songs, which offer a vivid commentary on the development of Sidney's image within his own circle. Two men who played important parts in the musical fashioning of his literary image were William Byrd and the learned author of some of the earliest English madrigals, Thomas Watson. They are slightly unexpected figures to emerge as mediators of the Sidney myth. Both had strong Catholic leanings or connections, and Watson had been associated with Sidney's arch-enemy the Earl of Oxford—of whom more anon. It cannot be shown for certain that either was personally acquainted with Sidney, though in neither case is it impossible. Byrd's position, as joint organist of the Chapel Royal from 1575, could have brought him into contact with Sidney, but we do not know that it did. Watson is likelier to have known him. A 'Mr. watsone' is among the 50 gentlemen who processed at Sidney's funeral,[7] but the surname is common, and we cannot be sure that all those who took part in the funeral were known to Sidney. However, Watson's association with the Walsingham family provides a reasonable basis for conjecture that he did, in fact, have some acquaintance with Sidney. According to his own account he met Thomas Walsingham, cousin to the Secretary of State, in Paris in 1581 and showed him some of his poems,[8] and by the later 1580s he seems to have come under his protection. Watson's allegiance to Sidney and his family is shown both by *Meliboeus* (1590), his joint elegy on Sidney and Sir Francis Walsingham, the English version of which was dedicated to Sidney's widow, and by his dying wish, recorded by the mysterious 'C. M.', that his *Amintae Gaudia* (1592) should be dedicated to the Countess of Pembroke.[9]

Whatever the personal standing of these two men in relation to Sidney, there can be little doubt that both Byrd and Watson had access to some poems from *Astrophel and Stella* well before its publication in 1591 and possibly also to a version of the *Arcadia*. It was Byrd who first published parts of *Astrophel and Stella*. The Sixth Song was included in his *Psalms, Sonnets, & Songs of Sadness and Piety* (1588), which had been entered in the Stationers' Register in November 1587, and the first three stanzas of the Tenth Song were included in his next volume, *Songs of Sundry Natures* (1589).[10] According to W. A. Ringler, Byrd's texts derive from manuscript

---

[6] *Miscellaneous Prose of Sir Philip Sidney*, ed. K. Duncan-Jones & J. van Dorsten, Oxford, 1973, p. 97.

[7] Oxford, Bodleian Library, MS Ashmole 818, f. 41ʳ.

[8] Thomas Watson, *An Eglogue upon the Death of the Right Honorable Sir Francis Walsingham*, London, 1590, sig. B3ᵛ.

[9] See *The Poems of Christopher Marlowe*, ed. Miller Maclure, London, 1968, pp. xxxix, 260–61, 263–4.

[10] All references to printed song books are from *English Madrigal Verse*, ed. E. H. Fellowes, 3rd edn., rev. Frederick W. Sternfeld & David Greer, Oxford, 1967.

anthologies, and he finds the first, the text of the Sixth Song, to be 'extremely corrupt'.[11] But there is more to be said about the first of these texts. It takes the form of a legal debate on the priority in excellence between Stella's singing voice and her face. It is a poem which has been little admired, but it is pre-eminently suitable for musical treatment. The appropriateness of its subject to a collection of songs is such that Byrd may have positively selected it for musical accompaniment, rather than setting it simply because it was the only one of Sidney's poems to which he had access. It is not obvious that its text is especially 'inaccurate', though it is true that half a dozen readings differ markedly from Ringler's text, which is based on the 1598 edition. Some examples: in line 5, where Ringler has 'Fear not to judge this bate' Byrd has 'Who dare judge this debate . . . ?' In line 26 Byrd has the more technical 'phrases finely placed' for Ringler's 'speeches nobly placed'. The most striking variant is in line 40, where Ringler, here following the Quarto editions, has 'The judgement of the eye', and Byrd has 'Eye witness of the eye'. On internal grounds, by-passing the complex arguments for textual descent made by Ringler, it is not obvious that Byrd's version must be inauthentic. Sidney was fond, to the point of obsession, of figures requiring the repetition of words in different senses; a famous example is the quadruple play on 'touch' in the Ninth Sonnet of *Astrophel and Stella* (lines 12–14). The idea of the 'eye' as a microcosmic 'eye witness' seems not uncharacteristic of Sidney's wit. The 1598 text, here rejected by Ringler, amalgamates the two readings, with 'Eye-judgement of the eye', which suggests that the 1598 editor drew on a text not unlike Byrd's here, or else conflated such a text with one having the other reading. Of the three versions of the line, Byrd's strikes me as the most coherent.

There is less to be said about Byrd's version of the first eighteen lines of the Tenth Song in his 1589 collection. It has at least one indefensible reading, 'Though my parting aught forgot' for Ringler's 'After parting ought forgot' in line 8, and Byrd's choice, or use, of poem here is unremarkable. This passionate meditation on an absent mistress circulated in manuscript during the later 1590s, most often in a shortened version, whose eroticism was less distinct. Sir John Harington transcribed it as a complete eight-stanza poem, subscribing it 'Sᵣ Phillip Syd. to the bewty of the worlde'.[12] Byrd's access to texts of Sidney's poems may well have been less privileged than Harington's, and the complete text may not have been available to him. It is possible, however, that he chose to print only the first three stanzas, assuming that users of his settings could supply further verses for themselves. Some other poems in his collections are very truncated, such as No. XXI of 1588 and No. XXXII of 1589. But neither personal knowledge of Sidney nor privileged

[11] *The Poems of Sir Philip Sidney*, ed. W. A. Ringler, Oxford, 1962, p. 561.
[12] *The Arundel Harington Manuscript of Tudor Poetry*, ed. Ruth Hughey, Columbus, Ohio, 1960, i. 116–17.

access to his texts can, finally, be claimed for Byrd with any confidence; there is simply too little evidence.

Watson's case is different. He is a poet who has been generally spurned by Elizabethan scholars, despite or because of his learning, love of music,[13] and pioneering of various genres—his translation of Sophocles's *Antigone* (1581), his Petrarchan 'sonnet' sequence (1581–2) and his early composition of words for madrigals in *Italian Madrigals Englished* (1590). According to C. S. Lewis,

One of the uses of Watson's work is to show that, as between a plain and a beautiful face, so between supreme and mediocre poetry, there can be a clear likeness. All the elements of Petrarch's beauty are present in the *Hecatompathia*, all those of *Lycidas* in *Meliboeus*, and nothing comes of them.[14]

Yet from a literary–historical point of view Watson's work may have other 'uses'. Though John Buxton has written that Watson 'was the only poet of ability writing in the 1580s who . . . never came directly under the influence of the Sidneys',[15] some definite threads link him with the Sidney circle. His Latin *Antigone* (entered in the Stationers' Register on 31 July 1581) was dedicated to Philip Howard, Earl of Arundel, who had taken part in the *Four Foster Children of Desire* entertainment along with Sidney earlier that same summer. Writers of commendatory verses for it include William Camden, who had been at Christ Church with Sidney. It seems likely that Sidney himself, who in his *Defence of Poesy* praised Sophocles as a statesman who was also a poet,[16] would have taken an interest in Watson's translation for its own sake, and would also have been impressed by Watson's citation of lines from several of Sophocles' other plays in *Hekatompathia*. Whether Sidney really admired Watson's sequence is very doubtful. It seems overall like just the kind of second-hand synthesis of Petrarch and other humanist poets that he had Astrophil dismiss in Sonnet 15 (lines 7–10):

> You that poore *Petrarch's* long deceased woes
> With new-borne sighes and denisend wit do sing;
> You take wrong waies, those far-fet helpes be such,
> As do bewray a want of inward tuch.

But the publication of *Hekatompathia* came, probably, just as Sidney was beginning to fashion his own sonnets into a coherent sequence. Ringler assigns the final shaping of *Astrophel and Stella*, perhaps a bit too neatly, to

---

[13] See Watson's & Byrd's *A Gratification unto Master John Case for his Learned Book Lately Made in Praise of Musicke*, London, 1589; also *Liber Lilliati*, ed. Edward Doughtie, London & Toronto, 1985, pp. 113–14, 189–90. Poems X–XVII of *Hekatompathia* are a celebration of the beauty of the mistress's singing voice.
[14] *English Literature in the Sixteenth Century*, Oxford, 1954, p. 483.
[15] *Sir Philip Sidney and the English Renaissance*, London, 1964, p. 198.
[16] *Miscellaneous Prose*, p. 110.

the summer of 1582.[17] Stephen Gosson's rabidly philistine *School of Abuse* (1579) helped to stimulate Sidney to pen his own cultivated and amusing *Defence of Poesy*; Watson's *Hekatompathia* may likewise have helped him, as he was shaping his own sonnet sequence, to see clearly how not to do it. The literary traffic between Watson and Sidney may have been two-way, for Passion XIX has strong echoes, hitherto unnoticed, of the eighth poem of Sidney's *Old Arcadia*, Dicus's description of Cupid as a monster. The poem's announced theme, in which 'The Author . . . reproveth the usuall description of love', is the same as Sidney's, and the poem itself has several apparent echoes of Sidney. The first two lines of Watson, 'If *Cupid* were a childe, as *Poets* faine, / How comes it then that *Mars* doth feare his might?', seem to pick up *Old Arcadia*, viii. 10: 'How is he young, that tam'de old *Phoebus* youth?' Watson's next two lines, 'If blind; how chance so many to theire paine / Whom he hath hitte, can witnesse of his sight?', expand Sidney's line 9: 'If he be blind, how hitteth he so right?' Watson's lines 7–8, 'If bowe and shaftes should be his chiefest tooles, / Why doth he set so many heartes on fire?', seem to recall *Old Arcadia*, xxx. 84: 'Those beames that set so many harts on fire', and his lines 13–14, 'If naked still he wander too and froe, / How doth not Sunne or frost offend his skinne?', seem a literal-minded variation on Sidney's *Old Arcadia*, viii. 8: 'Or naked he, disguis'd in all untruth?'

If Watson really had access to some 'Old' *Arcadia* poems at such an early date, his position was one of considerable privilege. Two other details in *Hekatompathia* support the possibility of his closeness to Sidney's world. In a curious sentence at the end of his dedicatory epistle to the Earl of Oxford Watson wishes him 'abundance of true Friends, reconciliation of all Foes, and what good soever tendeth unto perfect happines' (sig. A3ᵛ). Oxford's most notable 'foe' at this date was Sidney, with whom he had quarrelled on the tennis court at Whitehall in September 1579. In his 'Protrepticon' to his book, two pages later, Watson expresses the hope that Sidney and Edward Dyer, if the book reaches their desks, should not expect too much of his bucolic muse:

Hic quoque, seu subeas Sydnaei, siue Dyeri
  Scrinia, qua Musis area bina patet;
Dic te Xeniolum non diutius esse clientis,
  Confectum Dryadis arte, rudique manu.[18]

---

[17] *Poems*, pp. 439–40.
[18] *The Hekatompathia* [in Greek characters] or *Passionate Centurie of Love*, 1582, sig. *2ᵛ. A manuscript version of the sequence, apparently autograph, has only 70 poems rather than 100 and is addressed only to Oxford, with no allusion to Sidney or Dyer. The equivalent lines read: 'Ergo etiam timidus *Veri* perdocta subîto / scrinia, qua Musis area digna patet' (British Library, MS Harley 3277, f. 1ᵛ). I am indebted to Mr H. Woudhuysen for drawing my attention to this manuscript.

He goes on immediately to justify the book as one that has been shown to Oxford. Perhaps Watson hoped that the shared experience of reading *Hekatompathia* might reconcile Sidney and Oxford. It seems extremely unlikely that it did so, but Sidney may at least have perused it, and No. 15 of *Astrophel and Stella* may be a direct rebuke to his flattering plagiarizer.

In October 1586 Sidney died, and in 1587 his protégé Abraham Fraunce translated Watson's Latin poem *Amyntas* (1585) into English hexameters, without acknowledgement, dedicating it to Sidney's sister, the Countess of Pembroke. Whether this was an act of deliberate malice or arrogance by one who stood higher in Sidney's favour than Watson had done, we shall never know; it is certainly one of the most notorious cases of plagiarism to occur in the later Elizabethan period.[19] However, early in 1588 the first of three or more issues of Byrd's *Psalms, Sonnets, & Songs* was published, and in it Watson may have seized his chance of establishing his own place on the fringes of the Sidney circle. According to Kerman, supported by Sternfeld and Greer, Watson may have been the author of the two powerful funeral songs for Sidney that close the volume.[20] The first, 'Come to me grief for ever', is in a version of Aristophanic metre (used by Sidney in No. 25 of *Certain Sonnets*). The learnedness of this metre would certainly seem typical of Watson, and the lyric itself would sound well as a tribute from a subordinate who had enjoyed some part of his favour:

> He who made happy his friends,
> He that did good to all men.

The second funeral song, beginning 'O that most rare breast, crystalline, sincere', is in every sense more intimate. The first eight lines celebrate Sidney's princely virtues, his European fame and the fact that even his enemies bewailed him; lines 9–14 are a more personal tribute to Sidney as from a friend whose own life is desolated by his loss:

> The dolefull debt due to thy hearse I pay,
> Tears from the soul that aye thy want shall moan,
> And by my will my life itself would yield.

There is a text of this lyric in Robert Dow's manuscript part-books which suggests an explanation for this sense of immediate loss.[21] Where the 1588 printed text ends: 'Thou dead dost live, thy friend here living dieth' the Dow version has: 'Thou dead dost live, thy dier living dieth'. Dyer, who had been linked with Sidney in Watson's Latin poem before *Hekatompathia* may perhaps be the author of this lyric, as he probably is of No. XIV in *Psalms, Sonnets, & Songs*, 'My mind to me a kingdom is'. Alternatively, Watson, or

---

[19] H. O. White, *Plagiarism and Imitation during the Renaissance*, Cambridge, Mass., 1935, p. 114.

[20] *English Madrigal Verse*, p. 684.

[21] Oxford, Christ Church, MS Mus. 984, f. 61ᵛ.

some other poet, may have intended 'O that most rare breast' to be sung 'as if' by Dyer, rather as Spenser wrote the 'dolefull lay of Clorinda', appended to his *Astrophel* (1595), to be imagined as sung by the Countess of Pembroke. Once the 'dier' version has been read, its paradoxical play on Dyer dying and Sidney living lends a pointedness to the final elegy in Byrd's volume that is lacking in his printed version. One wonders how many more of the lyrics in such courtly collections as Byrd's may have had particular, personal connotations which were concealed from purchasers of the printed texts. Collaboration between Watson and Dyer would not be hard to envisage. According to Dyer's biographer, 'his allegiance seems to have been stronger to Secretary Walsingham than to any other courtier',[22] and by 1588, as we have seen, there can be little doubt that Watson too had come under Walsingham's protection.

The period 1586–90 saw the sudden endings of Sidney and all those to whom he was heir. Both his parents predeceased him, in the summer of 1586; his uncle, the Earl of Leicester, died in September 1588, his other uncle, the Earl of Warwick, in February 1590; and on 6 April 1590 Sidney's father-in-law, Sir Francis Walsingham, died, leaving his daughter an orphan as well as a widow. Three printed books that year signal Watson's double devotion to Walsingham and Sidney. First, Watson paid tribute to Walsingham and his son-in-law in a pastoral elegy in Latin, *Meliboeus*, dedicated to Thomas Walsingham. He avoided a repetition of his experience with *Amyntas* by making his own English version, *An Eglogue upon the death of the Right Honourable Sir Francis Walsingham*, which he dedicated to Sidney's widow, Walsingham's daughter. Very few printed dedications to Frances *née* Walsingham survive,[23] and she had to wait another five years before Spenser's belated tribute to Sidney, *Astrophel*, was addressed to her. Watson was explicit about his motives in translating his own elegy: 'I interpret my self, lest Meliboeus in speaking English by an other mans labour, should leese my name in his chaunge, as my *Amyntas* did'. He also offered a useful key to the meanings of his pastoral names:

I figure Englande in *Arcadia*; Her Majestie in *Diana*; Sir Francis Walsingham in *Meliboeus*, and his Ladie *Dryas*; Sir Phillipe Sidney in *Astrophill* and his Ladie in *Hyale*; Master Thomas Walsingham in *Tyterus*, and my selfe in *Corydon*.

We should remember that Sidney's *Astrophel and Stella* was not yet printed, so Watson's use of Sidney's poetic name, in the possibly more correct form 'Astrophill', confirms the suspicion aroused as early as *Hekatompathia* that

[22] R. M. Sargent, *At the Court of Queen Elizabeth: The Life and Lyrics of Sir Edward Dyer*, London, 1935, p. 91.
[23] According to F. B. Williams, *Index of Dedications and Commendatory Verses in English Books before 1641*, London, 1962, only three books were dedicated solely to Frances *née* Walsingham. Only one of the three, Jacques Le Moyne de Morgues's *La Clef des champs* (1586) is unrelated to Sidney. It is a picture-book of animals which might seem suited to her three-year-old daughter.

Watson had some knowledge of Sidney's poems. His elegy is in classical dialogue form, and ends with Christian consolation:

> His faith hath framd his spirit holie wings,
>   To soare with *Astrophil* above the Sun:
> And there he joies, whence every comfort springs,
>   and where the fulnesse of his blisse begun.

The poem ends with a plea to 'sweet Spencer' to celebrate the surviving great Elizabethan statesmen, Dametas (Hatton), Damon (Cecil) and Aegon (Howard). In the light of Watson's third and last publication in 1590, we may surmise that he felt that Spenser should devote himself to the cultivation of the elder statesmen, fast decaying, while he, Watson, turned his attention to the rising star. The most splendid of Watson's tributes to Sidney and his father-in-law are included in his last collaborative publication with Byrd, *Italian Madrigals Englished* (1590), but these elegies look as much to the present as to the past. The volume is dedicated to the Earl of Essex, whom Sidney had made his military heir in bequeathing to him his 'best sword',[24] and who married Sidney's widow shortly after her father's death, to the queen's chagrin. The fact that Sidney's widow had just re-married must surely have something to do with the extraordinarily sprightly tone of the tributes to Sidney in this volume. Song I, beginning 'When first my heedless eyes beheld with pleasure', is a variation on a theme from *Astrophel and Stella*; Stella sings, and celebrates her joy in Astrophel's wooing of her. Perhaps this cheerful adaptation of the names of Sidney's unhappy lovers is a wedding song for Essex and Frances Sidney, who might feel more entitled than anyone else to adopt those names. Song XIX, 'How long with vain complaining', written for a setting by Marenzio, is also relentlessly cheerful in both music and words, and has been thought puzzling in its effect as a lament for Sidney. However, if *Italian Madrigals Englished* was a wedding present for Essex, it would be highly appropriate to suggest, both musically and verbally, that the time for mourning is now over:

> Sweet Sidney lives in heaven, therefore let our weeping
> Be turned to hymns and songs of pleasant greeting.

If he was writing for Essex at the time of his marriage, it would be delicate, not tactless, for Watson to put such mirthful words to Marenzio's already mirthful music. Song XXIII, 'When Meliboeus' soul, flying hence, departed', is the most mirthful of all elegies on Sidney. Winifred Maynard points out that Tasso's original sonnet, set by Marenzio, was a love poem describing Amazons jousting, and thinks its theme of 'salutes between friends of the same sex' in a general way appropriate to this lyric on the heavenly encounter of father-in-law and son-in-law.[25] Perhaps it could be added that

---

[24] *Miscellaneous Prose*, p. 152.
[25] *Elizabethan Lyric Poetry and its Music*, Oxford, 1986, p. 44.

the Amazonian allusion, if picked up by the original audience, would also be apt for Sidney, whose hero Pyrocles in the *Arcadia* was disguised as an Amazon. Watson's lyric offers a picture of Sidney welcoming his father-in-law into heaven:

> Where, meeting with his friend, they both embraced,
> And both together joyfully were placed,
> O thrice happy pair of friends, O Arcady's treasure,
> Whose virtues drew them up to heavenly pleasure.

The real 'message' of this song, I suspect, is that the new Countess of Essex should feel no remorse or regret either for her first husband or for her father: they are happy in heaven, and she need have no sense of guilt about her new attachment. Song XXIV is a continuation of the same lyric on Meliboeus's apotheosis, but its consolation is addressed to 'Tityrus', i.e. Thomas Walsingham. Song XXVI, 'Love hath proclaimed war by trumpet sounded', warns 'Diana' (the queen) that her nymphs must be well guarded against the assaults of love; this could relate directly to the sudden marriage of her late Secretary's daughter. Song XXVII is another celebration of the heavenly joys of Walsingham and Sidney in heaven:

> worthy Meliboeus, even in a moment,
> With Astrophel was placed above the firmament.
> O they live both in pleasure,
> Where joys excel all measure.

Byrd's contribution to *Italian Madrigals Englished* (over and above his role as its publisher) was to furnish two settings, 'composed after the Italian vaine', of 'This sweet and merry month of May', addressed to the queen (Nos. VIII and XXVIII). These are described on the title-page as having been composed at Watson's request. We do not know the exact date of publication of *Italian Madrigals Englished*, but, since Walsingham had died only at the beginning of April 1590, it seems unlikely that the volume as a whole could have been ready as early as May. If the song was actually performed for the queen, it was probably before it reached print. Its refrain was used in the Elvetham entertainment the following year.[26] It is odd that one song should have received two different settings, though if any theme deserved such extra pains by the royal organist, the queen herself did. Watson may have been anxious that his lyrics should total 28, the number, according to Alastair Fowler, associated with 'virtue',[27] and a frequently recurring total in Elizabethan poetry—compare, for instance, Shakespeare's 'Dark Lady'

[26] *English Madrigal Verse*, p. 756.
[27] *Triumphal Forms: Structural Patterns in Elizabethan Poetry*, Cambridge, 1970, pp. 176–7.

sonnets.[28] It may have been in order to achieve this figure that Songs XXIII–XXIV, which are really continuous, were broken up into two, and the song to the queen set twice. Perhaps the volume as a whole was compiled with some haste, following the unexpected news of Essex's impending or actual marriage. The larger purpose of the twice-repeated 'This sweet and merry month of May' may have been to win royal approval for the volume as a whole, and in particular of its dedication to the newly wed Essex.[29] Just as there were hints in the preliminaries to *Hekatompathia* that Watson hoped that his poems might play a part in a reconciliation between Oxford and Sidney, there is a possibility here that *Italian Madrigals Englished* may have been intended to reconcile the queen to Essex's marriage. In neither case is it likely that the endeavour was effective. Nor is there any clear evidence that Watson succeeded in gaining favour with Essex or other survivors from the Sidney circle. His last employment was as a tutor with the Cornwallis family, who were recusants. By September 1592 he was dead.

Songs, which had punctuated important moments in Sidney's life and in particular his preparation for death, can be seen as marking also two distinct stages in the process of mourning for him. The two 'funeral songs' at the end of Byrd's *Psalms, Sonnets, & Songs* (1588), plausibly attributed to Watson, articulate the utter desolation felt by many of Sidney's closest friends in the immediate aftermath of his death. But Watson's three lyrics on Sidney and Walsingham in *Italian Madrigals Englished* (1590) mark a new stage in the development of grief. These cheerful lyrics, written for sprightly settings by Luca Marenzio, signal the moment when Sidney's widow, now an orphan, was ready to re-marry, and her husband, Sidney's military heir, was rising high in royal favour. Watson's songs can be seen as a propagandist celebration of Essex and his marriage. But for some surviving lovers of Sidney's memory 1590 may have been the most 'melancholie time' of all, for Essex was not a good husband, and he was eventually to leave Frances Walsingham a widow once more when he was executed in February 1601.

---

[28] See K. Duncan-Jones, 'Was the 1609 *Shake-speares Sonnets* really Unauthorized?', *Review of English Studies*, xxxiv (1983), 166.

[29] Essex's appearance in deep mourning for Sidney at the 1590 Accession Day Tilt (17 November) may also have been a bid for royal acceptance of his position as Sidney's successor 'in Love and Armes', as he is described in Peele's *Polyhymnia*; see D. H. Horne, *The Life and Minor Works of George Peele*, New Haven, 1952, pp. 235–6.

14

'And Who But Ladie Greensleeues?'

John M. Ward

GREEN SLEEVES, or WHICH NOBODY CAN DENY, has been, if we may judge by the constant allusions to it, a great favourite, from the time of Elizabeth down to the present; and it is still frequently to be heard in the streets of London, with the old burthen, 'Which nobody can deny'. It will also be easily recognized as the Air of CHRISTMAS COMES BUT ONCE A YEAR, and many another merry Song.[1]

IN the 1580s most of those who sang, whistled or played this most popular of English tunes must have known who the lady was and how her friend Donkin—if that was really his name—sought with extravagant gifts to win her love, and failed. After the young man's 'Courtly Sonet' had been answered by the lady, 'moralised to the Scripture' by an anonymous broadside poet, reprehended by another, and Green Sleeves described by a third ballad poet as 'worne awaie', few can have known that the tune was named after a lady. But although other names—'The Blacksmith', 'Which nobody can deny' and 'Bacca Pipes' among them—came to be associated with it, the tune has never lost what appears to be the first one it received.[2]

---

[1] William Chappell, *A Collection of National English Airs*, i (London, 1838), 38. As Iona & Peter Opie observe (*The Oxford Dictionary of Nursery Rhymes*, Oxford, 1951, p. 104), the line 'Christmas comes but once a year' 'was co-opted by the mummers for their Christmas entertainment'. It can still be heard in mummers' plays, but spoken, not sung. See, e.g., 'The Symondsbury Mumming Play', noted and recorded by Peter Kennedy, *Journal of the English Folk Dance and Song Society*, vii (1952), 3; also recording *The Songs of Christmas* ('The Folksongs of Britain', ix), Caedmon TC 1224, side A, band 12.

[2] On 3 September 1580 Richard Jones registered with the Stationers' Company 'A newe northen Dittye of ye Ladye Greene Sleves', probably the ballad reprinted in Jones's garland of 1584, *A Handefull of pleasant delites*, No. 7 (ed. Hyder Rollins, Cambridge, Mass., 1924, pp. 19–22). The same day Edward White registered 'ye Ladie Greene Sleves answere to Donkyn hir frende'. On 15 September Henry Carr entered 'Greene Sleves moralised to the Scripture Declaringe the manifold benefites and blessinges of God bestowed on sinfull manne'. Three days later White registered 'Greene Sleves and Countenaunce in Countenaunce is Greene Sleves'. On 14 December Jones registered 'a merry newe Northen songe of Greensleeves begynninge the boniest lasse in all the land' and on 13 February 1581 'A Reprehension againste Greene Sleves by William Elderton'. The list ended six months later with White's registration of 'Greene Sleves is worne awaie, Yellowe Sleeves Comme to decaie, Blacke

Describing with words the tune of 'Greensleeves' as written down during the decades around 1600 is not easy, for no two versions are note-for-note the same. Like almost all Elizabethan popular music, the tune was multiform, circulated without the constraints of print. One learnt it from balladmongers, tavern fiddlers, whistling apprentices, copied it from a friend's book of lute lessons; that is, picked it up in much the way those with an appreciation of the common muse acquired the musical ephemera of the day, casually.

The tune was simple enough to remember. Some versions consist of a single strain, most of two almost identical strains. Small differences apart —some begin with an anacrusis, several do not; half are in 4/4, half in 6/8 time, or their equivalents[3]—all of the versions have in common eight-bar strains in which bars 1 and 2 are the same as bars 5 and 6, or nearly so. When a version consists of two strains, the second usually differs from the first only in bars 1 and 5. The relationship between them can be illustrated by the tune as it appeared in William Cobbold's 'New Fashions' (Ex. 14.1):[4]

1st strain:	1	2	3	4	1	2	5	6
2nd strain:	7	2	3	4	7	2	5	6

Ex. 14.1

Sleeves I holde in despite, But White Sleeves is my delighte'. H. E. Rollins, *An Analytical Index to the Ballad-Entries (1557–1709) in the Registers of the Company of Stationers of London*, Chapel Hill, 1924 (repr. Hatboro, 1967), Nos. 1892, 1390, 1051, 1049, 1742, 2276, 1050. At least two broadside ballads of the 1580s were set to the tune of 'Greensleeves'; see Claude Simpson, *The British Broadside Ballad and Its Music*, New Brunswick, 1966, pp. 269–70, for details of these and other ballads sung to the tune.

[3] In the classified chronological list of all the versions of 'Greensleeves' known to the writer, appended to this paper, those in duple time include I.A.1, 2; B.1, 2; D.1; E.1; II.A.1, 2, 3, 4 etc.; those in compound time I.C.1, 2; II.B.1; C,1, 2 etc.

[4] Appendix I.E.1. Except for the change of tense, the first quatrain is identical with the refrain of the ballad printed by Jones; the second quatrain belongs to an otherwise unknown 'Greensleeves' ballad.

In addition, all versions share an underlying tonal framework, for 'Greensleeves' is a harmonic pattern in the form of a tune, in essence little more than an arpeggiated form of the romanesca (see Ex. 14.2c). When a version consists of two strains, the first sometimes begins with an older pattern, the one known as the passamezzo antico, which differs from the romanesca in its first note, occasionally also its fifth (see Ex. 14.2b). A few of the earliest settings of 'Greensleeves' begin with a mixed bar, half

Ex. 14.2

passamezzo antico, half romanesca.[5] An early seventeenth-century setting
for keyboard in Oxford, Christ Church, MS Mus. 92, is typical of a
double-strain version, one in which the chords established by the bass
pattern are baldly stated in the left hand and melodically elaborated in the
right (Ex. 14.2).[6]

'Greensleeves' was so closely identified with the romanesca that the name
sometimes accompanies settings that do not include the tune. For example, a
single statement of the harmonic pattern, without time values indicated,
appears alongside similar harmonic schemes in the Ridout commonplace

Ex. 14.3

[5] Neither bass pattern is English in origin; both date from the beginning of the sixteenth
century, if not earlier; and both acquired English names, as did other important Continental
bass patterns: for example, the passamezzo moderno became the 'Quadrant Pavan', its ¢
version 'John, come kiss me now'; the **C** version of the passamezzo antico became the
'Passing-measures Pavan', and the romanesca 'Greensleeves'. Versions of 'Greensleeves' set to
the romanesca include: I.A.1, 2; B.1; II.C.1, 2; D.1; E.1: 1685 ff., *c*.1730 (var.); F.1. Those set
to the passamezzo antico in strain 1, the romanesca in strain 2, include I.C.1; II.D.2; III.A.10:
1792; B.1; C.1; those with a mixed first bar, I.C.1; D.1; II.A.1, 2, 3, 4; B.1; G.1; those set to
free basses, I.C.2 (with passages based on the two grounds); E.1; II.H.1. Vars. 1 & 2 of II.E.1:
Balcarres are set to the romanesca, 3-7 the passamezzo antico.

[6] Appendix II.D.2, published with the permission of the Governing Body of Christ Church,
Oxford.

book.[7] How such raw material could be vamped into music can be seen in a set of three variations entitled 'Green-Sleeves. With division', the earliest known printed versions of 'Greensleeves', in John Playford's *A Book of New Lessons for the Cithern and Gittern* (1652) (Ex. 14.3).[8] The first of the variations is nothing more than the Ridout scheme with time values added, the second a figural enlivening of the chords; only the third variation contains a version of the 'Greensleeves' tune.

Both horizontal and vertical aspects of 'Greensleeves' are exploited in a much reprinted and copied set of fifteen divisions for violin first published by Playford in 1686 (see Ex. 14.4).[9] The anonymous work opens with a version of the double-strain tune, the two strains separated by a varied reprise of the first. There follows a string of twelve variations having nothing more in common than the romanesca harmonies; the tune is not referred to again. The pairing of variations with which the set begins does not recur; each self-contained variation has its own figural pattern, relentlessly pursued, the second half rigidly paralleling the first. The lack of a meaningful ordering, either musical or technical, of the fifteen divisions was recognized by at least one contemporary, a lute teacher active in Edinburgh during the 1690s, who incorporated six of the divisions in his set of nine, reordering the borrowed material in such a way that adjacent variations share a figure, occupy a similar position on the instrument or relate in some other way, the nine sections progressing from longer to shorter note values.[10]

The contents of *The Division-Violin* are described by the publisher as 'A Consort of Music which do not require many hands to perform'. In fact only two instrumentalists are required, one to play the divisions, the other the 'bassus' part (instrument unspecified) which provides the ground to each set. No accompaniment is actually required for 'Greensleeves': each division is self-sufficient, a précis of the essential notes of the chordal pattern differently arranged. As with any kind of music, context and performer determined the

[7] Harvard University, Houghton Library, MS * 79M-44 (4), f. [67]. The chordal patterns comprise the first eight cittern pieces in the MS and include 'Trenchmore', 'John come kisse me now' (= the ₵ passamezzo moderno), 'Seleingers [*sic*] Round', 'Halfe Hanikinge' (= a variant form of the ₵ passamezzo moderno), 'The hunt is up', 'Passamesures Galliard' (= the romanesca!) and 'Blame not my lute' (= the *Cara cosa* form of the folia). The tablatures are printed in John Ward, 'Sprightly & Cheerful Musick', *Lute Society Journal*, xxi (1983), 183–5.

[8] Appendix II.C.1. In *The First and Second Parts of the Division-Violin*, London (Wright), c.1730, f. 9, four tuneless figural outlinings of the chordal pattern are entitled 'New Greensleeves a Ground'.

[9] Appendix II.E.1; *The Division-Violin*, 'Green Sleeves', divisions 1 & 3. A similar set of divisions added about the same time in manuscript to a copy of Christopher Simpson's *The Division-Violist* (see Appendix II.F.1) begins with the ground, stated in minims; the tune of 'Greensleeves', double-strain version, constitutes the second and third divisions, disappears thereafter, figurations of the romanesca harmonies taking over, as in *The Division-Violin*.

[10] Appendix III.D.1. The first two divisions present a version of the double-strain tune set to the romanesca bass; the remaining seven are set to the ₵ passamezzo antico. Nos. 3–7 and 9 = Playford's Nos. 4, 11, 10, 15, 6 and 9, with occasional small differences.

way the notes were played. When David Young made a copy of the piece for Walter McFarlane's book of violin music at some time in the 1740s he left out the bassus part;[11] and when the Edinburgh lute teacher adapted six of the divisions for his instrument, he provided a single-line bass (chords occur only in the last bar of each variation) and substituted the passamezzo antico for the romanesca. Other sets from *The Division-Violin* were copied into manuscripts of the period, some with, some without the ground, some with a different ground, those arranged for keyboard with the harmonies spelled out, variation in the music begetting variation in the performance.[12]

The divisions on 'Greensleeves' published by Playford are player's and listener's music, distinct from the double-strain version of the tune included in the same publisher's *The Dancing Master*, 7th edition, 1686, and continuously in print for the next half century, which is music to accompany action.[13] The country-dance version is a bit livelier, in part smoother, and in the middle bars of its second strain more dramatic than the version in *The Division-Violin*, whose second strain is less tune and more figuration, thanks to the sequencing in bars 2–4 and echoed in bar 6 (Ex. 14.4).

Like the rest of the tunes in *The Dancing Master*, 'Green-Sleeves and Pudding-Pies' (the title given to the country-dance version) is advertised on the title-page of all editions as 'for the Treble-Violin', occasionally 'for the violin or flute' and once 'for Violin or Hautboy.' No bass parts are included, nor were they required, if we are to believe the title-page engraving, which depicts fiddlers providing music for the dancers. Bass parts were advertised as available from the publisher on the title-pages of the fifteenth and later editions, but no copy of them appears to survive, perhaps because they were in manuscript, not printed, and there was little request for them. What they

---

[11] Appendix II.E.1: McFarlane.

[12] The Balcarres MS (Appendix II.E.1) also contains arrangements of No.1, 'Readings ground' (= a form of the ciaccona ostinato; see Thomas Walker, 'Ciaccona and Passacaglia: Remarks on their Origin and Early History', *Journal of the American Musicological Society*, xxi (1968), 317 & *passim*; also Margaret Gilmore's 'Concordances' to the facs. edn. of Playford's *The Division Violin*, London, 1982), No. 4, 'Old Simon the King', No. 7, 'Tollets Ground', and No. 23, 'Johney Cock thy Beaver'; for details see Matthew Spring, 'The Lute in England and Scotland after the Golden Age 1620–1750' (dissertation), University of Oxford, 1986, pp. 334–43.

Twice in *A General History of the Science and Practice of Music* (1776) Hawkins writes disparagingly of the kind of music found in Playford's *Division Violin*. In his account (Book IV, pp. 380–81) of music heard in 'music-houses' in the time of Charles II (his source was the writings of man-about-town Ned Ward) he describes it as mostly 'that of violins, hautboys, or trumpets, without any diversity of parts, and consequently in the unison; or if at any time a bass instrument was added, it was only for the purpose of playing the ground-bass to those divisions on old ballad or country-dance tunes [he includes 'Green Sleeves' among them] which at that time were the only music that pleased the common people.' All of the illustrative examples Hawkins includes in the appendix to Book V, pp. 469–74, are first divisions of sets printed in *The Division-Violin*. I doubt if Playford's contemporaries would have read the evidence the same way.

[13] Appendix II.E.2.

Ex. 14.4

Ex. 14.5

may have been like can be seen in a copy of Pippard's *A Hundred and Twenty Country Dances for the Flute* (1711), to which a former owner has added unfigured basses to several of the tunes.[14] The first strain of 'Green-Sleeves and Pudding Pies' (the Playford tune transposed up a fourth) is set to a form of the passamezzo antico, the second to a poor substitute for the romanesca (Ex. 14.5).

I doubt if Playford's basses were much used by professional dance

---

[14] British Library shelf-mark b.49. The basses are added to Nos. 15, 19, 39, 58, 62, 79, 85, 88, 89, 91, 96, 99, 110 ('Green-Sleeves and Pudding Pies').

musicians, who were more likely to *'vamp a base* upon all occasions', as did the Shrewsbury town wait Burney recalled hearing early in his musical life. Since Burney's 'ears were seldom much offended by the dissonance', he supposed the man, who was unable to read music, 'by habit . . . contrived at least to begin and end in the right key, and was quick in pursuing accidental modulation'.[15]

Though it disappears from the country-dance books after the 1730s, the 'Pudding Pies' form of 'Greensleeves' continues to appear in occasional publications of fiddle and/or flute music—Oswald's *The Caledonian Pocket Companion* in the mid eighteenth century, Howe's *Second Part of the Musician's Companion* in 1850, Captain O'Neill's *The Dance Music of Ireland* in 1907, to name but three—and in the musical commonplace books of Scottish, Irish, English and American country musicians, the first strain identical or nearly so with Playford's, the second strain often varied, but never enough to obscure its derivation.[16]

Around the turn of the nineteenth century morris sides adopted the tune for one of their dances. The result was a distinctive form of the 'Greensleeves' tune, one usually called 'Bacca Pipes', after the crossed white-clay tobacco pipes over which the dance is performed. 'Bacca Pipes' is a slimmed-down form of the old tune, which gives the gist in roughly half the number of notes

Ex. 14.6

[15] *A General History of Music*, iii (London, 1789), 102 n. According to Vaughan Williams (*Journal of the [English] Folk-Song Society*, iv (1910), 64), 'generations of Castleton [Derbyshire] carol-singers were in the habit of adding "basses" to their carol-tunes'. And in the present century extemporary basses have been a speciality of the folk-singing Copper family of Rottingdean, Sussex, and can be heard in an album of recordings, *A Song for Every Season* (Leader LEAB 404), and seen in a book of the same title by Bob Copper (London, 1971), pp. 198–288 *passim*.

[16] Appendix III.E.1–19; IV.B.1–7; V.C.3–4.

Ex. 14.7

required for the country-dance form and substitutes liveliness for elegance. More than half the versions collected by Cecil Sharp, the chief authority for the morris dance in the first decades of this century, are in duple time, often in a jigging dotted rhythm (Ex. 14.6a),[17] the rest trochaic in compound time (Ex. 14.6b).[18] Sometimes Sharp notated a tune one way in his notebook and another when publishing it, which suggests that players sometimes per-

[17] Appendix V.C.13.
[18] Appendix V.C.7.

formed it one way, sometimes another, and sometimes somewhere in between.[19]

During the first century and a half of its recorded history 'Greensleeves' was the third most frequently named of the 1,766-plus broadside ballad tunes of which we have knowledge.[20] No particular form of the tune appears to have established itself as a favourite before the end of the seventeenth century. Ballads simply carried the rubric 'to the tune of "Greensleeves"' or something like, the assumption being everybody knew it. In the 1680s two forms began to appear in songsters, one the double-strain country-dance version known from Playford's *Dancing Master* (but without the 'Pudding Pies' in its title),[21] the other the far more popular ten-bar version that went variously by the name of 'The Blacksmith', after a ballad of that name, 'Which nobody can deny', after the refrain line of the same ballad and others sung to the tune, and the names of a great many ballads patterned after the original.[22]

James Smith's ballad 'The Blacksmith' appeared in print for the first time in *Wit and Drollery* (1656), but without music or the naming of a tune; it was reissued almost immediately with the tune identified as 'Greensleeves'. Only 30 years later was the distinctive form of the tune associated with the ballad printed, first in *The Second Part of the Pleasant Companion*, thereafter numerous times in D'Urfey's *Wit and Mirth: or, Pills to Purge Melancholy* and in several ballad operas.

A similar text and a variant form of 'The Blacksmith' tune occur together much earlier, in John Gamble's commonplace book, New York Public Library MS Drexel 4257, whose title-page is dated 1659;[23] but the relationship of this song to the ballad published by Playford is problematic. The melody (Ex. 14.7a), set to the romanesca bass (with the g–$b^\flat$ first bar), lacks the two-bar extension that distinguishes the 'Blacksmith' branch of the 'Greensleeves' tune family; and the text begins with a paraphrase of Smith's

---

[19] Of the 'Greensleeves'/'Bacca Pipes' tunes Sharp collected, six are in even note values in 2/4 (Sharp MSS, Clare College Library, Cambridge, pp. 1276, 2144, 2262, 2327, 2356), seven in dotted 2/4 (pp. 2062, 2187, 2305, 2789, 2378, 4968) and eight in 6/8 (pp. 1255, 1499, 1506, 1514, 2170, 2415, 2751, 2807). Those notated in 2/4 in the MSS and published in 6/8 are on p. 1276 (= *Morris Dance Tunes*, iv. 4) and p. 2262 (= v. 28).

[20] Roy Lamson, Jr., 'English Broadside Ballad Tunes of the 16th and 17th Centuries', *American Musicological Society: Congress Report New York, 1939*, ed. Arthur Mendel and others, New York, 1944, p. 144: 'A study . . . of 1,766 tunes reveals that 31 tunes appear in connection with 20 or more extant ballads up to 1700'. Of this top 31 only 'Packington's Pound', with 99, and 'Fortune my foe', with 91, appear more often than 'Greensleeves', with 80. Lamson provides full bibliographical details in 'English Broadside Ballad Tunes, 1550–1700' (dissertation), Harvard University, 1936.

[21] D'Urfey presents the tune twice (III.A.3, 9) in its Playford form, once (III.A.7) somewhat varied.

[22] Appendix II.G.2–3; III.A.2, 4–6, 8. Simpson, *The Broadside Ballad*, pp. 273–7, has an extended account of the different ballads associated with this form of the tune.

[23] Appendix II.G.1.

stanzas 1 and 4, continues with a third not found in his ballad, and breaks off after the first two words of a fourth stanza.

Gamble MS

1. Of all the Scienses vnder the sunn
   which haue beene since the world begunn
   a smith by his arte great praise hath wonn
   which noe body can deny.
2. The fairest goddess in the skyes
   To marry Vulcan did devise
   which was a cunning smith and wise
   which nobody can deny.
3. Then Mars cam downe for Venus sake
   And Vulcan did his Armor make
   In loue together he did them take
   which nobody &c
4. for he [poem breaks off]

Wit and Mirth

1. Of all the trades that ever I see,
   Ther's none with the *Blacksmith* compar'd may be,
   With so many several tools works hee,
      Which Nobody can deny.
4. The fairest Goddess in the Skies,
   To Marry with *Vulcan* did advise;
   And he was a *Blacksmith* Grave and Wise
   Which no Body &c.

The Gamble text may be the panegyric that inspired Smith's ballad; or it may be a polite rendering of the subject matter of 'The Blacksmith', abandoned after a few stanzas; it is certainly a different poem, or, rather, fragment of one, and not a variant of the ballad. The tune, however, belongs to the 'Blacksmith' branch of the 'Greensleeves' family, few of whose versions are

Ex. 14.8

note-for-note the same. Their multiformity, like that of other forms of the
family tune, is typical of urban popular music, and was in no way inhibited
by being continuously in print for more than half a century (see Exx.
14.7*b–d*).[24]

One of the few forms of 'Greensleeves' not always recognized (it escaped
Simpson, but not Chappell) is 'Tak' your auld cloak about you', whose
earliest recorded appearance is in Oswald's *The Caledonian Pocket Companion, c.*1755 (Ex. 14.8).[25] Both of its strains are divisions to the
romanesca ground, but none of those who set the tune recognized this fact,
least of all Haydn, whose elegant two- and three-voice counterpoint and

Ex. 14.9

[24] Appendix II.G.2, 3, 'The Blacksmith'; II.B.3, 4, 5, 'Which nobody can deny'; II.B.2,
'Which nobody can deny'.

[25] Appendix III.A.1. In a jig composed at the very end of 1601 and performed in several
parts of Yorkshire during the first half of 1602 the third scene is 'To the tune of *take thy old
Cloake about thee*'. The piece is printed in C. J. Sisson, *Lost Plays of Shakespeare's Age*,
Cambridge, 1936, pp. 135–40.

slight alterations in the melodic line (I assume they are his) to accommodate his harmonies have nothing in common with the old Renaissance bass pattern and the chords it generates.

Texts associated with Christmas and New Year were early set to 'Greensleeves', and this association has endured.[26] Before 1800 the evidence is verbal, words directed to be sung to the tune. In the nineteenth century words and music appear together in almost every one of the many printed collections of carols containing notes, some texts beginning 'As I sat on a sunny bank', others 'I saw three ships come sailing in', still others 'Dame, get up and bake your pies' and 'There was a pig went out to dig', all of their respective stanzas ending with the refrain 'On Christmas day in the morning' (see Ex. 14.9). The abac form of the quatrains parallels that of the 'Greensleeves' tune, as does the repetition of words from line a in line b and the repetition in bars 3 and 4 of elements from bars 1 and 2 of the tune, which suggests that the music came first, the words after; none of the other carols collected and published has anything like the same musical or textual pattern.[27]

Ex. 14.10

[26] Appendix V.A.3; also *New Christmas Carols* (*c.*1686), 'Another for Christmas-day at Night'.
[27] Appendix IV.A.1–9.

Like the 'Bacca Pipes' branch, what might be called the 'Sunny Bank' branch of the 'Greensleeves' family is a pared down form (Gilchrist describes it as 'denuded') of the old tune, jigs it rhythmically and matches with sequences the iterations of the carol texts.[28] Despite its frequent appearance in print, the shape of the 'Sunny Bank' tune remained remarkably variable. Printed versions, most of them collected from traditional singers, are multiform, identical versions the result of one editor's borrowing from another.

Presumably it was the association with a popular Christmas song and the simplicity of its tune that account for the appearance of the 'Sunny Bank' form of 'Greensleeves' in so many children's game songs, 'Here we go round the mulberry bush' and 'Here come three dukes a-riding' among the best known.[29] These share the 1 2 3 4 1 2 5 6 form, tonal contours and 6/8 time of the tune family and the a b a c (or a a a c) quatrain of the carol; in some instances music of carol and game song is identical, or nearly so.

Most of the carol and game songs differ from one another in the way each relates to the old bass patterns that begat the family. Ex. 14.10a fits the romanesca,[30] b the passamezzo antico;[31] c is a hybrid, the first half of bar 2 an extension of bar 1, the second half belonging to the romanesca.[32] Exx. 10d–f are versions in which the implied chords are chiefly tonic and dominant;[33] the tonal shape of the tune, while retaining the 'Greensleeves' contours, has been simplified.

The version of 'Greensleeves' that goes by the family name in the twentieth century is one written down sometime at the end of the sixteenth century by the unknown compiler of the so-called 'Ballet' lute book. It remained buried in Trinity College Library, Dublin, from early in the seventeenth century until disinterred by William Chappell, who published a diplomatic copy of the tablature and a transcription in staff notation in 1840, and again in 1855.[34] Thirty years later Bramley and Stainer published the tune coupled

---

[28] Anne G. Gilchrist, 'The Three Kings of Cologne (I saw Three Ships) and a Nursery Song, *Cuddy Alone*, With Some Notes on Refrains', *Journal of the English Folk Dance and Song Society*, v (1946), 38.

[29] Appendix IV.A.11–50. An actual joining of carol and children's game song is reported by a correspondent in *The Gentleman's Magazine*, n.s., XVI/1 (1823), 507–8, who quotes 'the song of "London Bridge is fallen down," which in . . . [his] remembrance, formed part of a Christmas Carol, and commenced thus: "Dame get up and bake your pies, On Christmas day in the morning," etc. The requesition goes on to the dame to prepare for the feast, and her answer "London Bridge is fallen down On Christmas-day in the morning," etc.' The writer adds, as well he might: 'why the falling of London Bridge should form part of a Christmas Carol at Newcastle-upon-Tyne, I am at a loss to know.'

[30] Appendix IV.A.4, 'Christmas day in the morning', first strain.

[31] Appendix IV.A.27, 'Milking Pails'.

[32] Appendix IV.A.6: Sandys, 'I saw three ships'.

[33] Appendix IV.A.1: Folktracks, 'As I sat on a sunny bank'; IV.A.33: Gomme, 'Poor Mary sits a-weeping'; IV.A.5: Bruce & Stokoe, 'Dame, get up and bake your pies', first strain.

[34] See Appendix I.C.1.

with W. C. Dix's verses, 'What child is this', in what became the most popular and influential collection of Christmas carols in a century much given to the production of such volumes.[35] Thereafter, in sources too numerous to list, the 'Ballet' version became *the* 'Greensleeves' tune.[36]

What is striking about this history of 'Greensleeves' is the way in which oral and written transmission have gone in tandem, the one feeding the other, throughout the four centuries the tune family has been kept alive. Byrd, the unknown compiler of the 'Ballet' lute book and their contemporaries acquired their versions, the earliest preserved, as have most of those who sang or played the tune over the years, either by ear or by copying from someone else who had. Printed books—*The Dancing Master* and *Pills to Purge Melancholy* among them—were responsible for the wide distribution and long life of specific forms of the tune. Ritual and seasonal associations established the 'Bacca Pipes' and 'Sunny Bank' branches. Oral transmission kept the tune variable, print established a few basic shapes. The resurrected 'Ballet' version has come near to pre-empting variation from the tradition, but not quite. One occasionally hears a traditional musician's version, like that of Stephen Baldwin, the village fiddler recorded by Peter Kennedy sometime in the 1950s, and a set of divisions like that of John Coltrane, recorded a decade or two later.[37]

Perhaps most surprising in this history of a tune family is the persistence of a Renaissance bass pattern and the tune it spawned, the underlying structure so firmly in place that one spots the romanesca even in the notes of a children's game song. It is clearly the presence of this tonal scaffolding, not always recognized by those who have made use of the tune—for example Vaughan Williams and Busoni in their respective operas—[38] that has discouraged the sometimes radical variation found in tune families untouched by harmonic restraints.[39]

[35] See Appendix IV.A.10 n.

[36] It is cited in this form, for example, in James Field, *The Book of World-Famous Music*, New York, 1966, p. 216.

[37] Appendix V.C.2; D.1.

[38] Appendix V.A.4–5a.

[39] I agree with Samuel Bayard ('A Miscellany of Tune Notes', *Studies in Folklore*, ed. W. Edson Richmond, Bloomington, 1957, p. 153) that 'The Delight of the men of Dovey' in Edward Jones' *Musical and Poetical Relicks of the Welsh Bards*, London, 1794, p. 129, is not 'an inferior copy of "Green Sleeves"', as proposed by Chappell (*Popular Music of the Olden Time*, i. 64 n.), but a version of 'Woodicock', found, e.g., in Playford's *The English Dancing Master*, 1650, p. 15, and elsewhere. But I cannot agree with Bayard (*Dance to the Fiddle, March to the Fife*, University Park, 1982, p. 550) that 'Johnny McGill', found, e.g., in Niel Gow & Sons' *Part First of the Complete Repository*, Edinburgh, [1799], p. 28, is a member of the 'Greensleeves' family; too many of the diagnostic features are lacking.

APPENDIX

'Greensleeves': a classified chronological list of versions

(Unless otherwise stated, the title of the piece is some form of 'Greensleeves', and the place of publication of works cited is London.)

I. SIXTEENTH CENTURY

A. For instrumental ensemble

1. William Byrd, 'Fantasia' *a 6* (*c.*1580s). For the dating, see Oliver Neighbour, *The Consort and Keyboard Music of William Byrd*, 1978, p. 79; for the sources, Warwick Edwards, 'The Sources of Elizabethan Consort Music' (dissertation), University of Cambridge, 1974, ii. 33–4; for the music, *The Collected Works of William Byrd*, vii: *The Consort Music*, ed. Kenneth Elliott, 1971, pp. 87–8.
2. *GB-Cu*, MSS Dd. 5.30 (bass viol), f. 6, and Dd. 5.21 (treble violin), f. 10 (*c.*1585). The rest of the instrumental parts appear to be lacking.

B. For two lutes

1. *US-Ws*, MS V.b.280 (olim 1610.1; *c.*1590s), f. 5, 'the terble [*sic*] to grien slivis', and 'the ground to grien slivis'. 5 vars. A diplomatic copy is in *12 Duets of Anonymous Elizabethan Composers*, ed. Nigel North ('Tablature for Two Lutes', i), 1983, No. 1; transcription in John Ward, 'Music for *A Handefull of pleasant delites*', *Journal of the American Musicological Society*, x (1957), 156 (errata: bar 2, note 3, *f* not *b♭*; 5th var., last bar, *b♮*). Library of Robert Spencer, the Mynshall MS, ff. 3–3ᵛ, treble part. Facs. in *Reproductions of Early Music*, iii (Leeds, 1975); comprises vars. 1, 4, 2 and a variant of 5.
2. *GB-Cu*, MS Dd. 3.18, (*c.*1595), ff. 8ᵛ–9, treble part only. 24 vars. (1–16 in 4/4; 17–24 in 6/4).

C. For solo lute

1. *EIRE-Dtc*, MS D.1.21/i (the 'Ballet' MS, *c.*1590s), p. 104. 2 vars. Diplomatic copy in William Chappell, *A Collection of National English Airs*, ii (1840), frontispiece; transcription on p. 118; also *The Ballad Literature and Popular Music of Olden Time*, i (1855), 233; repr. in Oscar Chilesotti, *Lautenspieler des XVI. Jahrhunderts*, Leipzig, 1891, p. 17. Facs., reconstruction of the tablature and transcription in *Elizabethan Popular Music*, ed. Brian Jeffery ('Music for the Lute', 1), 1968, p. 11.
2. *GB-Lbm*, Add. MS 31392, f. 29, Francis Cutting. 4 vars. Facs. and transcription in Jeffery, 1968, p. 12.

D. For cittern

1. *GB-Cu*, MS Dd. 4.23 (*c.*1595), f. 25. 2 vars.

E. For voices & instruments

1. William Cobbold, 'New Fashions', *a 5*. *GB-Lbm*, Add. MS 18936 (cantus), ff. 58–58ᵛ; *GB-Lcm*, MS 684 (cantus), f. 94ᵛ. Pr. in *Consort*

Songs, ed. Philip Brett ('Musica Britannica', xxii), 1967, pp. 158–60, bars 48–60; also Ex. 14.1 above.

II. SEVENTEENTH CENTURY

A. For solo lute

1. *NL-Lt*, MS 133.K.63 ('Luitboek van Johan Thysius', *c.*1600), f. 390, 'Gruen sleefs ey touiou met all myn here'. 4 vars.
2. Ibid., f. 390ᵛ, 'Greene sleeves is al my joye'. 4 vars. Tablature & transcription in *English Ballad Tunes for the Lute*, ed. Diana Poulton ('The Cambridge Lute Series', ii), 1965, No. 9.
3. Ibid., ff. 390ᵛ–391, no title. 2 vars.
4. Joachim vanden Hove, *Florida*, Utrecht, 1601, f. 107ᵛ, 'Griensliefs'. 2 vars.

B. For bandora

1. Vilnius, Centrine Biblioteka, TSR Moslu Akademijos MS F15/285 (olim Königsberg, Staatsarchiv MS A 116 fol.), f. 40. Consort part.

C. For cittern

1. *A Booke of New Lessons for the Cithern & Gittern* (Playford, 1652), p. 31. 3 vars.
2. *US-CA*, MS *79M-44 (John Ridout's commonplace book), f. [67]. Tablature pr. in John Ward, 'Sprightly and Cheerful Musick', *Lute Society Journal*, xxi (1983), 184.

D. For keyboard

1. *F-Pn*, MS Rés. 1186, f. 101. 2 vars. Pr. *English Pastime Music, 1630–1660*, ed. Martha Maas (Collegium Musicum, Yale University, 2nd ser., iv), Madison, 1974, p. 58. *US-NYp*, Drexel MS 5609, p. 71, is an 18th-century copy of the piece.
2. *GB-Och*, Mus. MS 92, f. 3. 2 vars. Ex. 14.2.

E. For violin

1. *The Division-Violin*, 2nd edn. (Playford, 1685), No. 27, 'Green Sleeves, to a Ground with Division'. 16 vars. Also ibid., 3rd edn. (1688), No. 27, 'A Division on a Ground, call'd Green-sleeves and Pudding-pyes'; ibid., 4th edn. (1695); ibid., 5th edn. (1701); *The First Part of the Division Flute* (Walsh, 1706), ff. 9–10 (transposed up a fourth; 'ground bass' printed as 1st var.); *The First and Second Books of the Division Violin* (Young, *c.*1710), No. 10, 'Green Sleves to a Ground with a Division in Gamut b 3d'; *The First and Second Division Violin* (Wright, *c.*1730), No. 4, 'Green Sleves to a Ground'; *GB-En*, MS 2084 (Walter Mc'Farlane's MS, *c.*1740), pp. 258–61 (vars. 2–16). *GB-Mr*, Balcarres lute book (*c.*1700), pp. 62–3, 'Green sleeves, with the 9ᵗʰ string lowered, halfe a note, by mʳ beck'. 9 vars. (vars. 3–7, 9 = Playford's Nos. 4, 11, 10, 15, 6 and 9, with small differences).
2. *The Dancing Master*, 7th edn. (Playford, 1686), p. 186, 'Green-Sleeves and Pudding-Pies'. Also ibid., 8th edn. (1690), p. 172; ibid., 9th edn. (1695), p. 113; ibid., 10th edn. (1698); ibid., 11th edn. (1701); ibid., 12th edn. (1703); 13th edn. (1706); 14th edn. (1709); *A Hundred and*

Twenty Country Dances for the Flute (Pippard, 1711), p. 29, No. 110
(transposed up a fourth); *The Dancing Master*, 15th edn. (1713), p.
113; ibid., 16th edn. (1716); *The Compleat Country Dancing-Master*
(Walsh, 1718), p. 113; *The Dancing Master*, 17th edn. (1721), p. 113,
'Green Sleeves and Yellow Lace'; ibid., 18th edn. (post-1728); *The
Compleat Country Dancing-Master* (Walsh, 1731), p. 36, 'Green
Sleeves and Pudding Pyes'; ibid., 3rd edn. (1735).

The two forms of the title come from popular verses associated with the tune,
versions of which were written down sometime in the late 18th century by
David Herd, folksong collector. The first stanza reads:

> Green sleeves and pudden-pyes,
> Come tell me where my true love lyes,
> And I'll be wi' her ere she rise:
> Fidle a' the gither!

And the third stanza reads:

> Green sleeves and yellow lace,
> Maids, maids, come, marry apace!
> The batchleors are in a pitiful case
> To fiddle a' the gither.

Songs from David Herd's Manuscripts, ed. Hans Hecht, Edinburgh, 1904, p.
177.

3. *The Compleat Country Dancing-Master*, ii (1719), 151, 'Buckingham
   House. Longways for as many as will'.

F. For viol
   1. *GB-Lcm*, MS adds. to Christopher Simpson, *The Division-Violist*,
      1659, pp. 114–16. 16 vars.

G. Texted single songs
   1. *US-NYp*, MS Drexel 4257 (John Gamble's musical commonplace
      book, dated 1659), No. 121, 'Of all the Scienses under the sunn'. Ex.
      14.7a.
   2. *The Second Book of the Pleasant Musical Companion*, 2nd edn.
      (Playford, 1686), sig. M^v–M2, 'A Song made on the Power of Women.
      To the Tune of the Blacksmith', beg. 'Will you give me leave, and I'le tell
      you a Story'.
      Repr. without the music in *Wit and Mirth: or Pills to Purge Melancholy*, 1699,
      pp. 41–3, to the tune of 'The Blacksmith'; also ibid., 2nd edn. (1705); ibid., i,
      3rd edn. (1707); ibid., 4th edn. (1714); ibid., iii, 3rd edn. (1712), 27–9; ibid.,
      (1719).
   3. *Wit and Mirth: or, Pills to Purge Melancholy*, 1699, pp. 28–31, 'Of all
      the Trades that ever I see'; also ibid., i, 2nd edn. (1705); ibid., 3rd edn.
      (1707); ibid., 4th edn. (1714); *Songs Compleat, Pleasant and Diver-
      tive*, iii (1719), 20; *Wit and Mirth*, iii (1719).
      Sung to the same tune, the music printed elsewhere in the volume: (1) 'There's
      many Clinching Verse is made', *Wit and Mirth* (1699), pp. 32–4; ibid., 2nd edn.
      (1705); ibid., i (1707); ibid., 4th edn. (1714); ibid., iii, 3rd edn. (1712), 24–6;
      ibid. (1719); (2) 'I'll tell you a Story if it be true', in the same sources, pp.
      140–43, 121–4 respectively; (3) 'I'll sing you a Sonnet that ne'er was in Print',
      same sources, pp. 156–8, 138–40 resp.; (4) 'You talk of New England, I truly
      believe', same sources, pp. 139–40, 119–21 resp.; (5) 'A late Expedition to

Oxford was made', *Wit and Mirth*, Part II (1700), 176–8; ibid., ii, 2nd edn. (1707); ibid., 3rd edn. (1712); *Songs Compleat*, iv (1719), 174–6; *Wit and Mirth*, iv (1719); (6) 'Prey lend me your Ear if you've any to spare', in the same sources, pp. 24–5, 18–19 resp.; (7) 'Let's Sing as one may say the Fate', *Wit and Mirth*, v (1714), 91–4; ibid., vi (1720), 226–9; (8) 'A World that's full of Fools and Madmen', *Wit and Mirth*, v (1714), 151–3; ibid., vi (1720), 229–31.

The 'Blacksmith' tune found in the 'Ballet' MS, p. 84, the Boteler MS (*US-CA*, MS *79M-44 [7]), f. 43A, *Oude en Nieuwe Holantse Boeren Lietjes en Contredansen*, Amsterdam, n.d., vii, No. 561, and *An Extraordinary Collection of Pleasant & merry Humours* (Wright, c.1713), No. 3, belongs to the morris tune family, not 'Greensleeves,' as stated in Simpson, *The British Broadside Ballad*, p. 277; see John Ward, 'The Morris Tune,' *Journal of the American Musicological Society*, xxxix (1986), 294–331.

H. Untexted setting *a* 4
  1. *US-Lau*, Robert Taitt MS, f. 151ᵛ, No. 132. Pr. Walter Rubsamen, 'Scottish and English Music of the Renaissance in a Newly-Discovered Manuscript', *Festschrift Heinrich Besseler zum 60. Geburtstag*, Leipzig, 1961, p. 269.

III. EIGHTEENTH CENTURY

A. Texted single songs
  1. 'Tak' your auld cloak about you' (representative sources)
     c.1755 James Oswald, *The Caledonian Pocket Companion*, ii. 29. 4 vars. Repr. Frederick Sternfeld, *Music in Shakespearean Tragedy*, 1963, p. 148 (first two vars.).
     1757 Robert Bremner, ed., *Thirty Scots Songs* (Edinburgh), i. 14. The tune is repr. Sternfeld, *Songs from Shakespeare's Tragedies*, 1964, p. 2.
     1790 John Johnson, ed., *Scots Musical Museum* (Edinburgh), iii. 258–9, No. 250.
     1799 George Thomson, ed., *A Select Collection of Original Scotish Airs* (Edinburgh), iii, No. 142; arr. Joseph Haydn.
     1853 *Davidson's Universal Melodist*, i. 373.
     1881 Helen K. Johnson, ed., *Familiar Songs* (New York), pp. 66–8.
  2. 'Come listen, good people, the while I relate'
     1700 *Wit and Mirth . . . The Second Part*, pp. 21–3; also ibid., ii, 2nd edn. (1707); ibid., 3rd edn. (1712); *Songs Compleat*, iv (1719), 15–17; *Wit and Mirth*, iv, 4th edn. (1719).
  3. 'A Country Bumpkin that Trees did grub'
     1700 *Wit and Mirth . . . The Second Part*, pp. 277–79; also ibid., ii, 2nd edn. (1707); ibid., 3rd edn. (1712); *Songs Compleat*, iii (1719), 164–6; *Wit and Mirth*, ii, 4th edn. (1719).
  4. 'In the Devil's Country there lately did dwell'
     1706 *Wit and Mirth*, iv. 38–9; also ibid. (1707); ibid., 2nd edn. (1709); *Songs Compleat*, v (1719), 270–71; *Wit and Mirth* (1719).
  5. 'Bold impudent Fuller invented a Plot'
     1707 *Wit and Mirth*, iii, 2nd edn., 76–8; also ibid., 3rd edn. (1712); *Songs Compleat*, v (1719), 5–6; *Wit and Mirth* (1719).

6. 'Once more to these Arms my lov'd Pick-ax and Spade'
    1707   *Wit and Mirth*, iii, 2nd edn., 170–71; also ibid., 3rd edn.
           (1712); *Songs Compleat*, v (1719), 92–3; *Wit and Mirth*
           (1719).
7. 'Three merry Lads met at the Rose'
    1707   *Wit and Mirth*, iii, 2nd edn., 6–8; also ibid., 3rd edn. (1712);
           Songs Compleat, iv (1719), 259–61; *Wit and Mirth* (1719).
8. 'Let's wet the whistle of the Muse'
    1714   *Wit and Mirth*, v (1714), 89–91; ibid. (1719).
9. 'Whilst favour'd Bishops new Sleeves put on'
    1719   *Songs Compleat*, v. 257–60; *Wit and Mirth*, i (1719).
10. 'Ye watchful Guardians of the Fair' (representative sources)
    *c.*1725   Alexander Stuart, ed., *Musick for Allan Ramsay's Collection
               of Scots Songs* (Edinburgh), p. 82.
    1792   Johnson, *Scots Musical Museum*, iv. 402, No. 388, headed
               'Green Sleeves'.
    1795   *A Selection of Original Scots Songs* (W. Napier), i. 12; arr.
               Joseph Haydn.

B. Ballad opera airs
   1. 'Since laws were made for ev'ry degree'
       1728   John Gay, *The Beggar's Opera*, Air LXVII. Facs. in *The Ballad
              Opera*, ed. Walter H. Rubsamen, New York, 1974, I, A.
   2. 'O! Mother, O! Mother, no longer complain'
       1728   Thomas Cooke & John Mottley, *Penelope*, [Air No.] 9, 'Which
              no Body can deny'. Facs. ibid., VII, A.
   3. 'That all Men are Beggars, you plainly may see'
       1731   Richard Brome, *The Jovial Crew*, Air XLII, 'Which no body can
              deny'. Facs. ibid., XVII, B.
   4. 'For our Poultry and Flocks we oft break our Repose'
       1731   George Lillo, *Silvia*, Air XXVIII, 'At *Rome* there was a terrible
              Rout'. Facs. ibid., XVII, A.
   5. 'Here's Nick the poor Tinker, Maids, what do you lack?'
       1735   Charles Coffey, *The Merry Cobler*, Air XV, 'Which no body
              can deny'. Facs. ibid., X, D.

C. Cantata
   1. Anon., *The Roast Beef Cantata* (Skillern, *c.*1770), bars 16–19, a
      single-strain instrumental interlude.

D. For lute
   1. See Appendix II.E.1: Balcarres MS.

E. For violin
   ENGLISH
   1. *GB-Lcs*, MS 34 (extracts from MSS made by Anne Gilchrist, unpagi-
      nated), from the 'Livre de Jean Doeg', dated 'after 1798'.
   2. *A Choice Collection of Country Dances with Their Proper Tunes*,
      Dublin (Neal), *c.*1726, p. 12. 2 vars.

3. *The first and Second Parts of the Division Violin* (Wright, *c*.1730), f. 19, 'New Green Sleeves a Ground'. 4 vars.
4. *GB-Lbm*, Add. MS 29371, f. 46, No. 156. 2 vars.
5. Newcastle upon Tyne, Library of the Society of Antiquaries, Atkinson MS (*c*.1700), p. 120.
6. *GB-Lcs*, MS QM 3049, No. 76. 2 vars.

SCOTTISH

My dating of the Scottish sources is based largely on the 'Bibliography of Scottish manuscripts containing folk-tunes, 1680–1840', in David Johnson, *Music and Society in Lowland Scotland in the Eighteenth Century*, 1972, pp. 209–11.

7. *GB-En*, MS 2833 (James Thomson MS, *c*.1702–*c*.1720), pp. 18–19. 5 vars.
8. *GB-En*, MS 3296 (Margaret Sinkler's violin MS, dated 1710), f. 63, 'Green Sleivis and pudding pys'. 2 vars. Pr. Mary A. Alburger, *Scottish Fiddlers and Their Music*, 1983, p. 35.
9. *GB-En*, MS 2084—see II.E.1: Mc'Farlane.
10. *GB-En*, MS Ing. 153 (the Sharpe MS, *c*.1790), p. 22. 4 vars.
11. Ibid., p. 200. 2 vars.
12. *GB-En*, MS 808 (James Gillespie MS, 1768), p. 96. 3 vars. Pr. Johnson, *Scottish Fiddle Music in the 18th Century*, pp. 228–9, No. 84.
13. Oswald, *The Caledonian Pocket Companion*, viii (*c*.1755), 4. 6 vars.
14. 'Jenny's Bawbie' (representative sources)
    1779   Joshua Campbell, *A Collection of the Newest & best Reels and Minuets* (Glasgow), p. 79. Repr. in *The Glen Collection of Scottish Dance Music*, ed. John Glen, i (1891), 5.
    c.1795   Archibald Duff, *A Collection of Strathspey Reels* (Edinburgh), p. 23, 'Jenny Babee, or Miss McDonald's favourite'.
    c.1817   Thomas Wilson, *A Companion to the Ball Room*, p. 67, 'Jennys Bawbee (Old Scotch)'.
15. James Aird, *A Selection of Scotch, English, Irish and Foreign Airs*, i (Glasgow, 1782), 46, No. 130. 2 vars.
16. Ibid., v (*c*.1796), 35, No. 90, 'The Basket of Oysters, Irish' (first strain 'Greensleeves', second strain 'Paddy the Weaver'). Also in *Forty Eight Original Irish Dances*, Dublin (Hime), *c*.1800, Book II, No. 2.
    This popular medley of two tunes is also found in IV.A.4, 5: Bruce & Stokoe, Whittaker, pp. 118–19, 6: Whittaker, 51; B.4.

WELSH

17. *GB-AB*, J. Lloyd Williams MS 39 (John Thomas's fiddle MS, 1752), f. 49^v.
18. Ibid., f. 73^v (in tablature).
19. *GB-AB*, Morris/Maurice Edwards MS ('Morris y fidler' MS, dated 1776–9), p. 38, 'Cants y nhaid' (as my grandfather sang it), a discant to each of the two grounds.

FRENCH

20. Raoul Feuillet, *Recueil de contredances mises en chorégraphie*, Paris, 1706, pp. 17–26, 'Les Manches vertes'.
    'Les Manches vertes' is also among the dances named in André Lorin's 'Livre de la contredance du roy', *F-Pn*, MS fr. 1698.

AMERICAN
21. *US-Wc*, Henry Beck's German flute MS (1786), p. 44, 'Green Sleaves & Mutton pies'. Facs. in Joy Van Cleef & Kate Van Winkle Keller, 'Selected American Country Dances and their English Sources', *Music in Colonial Massachusetts, 1630–1820*, Boston, 1980, p. 40.
22. *US-NYcu*, MS X780.973/C68 (Whittier Perkins violin MS, Massachusetts, 1790), p. 16. Facs. in Van Cleef & Keller, 1980, p. 39.
   Two MSS include a description of the dance but no music: (1) *US-WOa*, Clement Weeks MS 'Figures of Contra Dances' (New Hampshire, 1783), p. 20; facs. in Van Cleef & Keller, 1980, p. 40; (2) *US-Cn*, Case MS V 168.971, Asa Willcox's MS 'book of Figures' (Connecticut, 1793), p. 21.

F. For keyboard
   1. 'Nancy Dawson' (first strain only; representative sources)
      c.1760   Anon., *Miss Dawson's New Hornpipe as Performed at Drury Lane.*
        1763   Isaac Bickerstaff, *Love in a Village*, Act I sc. x, part of the medley beg. 'I pray ye, gentles, list to me'.
      c.1764   *Rutherford's Compleat Collection of 200 ... Country Dances*, ii. 13.
        1764   Kane O'Hara, *Midas*, Act III, set to the words 'The Gods were all call'd in to see'.
      c.1800   *Forty Eight Original Irish Dances* (Dublin), Book II, No. 2.
        1817   Thomas Wilson, *A Companion to the Ball Room*, p. 89.
        1878   H. M. Mason, *Nursery Rhymes and Country Songs*, 2nd edn., 1908, p. 13, 'Nancy Dawson's grown so fine'.
                 Lees Kershaw's version of 'Nancy Dawson', pr. in *Lancashire Morris Dance Tunes*, ed. Maud Karpeles (1930), p. 7, is based entirely on the second half of the tune, which is unrelated to 'Greensleeves'. Chappell (*Popular Music of the Olden Time*, ii. 718–20), Simpson (*The British Broadside Ballad*, p. 505) and other writers have noted that 'the first strain of the tune is still used in "Here we go round the mulberry bush" and several other songs, including "I saw three ships a-sailing"', but not all of them observed the 'Greensleeves' connection.

IV. NINETEENTH CENTURY

A. With text
   CHRISTMAS SONGS
   1. 'As I sat on a sunny bank
      On Christmas day in the morning'
      William Sandys, *Christmas Carols*, 1833, p. 24: 'This carol enjoys a very extensive popularity. It is found, under various forms, in nearly every collection of sheet carols. One of the most frequently printed versions is entitled, "The Sunny Bank". This is said to be of Warwickshire or Staffordshire origin; but its use is not confined to those, or the neighbouring, counties, as it is printed both in the North and West of England.'
        1863   Edward Rimbault, ed., *A Collection of Old Christmas Carols with the Tunes to which They are Sung*, p. 55.
        1882   *Cecil Sharp's Collection of English Folk Songs*, ed. Maud Karpeles, 1974, ii. 478.

'As sung by Charles Poole of Wooton under Edge, Gloustershire in 1882. Noted from Mrs Cecil Sharp, October 1911.'

1893 *English County Songs,* ed. Lucy Broadwood & J. A. Fuller Maitland, p. 111.

1905 *Journal of the English Folk Dance & Song Society* (hereafter *JEFDSS*), v (1946), 32, 'As I sat under a holly tree'.

1910 Alice E. Gillington, *Old Christmas Carols of the Southern Counties,* pp. 12–13.

1911 Sharp–Karpeles, ii. 477; also Cecil Sharp, *Folk-Song Carols,* 1913, pp. 14–15. Ibid., ii. 478. Cecil Sharp MS notebooks, *GB-Cclc* (photostatic copy in *US-CA*) (hereafter Sharp MSS), p. 2732.

1912 *JEFDSS,* v (1946), 31.

1916 *The Oxford Book of Carols,* No. 2 (collected by J. M. Blunt from Mr Samuel Newman, at Downton, Wilts.).

1939 George B. Gardner, *Folk Songs from Hampshire,* p. 368.

1965 *The Bitter Withy—Folk Carols,* Folktracks FSB-60-504, side A, band 5; also Caedmon TC 1224, *The Folksongs of Britain,* ix: *Songs of Christmas,* side A, band 8.

2. 'At last the ship came sailing in
   On Christmas day in the morning'
   1907 Frank Kidson & Alfred Moffat, *Eighty Singing Games,* pp. 16–17.

3. 'Christmas comes but once a year'
   c.1840 *GB-Lcs,* MS QM 7416 (a partial copy of William Irwin's folio MS), p. 40, described as an 'Old English Dance'.
   1907 Kidson & Moffat, p. 66, headed 'The Christmas Pudding'.

4. 'Christmas day in the morning' (first strain only)
   c.1812 Newcastle upon Tyne, Library of the Society of Antiquaries, John Bell's MS, p. 111.

5. 'Dame, get up and bake your pies,
   On Christmas day in the morning'
   n.d. Rimbault, ed., *A Collection of Old Nursery Rhymes,* p. 37; also Walter Crane, *The Baby's Opera,* [1877], p. 30.
   1882 J. Collingwood Bruce & J. Stokoe, eds., *Northumbrian Minstrelsy* (Newcastle upon Tyne; repr. Hatboro, 1965), p. 111 (first strain only).
   1904 Moffat & Kidson, *Seventy-five British Nursery Rhymes,* p. 80; also Kidson & Moffat, 1907, p. 66.
   1909 Alice B. Gomme & Cecil Sharp, eds., *Children's Singing Games,* ii. 16.
   1921 W. G. Whittaker, ed., *North Countrie Ballads, & Pipe-Tunes,* p. 37. Ibid., pp. 118–19, from a MS belonging to the Society of Antiquaries, Newcastle upon Tyne (first strain only).

6. 'I saw three ships come sailing by
   On Christmas day in the morning'
   Something like the carol text occurs in 'All sons of Adam', a medley of snippets from popular and other types of song preserved in Scottish sources. The passage reads:

ther cam a ship fair sailland then
Sanct Michaell was the stieres man
sanct Jon satt in the horne
our lord harpit, our ladie sang
and all the bells of heavn they rang
on Chrysts sonday at morn

The lines are set to music unrelated to anything like the romanesca; see *Music in Scotland, 1500–1700*, ed. Kenneth Elliott & Helena M. Shire ('Musica Britannica', xv), 1957, p. 153.

1833   William Sandys, *Christmas Carols*, No. 9; also William Husk, *Songs of the Nativity*, 1868, No. 9.

1847   Rimbault, ed., *A Little Book of Christmas Carols*, p. 16 ('It has always been a great favourite with the illiterate . . .'); also in Rimbault, 1863, p. 38.

n.d.   Rimbault, *A Collection of Old Nursery Rhymes*, p. 52; also in Crane, 1877, p. 18; Moffat & Kidson, 1904, pp. 28–9.

1895   Sabine Baring Gould & H. Fleetwood Sheppard, eds., *A Garland of Country Songs*, p. 27.

1921   Whittaker, pp. 41–2 (first strain only).

7. 'There was a pig went out to dig
   On Christmas day in the morning'

   1878   Mason, *Nursery Rhymes and Country Songs*, p. 25; also Broadwood & Fuller Maitland, 1893, p. 28; *JEFDSS*, v (1946), 37. 'Hunt the Squiril' in *The Dancing Master*, 17th edn. (1921), p. 357, is a variant of 'There was a pig'.

8. 'Three little boats went out to sea
   On Christmas day in the morning'

   1926   *Journal of the Folk Song Society* (hereafter *JFSS*), vii/5, 291 (Manx; collected during the latter part of the 19th century).

9. 'Three little ships come sailing by
   On Christmas day in the morning'

   1898   Gomme, *The Traditional Games of England, Scotland, and Ireland*, ii. 279.

10. 'What child is this?'

    1871   H. R. Bramley & J. Stainer, eds, *Christmas Carols New and Old*, pp. 32–3.
            'The influence of this book was enormous: it placed in the hands of the clergy . . . a really practicable tool, which came into general use, and is still in use after nearly sixty years. The great service done by this famous collection was that it brought thirteen traditional carols, with their proper music, into general use at once . . . It is . . . mainly to Bramley and Stainer that we owe the restoration of the carol . . .' (Percy Dearmer, *The Oxford Book of Carols*, 1928, pp. xvi–xvii).

CHILDREN'S GAME SONGS

Frank Rutherford, *All the Way to Pennywell: Children's Rhymes of the North East*, Durham, 1971, p. 14, includes in the list of songs belonging to the 'Greensleeves' family: 'Here I sit on a cold green bank', 'Glasgow ships', 'Poor widow', 'My ship's home from China', and 'Oh lady, oh lady, keep off the tramlines' (tune: 'Queen Mary'—cf. hymn tune 'Stella'), copies of which I have not seen.

11. 'Babbity Bowster'

    1894   Gomme, i. 9.

12. 'Dilsey Dolsey Officer, The'
    1907 Kidson & Moffatt, p. 25.
13. 'Going over the sea'
    1959 Edith Fowke, *Sail Go Round the Sun* (New York), p. 84.
14. 'Here comes a lusty wooer'
    1846 Rimbault, *Nursery Rhymes*, p. 38.
    1894 Gomme, i. 202.
15. 'Here comes three dukes a-riding'
    1888 Heywood Sumner, *The Besom Maker & Other Country Folk Songs*, p. 21, 'Forty dukes a-riding'.
    1898 Gomme, ii. 233 (four versions).
    1909 Gomme & Sharp, i. 20–21. Gillington, *Old Surrey Singing Games and Skipping-Rope Rhymes*, p. 4.
    1951 *One-Two-Three-a-Loopah*, Folktracks FSC-30-201, Side A, no. 11.
16. 'Here we come up the green grass'
    1909 Gillington, *Old Surrey Singing Games*, pp. 18–19.
17. 'Here we go gathering nuts in may'
    1883 William Newell, *Games and Songs of American Children* (New York; repr. New York, 1963), p. 236.
    1894 Gomme, i. 424.
    1907 Kidson & Moffat, p. 31.
    1909 Gillington, *Old Hampshire Singing Games and Trilling the Rope Rhymes*, p. 14. Gomme & Sharp, ii. 3–5.
    1969 Fowke, p. 16.
18. 'Here we go round the mulberry bush'
    1883 Newell, p. 86.
    1894 Gomme, i. 404.
    1907 Kidson & Moffat, p. 75.
    1952 *Ipetty Sipetty*, Folktracks FSC-45-181, Side B, No. 9.
19. 'Here's a poor widow of Babylon'
    1933 Moffat, *Fifty Traditional Scottish Nursery Rhymes*, p. 16.
20. 'The Holly, Holly O'
    1909 Gillington, *Old Hampshire Singing Games*, p. 24.
21. 'Jing-a-ring'
    1907 Kidson & Moffat, p. 10.
    1933 Moffat, p. 10 (alternative title 'The Merrie-matanzie').
22. 'Jolly Roger'
    1894 Gomme, i. 293.
23. 'Lady of the Land'
    1894 Gomme, i. 313.
24. 'London Bridge is falling down'
    1846 Rimbault, p. 34; also Rimbault, n.d., p. 38.
    1894 Gomme, i. 333.
    1904 Moffat & Kidson, p. 13.
    1909 Gillington, *Old Hampshire Singing Games*, p. 17.
25. 'The Lone Widow'
    1907 Kidson & Moffatt, p. 61.

26. 'Mary Went to School'
    1978   Folktracks FSC-45-181, Side A, No. 7.
27. 'Merry-ma-tansa'
    1894   Gomme, i. 369.
28. 'Milking Pails'
    1894   Gomme, i. 376.
    1909   Gillington, *Old Surrey Singing Games*, p. 13 ('The Milking Pail').
29. 'Muffin Man, The'
    1894   Gomme, i. 402.
    1907   Kidson & Moffat, pp. 8–9 (two versions).
30. 'Now my dorn is ended'
    1910   Gillington, *Old Christmas Carols of the Southern Counties*, p. 10.
31. 'Nuts Away'
    1909   Gillington, *Old Hampshire Singing Games*, p. 14.
32. 'Oats and beans and barley'
    1898   Gomme, ii. 2.
33. 'Old Roger's Dead'
    1898   Gomme, ii. 16.
    1909   Gillington, *Old Hampshire Singing Games*, pp. 4–5. Gomme & Sharp, i. 6.
34. 'Poor Mary Sits a-weeping'
    1898   Gomme, ii. 46.
    1912   Gomme & Sharp, iii. 18–19.
35. 'The Posy'
    1907   Kidson & Moffat, p. 90.
36. 'Push the Business On'
    1909   Gomme & Sharp, ii. 18.
37. 'Robert Burns was born in Ayr'
    1978   Folktracks FSC-45-181, Side A, No. 5.
38. 'Shotman'
    1907   Kidson & Moffat, pp. 44–5.
39. 'The ship goes through the Illey Alley O'
    1978   *Somebody Under the Bed*, Folktracks FSC-30-202, Side A, No. 3.
40. 'Silly Old Man'
    1898   Gomme, ii. 196–7 (two versions).
41. 'Thread the Needle'
    1898   Gomme, ii. 228.
42. 'The Two Young Men of Kenilworth'
    1888   Sumner, p. 18.
43. 'Up Again the Wall'
    1978   Folktracks FSC-45-181, Side B, No. 10.
44. 'Walking Up the Hillside'
    1909   Gomme & Sharp, i. 12. Gillington, *Old Surrey Games*, pp. 2–3 ('Climbing up the Hillside').
45. 'We come to see Miss Jennie Jones'

1883 Newell, pp. 243–4 (two versions).

1909 Gillington, *Old Hampshire Singing Games*, pp. 6–7 ('Jenny Jones').

1912 Gomme & Sharp, iii. 2–3.

46. 'When I Was a Baby'

1969 Fowke, p. 22.

47. 'When I Was a School Girl'

1909 Gillington, *Hampshire Singing Games*, pp. 20–21. Gomme & Sharp, ii. 10.

48. 'When I Was a Young Girl'

1898 Gomme, ii. 363 (two versions).

49. 'When I Was One'

1978 Folktracks FSC-30-202, Side B, No. 1.

50. 'Where are you three foxes going?'

1909 Gillington, *Old Hampshire Singing Games*, p. 17 ('London Bridge').

OTHER TEXTS

According to Chappell (*Popular Music of the Olden Time*, i. 232) 'there is scarcely a collection of old English songs in which at least one may not be found to the tune of *Green Sleeves*. In the West of England it is still sung at harvest-homes to a song beginning, "A pie sat on a pear-tree top"; and at the Maypole still remaining at Ansty, near Blandford, the villagers still dance annually round it to this tune.'

51. 'Oh! could we do with this world of ours'

1834 Thomas Moore, *A Selection of Irish Melodies*, x. 118–22 (first strain only; for the tune, see III.B.16).

52. 'The Brisk Young Lad'

1849 *Davidson's Universal Melodist*, ii. 196 (first strain only). The second strain is that of 'Bung your eye', both strains of which provide the setting for 'The brisk young lad' in Johnson's *Scots Musical Museum*, No. 219.

53. 'Ushag Veg Ruy' ('Little Red Bird')

1896 A. W. Moore, ed., *Manx Ballads & Music* (Douglas, Isle of Man), p. 253; repr. *JFSS*, vii/28 (1924), 166, together with other versions on p. 165 and vii/30 (1926), 310.

B. For violin or flute

ENGLISH

1. *GB-Lcs*, MS QM 7410 (a partial copy of Joseph Kershaw's MS, *c*.1820), f. 8. 2 vars.

2. Frank Kidson & Mary Neal, *English Folk-Song and Dance*, Cambridge, 1915, p. 28 (from a MS of 'fiddle airs dated 1838'). The tune entitled 'Green Sleaves' in *GB-Lcs*, MS 7411 (extracts from Will. Irwin's 1838 MS), p. [23], is a version of 'Green grow the rashes O', no relative of 'Greensleeves'.

IRISH

3. P. W. Joyce, *Old Irish Folk Music and Songs*, Dublin, 1909 (repr. New York, 1965), p. 72, No. 142 (taken down 'from James Buckley, a Limerick piper, about 1852'). 3 vars.

4. George Petrie, *The Complete Collection of Irish Music*, ed. Charles V.

Stanford, ii (1902), 192, No. 769, 'Behind the bush in the garden' (collected some time before 1866; first strain only).
Francis O'Neill, *The Dance Music of Ireland*, Chicago, 1907, p. 79, No. 398, 'Behind the bush in the garden', is a different tune.

AMERICAN

5. *Flute Melodies: Consisting of Airs, Duets, Cotillions, Waltzes, Marches, &c.*, Utica, 1822, p. 17, 'Green Sleeves, with variations'. 9 vars.

6. Elias Howe, *Second Part of the Musician's Companion*, Boston, 1850, p. 150. 2 vars.

7. *Ryan's Mammoth Collection: 1050 Reels and Jigs, Hornpipes, Clogs, Walk-arounds, Essences, Strathspeys, Highland Flings and Contra Dances*, Boston, 1883 (partial repr. Chicago, 1967), p. 75. 2 vars.

V. TWENTIETH CENTURY

A. With text

SONGS

1. 'There was a squire of high degree'
JFSS, i/5 (1904), 253; also Bertrand H. Bronson, *The Traditional Tunes of the Child Ballads*, i (Princeton, 1959), 164.

2. 'Oh shepherd, oh shepherd, will you come home?'
JFSS, iii/2 (1906), 122 (Mrs Davis). Frank Purslow, ed., *More English Folk Songs from the Hammond & Gardiner MSS*, 1972, p. 90 (collected in 1906).

3. 'The old year now away is fled'
Percy Dearmer and others, eds, *The Oxford Book of Carols*, 1928, No. 28, the text from 'A Caroll for New-yeares day' in *Good and True, Fresh and New, Christmas Carols* (1642); tune from I.C.1 above.

OPERA

4. Ferruccio Busoni, *Orchester Suite aus der Musik zu Gozzis Märchen-drama Turandot*, Op. 41, Leipzig, 1906, No. 5, 'Das Frauengemach'.

4a. Busoni, *Elegien: 6 neue Klavierstücke*, Leipzig, 1908, No. 4, 'Turandots Frauengemach. Intermezzo'.

4b. Busoni, *Turandot: Eine chinesische Fabel in zwei Akten nach C. Gozzi*, Leipzig, 1918, Act II sc. iii, No. 1, 'Lied und Chor'.
The version of 'Greensleeves (I.C.1) used by Busoni in these three works almost certainly came from Chappell via Chilesotti's *Lautenspieler*.

5. Ralph Vaughan Williams, *Sir John in Love* (1928), Act III sc. ii (Mrs Ford & Falstaff each sing the 'Ballet' version (I.C.1) to a bit of the *Handefull of pleasant delites* text); Act IV, the interlude between sc. i & ii (based on the same tune).

5a. Vaughan Williams, *Fantasia on 'Greensleeves'*, arr. Ralph Greaves from the score of the opera (1934); combines the interlude between sc. i & ii of Act IV with the one between sc. i & ii of Act I, which is based on the tune 'Lovely Joan'.

B. For piano

1. Gustav Holst, *Chrissemas day in the morning* (1926). The tune is from IV.A.5: Whittaker, pp. 118–19.

C. For violin

ENGLISH

1. *US-Wc*, a copy of Percy Grainger's cylinder recordings, No. 166 (Mr Bennett, Gloustershire, 1908).

2. *Stephen Baldwin: English Village Fiddler*, Leader LED 2068 (1976), Side A, band 2.

IRISH

3. *Francis O'Neill's Music of Ireland*, Chicago, 1903 (repr. Ho-Ho-Kus, 1979), p. 185, No. 994. 2 vars.

4. Francis O'Neill, *The Dance Music of Ireland*, Chicago, 1907, p. 49, No. 209 (double jig). 2 vars.

5. Breandán Breathnach, ed. *Ceol Rince na hÉireann*, i (Baile Átha Cliath, 1977), 4, No. 4, 'Pingneacha Rua agus Prás'.

MORRIS DANCE (by county)
It is not clear from Sharp's notebooks whether the informant or the collector suplied the title for each tune.
Derbyshire

6. Sharp MSS, p. 2378 (Blackwell, 1909).

Gloucestershire

7. Sharp MSS, p. 1276 (Cheltenham, 1907).

8. Ibid., p. 4968 (Idbury, 1923).

9. Ibid., p. 1276 (Longborough); also Sharp & Herbert C. Macilwaine, *Morris Dance Tunes*, iv (1909), 4–5 (first figure); Lionel Bacon, *A Handbook of Morris Dances* (1974), p. 197; also p. 251 (Headington). The 'Bacca Pipes (Green Sleeves)' jig in Sharp & Macilwaine, *The Morris Book*, ii, 2nd edn. (1919), 34–5 (description), and *Morris Dance Tunes*, iv, rev. edn. (1919), 4–7 (music), is a medley of four distinct tunes, comprising those of Longborough (Glos.), Nattlebridge (Northants.), Stow-on-the-Wold (Glos.) and Headington (Oxon.). Bacon 1974, pp. 197–200, reprints the medley (under Headington), and the Stow-on-the-Wold tune a second time (under Longborough), referring the reader to the Headington section for a description of the dance.

10. Sharp MSS, p. 1255 (Stow-on-the-Wold, 1907); also Sharp & Macilwaine, iv. 6 (third figure); Bacon, 1974, p. 197.
The following words were associated with the tune:

> Green sleeves and yellow lace
> Boys and girls they work a pace
> They save some money to buy some lace
> To lace the lady's green sleeves.

11. Sharp MSS, p. 2144 (Winchcombe, 1909).
The following words were associated with the tune:

> Some says the Devil's dead
> The Devil's dead, Devil's dead,
> Some says the Devil's dead
> And buried in cold harbour.

> Some says he's rose again [3 times]
> And prenticed to a barber.

Sharp collected still another set of words to 'Greensleeves' from Tom Harris (Armscote, 1910), word-book pp. 2205–6:

Toby Colbourn had a wife,
Had a wife, had a wife,
Toby Colbourn had a wife
And then at last he killed her.

Colbourn's wife she rosed again
And brought him forth two children.

These two children were two fine boys,
As ever were borne of a mother.

Little John was the name of one
And Tom the name of the other.

These two boys they went to church
Whenever they thought fit, Sir.

Little John in the gallery sat,
And little Tom in the pit, sir.

12. Ibid., p. 1506 (Nattlebridge, 1907); also Sharp & Macilwaine, iv. 5 (second figure); Bacon, 1974, p. 197.

Herefordshire

13. Sharp MSS, p. 2415 (Leominster, 1909).

14. Ella Mary Leather, *The Folk-Lore of Herefordshire*, Hereford, 1912, p. 137; also *English Song & Dance*, xxvi (1964), 85.
    Sharp noted Nos. 13 and 14 from the playing of John Locke, gypsy fiddler.

Lancashire

15. Sharp MSS, p. 2807 (Wyresdale); also Sharp & George Butterfield, *Morris Dance Tunes*, x (1913), 18–19.
    Copied from a MS notebook belonging to the father of Sharp's informant.

Northamptonshire

16. Sharp & Macilwaine, *The Morris Book*, iii, 2nd edn. (1924), 106–8 (Brackely; second strain only); also Bacon, 1974, p. 204 (Hinton-in-the-Hedges; both strains).

Oxfordshire

17. Sharp MSS, p. 2683, 'Bacca Pipes' (Ascot-under-Wychwood); also Bacon, 1974, p. 26.
    According to Sharp, his informant 'gave me this [the music on p. 2683] as the pipe tune but when he danced it [i.e. 'Bacca Pipes dance'] he sang a version of Green Sleeves', which Sharp failed to write down. Apparently the collector failed to recognize the tune he wrote down as also a version of 'Greensleeves', one belonging to the 'Sunny Bank' branch of the family.

18. Sharp MSS, p. 2262, 'Bacca Pipes Jig' (William Wells, Bampton, 1909; in 2/4); also Sharp, *Morris Dance Tunes*, v, rev. edn. (1910), 28–9 (in 6/8); the latter also in Bacon 1974, p. 57.

19. William Wells, *Constant Billy: Music & Memories of a Morris-Man*, ii, 'The Pipe Dance (Bacca Pipes)', Folktracks FSA-90-084 (1974), Side A, band 12 (Bampton, 1952). The tune is first sung with the words also found with V.B.11, then with vocables.

20. Sharp MSS, p. 2187 (Noke, 1909).

21. Ibid., p. 2751 (Oxford, 1912).

22. Ibid., p. 2444, 'Bacca Pipes' (William Kimber, Oxford 1910); see also *William Kimber*, English Folk Dance & Song Society LP 1001, Side A, band 1, recorded some time in the 1950s.

23. Bacon 1974, p. 295 (Stanton Harcourt).
Shropshire
24. Sharp MSS, p. 2789 (Newport, 1912).
Somersetshire
25. Sharp MSS, p. 1499 (Shepton Mallet, 1907).
26. Ibid., p. 2170 (Wells, 1909).
Warwickshire
27. Sharp MSS, p. 2062 (Ilmington, 1909).
28. Ibid., p. 2305 (Shipton-on-Stour, 1909).

SWORD DANCE
29. Sharp, *Sword Dance Tunes*, iii (1913), 9, Song-Air No. 4, 'When first King Henry ruled this land'.
30. M. K[arpeles], ' "The 'owd Lass of Coverdill" and Other Sword-Dance Fragments', *Journal of the Folk Dance Society*, 2nd ser., ii (1928), 32, 'When first King Henry ruled this land'.

D. For saxophone
1. The John Coltrane Quartet, *Africa/Brass*, Impulse recording A-6, Side B, band 1.
   The piece is described in the notes accompanying the record as 'an updating of the old, revered folk song'; and in the words of Coltrane, 'we do it just about as written [i.e. in "the arrangement . . . based on (McCoy) Turner's chords. (Eric) Dolphy notated it"]. There's a section [the piece lasts 9 minutes 55 seconds] with a vamp to blow on.'

E. For instrumental ensemble
1. Gustav Holst, *St Paul's Suite*, for string orchestra, finale (combines the 'Ballet' version of 'Greensleeves' with the country-dance tune 'Dargason') = Second Suite in F for Military Band, No. 4, 'Fantasia on the "Dargason" '.

F. Miscellaneous arrangements
Of the dozens of recordings of the 'Ballet' lute-book version (I.C.1) in various guises, the 'Medley: Love in Blue/Greensleeves' can be the representative. It is included in The Lettermen's album, *Goin' Out of My Head*, Capitol/EMI St 2865, Side B, band 2.
The definitive pseudo-history of 'Greensleeves' is included on Michael Flanders & Donald Swann's recording *At the Drop of a Hat*, Angel 35797, Side A, band 3.

15

Five Variations on 'Farewel dear loue'

David Greer

TO.	Farewell deere heart, since I must needs be gone.
MAR.	Nay good Sir *Toby*.
CLO.	His eyes do shew his dayes are almost done.
MAL.	Is't euen so?
TO.	But I will neuer dye.
CLO.	Sir *Toby* there you lye.
MAL.	This is much credit to you.
TO.	*Shall I bid him go.*
CLO.	*What and if you do?*
TO.	*Shall I bid him go, and spare not?*
CLO.	*O no, no, no, no, you dare not.*

THE earliest editors of Shakespeare—Rowe, Pope, Theobald, Hanmer —realized that this passage in *Twelfth Night* (II. iii) incorporates lines of song. But it is by no means certain that they knew the identity of the song. And when Thomas Percy included the complete text of it among the 'Ballads that illustrate Shakespeare' in his *Reliques of Ancient English Poetry* (1765)[1] he took it from Richard Johnson's black-letter miscellany *The Golden Garland of Princely Pleasures* (1620) and made no mention of its true source. This was revealed only when John Stafford Smith printed Robert Jones's air 'Farewel dear loue' (*First Book of Songes*, 1600, No. 12) in his *Musica antiqua* (London, 1812) with the comment 'Quoted by Shakespeare, "Twelfth Night"'.[2] Since then its appearance in the play has been much commented on by scholars, both from the point of view of its dramatic function and as evidence in the dating of the play.[3]

---

[1] *Reliques*, i. 187–9; ed. Henry B. Wheatley, London, 1887, i. 209–11.
[2] *Musica antiqua*, pp. 10, 204–5. Edward F. Rimbault later included the air in his *Musical Illustrations of Bishop Percy's Reliques of Ancient English Poetry*, London, 1850, pp. 9–10, 52.
[3] For a summary of critical comment see Peter J. Seng, *The Vocal Songs in the Plays of Shakespeare: A Critical History*, Cambridge, Mass., 1967, pp. 105–8. The dates for the play's composition given in Alfred Harbage, *Annals of English Drama 975–1700*, rev. S. Schoenbaum, London, 1964, p. 76, reflect the consensus of modern scholarly opinion: 1600–1602.

After an inauspicious start Jones's composing career proceeded downhill all the way. Against this indifferent background the story of 'Farewel dear loue' is all the more striking. Together with some of Dowland's airs it was one of the most successful of all the English lutenist songs. It was arranged for cittern, lute, mandora and keyboard; both words and music were parodied; new words were composed to the tune; and within a short time of

Ex15.1

The latter date is fixed by a reference in the diary of a barrister, John Manningham, to a performance of the play at the Middle Temple on 2 February 1602; the earlier is based on various pieces of circumstantial evidence, including the publication date of 'Farewell dear loue'. Attempts have also been made to link the song 'O Mistris mine' (II. iii) with the tune so titled in Thomas Morley's *First Booke of Consort Lessons* (1599), but apart from the difficulty of fitting the words to that tune, Stephen D. Tuttle has pointed out (*Musica Britannica*, v. 158) that in Tomkins's list in Paris, Bibliothèque Nationale, Rés. 1122, the tune is entitled 'O mistris myne I must'.

its publication it was taken up in Scotland and the Netherlands. In this article I examine five aspects of its history.[4]

I

In 1603 the Edinburgh publisher Robert Charteris brought out *Ane Godlie Dreame, Compylit in Scottish Meter be M. M. Gentelwoman in Culros, at the requeist of her freindes.* 'M.M.' was Elizabeth Melville, Lady Comrie, devout wife of John Colville of Wester Comrie in the parish of Culros, and this slim volume contains two poems—'Ane Godlie Dreame', and 'A Comfortabill Song'. The first of these was enormously successful and was regularly reprinted right through to the end of the last century. According to Rimbault, 'Armstrong relates in his Essays, that he recollected having heard it sung by the peasants to a plaintive air'.[5] But it is the second poem that interests us here, for it is directed to be sung 'to the tune of *Sall I let her Go*', i.e. 'Farewel dear loue', and it is a parody of Jones's lyric:

> Away vaine warld bewitcher of my heart,
> My sorrow shawes my sinnes maks me to smart:
> 3it will I not dispair, bot to my God repair,
> He hes mercie ay, thairfor will I pray:
> He hes mercie ay, and loves me,
> Thouch be his troubling hand he proves me.
> (four more verses)[6]

The year this song appeared marked a watershed in the history of part-music—'musik fyne'—in Scotland.[7] Until 1603 Scotland had its own court, which formed a focal point for poets and musicians. The cultivation of courtly song reached its apogee in the years after James VI attained the age of seniority in 1579, when he became the centre of a group of courtly *makars*—including Alexander Montgomerie, Patrick Hume, Alexander Hume, John Stewart and William Fowler—who formed the 'Castalian Band', dedicated to the creation of a new Scottish poetry that married together the best traditions of the Scottish tongue and the refined art of

---

[4] The original air is given as Ex. 15.1, and a list of other musical sources is given in the Appendix, pp. 227–9 below.

[5] Op.cit., p. 10 n.

[6] Included as Appendix D in *The Poems of Alexander Hume (?1557–1609)*, ed. Alexander Lawson (Scottish Text Society, xlviii), Edinburgh & London, 1902, pp. 184–98. The same poem is attributed to Alexander Hume in Edinburgh University Library MS Drumm. De.3.70, Margarat Ker's Manuscript, formerly owned by William Drummond of Hawthornden and presented to the university by him in 1627. It was printed from this source in *The Poems of Alexander Montgomerie*, ed. James Cranstoun (Scottish Text Society, ix–xi), Edinburgh & London, 1887, pp. 237–8; but the scholarly consensus upholds Elizabeth Melville's claim to authorship.

[7] See Helena Mennie Shire, *Song, Dance and Poetry of the Court of Scotland under King James VI*, Cambridge, 1969; a selection of the music is printed in *Music of Scotland 1500–1700*, ed. Kenneth Elliott ('Musica Britannica', xv), London, 1957 (3rd edn. 1975).

Ronsard and Du Bellay. For musical settings the poets turned to composers close to court, such as Andro Blackhall or James Lauder, or to music imported from England or France. In the case of Montgomerie, music survives for about 30 of his poems, ranging from adaptations of chansons by Lassus and La Grotte to ballad tunes such as 'The Nine Muses'.[8] Elizabeth Melville was on the fringe of this courtly songmaking activity. She was a friend of the poet Alexander Hume, who dedicated his *Hymnes, or Sacred Songs* of 1599 to her. In his address 'To the Scottish youth' he reflects that

... in Princes courts, in the houses of greate men, and at the assemblies of young gentilmen and yong dameshels, the chiefe pastime is, to sing prophane sonnets, and vaine ballats of loue, or to rehearse some fabulos faits of Palmerine, Amadis, or other such like raueries ...[9]

Alexander's brother Patrick was the 'Polwart' who engaged in the famous *flyting*—match of poetic invective—with Montgomerie.[10]

But in the same year that Elizabeth Melville brought out 'Away vaine warld' James VI travelled south to become James I of England; Scotland no longer had a court of its own, and without this focal point poetry and songmaking all but ceased.[11] As a result, seventeenth-century Scottish sources tend to contain music from two distinct repertories: one is the old court repertory just described; the other consists of English songs by the lutenists and their successors, which filled the lacuna when the courtly well dried up. One such source is John Forbes's *Songs and Fancies* (Aberdeen, 1662), the only printed music from Scotland in this period. This collection represents the repertory of the Aberdeen song school, with an introduction (largely lifted from Morley) by Thomas Davidson, master of music at the school from 1640 to 1675. Such song schools existed in a number of Scottish burghs; they had been suppressed at the time of the Reformation but were

[8] Musical settings of Montgomerie's poetry are discussed in Shire, op. cit., pp. 139–80. There is (or was) music for at least two of the poems attributed to him in *Poems of Alexander Montgomerie: Supplementary Volume*, ed. George Stevenson (Scottish Text Society, lix) Edinburgh & London, 1910: 'Glade am I, glade am I' (No. 18) occurs as a round in Thomas Ravenscroft's *Deuteromelia* (1609), No. 11 (C. S. Lewis praises the opening of this poem in *English Literature in the Sixteenth Century*, p. 111, but it is unlikely to be by Montgomerie); 'Some men for suddane Joy do weip' (No. 29) is the ballad of John Careless, the tune of which seems to be lost. See Claude M. Simpson, *The British Broadside Ballad and its Music*, New Brunswick, 1966, p. 534 n. 3. The words cannot be by Montgomerie.
[9] *Poems of Alexander Hume*, p. 6.
[10] *Poems of Alexander Montgomerie*, pp. 55–86.
[11] Something of the Castalian spirit lingers in the work of Sir Robert Ayton (born c.1570), who travelled south and whose poems were set to music by Henry Lawes, John Wilson, John Playford and others. See *The English and Latin Poems*, ed. C. B. Gullans (Scottish Text Society, ser. 4, i), Edinburgh, 1963; *Musa jocosa mihi* (twelve songs to words by Ayton), ed. Kenneth Elliott, London, 1966; Shire, op. cit., pp. 215–54. Sources for 'Thou sent'st to me' not mentioned by Elliott or Shire are: Oxford, Bodleian Library, MS Mus. Sch. F.575, f. 6; Carlisle Cathedral Library, Bishop Smith's Partbooks, p. 102; New York Public Library MS Drexel 4175, No. 14.

Ex. 15.2

*MS: Altus a´

reopened by a royal edict of 1579. In them part-music was taught alongside the general curriculum. A source with similar connections is the Taitt Manuscript, compiled *c.*1676 by Robert Taitt, master of music at the song school at Lauder. Here the music of 'Farewel' occurs twice, to the words of 'Away vain world' and to another poem—'Farewell fond fancies'—not found elsewhere. This version is in four parts, the lower three untexted (Ex. 15.2). Here, as elsewhere in the manuscript, various changes are made to the original part-writing (compare Ex. 15.1). Some of these are trivial, and not all for the better, but in the final strain (bb. 13–19) there is a significant elaboration of the texture, which is anticipated by the rising quavers in bars 10–11.

Of the other Scottish manuscripts, the Wode Partbooks are noteworthy as the only source which brings together 'Farewel' and the parody of his own air which Jones brought out in 1609—indicating a good knowledge of English songbooks on the part of the compiler.[12] In another source, the Skene Manuscript, the title 'O sillie soul alace' suggests that the tune was used for yet another poem, now lost.

II

'Farewel dear loue' is also one of the English tunes that found their way to the Netherlands in the early seventeenth century.[13] In view of the many English composers employed on the Continent in this period (Dowland, Bull, Philips etc.) it is hardly surprising that English tunes appear in Continental sources. But an equally potent agent in the process of transmission was the constant stream of English acting companies that travelled on the Continent. Occasionally we have clear evidence that this was indeed the means by which a tune was transmitted, as is the case with 'What if a day', which is entitled 'Comedianten dans' in Valerius's *Neder-Landtsche Gedenck-Clanck*. From Denmark to Italy the mainland was criss-crossed by troupes of English players seeking to make a living in the courts, town squares and fairgrounds of Europe—a pursuit which became an urgent necessity for many when English theatres closed in 1642.[14] Among the leading English actors who

[12] These part books also bring together 'What if a day' and Alison's parody of verse 2 (see below, p. 221).

[13] Dutch sources containing the music are listed in the Appendix. Florimond van Duyse (*Het oude nederlandsche Lied*, The Hague, 1903–22, i. 603–7) mentions twelve other Dutch songbooks between 1605 and 1664 in which the tune is cited without the music, usually under the name 'Wanneer ick slaep' or 'O slaep, o soeten slaep'. The first of these is *Tweede nieuw amoreus liedtboek*, Amsterdam, 1605, p. 131, where 'Wanneer ick slaep' appears as 'Een nieu liedekin'—just five years after the tune's first publication in London.

[14] The first writer to take an interest in this phenomenon was Johann Ludwig Tieck in his *Deutsches Theater* of 1817. Later in the nineteenth century the subject was mapped out by a succession of German literary scholars. Their findings are summarized in E. K. Chambers, *The Elizabethan Stage*, Oxford, 1923, ii. 270–94. More recent studies are: J. G. Riewald, 'New Light on English Actors in the Netherlands, *c.*1590–*c.*1660', *English Studies*, xli (1960), 65–92; Jerzy Limon, *Gentlemen of a Company: English Players in Central and Eastern*

worked on the Continent were Will Kempe, Robert Browne (whose travels extended over 30 years, from 1590 to 1620), John Greene, Richard Jones, Thomas Sackville, John Spencer and Robert Reynolds. The last three were famous as clowns, 'John Bouset' (or 'Posset'), 'Stockfish' and 'Pickleherring' respectively. The entertainment offered by such players ranged from adaptations of plays by Kyd, Marlowe, Shakespeare, Heywood and others to jigs and other musical diversions. The popularity of these entertainments led to German translations and imitations.[15] In 1620 a collection of plays and jigs was published in Leipzig under the title *Engelische Comedien und Tragedien*. There was a second edition in 1624, and in 1630 there was a further collection, *Liebeskampff oder Theil der engelischen Comoedien und Tragoedien*. Of particular interest to us are the jigs—miniature dramas sung to popular tunes: through these many English melodies must have become familiar on the Continent.[16]

Not surprisingly, it is often the music, dancing and acrobatics—elements that transcend the language barrier—which seem to have made the strongest impression on foreign audiences. Balthasar Paumgartner the Younger witnessed Robert Browne's company at the Frankfurt Autumn Fair in 1592 and wrote to his wife: 'The English comedians have a splendid band and are so perfect in their acrobatics and dancing that I have never heard or seen the like'.[17] Expressions such as 'lieblicher musica' occur in a number of contemporary accounts.[18] A description of an English company at Münster in 1599 recounts how eleven actors performed five comedies in English on successive days.[19] They had lutes, citterns, fiddles, pipes etc. and performed 'many new and strange dances' before and after the plays. Some accounts distinguish between players and musicians: Spencer had nineteen players and sixteen musicians at Königsberg in 1611, and nineteen players and fifteen musicians at Frankfurt in spring 1614.[20]

Europe, 1590–1660, Cambridge, 1985; and Willem Schrickx, *Foreign Envoys and Travelling Players in the Age of Shakespeare and Jonson*, Ghent, 1986. Concerning English musicians on the Continent see Thurston Dart, 'English Music and Musicians in 17th-Century Holland', *Internationale Gesellschaft für Musikwissenschaft: Kongress-Bericht Utrecht 1952*, Amsterdam, 1953, pp. 139–45; and Alan Curtis, *Sweelinck's Keyboard Music*, Leiden & Oxford, 1969, pp. 10–34.

[15] A German *Twelfth Night* was performed and published in Brunswick in 1677 as *Tugend und Liebesstreit, oder Was Ihr Wollt*. According to Ernest Brennecke, there was probably an earlier version: see his *Shakespeare in Germany 1590–1700*, Chicago, 1964, pp. 190–245.

[16] Johannes Bolte, *Die Singspiele der englischen Komödianten und ihrer Nachfolger in Deutschland, Holland, und Skandinavien*, Hamburg & Leipzig, 1893; Charles Read Baskervill, *The Elizabethan Jig and Related Song Drama*, Chicago, 1929.

[17] Schrickx, *Foreign Envoys*, p. 188.

[18] Curtis, *Sweelinck*, p. 12.

[19] Baskervill, *The Elizabethan Jig*, p. 129.

[20] Charles Harris, 'The English Comedians in Germany before the Thirty Years War: The Financial Side', *Publications of the Modern Language Association of America*, xxii (1907), 455.

Whether their final destination was Denmark, Germany or Poland, the route taken by the travelling companies took them through the Netherlands, and there are records of their activities in all the main centres: Utrecht, Leiden, Arnhem, Groningen, Franeker, Amsterdam, Nijmegen, The Hague and Zutphen in the north, and Lille, Ghent, Héverlé and Brussels in the Spanish Netherlands to the south. As in Germany, the success of English plays in the Netherlands led to imitations in the vernacular. Jan Janszoon Starter's *Kluchtigh t'samen-Gesang van dry Personigien* (called *Der betrogene Freier* by Bolte), published in 1621, uses nine tunes, some of which are of English origin.[21] Starter was born in London in 1594, and his famous songbook *Friesche Lust-Hof* (1621) uses a number of English tunes, including 'Farewel'.[22] Another jig-like piece is Jan van Arp's *Singhende Klucht, van Droncke Goosen* (Amsterdam, 1639), which uses three tunes, all of them found also in Starter's piece.[23] On awakening, the drunken Goosen sings 'O Slaep / o slaep / o soete slaep'—a striking recollection of the refrain of 'Wanneer ick slaep', though the tune here is not 'Farewel'.

Ex. 15.3

[21] Printed in Starter's *Boertigheden*, bound in with his *Friesche Lust-Hof* (1621); reprinted in Baskervill, op.cit., pp. 590–600 (with comment on p. 313).

[22] On page 42 'Wanner ick slaep &c' is cited as the tune for verses beginning 'Seght dogh mijn licht' (no music is given). See also *Friesche Lust-Hof*, i: *Teksten*, ed. J. H. Brouwer ('Zwolse Drukken en Herdrukken voor de Maatschappij der Nederlandse Letterkunde te Leiden', xlix A), Leiden, 1966, pp. 72–3, and Marie Veldhuyzen, *De Melodieën bij Starters Friesche Lust-Hof* (ibid., xlix B), Leiden, 1967, p. 61.

[23] Reprinted in Baskervill, op.cit., pp. 601–5 (with comment on pp. 314–15).

It has been suggested that Jones himself may have travelled on the Continent: a Robert Jones was a member of Robert Browne's company at Frankfurt in September 1602.[24] But the commonness of the name makes identification very uncertain. We are perhaps on surer ground with another English lutenist composer, William Corkine. A Privy Council document dated 22 June 1617 grants

A passe for the sayd Geo Vincent to goe over to the Prince of Poland, and to carry over with him to the sayd Prince his master these musicians, Richard Jones, Wm. Corkin, Donatus O'Chaine, Thomas White, Wm. Jackson, Tho. Sutton, Valentine Flood and John Wayd.[25]

III

The history of 'Farewel dear loue' has close parallels with that of another popular Elizabethan air already mentioned in this paper—'What if a day'.[26] Both travelled to Scotland in the same year, 1603, first appearing there in publications of the Edinburgh publisher Robert Charteris. Both became popular in the Netherlands and are found in the same Dutch songbooks. And both are unusual in the air repertory in that they were treated to musical parody. Jones provided his own parody of 'Farewell dear love' in his fourth book of airs, entitled *A Musicall Dreame*, in 1609. In general, he imitates the rhythms and phrase-lengths of the original, with occasional reminiscences of the melody also. Extracts are given in Ex. 15.3, with the original tune for comparison. Richard Alison's parody of 'What if a day' occurs in his *Howres Recreation in Musicke* of 1606, and in setting the second stanza, 'Earthes but a point', he produces a further parody. These pieces have been discussed elsewhere,[27] but the openings of both verses are given in Ex. 15.4*a* and *b*

[24] Curtis, *Sweelinck*, p. 16.

[25] *Acts of the Privy Council of England*, ed. J. V. Lyle, London, 1927, p. 267. For more new information on Corkine see David Greer, 'Two Songs by William Corkine', *Early Music*, xi (1983), 346–9.

[26] David Greer, '"What if a day"—An Examination of the Words and Music', *Music & Letters*, xliii (1962), 304–19. To the versions there listed the following can now be added: (i) keyboard variations by Thomas Tomkins (ed. Stephen D. Tuttle, *Musica Britannica*, v (London, 1955, rev. 1964), No. 64); (ii) lute variations by (?)John Dowland (ed. Diana Poulton in the *Complete Works for Lute*, London, 1974, No. 79). Concerning this piece and other versions of the music in Washington, DC, Folger Shakespeare Library, MS V.b.280, see John M. Ward, 'The so-called "Dowland Lute Book" in the Folger Shakespeare Library', *Journal of the Lute Society of America*, ix (1976), 5–29, and the same author's 'Dowland Miscellany', *Journal of the Lute Society of America*, x (1977), 48–9; (iii) four-part setting in Edinburgh, National Library of Scotland, MS Acc. 2764 (Edward Millar's Manuscript), ff. 65ᵛ–66; (iv) four-part setting in the Taitt Manuscript (see Appendix, p. 228), ff. 34ᵛ, 51–51ᵛ; (v) British Library Add. MS 33933, discussed in Greer, '"What if a day"', p. 316, is the altus of the Wode Partbooks which are fully listed in *Musica Britannica*, xv. 202; (vi) for other sources see: Walter H. Rubsamen, 'Scottish and English Music of the Renaissance in a Newly-Discovered Manuscript', *Festschrift Heinrich Besseler*, Leipzig, 1961, pp. 277–8; Kenneth Elliott, letter in *Music & Letters*, xliv (1963), 206; Simpson, *The British Broadside Ballad*, pp. 752–4.   [27] Greer, '"What if a day"', pp. 314–16.

Ex. 15.4

alongside the original tune (*c*). The effect of this technique is to produce a second verse which is like a variation on verse 1. This also happens in Alison's 'My prime of youth' / 'The spring is past', and it is hinted at elsewhere in his pieces in two or more verses.

Of course, parody is to be found in the works of the madrigalists: Wilbye imitated Ferrabosco just as Ferrabosco imitated Rore, and Morley imitated Gastoldi and Anerio. The whole process of importing the madrigal style to England was facilitated by such parodies. A comparison of one of Morley's canzonets, 'Flora, wilt thou torment me', with its model (Anerio's 'Flori morir debb'io') shows the similarity to Alison's and Jones's methods (Ex. 15.5).[28]

One other feature links these pieces. Joseph Kerman points out that in setting his first collection of canzonets for two voices Morley chose a highly uncharacteristic—for the canzonet—texture, and he remarks that in this respect the canzonets are more closely allied to the didactic *bicinium*, a species of music represented in England by such collections as Whythorne's *Duos* of 1590.[29] Jones's parody belongs to the small category of lutenist duet-air. Alison's pieces are for four or five voices, but they are mostly scored for two cantus parts, a feature to which he draws attention in his title page and for which he gives the following explanation: 'All for the most part with two trebles, necessarie for such as teach in priuate families . . .'. It may be that the didactic strain running through English music of this period is stronger than is generally recognized.

---

[28] Joseph Kerman, *The Elizabethan Madrigal: A Comparative Study*, New York, 1962: the two pieces are given complete on pp. 283–4.   [29] Ibid., p. 159.

Ex. 15.5

IV

We return to Shakespeare. The fact that a man of the stage should use an air for theatrical effect is another indication of its appeal. Nor was Shakespeare the only playwright to do so, for it is also alluded to in Beaumont's *Knight of the Burning Pestle* (1607–c.1610)—

> Why an if she be, what care I?
> Or let her come or go, or tarry.
> (II. 470–71)

—though in this play it shares the distinction with some 40 other airs, madrigals, ballads and rounds.[30] In the case of *Twelfth Night*, however, there is a minor puzzle: how much of it was actually sung? The extract from the play at the head of this article gives the text as it was printed in the First Folio of 1623. If we compare this with the complete text of Jones's air we see that Shakespeare has conflated the first and second stanzas. Lines 1, 3, 5–6 of the dialogue derive from lines 1–4 of the first stanza, and lines 8–11 derive from lines 5–8 of the second:

---

[30] Ed. Cyrus Hoy in *The Dramatic Works in the Beaumont and Fletcher Canon*, general ed. Fredson Bowers, i (Cambridge, 1966), 1–110; most of the songs are identified in the textual notes, pp. 89–95.

Farewel dear loue since thou wilt needs be gon,
mine eies do shew my life is almost done,
    nay I will neuer die,
    so long as I can spie,
    there be many mo   5
though that she do go,
there be many mo I feare not,
why then let her goe I care not.

Farewell, farewell, since this I finde is true,
I will not spend more time in wooing you: 10
    But I will seek elswhere,
    If I may find her there,
    Shall I bid her goe,
    What and if I doe?
Shall I bid her go and spare not,   15
O no no no no I dare not.

Ten thousand times farewell, yet stay a while,
Sweet kisse me once, sweet kisses time beguile:
    I haue no power to moue,
    How now, am I in loue?   20
    Wilt thou needs be gone?
    Go then, all is one,
Wilt thou needs be gone? oh hie thee,
Nay, stay and doe no more denie mee.

Once more farewell, I see loth to depart,   25
Bids oft adew to her that holdes my hart:
    But seeing I must loose,
    Thy loue which I did chuse:
    Go thy waies for me,
    Since it may not be,   30
Go thy waies for me, but whither?
Go, oh but where I may come thither.

What shall I doe? my loue is now departed,
Shee is as faire as shee is cruell harted:
    Shee would not be intreated,   35
    With praiers oft repeated:
    If shee come no more,
    Shall I die therefore,
If shee come no more, what care I?
Faith, let her go, or come, or tarry.   40

The conflated lines make up a complete 'stanza', and it is reasonable to suppose that the whole tune was sung through once by Sir Toby and the clown, with spoken interpolations by Maria and Malvolio.[31] This indeed is

[31] This point is discussed by John P. Cutts in 'A Reconsideration of the *Willow Song*', *Journal of the American Musicological Society*, x (1957), 14–24.

how the passage is interpreted in modern editions. But the typographical layout suggests something different. As a rule the First Folio follows the convention of printing sung text in italic typeface, implying in this case that only the second strain of the tune (from 'Shall I bid . . .') is to be sung. This is not an infallible guide, however, and it could well be that owing to the interspersed prose the compositor did not recognize lines 1, 3, 5–6 to be lines of a song. But there is one curious fact that lends some weight to the notion that the compositor was right and the singing should not begin until line 8. When Elizabeth Melville used the tune for her poem in 1603 she called it 'Sall I let her Go' (see p. 215), and in Camphuysen's *Stichtelycke rymen* it is also known as 'Shal I bed' or (later editions) 'Shal I bed her go'. So for some reason the tune acquired a title from an otherwise unremarkable line in the middle of the second stanza. Could it be that this was because this was the point where—in the play—the singing actually began? It is not difficult to imagine the preceding lines being burlesqued in exaggerated speech.

V

Accounting for the popularity of a tune is often a difficult matter, and of course it involves factors which have nothing to do with the music *per se*. That said, it is interesting to note that 'Farewel' shares a number of features with other tunes in the popular repertory. The opening phrase (Ex. 15.6*a*) belongs to a type which is found in several other pieces, which are set out for comparison. Ex. 15.6*b* is from a piece entitled 'La doune cella' in the Mulliner Book (compiled in the mid sixteenth century).[32] It is one of three adjacent pieces with what appear to be French titles, the other two being 'La bounette' and 'La shy myze'. A reference to two of them in Giles Farnaby's *Canzonets to Fowre Voyces* (1598) seems to indicate that they were well known:

> Pearce did daunce with Petronella,
> *Lasiamiza* and *Laduncella*,
> Pretty Almans that weare new.

Ex. 6*c* is from the ballad tune 'Fortune my foe'.[33] The similarity of this and 'Farewel' seems to have been recognized—or to have led to confusion—on at least one occasion: when copying a setting of 'Fortune my foe' into his virginal manuscript in 1612 Clement Matchett gave it a double title—

---

[32] *The Mulliner Book*, ed. Denis Stevens ('Musica Britannica', i), London, 1951, No. 14; see also the same author's *The Mulliner Book: A Commentary*, London, 1952, pp. 67–8.

[33] Simpson, op. cit., pp. 225–31; and John M. Ward, 'Curious Tunes for *Strange Histories*', *Words and Music: the Scholar's View . . . in Honor of A. Tillman Merritt*, ed. Laurence Berman, Harvard University, 1972, pp. 339–58. A few other English lute airs have openings that closely resemble ballad tunes: for example, compare Thomas Ford's 'What then is loue sings Coridon' (*Musicke of Sundrie Kindes*, 1607, No. 2) with 'Bara Faustus' Dream' (Simpson, op. cit., pp. 34–6).

'Farwell delighte: Fortune my Foe'.[34] Ex. 15.6d is from an anonymous lute piece (or, more likely, the lute part of an ensemble piece) entitled 'Ballet Englese' in Joachim van den Hove's *Delitiae Musicae* (1612), f. 59.[35] Ex. 15.6e is from a piece entitled 'Littawe Engelsche Leuffer' in a collection of English lute music compiled c.1640 by Johann Stobaeus of Königsberg (now British Library MS Sloane 1021, f. 77ᵛ). Openings analogous to these are to be found in two lute airs, Michael Cavendish's 'Curst be the time' (1598, No. 10) and Thomas Greaves's 'Ye bubling springs' (1604, No. 3).

As for the poem, the notion of farewell was a popular theme in sixteenth-century verse, courtly and popular, and Jones's lyric employs motifs that were part of the stock-in-trade of the genre. 'Loth to depart' (line 25) was an expression used for any song of farewell, and a tune with that title is found in the Fitzwilliam Virginal Book and elsewhere.[36] Lines 15–16 find an echo in the refrain of Walter Davison's poem 'At her faire hands how have I grace intreated' in *A Poetical Rhapsody* (1602):

Ex. 15.6

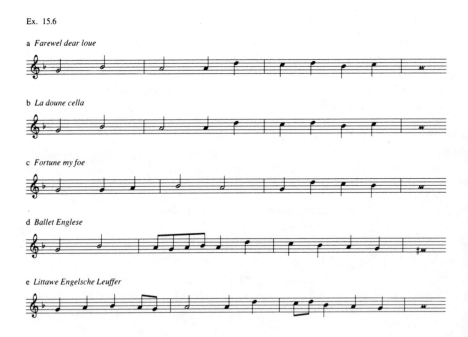

a *Farewel dear loue*

b *La doune cella*

c *Fortune my foe*

d *Ballet Englese*

e *Littawe Engelsche Leuffer*

[34] *Clement Matchett's Virginal Book*, ed. Thurston Dart, London, 1957, No. 8. No. 12 in this collection has the odd title 'Tille valle Monye grow'; Dart suggests a connection with the expression 'tilly vally' in *Twelfth Night*, II. iii. 79.

[35] Ed. Helmut Mönkemeyer, Hofheim am Taunus, 1967–77, iv. 10. Hove took the lute part alone from several pieces in Dowland's *Lachrimae or Seauen Teares*: see Diana Poulton, *John Dowland*, London, 1972, p. 111, and Ward, 'A Dowland Miscellany', p. 80.

[36] Simpson, op. cit., pp. 456–7; John M. Ward, 'Apropos *The British Broadside Ballad and its Music*', *Journal of the American Musicological Society*, xx (1967), 57.

> Say, shal shee goe?
> Oh no, no, no, no, no.[37]

Phrases like 'Be gone', 'needs be gone', 'needs depart', and other variants, were part of the standard vocabulary:

> But since we needs must part,
> Once again, adieu, sweet heart.[38]

> And in fayth will you needes be gon,
> . . .
> Farewell frost, will you needes be gone,
> Adue since that you will needes away.[39]

> And must I goe, and must I needs depart?[40]

These last two examples both come from plays, in which such farewells are common enough. In introducing Jones's recently published air into *Twelfth Night* Shakespeare was guided by his instinct for what would entertain and amuse. In sending up 'Farewel dear loue' he was burlesquing not just one song but a whole tradition.

APPENDIX
List of musical sources

ENGLISH

Robert Jones, *The First Booke of Songes & Ayres*, London, 1600, No. 12
    See *The English School of Lutenist Song Writers*, ed. Edmund H. Fellowes, ser. 2, iv (London, 1925, rev. 1959), 24–5; *Collected English Lutenist Partsongs: I*, ed. David Greer ('Musica Britannica', liii), London, 1987, pp. 51–2.

Robert Jones, *A Musicall Dreame*, London, 1609, No. 8: parody, 'Farewell fond youth'
    See *The English School of Lutenist Song Writers*, ser. 2, xiv (London, 1925), 23–5.

Thomas Robinson, *New Citharen Lessons*, London, 1609, No. 4: for cittern, with divisions
    Concerning Robinson's collection, see John M. Ward, 'Sprightly and Cheerful Music', *Lute Society Journal*, xxi (1979–81), 60–82.

GB-Ob, MS Mus. 439, p. 98: untexted bass
    75 songs with bass, including pieces by Byrd, Weelkes, Dowland and Ferrabosco II. The date '1634' occurs in the margin of p. 114. See Mary Chan, 'Cynthia's Revels and Music for a Choir School: Christ Church Manuscript Mus. 439', *Studies in the Renaissance*, xviii (1971), 134–72.

---

[37] Ed. Hyder Edward Rollins, Cambridge, Mass., 1931–2, i. 110–11. This poem was also set to music by Jones (*Ultimum Vale*, 1605, No. 19) and Martin Peerson (*Priuate Musicke*, 1620, No. 19).
[38] Thomas Bateson, *First set of English Madrigales* (1604), No. 10.
[39] *The Tide Tarrieth no Man* (1576), sig. E.
[40] *Mucedorus* (1598), III. i; ed. James Winny, *Three Elizabethan Plays*, London, 1959, p. 127.

F-Pn, MS Rés. 1186, f. 118: for keyboard
A large collection of keyboard music, including many arrangements of vocal pieces, compiled by Robert Creighton *c.*1630–40.

SCOTTISH

EIRE-Dtc, MS 412 (formerly F.5.13), ff. 58ᵛ–59ᵛ: cantus. On f. 59ᵛ there is 'the anser to the former letter, "Fairwell fond youth if thou had not been blind"' (from Jones's *Musicall Dreame*, No. 8).
The quintus of the MS psalter compiled by Thomas Wode, 1562–*c.*1592, with songs added in the early seventeenth century. For the locations of the other partbooks see *Musica Britannica*, xv. 202.

GB-En, MS Adv. 5.2.15, pp. 6–7: tablature for mandora entitled 'O sillie soul alace'
The Skene MS, compiled *c.* 1615–35. Some pieces, including this one, transcribed in William Dauney, *Ancient Scotish Melodies*, Edinburgh, 1838.

GB-En, MS Panmure 11: cantus without text, entitled 'Faire weill my deire'
The commonplace book of Robert Edwards, compiled *c.*1630–65.

GB-En, MS Adv. 5.2.14, f. 8: cantus
William Stirling's cantus partbook, also known as 'John Leyden's MS', 1639. See Nelly Diem, *Beiträge zur Geschichte der schottischen Musick im XVII. Jahrhundert*, Zurich & Leipzig, 1919, pp. 21–4, 86–7.

John Forbes, *Songs and Fancies*, Aberdeen, 1662 (rev. 1666 and 1682, facsimile of 1682 edn. Paisley, 1879), No. 35: cantus, 'Away vain world, bewitcher of my heart'
Only the cantus partbook was published. For a description of the contents see Charles Sanford Terry, 'John Forbes's "Songs and Fancies"', *The Musical Quarterly*, xxii (1936), 402–19.

US-LAuc, MS T 135Z B724 1677–99, two versions: (a) f. 50, 4 parts, only the cantus texted, 'Farewell fond fancies' (verses 1–3 on f. 58ᵛ); (b) f. 75, cantus, 'Away vain world' (verses 2–5 on ff. 86ᵛ–87)
A collection of part-songs, catches and instrumental pieces compiled in the last quarter of the seventeenth century by Robert Taitt. See Walter H. Rubsamen, 'Scottish and English Music of the Renaissance in a Newly-Discovered Manuscript', *Festschrift Heinrich Besseler*, Leipzig, 1961, pp. 259–84.

DUTCH

NL-Lt, MS 1666, f. 402ᵛ: lute, entitled 'Wanner ick slaep'
The Thysius lute book, compiled 1595–1620. See J. P. N. Land, *Het Luitboek van Thysius*, Amsterdam, 1889.

Nicolas Vallet, *Het Tweede Boeck van den Luyt-Tablatuer. Ghenoemt Het Ghehy-menisse der Sangh-Goddinen*, Amsterdam, 1616; repr. as *Le second livre de tablature de luth, intitulée Le Secret des Muses*, Amsterdam, 1619, p. 9: lute, entitled 'Slaep soete slaep'
Ed. André Souris & Monique Rollin, *Oeuvres de Nicolas Vallet pour luth seule: Le Secret des Muses*, Paris, 1970.

Het gheestelick Paradiisken, Antwerp, 1619, i. 15: cantus with incipit 'Wy looven u, en belyden u Heer'

Dirk Rafaelszoon Camphuysen, *Stichtelycke rymen*, Hoorn, 1624, p. 4: cantus headed 'zang: Shal I bed; of: O slaep. o zoete slaep', with words 'Heylgierigh mensch'

> Also in later edns., of which there were at least 34 before 1700. In the 1652 edn. (two partbooks), sig. A2ᵛ, there is a 'gebroken' version of the music. A note on sig. Ee2 states that 'Hoogheyts minnaer' on sigs. S3ᵛ–S4 can also be sung to this tune. See Curtis, *Sweelinck*, pp. 20–21, for a facsimile of the 1652 version.

Adriaen Valerius, *Neder-Landtsche Gedenck-Clanck*, Harlem, 1626, pp. 68–9: cantus with bass, headed 'Stem: Engels Farwel, met den Bes daer by gestelt', with words 'Almachtig God! ghy die ōs met u hād'; also untexted versions for lute and cittern

> Ed. P. J. Meertens, N. B. Tenhaeff & C. Compter-Kuipers, Amsterdam & Antwerp, 1947.

Amsterdamsche Pegasus, Amsterdam, 1627, p. 41: cantus headed 'Kus-Liedt, Stemme: Wanneer ick slaep, voel ick &c.', with words 'Wanneer ick kus'

Dirck Pieterszon Pers, *Bellerophon*, Amsterdam, 1633, p. 115: cantus headed 'stem: Slaep, ô soete slaep, etc.', with words 'Die in 't ghewoel'

> In the 1657 edn. the tune is also cited in Book II (*Urania*), p. 19, for a poem beginning 'Wat strijdt en ramp', and again in Book III (*Gesangh der Zeeden*), pp. 172–3, for a poem beginning 'Ick heb geseydt'.

S. Theodotus, *Het Paradys der geest. en kerck. lof-sanghen*, 1648, p. 80: cantus, headed 'op de wijse: Ick slaep, ik waeck', with words ''t Nieuw jaer begint'

Cornelis Janszoon de Leeuw, *Christlycke plicht-rymen*, Amsterdam, 1649, p. 133: cantus with words 'Besit van heerelycke staten'

> See J. W. Enschedé, 'Cornelis de Leeuw', *Tijdschrift der Vereeninging voor Noord-Nederlands musiekgeschiedenis*, vii (1901–4), 89–148, 157–232. This gives another setting in four parts by Leeuw, beginning 'Wie kan van die op Aerden woonen' (pp. 210–11).

G[uilliemus] D[e] S[waen], *Den Singende Zwaan*, Leiden, 1728, pp. 519–21: cantus, headed 'Stem: Rijst uyt den slaep. Ofte: Wanneer ik slaep. Ofte: 't Nieuw Jaer begint', with words 'Hort Herders! hoort'

16

A Mid-Seventeenth-Century Music Meeting and Playford's Publishing

Mary Chan

DURING the middle years of the seventeenth century the role of professional musicians in English society underwent a major cultural upheaval. Apart from musicians in Court or private employment, many had formerly found employment in the theatres and the Church. With the closing of the theatres in 1642 and the Ordinance of 1644 ordering the removal of organs from churches, many were without employment. Court activities were dislocated during the Civil Wars, first when the Court moved to Oxford and then later when the queen was in France and King Charles forced to move about England for his safety. This meant the end of Court masques and entertainments and thus a loss of places for Court musicians.

Some of the Court musicians may have joined with former actors for the surreptitious performance of plays.[1] Some became private music teachers. Edward Lowe, who was organist at Christ Church, Oxford, from about 1630, was later music teacher to Anne Baylie and to Barbara Fletcher.[2] John Wilson left Oxford after the surrender of the garrison there in 1646 and, as Anthony Wood recounts, 'spent some years in the family of Sir *Will. Walter* of *Sarsden* in the Parish of *Churchill* in *Oxfordshire*, who, with his Lady, were great lovers of Musick'.[3] There must have been many who had now no regular employment and who were thrown on their own enterprise to make a living. Edmund Chilmead provides an example. Wood describes him as a petty canon at Christ Church from 1632 to 1648, when he 'was forced, such

---

[1] See *The Wits, or Sport upon Sport*, ed. John James Elson ('Cornell Studies in English', xviii), New York & London, 1932, Introduction; Mary Chan, 'Drolls, Drolleries and Mid-Seventeenth-Century Dramatic Music in England', *RMA Research Chronicle*, xv (1979), 117–73.

[2] Ann Baylie's Manuscript, partly in Lowe's hand, is preserved in Christ Church Library, Oxford, MS Mus. 438. Barbara Fletcher's Manuscript was once preserved among the Le Fleming papers in Cumbria.

[3] *Athenae Oxonienses: An Exact History of all the Writers and Bishops who have had their education in the most ancient and famous University of Oxford . . . to which are added the Fasti or Annals, of the said University, for the same time*, London, 1691, ii. 724.

were the then times, to obtain a living by that, which before was only a diversion to him, I mean by a weekly music meeting, which he set up at the *Black Horse* in *Aldersgatestreet* in *London*'.[4]

In Wood's remark we glimpse a new enterprise and a new direction for English music, one which appears to grow directly out of the social and political upheaval of the times. Music meetings among friends were not, of course, a new activity. What is significant in Wood's remark is the implication that one might charge admission and that the meeting would therefore be a public, or at least a semi-public, affair. How typical was Chilmead's enterprise among professional musicians during the late 1640s and 1650s? Records which might provide evidence of music meetings are scant: musical activity might appear to have been submerged. Yet this cannot be an accurate picture, for it was this period that saw the emergence of one of the most important phenomena in English music history, that is, John Playford's publishing venture which began in 1651. So a second question arises: why did Playford begin his publishing business at this time?

Several scholars have written about Playford's publishing career at some length. D. W. Krummel makes clear that he not only re-established music printing in England but that he was primarily concerned with music publishing (as distinct from printing). Krummel draws a distinction between the partbooks published earlier in the seventeenth century, which 'bore their dedication to the noble patron; this may have been followed by a note of instructions to the reader', and Playford's editions where the 'dedication and the instructions are typically addressed to the reader'.[5] That is to say, Playford was concerned primarily with promoting and selling his books. His was a commercial venture, and as such it highlights the issue of the creation and fulfilment of demand.

This essay is an attempt to answer both questions: how typical was Chilmead's enterprise, and why did Playford begin publishing in 1651? The arguments presented are largely conjectural, based mainly on a new investigation of the available documents—that is, the manuscript and printed songbooks of the period. These materials suggest that public concerts were an important part of social life in London in the late 1640s and early 1650s, and that Playford's publishing business was a direct result of such concerts.

Three manuscript collections indicate by their contents that they belonged at one time to a group of musicians and together formed the basis of its repertoire; at a time when there was no such thing as a standard text for songs, close similarities and identical versions imply either a single common source or that one was copied directly from another. The group was centred on the composers John Hilton, Henry Lawes, Nicholas Lanier, John Wilson and possibly Robert Ramsey, although it is not known whether he was still

---

[4] Ibid., ii. 99.
[5] *English Music Printing 1553–1700*, London, 1975, p. 116.

alive in 1650. Evidence for public performance before an audience is provided by the texts of some of the songs. The work of those composers, especially of Hilton and Henry Lawes, dominated Playford's early song-books of 1651–3. Detailed comparison of the three manuscripts with Playford's early publications suggests that it was this same group of musicians, giving public concerts, that created the demand for Playford's publications and gave the impetus to his commercial venture.[6]

The three manuscripts are London, British Library, Add. MS 11608, a manuscript mainly in the hand of John Hilton and containing a number of his songs;[7] Oxford, Bodleian Library, MS Don. c.57;[8] and British Library Egerton MS 2013. The manuscripts have several songs in common. Some occur in versions that are close only in a very general sense. Others, however, are found in versions of which at least parts are almost identical, implying that one has been copied from the other. These songs, which indicate the closest concordances between the three manuscripts, are listed in Table 16.1. Hilton's manuscript (Add. 11608), a large part of which is in his own hand, was compiled both as a record and as a working copy. While most of the songs are in Hilton's own hand, other people too have entered the occasional song or added ornamental versions of a phrase or a passage at the end of a song in several parts of the manuscript. Two songs are annotated thus: 'The treble I tooke & prickt downe as mr Thorpe sung it' (f. 63ᵛ) and, above a rewritten phrase from the song on folios 75ᵛ–77, 'The last close of ye third verse as mr Elliston sung it' (f. 77). Hilton entered songs from both ends of the book, beginning at about the same time. Those entered from what is now the back (turning the volume upside-down) are mainly catches and rounds.

Bodleian Don. c.57 is a large folio manuscript which appears to have been started as a record of songs by Robert Ramsey. Of the first eight entries, six are by him, written with great care and formally ascribed 'Mr Robert Ramsey. Bach: of Mus:', although in fact they are carelessly notated. The songs in treble and bass have been entered by one person, consecutively and apparently over a period of time, to judge by the handwriting. These songs

---

[6] We know that more than fifteen years after he began his music publishing business Playford based one of his largest publications, *The Musicall Companion* (1677), on the repertoire of a group of musicians, for the book is dedicated to members of the group, and Playford's connection with it is established by the existence of a set of manuscript partbooks, in his hand, which formed the basis of the printed text. These are now University of Glasgow, Euing Music Library, Anderson MSS R.d. 58–61. See Ian Spink, 'The Old Jewry "Musick-Society": A Seventeenth-Century Catch Club', *Musicology*, ii (1967), 35–41. Spink argues that the 'Musick-Society' was meeting in the late 1650s. I argue that a different group, meeting in the early 1650s, was responsible for the demand for Playford's publications.

[7] See Mary Chan, 'John Hilton's Manuscript British Library Add. MS 11608', *Music & Letters*, lx (1979), 440–49.

[8] See John P. Cutts, 'A Bodleian Song-book: Don. c. 57', *Music & Letters*, xxxiv (1953), 192–211; George Thewlis, 'Some Notes on a Bodleian Manuscript', *Music & Letters*, xlii (1961), 32–5.

TABLE 16.1

First Line	Hilton MS	Ramsey MS	Egerton 2013	Notes
Amarillis by a spring (Herrick)	ff. 10ᵛ–11, treble & bass: Henry Lawes		ff. 22–22ᵛ, treble & bass: John Wilson	Very similar despite different ascriptions: three small variants in bass, two in treble. Same error in note values in both MSS (Hilton, f. 11; Egerton, f. 22ᵛ).
Ardens est cor meum	ff. 31ᵛ–32, 2 voices, treble & bass: Richard Dering		f. 7, treble & tablature	Similarities in upper voice part only. In Hilton some marked bars reproduced in ornate versions, f. 32; Egerton marks two but does not give ornate versions.
Charon, come hither Charon	ff. 13ᵛ–14ᵛ, treble & bass: John Hilton	pp. 10–13, treble & bass		Ramsey one tone higher than Hilton: otherwise only slight variants in some note values.
Hither we come into this world of woe	f. 9, treble & bass: Henry Lawes	p. 61, treble & bass	f. 15, 2 bars treble & tablature then treble & bass: Henry Lawes	Treble very similar in all three; Hilton has ornament in antipenultimate bar lacking in Ramsey, Egerton. Bass also very similar in Hilton, Ramsey.
I saw fair Chloris walk alone		p. [118], treble & bass: John Hilton	ff. 23–23ᵛ, treble & bass: John Hilton	Two small variants in treble, several in bass. (Paris, Conservatoire, MS Rés. 2489, p. 296, is very close to Egerton.)

First line				Notes
No sad thought his soul affright		p. 33 (and, words only, p. 53), treble & bass	f. 3, treble & bass: John Hilton	Two small variants in bass only; ornaments at bb. 13, 17 in both MSS.
Swift through the yielding air I glide	ff. 11v–12, treble & bass: Henry Lawes	pp. [125–6], treble & bass		Treble almost identical; slight variants in bass.
Three score and ten the life and age of man		p. 59, treble & bass	ff. 59v–60, treble & tablature: John Hilton	Only treble similar; variant note values appear to be errors in Egerton.
What tears (dear Prince) can serve	f. 26, treble & bass: Robert Ramsey	p. 37, treble & bass: Robert Ramsey		Identical apart from some ornamentation in Hilton.

run from pages 1 to 145 (i.e. to page [159], for the pagination is sometimes erratic), after which there is a gap of ten folios (filled up by entries in a much later hand), and then, towards the end of the book, there are more entries in the main hand of the manuscript. These last entries consist of thirteen songs for voice and tablature and were apparently (again to judge from the handwriting) entered at about the time the book was begun. The writer divided the book, entering songs in treble and bass at the front and songs in treble and tablature towards the back.[9] Despite the prominence of songs by Robert Ramsey, particularly in the early part of the book, it is hard to imagine that entries made by him of his own songs would contain the errors they do.

Little is known about Ramsey's life, except that from 1628 to 1644 he was organist at Trinity College, Cambridge.[10] His connection with John Hilton has been commented on by Basil Smallman, who suggested that they met at Cambridge.[11] Although this is possible, Hilton had left Cambridge by 1628, the year Ramsey took up his appointment at Trinity College. That a common interest or friendship of some kind drew them together is, nevertheless, indicated by the fact that Hilton and Ramsey were, between them, responsible for almost the entire extant repertoire of biblical and mythological dialogue songs in England in the mid seventeenth century. Don. c. 57 and Hilton's manuscript contain all their extant dialogues and are the only extant sources for them. For this reason Don. c. 57 may be referred to as Ramsey's manuscript, for if it was not compiled by him, its unique source for his dialogues implies his influence in its compilation. Ramsey's songs at the beginning of the manuscript are mainly these dialogues; and although the entries could have been made as early as 1631, the date of John Hilton's 'Charon' dialogue on the death of Hobson, the famous Cambridge water carrier (pp. 10–13), there is no indication of any date for the collection's compilation. The manuscript contains none of Ramsey's church music.

Hilton's and Ramsey's manuscripts contain several songs in common, and four songs occur in both in almost identical versions. Because these songs occur near the beginning of Hilton's manuscript but are scattered in Ramsey's I infer that Hilton's book contains the copies. The versions in Hilton's manuscript differ mainly in that two contain some ornamentation of the vocal line, and one is a tone lower than Ramsey's version (see Table 16.1). The first entry in Hilton's manuscript can be dated c.1640.[12] Each manuscript was, then, begun separately. Ramsey is known to have left his

---

[9] The manuscript was later used as a plant catalogue: about half the book has been written over with times and instructions for planting various herbs.

[10] For details see Edward Thompson in *The New Grove*, xv. 579.

[11] 'Endor Revisited: English Biblical Dialogues of the Seventeenth Century', *Music & Letters*, xlvi (1965), 137–45.

[12] Up to folio 11ᵛ the songs are numbered consecutively, and Nos. 2 and 5 can be dated 1641 and 1640 respectively. See Chan, 'John Hilton's Manuscript', p. 442.

post as organist at Trinity College in 1644. Was it after this that his and Hilton's manuscripts formed the basis for a single repertoire?

Egerton 2013 is a folio collection of songs in both treble and bass and treble and tablature. The majority of the song texts are written in Elizabethan secretary hand. Another, italic, hand which occasionally seems to suggest the same writer has added ascriptions at the ends of some songs, the occasional 'correction' of a word in the margin and two additional stanzas for the song on folio 61. The last song in the manuscript (ff. 66–8), the 'Dialogue' ascribed to 'Jo: Lenton', has been entered in a later hand. This manuscript has attracted little notice from scholars, because the songs in it appear to have been very carelessly entered and therefore to be unreliable sources.

This manuscript contains two songs whose versions are very close to versions in Hilton's manuscript, four whose versions are very close to those in Ramsey's manuscript and one in common with both the others (see Table 16.1). A comparison of the songs that occur in very similar versions in either of the other two manuscripts reveals not so much carelessness in notating the songs as the fact that in Egerton 2013 the bass part at least was taken down aurally; and the occurrence of four songs towards the end of the book (ff. 59, 60^v, 63, 65) with texts entered in a kind of shorthand (i.e. with many of the words represented by the first letter only) supports a suggestion of hasty or aural transcription. The song which all three manuscripts have in common in very similar versions provides an illustration of this point. The version of Henry Lawes's 'Hither we come into this world of woe' in the Egerton manuscript is similar to the other two only in the vocal part. Its accompaniment begins in lute tablature but after two bars is written in very rough staff notation. The way in which the bass has been entered, with disregard for time values in alignment with the voice part, implies that it was added after the vocal line and in some haste, even as the song was performed. The copyist changed from tablature to unfigured bass because tablature is slow to write.[13]

The Egerton manuscript has more in common with Ramsey's book than with Hilton's. As was the case with Hilton's manuscript, the fact that songs in common occur in the Egerton manuscript in groups but are scattered in Ramsey's implies that this latter manuscript was the earlier. However, two consecutive songs in Ramsey's book (pp. [118] and [119]) are in versions very similar to those of two songs in the Egerton manuscript which are not consecutive (Egerton 2013, ff. 23–23^v and 25^v–26), so if Ramsey's book was begun early and then used as a source book for a group of musicians, pieces were also added to it later from either of the other two manuscripts associated with that group.

---

[13] Hilton's manuscript also contains examples of aural transcription, ff. 63^v, 77; see above, p. 233.

Only some of the composers of songs in the Egerton manuscript are identified, and apart from Ramsey, who is not mentioned, those identified are the composers most represented in both the other manuscripts: John Hilton, Henry Lawes, John Wilson and Nicholas Lanier. While the other manuscripts also contain several songs by William Lawes, only one song in the Egerton manuscript is ascribed to him. If the named composers also formed the basis of the group performing the songs, then the lack of songs by William Lawes in the Egerton manuscript implies that it was compiled after William Lawes's death in 1645.[14]

Comparison of the three manuscripts suggests a date towards the end of the 1640s for the flourishing of a group of musicians centred on Hilton, since his manuscript, more than the other two, has the appearance of a working copy, with its added passages at the ends of some songs referring to particular performances and working out details of ornamentation. We know that Nicholas Lanier was not in England continuously during the 1640s: in 1645 and 1646 he was in Antwerp.[15] Anthony Wood tells us that John Wilson left Oxford in 1646 and spent 'some years' with Sir William Walter in Oxfordshire. Was he in London before he returned to Oxford in 1656, the year he was made Professor of Music?

Many songs in the two largest of the three manuscripts (i.e. Hilton's and Ramsey's) imply public performance. An audience is implied not only by the number of dramatic pieces and dialogues but also by songs with veiled political reference, for such songs lose their point unless sung before an audience, some of whom (but not all) must understand the allusions. References to the execution of Charles I in 1649 confirm 1649 and 1650 as dates for many of the songs. While the two larger manuscripts contain several royalist and overtly political songs, it is those with covert political reference which are the more important in discussing their public function.

Elsewhere I have considered the possibility of covert reference in one very popular dialogue song, the Witch of Endor dialogue ascribed to Robert Ramsey which occurs in both Hilton's (ff. 23ᵛ–25ᵛ) and Ramsey's (pp. 14–18) manuscripts.[16] In Hilton's manuscript the song occurs near another which suggests political reference, 'Cloris sigh'd, & sunge, & wept' (ff. 26ᵛ–27), ascribed to 'Mr Balls'.[17] In this song two characters are named, Chloris and Amintor. Although the song dates from well before the 1640s,

---

[14] Further evidence for a group centred on those named composers may exist in Lanier's recast version of Ramsey's Witch of Endor dialogue, which dates from the 1660s. See Mary Chan, 'The Witch of Endor and Seventeenth-Century Propaganda', *Musica disciplina*, xxxiv (1980), 205 n. 2.

[15] See Gordon James Callon, 'Nicholas Lanier, his Life and Music: A Study and Edition' (dissertation), University of Washington, 1983, pp. 77–80, 96.

[16] 'In guilty night', a dialogue between Saul and the Witch of Endor. See Chan, 'The Witch of Endor and Seventeenth-Century Propaganda'.

[17] The song also occurs in Ramsey's manuscript, p. 26.

its placing here draws it into what became a little genre of Chloris and Amintor (or sometimes Amintas) laments, almost all of which are by Henry Lawes and many of which occur in the three volumes of his *Ayres and Dialogues* (1652, 1653, 1658) as well as in Playford's *Select Musicall Ayres and Dialogues* (1652, 1653, 1669). A study of these Chloris and Amintor songs reveals a group of songs with covert political reference. The inclusion of songs from this genre in the repertoire of Hilton's group provides one instance of the kind of song which requires performance before an audience.

The association of the Chloris and Amintor laments with the execution of Charles I was a development from two traditions. Two songs by Henry Lawes use the names in clear and overt reference to Henrietta Maria (Charles's queen) and Charles: 'Help, help, O help, Divinity of Love', entitled 'A Storm: Cloris at sea, near the Land, is surprized by a Storm: AMINTOR on the shore, expecting her Arrival, THUS COMPLAINS', in *Ayres and Dialogues* (1655), pp. 1–3, and 'See, see! my Chloris, my Chloris comes in yonder bark' entitled 'Chloris *landing at* Berlington', in *Ayres and Dialogues* (1658), pp. 1–2. Both songs refer to the return of Henrietta Maria to England from the Low Countries in February 1643, whence she had gone at the outbreak of civil war in 1642.[18]

Another song by Henry Lawes builds on this already established allusion, but now it uses the names as disguise; for this song almost certainly refers to Charles I's death. 'Chloris since thou wert fled away' was first printed in *Ayres and Dialogues* (1658), p. 10, entitled 'Amintor's welladay' because it makes use of the 'welladay' refrain. The song also occurs in several manuscript sources dating from the middle of the seventeenth century. A ballad tune (different from that of 'Chloris since thou wert fled away') called 'Welladay', popular throughout the first half of the seventeenth century, was first associated with 'A lamentable Dittie composed vpon the death of Robert Lord late Earle of Essex . . .' (1601), beginning 'Sweet England's pride is gone / welladay welladay'.[19] The same tune was used in 1618 for a ballad on the execution of Sir Walter Ralegh and in 1641 for a ballad on the execution of Sir Thomas Wentworth. A fragmentary ballad to the tune survives from 1649 entitled 'King Charles His Speech, and last Farewell to the World . . . January 30. 1648 [1649 NS]' which begins 'Faire England's joy is fled, Weladay, weladay'. The echo of this in the first line of 'Chloris since thou wert fled away' and the use of the 'welladay' refrain link the Chloris song to this ballad tune of 'Welladay', associated for nearly 50 years with ballads on the deaths of popular martyrs. The reference to Charles's execution is covert, for here Chloris, a woman's name, is given to Charles, while it is, nevertheless, a close anagram on his name, containing all the

---

[18] See Ian Spink, *English Song: Dowland to Purcell*, London, 1974, p. 96.
[19] See Claude M. Simpson, *The British Broadside Ballad and its Music*, New Brunswick, 1966, p. 206.

consonants but changing the vowels. Amintas (or Amintor as he is called in the printed texts) then refers to England in mourning, as that other 'Welladay' ballad began 'Faire England's joy is fled'. But there is another role for Amintas too: in Virgil's eclogues he is the shepherd referred to as the musician. The song is the lament of Henry Lawes himself, one of King Charles's most famous musicians. Not only, then, are the names Chloris and Amintas anagrammatically and allegorically appropriate: the original use of the names Chloris and Amintor to refer to the queen and the king make the later reference part of a shared, coterie, allusion. If one accepts the hypothesis that this 'Welladay' lament refers to Charles and England (or Henry Lawes), then others of Henry Lawes's 'Chloris' songs share the reference of mourning for the dead King.[20] Ramsey's manuscript (pp. 48–9) contains another lament in this genre, 'Come Sorrow wrap me in thy sable cloake', although there Chloris is not referred to by name, only Amintas.

Henry Lawes's use of Chloris and Amintor suggests reasons for the inclusion of that earlier seventeenth-century Chloris song in Hilton's manuscript ('Cloris sigh'd') near the Witch of Endor dialogue.[21] Although originally without allegorical significance, by association with the genre of Chloris songs it is drawn into that genre. But this is unlike those laments which refer to the dead Chloris: in this song Amintas is dead, lamented by Chloris. One can only conjecture whether, in its revival in the 1640s, this reversal of the mourner and the mourned had any significance. The original specific reference of Amintor/Amintas by Henry Lawes in those two songs dating from the early 1640s was to Charles; but Amintas in Virgil was the musician, and this formed the basis for the mourning of Amintas at the death of Chloris in those songs written after Charles's execution. The anagram on Charles/Chloris, however, may have been current earlier than Charles's death, and here, where Chloris is mourning Amintas's death, we may see in Amintas that other Lawes musician, Henry's brother William. The song was perhaps revived on behalf of the King when William Lawes was killed fighting in his service in 1645, and then became part of that coterie allusion and part of the genre of Chloris songs which Henry Lawes developed after

---

[20] Three songs of this kind occur in a group in *Ayres and Dialogues* (1658): p. 24 'A description of Chloris', beginning 'Have you e're seen the morning sun'; p. 27 'Amintor's Dream', beginning 'As sad Amintor in a Medow lay'; p. 28 'Chloris *dead, lamented by Amintor*', beginning 'Mourn, mourn with me, all true Enamour'd hearts'. Another was first printed in Playford's *Select Musicall Ayres, and Dialogues* (1652, p. 17, 1653, p. 13, 1659, p. 41): 'Tell me you wandering spirits of the air' by Henry Lawes. Exactly the same version of the treble part occurs in Ramsey's manuscript (treble only), p. [157]. The printed version is entitled 'Amintor *for his* Chloris *absence*'. A dialogue lament by Simon Ives (a contributor to both Hilton's and Ramsey's manuscripts) occurs in *Select Ayres and Dialogues . . . The Second Book* (1669), pp. 118–20, in which the dead nymph is referred to as Clorin.

[21] Other sources for this song are Trinity College, Dublin, MS F.5.13., f. 30; Christ Church, Oxford, MS Mus. 87, f. 1; New York Public Library MS Drexel 4175, No. viii; British Library Add. MS 10337, f. 21[v].

the execution of Charles I. One other song in the Amintas group supports the
conjecture that William Lawes is referred to here. Ramsey's manuscript (pp.
5–8) contains a setting by Ramsey of a Charon dialogue beginning 'Charon
O Charon heare a wretch opprest'. A setting of the same text by William
Lawes was published in *Select Ayres and Dialogues . . . The Second Book*
(1660), pp. 112–13, and in this printed version the characters in the dialogue
are both identified: Charon and Amintor. The continued popularity of this
particular dialogue song must have encouraged its publication in 1669, 24
years after William Lawes's death. Does this mean that William Lawes's
association with Amintor—as the reason for the revival of 'Cloris sigh'd'—
led to the later identification, by Playford, of the other character in his setting
of the Charon dialogue as Amintor?

Immediately preceding 'Cloris sigh'd' in Hilton's book, and immediately
following Ramsey's Witch of Endor dialogue, on folio 26, is another Ramsey
song: 'What teares (deere Prince) can searve'. The text, sometimes, although
dubiously, attributed to Sir Walter Ralegh, is believed to date from 1612, a
poem written on the death of Prince Henry. Ian Spink has pointed out that
stylistically this is rather too early a date for Ramsey's setting and suggests
instead that its entry in Ramsey's manuscript (which he dates *c*.1631)
indicates a setting for the death of Charles I's son, a few hours after his birth
in 1629.[22] Whatever its earlier history, the placing of this song in both
Hilton's and Ramsey's manuscripts makes clear that its purpose has been
correctly identified by the nineteenth-century reader of Hilton's manuscript
who pencilled a note indicating that the song commemorates the execution
of Charles I.

Two more songs in Hilton's manuscript following 'Cloris sigh'd' imply,
by their placing, veiled reference to the king and thus belong to the period of
mourning for his death. One of these, 'Come sylent night, & in thy gloomy
shade' (ff. 28ᵛ–29) is ascribed to John Wilson. This is preceded by a song
beginning 'Marke how ye blushfull Morne in vayne' (f. 28), headed 'By his
Majesty'. The text is by Carew, and in *Select Ayres and Dialogues . . . The
Second Book* (1669), p. 53, the same setting is ascribed to Nicholas Lanier.
While the song is more probably Lanier's, Hilton may have included it in a
group of songs commemorating Charles I because it was a favourite with
him or set at his request.

The repertoire of the music group represented by the three related manuscripts is closely related to Playford's early publications. Playford's first
publications containing songs were *A Musicall Banquet* and *Musick and
Mirth* (both 1651). *A Musicall Banquet*, in three sections, consisted mainly
of music for viols, but Part III contained 'New and Choyce Catches'; *Musick
and Mirth* was a 'choyce collection of rounds and catches for three voyces'.

[22] *English Song*, p. 67.

In the following year Playford devoted an entire book to catches, or rounds: Hilton's *Catch that Catch Can* (1652). The last part of Hilton's manuscript (ff. 79–86ᵛ) consists almost entirely of catches.²³ With the exception of three, the entries were made by Hilton himself, and all but three were published in *Catch that Catch Can*. There are few variants between the printed and manuscript versions, the most significant being in the words of the songs. In these cases Hilton's manuscript version makes more sense. Since Hilton is unlikely to have copied his own songs from the printed book, this manuscript is the source for *Catch that Catch Can*.²⁴

Playford began his song publishing with the simplest part-songs, the catches. Their popularity indicates a market: in 1658 and again in 1663 he published enlarged editions of *Catch that Catch Can*. By the edition of 1667 it had changed its title to *The Musical Companion*, although in this first mutation it retained its original title as an alternative. Simple part-songs and rounds remained the staple of Playford's early books, even of his more serious collections. The format that was to remain constant throughout the various editions of his second type of popular collection, the *Select Musicall Ayres and Dialogues* (1652, 1653, 1669)—a section of solo songs, a section of dialogue songs and a section of rounds, catches and simple part-songs—is also the format of Hilton's manuscript. Furthermore, Playford's early songbooks centre on the work of the composers most represented in the three manuscripts (with the exception of Robert Ramsey);²⁵ Henry Lawes, Nicholas Lanier, John Hilton and John Wilson.

Hilton's manuscript collection of catches and the kinds of songs in the manuscript as a whole do not, however, provide the only link between these three manuscripts and Playford's publishing. One song in Ramsey's manuscript, 'Ladyes fly from Loues smooth tale' (p. [134]) was printed in *Select Musicall Ayres and Dialogues* (1653), p. 21, in a version very similar to that in the manuscript. There is only one variant in note values in the treble, but the more frequent variants in the bass suggest that Playford used the manuscript as his source rather than that the manuscript copied the printed text. It appears that Playford altered what is, in places, an idiosyncratic bass in the manuscript to a more simple and regular one. The variants in Playford's bass indicate the kind of editing that Charles Pigeon, writing a commendatory verse to *Select Ayres and Dialogues . . . The Second Book* (1669), implies was Playford's usual procedure:

> Nor let vain *Momus* Carp and Cry
> This Work speaks thee a *Plagiary*;
> For don't we know thy depth, and skill

²³ See above, p. 233.
²⁴ See Chan, 'John Hilton's Manuscript', pp. 443–4.
²⁵ Does this indicate that Ramsey was dead by the late 1640s and therefore no longer a member of the group?

In *Musick*? thou dost change, or fill
What pleaseth not, or where it wants,
And regulate the false Descants.
Thou art as ready to translate,
As to transcribe, thy Book can say't.

Further evidence for a link between Playford and the group can be adduced from a manuscript which is in Playford's own hand, Paris Conservatoire Rés. 2489.[26] The connection of this Playford manuscript with the three manuscripts of Hilton's group is clear in the versions of two songs, both by John Hilton himself.[27] The first of these, 'I saw faire Chloris walke alone', occurs in Rés. 2489, p. 296, and also in Egerton 2013, ff. 23–23ᵛ, and in Ramsey's manuscript, p. [118]. The two latter versions are very similar, although there are some variants in the bass parts; the version in the Paris manuscript has clearly been made from the Egerton manuscript, for it is very close indeed. The other Hilton song is 'Thou maist be proud', Rés. 2489, p. 353, ascribed to 'J Hilton'. The Egerton manuscript version (f. 10) is also ascribed to Hilton, although it is not the same as that in Rés. 2489. Ramsey's manuscript (p. 79) contains a version ascribed to Robert Ramsey, and this is the same version as, and almost identical to, that ascribed to Hilton in the Paris manuscript: the similarity extends to the reproduction of an error in the bass part of bar 7. These two Hilton songs, then, establish a link between the manuscript in Playford's hand and the Egerton and Ramsey's manuscripts.

That the Playford manuscript is later than both these and therefore contains the copies rather than the sources of these songs is suggested by the fact that the early part of Rés. 2489 contains eighteen songs which occur also in *Select Ayres and Dialogues . . . The Second Book* (1669), fifteen of which occur there in versions exactly the same as those in the manuscript. Since it would be unlikely that Playford would copy from his own printed book, Rés. 2489 is the source for the printed versions. All the other songs in the manuscript which also occur in printed books are found in publications later than 1669.

The recognition of part of Rés. 2489 as a source for *Select Ayres and Dialogues . . . The Second Book* (1669) points to a further link between that manuscript and the three manuscripts of Hilton's group. The 1669 text contains a song which occurs in both Hilton's and Ramsey's manuscripts,

---

[26] See John P. Cutts, 'Seventeenth-Century Songs and Lyrics in Paris Conservatoire MS Rés. 2489', *Musica disciplina*, xxii (1969), 117–39. Cutts did not identify the hand as Playford's but observed only that 'John Playford may have been the compiler' (p. 118). Identification of the handwriting is made by comparison with the manuscript partbooks in the Euing Music Library, University of Glasgow (Anderson MS R.d. 58–61), which the library claims to be in Playford's hand. See Spink, 'The Old Jewry "Musick-Society"', and note 6 above.

[27] The two songs by Hilton in the Paris manuscript are the only Hilton songs in any manuscript other than the three discussed in this essay.

and which is very similar in all three copies. This is Henry Lawes's 'Swift through the yeilding aire I glide' (Hilton, ff. 11^v–12; Ramsey, pp. [125–6]).[28] The major variant between the printed and manuscript versions is in the opening run, part of which is omitted in the printed text. Nevertheless, this first bar is closer to the two manuscript versions than to that in Lawes's autograph: these two, like the printed version, begin the bar with a rest. The printed version, then, is a copy of those belonging to Hilton's group, the first bar either containing a misreading of the manuscripts or indicating that the typesetter lacked the piece of type for the first two notes.

Any answers to the questions with which I began can be only hints. Nevertheless, this paper is also presented to suggest ways in which new demands can be made of the documents which survive from this period; for by asking questions of the songs themselves and of the physical form (manuscript or printed) in which they survive, more details of a period of major cultural disruption, with consequences for music both social and aesthetic, may be illuminated. The three major manuscript sources of songs for the middle years of the seventeenth century were of greater influence than collections made for purely private use would have been. The burgeoning of musical publishing in the 1650s was rooted in, and nourished by, the public or semi-public concerts of which these manuscripts formed the repertoire. The 1650s saw a strong development of musical culture in England, its very strength dependent on forces which, in the past, were thought to have weakened it since they removed musicians from public positions in the Church, the theatres and at Court.

---

[28] Henry Lawes's own version of the song occurs in his autograph manuscript British Library Add. MS 53723, ff. 68^v–69; while this is basically the same, it varies from these other three in many details.

17

Milton's Harmonious Sisters

John Carey

DID Milton like music? The answer seems so clearly yes as to make the question hardly worth asking. Milton's knowledge and love of music have always been standard ingredients in accounts of his life and work. His father, as everyone knows, was a musician and composer. Jonathan Richardson, among early biographers, tells us that Milton inherited this paternal taste. He loved music 'extreamly', Richardson attests, and ' 'tis said' he composed, though none of his music survives. Richardson's informants also told him that Milton played the organ and the bass viol.[1] From Milton himself we learn how eagerly he followed new developments in music. He recalls, in *Defensio secunda*, that when living at his father's country house after leaving Cambridge he would go up to London to buy books or learn something new about mathematics or music, 'in which I then took the keenest pleasure'.[2] Edward Phillips, Milton's nephew, remembers that his uncle brought back 'a Chest or two of choice Musick-books' from his Italian trip, including works by Luca Marenzio, Claudio Monteverdi, Orazio Vecchi, Antonio Cifra and Don Carlo Gesualdo, Prince of Venosa.[3] Music seems to have been inseparable from Milton's understanding of ultimate reality. The theory of world harmony and the mythical music of the spheres repeatedly attract his poetic attention, as many commentators have noted, and the divine musician Orpheus was a dominant presence in his personal pantheon.[4]

Despite this weight of evidence, the question of Milton's attitude to music seems worth raising, because he ventures, in his Latin poem *Ad patrem*, a distinction and a criticism which would seem by no means self-evident to most music-lovers. His intent in the poem (written when he was about 24 and still unemployed after university) was to defend poetry, and his own

---

[1] *The Early Lives of Milton*, ed. Helen Darbishire, Oxford, 1932, p. 204.
[2] *Complete Prose Works of John Milton*, ed. Don M. Wolfe and others, New Haven, 1953–82, iv. 614.
[3] Darbishire, *Early Lives*, p. 59.
[4] See for example John Hollander, *The Untuning of the Sky: Ideas of Music in English Poetry, 1500–1700*, Princeton, 1961, and Leo Spitzer, *Classical and Christian Ideas of World Harmony*, Baltimore, 1963.

resolution to become a poet, against his father's worldly misgivings. He
mentions his father's proficiency in music only to argue that music is
subordinate to and dependent on poetry. True music, Milton affirms, is not
melody but words:

After all, what use is the voice if it merely hums an inane tune, without words,
meaning, or the rhythm of speech? That kind of song is good enough for the
woodland choirs, but not for Orpheus, who with his singing, not his lyre, held
streams spellbound and gave ears to the oak trees, and moved lifeless phantoms to
tears. It is to his singing that he owes his reputation.[5]

Milton may have been influenced here by his beloved Plato, though it is a
possibility which, to judge from the *Variorum Commentary*, critics and
editors have ignored.[6] The Athenian stranger who is the protagonist in
Plato's *Laws* (ii. 669–70) refers, like Milton, to Orpheus, while assuring his
companions that it is a mistake to compose tunes without words. Wordless
music is not permissible because it lacks meaning: 'it is almost impossible to
understand what is meant by this wordless rhythm and harmony'. Accordingly, to employ musical instruments without the accompaniment of song is
'clownish in the extreme', the stranger concludes, and 'the mark of the
mountebank or the boor'.[7]

Young Milton in *Ad patrem* was not just aping Plato, though, nor was he
making a debating point. His doubts about the status and value of music,
except as an accompaniment to song, seem to have been real, permanent,
and connected to some of his deepest anxieties. As Sigmund Spaeth has
observed,[8] the references to song in his poems far outnumber those to
instrumental music. The poems Milton wrote about music bear out this
preference. The only musical performer who stirred him to poetic applause
was a singer, not an instrumentalist—Leonora Baroni, whom he had heard
in Italy.[9] Milton's sonnet to Henry Lawes insists on the priority of words to
music. Musical accompaniment, the sonnet advises, should not be so
elaborate as to obscure the sense of the words or upset their natural
rhythm.[10] This judgement implies Milton's disapproval of contemporary
madrigalists and also, as William Riley Parker notes,[11] of some of his father's
settings.

The Lawes sonnet, it has been argued, shows Milton's musically pro-

---

[5] Translation from *The Poems of John Milton*, ed. John Carey & Alastair Fowler, London,
1968, p. 154.
[6] See *A Variorum Commentary on the Poems of John Milton*, i, ed. Douglas Bush and
others, London, 1970, p. 248.
[7] Plato, *Laws*, ed. & trans. R. G. Bury (Loeb Classical Library), London, 1926, i. 146–7.
[8] *Milton's Knowledge of Music: its Sources and its Significance in his Works*, Princeton,
1913, p. 48.
[9] See *Poems*, pp. 254–7.
[10] Ibid., pp. 292–3.
[11] *Milton: a Biography*, Oxford, 1968, i. 302.

gressive taste.[12] Lawes was breaking from the traditions of polyphony, which, for all its beautiful interlacing of melodies, sacrificed textual clarity. The composers whose works Milton brought back from Italy can also be seen as part of this movement. Though diverse, they all wrote vocal music in the new homophonic, harmonic style which had been flourishing in Italy for several decades but was only beginning to evolve in England. The emergence in Italy, around the turn of the century, of the *stile rappresentativo* has been seen as a turning point in the history of music. The renunciation of the polyphonic style marked the end of the Renaissance and was closely connected with the advent of opera. The whole development was essentially part of the triumph of rhetoric, of persuasive word-power, with its potential for serving the sectional and propagandist interests of the post-Reformation world, as against the relative consensus of the purely musical. Giulio Caccini, in the preface to his *Nuove musiche* (1602), condemned 'that sort of music which, preventing any clear understanding of the words, shatters both their form and content'.[13]

Of course, Milton's opinions in the Lawes sonnet might amount to no more than poetic prejudice—a natural anxiety on the part of a young writer to protect the integrity of his words against the distortions of a fancy musical setting. But a survey of Milton's poetry, early and late, suggests that his elevation of words above music reflects a more basic judgement, which involved not just his authorial pride but the nature of his intelligence. The idea of song, and of song as opposed to songless music, was vital to his creative impulse and can be traced in the choices his imagination made. In conceiving, for example, of the music of the spheres, Milton found that his classical sources offered him two alternative accounts of how the sound was produced. Plato, in the *Republic* (x. 617), recounts Er's vision of the universe as a system of eight concentric whorls, fitting into one another like a nest of boxes. These, Er reports, revolved round a spindle of adamant which rested on the knees of Necessity, and around her sat the Fates, her daughters.

On each of the rims of the whorls a Siren stood, borne around in its revolution, and uttering one sound, one note, and from all the eight there was the concord of a single harmony.[14]

According to Cicero in the *Somnium Scipionis*, however, the music of the spheres is produced not by the voices of the Sirens but by 'the onward rush and motion of the spheres themselves'. For, it is explained:

---

[12] I am indebted in this paragraph to Mortimer H. Frank, 'Milton's Knowledge of Music: some Speculations', *Milton and the Art of Sacred Song*, ed. J. Max Patrick & Roger H. Sundell, Madison, 1979, pp. 83–98.

[13] *Le nuove musiche*, ed. H. Wiley Hitchcock ('Recent Researches in the Music of the Baroque Era', ix), Madison, 1970, p. 44.

[14] Plato, *Republic*, ed. & trans. Paul Shorey (Loeb Classical Library), rev. edn., London, 1937, ii. 502–5.

Such mighty motions cannot be carried on so swiftly in silence; and nature has provided that one extreme shall produce low tones while the other gives forth high. Therefore this uppermost sphere of heaven, which bears the stars, as it revolves more rapidly, produces a high shrill tone, whereas the lowest revolving sphere, that of the Moon, gives forth the lowest tone.[15]

Cicero's explanation, which attributes sphere-music to a mechanical or instrumental, rather than a supernatural and vocal source, had been accepted by a number of later expositors, including Boethius in his *De musica* (I. 2).

Despite this more modern tradition, Milton's account in *Arcades* of the music of the spheres is modelled on Plato's. The Attendant Spirit listens to

> . . . the celestial sirens' harmony
> That sit upon the nine enfolded spheres,
> And sing to those that hold the vital shears,
> And turn the adamantine spindle round . . .
> (*Arcades*, ll. 63–6)

Given Milton's apparent view of the respective merits of vocal and instrumental performance, that is what we should expect. The sphere-music is song.

Matters are not, however, quite so straightforward. Invoking the sphere-music in the Nativity Ode, Milton apparently inclines to the alternative, Ciceronian tradition:

> Ring out, ye crystal spheres,
> Once bless our human ears,
>   (If ye have power to touch our senses so)
> And let your silver chime
> Move in melodious time;
>   And let the base of heaven's deep organ blow,
> And with your ninefold harmony
> Make up full consort to the angelic symphony.
> (*On the Morning of Christ's Nativity*, ll. 125–32)

No mention here of sirens or the song they sang. The words 'chime' and 'organ' imply that the cosmos emits sound by some kind of mechanical operation, without a vocal component. Is Milton then deviating from his tenet that melody, without words, is inferior?

We need not, in fact, suppose so. The difficulty of reconciling the Nativity Ode's sphere-music with what had seemed to be Milton's preference elsewhere is only apparent. For the spheres are called on to 'ring out' in the ode only as an accompaniment to choral song. Song is already happening in the poem: the Christmas angels are performing:

[15] Cicero, *De republica*, ed. & trans. Clinton Walker Keynes (Loeb Classical Library), London, 1928, pp. 272–3.

Divinely-warbled voice
Answering the stringed noise.
(ll. 96–97)

It is with this 'angelic symphony'—voices and instruments together—that the sphere-music is required to harmonize.

What seems to be the case is that Milton's opinion about the sphere-music was a relatively subordinate concern. Though it has often, and rightly, been thought of as having profound imaginative importance for him, he was really indifferent about its working details. He was quite prepared to entertain the idea that it came from voices, and equally willing to present it as coming from the spheres themselves. For that matter he was ready to argue that it did not exist at all, but was just a kind of allegory, as he concedes in *Prolusion* II, 'On the Harmony of the Spheres'.[16] But his imaginative attachment to the presence of the voice in musical performance was, by comparison, fundamental. The spheres could do without their singing sirens, so long as singing was being supplied from elsewhere—and that is what happens in the Nativity Ode. The pagan sirens, like the Fates and Necessity, would have looked odd in the ode beside the angel choir, which may be why Milton left them out. And he could leave them out because the vocal component was already present, before the spheres were told to ring, or blow.

Following this train of thought brings us to *At a Solemn Music*, a poem close in date to *Arcades* and which, unlike the Nativity Ode, seems actually to identify the music of the spheres with the angelic song. True, 'sirens' are mentioned at the start of the poem, but their status, it soon becomes apparent, is metaphoric. These sirens are 'Voice, and Verse': they belong to a thinner, more safely rhetorical region of reality than the awesome beings the Genius in *Arcades* listened to. The idea of a music which humans could once hear, but cannot now, because of mankind's corruption—an idea which was rightly part of the music-of-the-spheres syndrome—is in this poem re-allocated to the song of the angels. It is their song which we might, suitably transported, come to hear again, 'as once we did'. This poetic merger (for which Milton was indebted to Dante, *Purgatorio*, xxix. 22–30) was a natural development of the Nativity Ode situation, where the spheres and the angels were called on to blend or harmonize. Now the angels swallow up the spheres. It is a solution that circumvents the dilemma of having two heavenly musics, one pagan, one Christian, and it also makes the sphere-music firmly and finally vocal—angels' voices.

The surprising thing about *At a Solemn Music*, however, is that it is not a celebration of the power of music, though if read carelessly it can appear to be so. The solemn music to which, the title implies, the poet was listening when he wrote the poem is not so much as mentioned—not 'heard' at all.

[16] *Prose Works*, i. 234–9.

The music in the poem is all imagined music, future music, silent like Keats's unheard melodies. Being present at a musical performance does not, apparently, make Milton think about the potential of music, but about the potential of words without music:

> Blest pair of sirens, pledges of heaven's joy,
> Sphere-borne harmonious sisters, Voice, and Verse,
> Wed your divine sounds, and mixed power employ
> Dead things with inbreathed sense able to pierce,
> And to our high-raised phantasy present,
> That undisturbed song of pure concent,
> Ay sung before the sapphire-coloured throne
> To him that sits thereon
> With saintly shout and solemn jubilee,
> Where the bright seraphim in burning row
> Their loud uplifted angel trumpets blow,
> And the cherubic host in thousand choirs
> Touch their immortal harps of golden wires,
> With those just spirits that wear victorious palms,
> Hymns devout and holy psalms
> Singing everlastingly.

The tumultuous effect of music in these lines, an effect of Milton's baroque, illusionistic rhythmic and metrical craft, can distract our attention from the fact that the 'sirens' he invokes are Voice and Verse, not voice and music. It is the speaking—or, at most, singing—voice, unaccompanied by any instrument, that Milton conceives of as being used to make us imagine (with our 'high-raised phantasy') trumpets, harps, choirs and the whole harmonious uproar of heaven's noise. That, of course, is what happens in the poem itself, which has no music, but only voice and verse to make us imagine music. Whether 'Voice and Verse' means, in the context, song, or simply metrical composition, remains uncertain. The fact that Voice and Verse are called 'sirens' suggests song, but Milton, as the Trinity Manuscript shows, altered the third line from 'Mix your choice chords, and happiest sounds employ' to the present version,[17] and that emendation could be seen as purposely switching his poem away from any definite identification of Voice with the singing voice. If the invocation of Voice and Verse at the start of *At a Solemn Music* is, like the invocation of the Heavenly Muse at the start of *Paradise Lost*, to be thought of as followed by a poem which the invoked power or powers 'perform' or are responsible for, then Voice and Verse do not amount to song, for what we have is an unsung poem. Alternatively, of course, Milton could be referring to the solemn music which he is ostensibly hearing or about to hear, and he could be wishing for voice and verse to blend in that music in a particularly transporting way. Presumably the solemn music did not involve the use of instruments but was an unaccompanied choral or solo

---

[17] See *Poems*, pp. 161–2.

performance; otherwise its components would not be just voice and verse. We cannot, admittedly, be sure about this, or about whether there ever was any solemn music at all. What we can be sure of, though, is that thinking about music led Milton to consider what could be done without music —with only voice and verse—and he proceeded, in the poem, to do it.

Another curious thing about the start of the poem is that Voice and Verse are asked to 'wed' their 'sounds'. Voice, of course, has, or is, a sound. But what sort of sound could 'Verse' have by itself, before being spoken by a voice? 'Verse' can only mean, and could only mean in Milton's day, versification, or verse composition, and neither of these, one would have thought, could exist as a sound independent of a voice reciting or singing. Yet Milton does clearly imagine verse as having an independent sound. For there would be no point in asking it to wed its sound to the sound of voice unless it had a sound, and a sound which could, conceivably, exist apart from the sound of voice. Was it a sound Milton heard only in his head—a Platonic idea of sound, pre-sonic, intellectual? Was it a rhythm that he felt or 'heard' before he fitted words to it (and should we remember, in this context, the young W. H. Auden's observation that poems came to him, first, as rhythms or metrical patterns, for which he would later find words)? Whatever its nature, 'Verse' was for him a separate entity, audible and 'divine'. It was not music, although, like music, it was able to transform the voice by combining with it. United with verse, voice, like Orpheus's song, could become supernatural—'Dead things with inbreathed sense able to pierce', or so Milton imagined.

At a Solemn Music seems, then, to be a poem which draws our attention rather forcibly to the sufficiency and independence of the human voice, in a context where prominence might have been expected, instead, to be given to music and what it could add to the voice's resources. From this viewpoint, the corresponding moment in *Paradise Lost* occurs when Adam and Eve emerge from their bower to perform their morning worship. Their prayer or hymn (based on the Benedicite and Psalm 148) calls on all creatures to extol God's glory. Some of the creatures, such as birds, can communicate their praise through sound. Others, Adam and Eve realize, will have to use signals. The elements—earth, air, fire and water—will convey their worship by interchanging one with another, which is what they always do anyway:

> let your ceaseless change
> Vary to our great maker still new praise.
> (v. 183–4)

The 'mists and exhalations' will praise God by rising and falling, which is what mists and exhalations normally do. The trees and plants will sway in the wind as usual, but with a glorifying purpose: 'wave your tops . . . in sign of worship' (v. 193–4). The fountains, rivers and watercourses that 'warble,

as ye flow' will still flow and warble, and 'warbling, tune his praise'
(v. 195–6).

The point of the hymn seems to be that creation will praise God by being
itself. Each creature, by expressing its own nature unaltered, unaided,
unaugmented, will naturally express the glory of the Maker, who made
it needing no alteration, aid or addition. This idea represents an adjustment,
or clarification on Milton's part, of his biblical and liturgical sources. In the
Benedicite, for example, the dews and frosts, lightnings and clouds, and so
on, are called on to praise and magnify the Lord, but whether they will do so
by some special effect, some unusually impressive meteorological demon-
stration, or just by being themselves, is left to us to imagine. Milton does not
so leave it, and he is correspondingly explicit about how Adam and Eve
perform their praise. Like other creatures, they use only their own means,
without accompaniment, and they praise spontaneously, their words spring-
ing from their inner natures, without passing through the distorting glass of
thought, just like the praise of winds, plants and so forth:

> Lowly they bowed adoring, and began
> Their orisons, each morning duly paid
> In various style, for neither various style
> Nor holy rapture wanted they to praise
> Their maker, in fit strains pronounced or sung
> Unmeditated, such prompt eloquence
> Flowed from their lips, in prose or numerous verse,
> More tuneable than needed lute or harp
> To add more sweetness, and they thus began.
>   (v. 144–52).

'Prose' is the surprising word here—partly because Milton, by representing
Adam and Eve speaking verse, leads us to suppose they spoke it. His
insistence that they sometimes worshipped in prose (though they never can
in his poem) warns us against taking his medium at face value, just as
Raphael warns Adam that the description of heaven is necessarily inaccurate
(v. 571–4). Milton is intent, in the whole passage, on making a point which is
not just anti-poetic, or just anti-liturgical (supporting the Puritan preference
for unpremeditated prayer as against set forms), but which also relates to the
rightness of the natural—a key theme in *Paradise Lost*, in sexual and other
matters. Prose is natural human utterance, just as rising and falling is natural
behaviour for mists and exhalations. It must therefore, Milton's logic runs,
be fit for worship, and fitter than music ('lute or harp') could make it. The
way God has arranged for people naturally to speak, like the way He has
made trees and plants naturally to sway in the wind, cannot be in need of
improvement, otherwise He would have improved it. It must, just as it is,
advance His glory. Adam and Eve sometimes use 'numerous verse' as well as
prose, for that, Milton implies, is a natural, spontaneous and independent

expression of the human organism too. What they never use is musical instruments—any more than trees or fountains do.

Or than the planets do: for the planets figure in Adam and Eve's morning hymn along with the other creatures, and Milton, changing his mind yet again about the music of the spheres, represents them as singing—not sat on by singing sirens, not chiming, not relinquishing their singing role to an angel choir, but singing. Adam and Eve, being unfallen, can hear the song, and they take it for granted like the other natural phenomena of Eden:

> Thou sun, of this great world both eye and soul,
> Acknowledge him thy greater, sound his praise
> In thy eternal course, both when thou climb'st,
> And when high noon hast gained, and when thou fall'st.
> Moon, that now meet'st the orient sun, now fly'st
> With the fixed stars, fixed in their orb that flies,
> And ye five other wandering fires that move
> In mystic dance not without song, resound
> His praise . . .
>
> (v. 171–9)

In Eden the sky made a noise: the planets (including, of course, in Adam and Eve's pre-Copernican cosmology, the sun) sang. It was never quiet. A divine, ethereal muzak accompanied all human activity. But the incessant sound was vocal and meaningful. The wandering fires danced 'not without song' and praised God. Though Milton himself had never heard them sing, the idea of their song—of light as sound—remained so powerful for him that (to digress for a moment) it provided, in *Samson Agonistes*, one of his most haunting evocations of loss, as the blind Samson laments:

> The sun to me is dark
> And silent as the moon,
> When she deserts the night
> Hid in her vacant interlunar cave.
> (ll. 86–9)

The emptiness of the sky becomes for Samson an emptiness of sound, not light. The sun no longer makes a noise. His personal loss confuses with the loss all humankind suffered at the Fall.

Apart from Milton's theories about the sufficiency of the voice, one reason Adam and Eve did not play musical instruments in Eden was that they had not been invented. The invention of the arts comes later in the biblical story when (Genesis 4: 19–20), of the three sons of Cain's descendant Lamech, Jubal is named as 'the father of all such as handle the harp and organ'. The visions of the future development of mankind that Michael organizes for Adam in Book 11 of *Paradise Lost* include a foretaste of Jubal's instrumental music. Adam sees tents

> whence the sound
> Of instruments that made melodious chime
> Was heard, of harp and organ; and who moved
> Their stops and chords was seen: his volant touch
> Instinct through all proportions low and high
> Fled and pursued transverse the resonant fugue.
>
> (xi. 558–63)

Adam greets the performance ecstatically but is swiftly put right by Michael:

> Those tents thou saw'st so pleasant, were the tents
> Of wickedness, wherein shall dwell his race
> Who slew his brother; studious they appear
> Of arts that polish life, inventors rare,
> Unmindful of their maker . . .
>
> (xi. 607–11)

Milton has manipulated the episode as if deliberately to discredit instrumental music. It has been noted that Jubal's organ, together with his brother Tubalcain's metal-smelting (another art described in this passage), aligns him with the devils in hell, whose contrivance for metal-smelting is compared to the pipes and soundboard of an organ (i. 708). The 'melodious chime' of Jubal's organ inevitably, and at first startlingly, reminds us of the sphere-music invoked in the Nativity Ode:

> let your silver chime
> Move in melodious time
> And let the base of heaven's deep organ blow.
>
> (ll. 128–30)

But that music, we recall, was redeemed by voices—the 'divinely-warbled voice' of the angel choir. Jubal's 'chime' has no voice to give it meaning. It belongs with the purely sensuous seductions of voiceless music—the 'inane tune, without words' scorned by Milton in *Ad patrem*. Its chiming is like the voiceless music 'of chiming strings, or charming pipes' with which Satan in *Paradise Regained* (ii. 363) sets off his diabolical banquet temptation.

If my argument holds good so far—if, that is, we can accept that Milton had serious misgivings, moral and intellectual, about music, it may help us to reach a better understanding of an episode in *Paradise Lost* which has provoked some unease among commentators. When Satan rouses his fallen angels to military fervour, using rhetoric that (Milton carefully points out) 'bore / Semblance of worth, not substance', the devils march to music:

> anon they move
> In perfect phalanx to the Dorian mood
> Of flutes and soft recorders; such as raised
> To highth of noblest temper heroes old
> Arming to battle, and in stead of rage
> Deliberate valour breathed, firm and unmoved

> With dread of death to flight or foul retreat,
> Not wanting power to mitigate and swage,
> With solemn touches, troubled thoughts, and chase
> Anguish and doubt and fear and sorrow and pain
> From mortal or immortal minds. Thus they
> Breathing united force with fixed thought
> Moved on in silence . . .
>
> (i. 549–61)

The worrying thing about this passage, of course, is that the devils seem to have the good tunes. Milton seems positively to approve of the diabolic music, and that impression is strengthened when the puzzled reader looks up 'Dorian mood' in the notes, for he finds that Plato favourably contrasted this musical mode with the soft and indolent Ionian and Lydian (*Republic*, iii. 398–9). The reader, at this stage, is rather like Adam admiring Jubal's organ playing. A clear-minded Michael is needed to point out what is wrong with the devils' music, and why the praise Milton accords it is deceptive— 'semblance of worth, not substance'. The music rouses the devils to military defiance of the Almighty—which is irrational, hopeless and evil. Anguish, doubt, fear, sorrow and pain are exactly what, as fallen angels, they should feel, and would have to feel were they to have any chance of redemption. To dull these healthful sensations, as music does, is to doom the devils. Music clouds their minds and hides them from reality. That similar music raised 'heroes old' to war-like deeds is, of course, no sort of recommendation within the rationale of Milton's poem. He warns us more than once that classical military heroism is just the ideal he is out to discredit and supplant. He is

> Not sedulous by nature to indite
> Wars, hitherto the only argument
> Heroic deemed.
>
> (ix. 27–29)

It is not, he insists, military virtue that 'justly gives heroic name / To person or to poem' (ix. 40–41). The punch-drunk old devils, blotto but unbowed, their minds swept clean of every glimmer of rationality by the music of their military band, are meant to be a warning not an ideal. The music the passage makes is seductive because that is precisely what Milton wants us to see that music is.

But it is not only the fallen angels in Book 1 who illustrate music's dangers. The parallel to the dumb devils, following their band, is supplied by the dumb good angels following theirs at the start of the war in heaven, when

> moved on
> In silence their bright legions, to the sound
> Of instrumental harmony that breathed

Heroic ardour to adventurous deeds
Under their godlike leaders.

(vi. 63–67)

The repetition of the phrase 'moved on in silence' can leave us in no doubt we are meant to connect the two passages, and that is, at first, disconcerting. Surely, we may object, the good angels can only be contrasted with the devils, not likened to them? But if we see the angels' actions at this point in the whole context of the war in heaven, and what it implies, it allows us to read their 'heroic ardour' in a less simple light. As Stanley Fish has argued,[18] the war in heaven is in some respects a comic episode, its purpose being to show, among other things, the futility of war. The good angels can, in fact, achieve nothing unless God wills it, and if He wills it He can achieve it without their aid. Raphael later explains this to Adam (viii. 237–40). The 'heroic ardour' of the angels is, therefore, useless. God deceives them by making them think they can really effect something. He commands them to drive the rebel angels out of heaven (vi. 52), but He knows they cannot—it is a role He has reserved for His Son. When the good angels have fought for two days to no avail, God blandly points out to the Son that 'War wearied hath performed what war can do' (vi. 695)—that is, nothing—and that it remains for the Son to drive out the rebel angels and end the war—'since none but thou / Can end it'—a piece of information God certainly did not divulge to the hopeful good angels when He sent them off on their impossible task. When it comes to being deluded, there is little to choose in the war in heaven between the good angels and the bad. Though the good angels are, of course, entirely virtuous, they are also deceived, and the music that stirs them to heroic ardour is, as with the fallen angels, an aid to their deception.

Milton's doubts about music, and his preference for words, seem—to conclude—to be vitally bound up with the polarization of Reason and Passion which is built into the thesis of *Paradise Lost*. Wordless music acts upon the passions and excites them with the unreal. Even when music is accompanied by words—or even when it is purely vocal, consisting only of words—it has for Milton perplexing ramifications. He apprehends it not as pleasure but as power, and power hostile to the self. It overcomes, subdues, dominates. It makes its hearers forsake their natures. Comus, hearing the Lady's song, recognizes and falls in love with sanctity—'Sure something holy lodges in that breast' (*Comus*, l. 245). The song his mother and the sirens used to sing robbed monsters of their monstrosity:

Scylla wept,
And chid her barking waves into attention,
And fell Charybdis murmured soft applause.

(ll. 256–8)

---

[18] See Stanley E. Fish, *Surprised by Sin*, Berkeley, 1967, pp. 180–96.

Milton persistently relates music to moral issues—law and freedom, determinism and autonomy. Music is access; it can 'dissolve' the self in ecstasies and give a sight of heaven (*Il Penseroso*, ll. 165–6), but another of its narcotic powers is that it can cancel the will and remove the self from the self's control, drawing 'iron tears down Pluto's cheek' (*Il Penseroso*, l. 107). At times the confusion of Milton's language when he writes about music can alert us vividly to his dilemma, as with the Genius's speech in *Arcades*:

> Such sweet compulsion doth in music lie,
> To lull the daughters of Necessity,
> And keep unsteady Nature to her law.
>
> (ll. 68–70)

Milton here diverges from his Platonic source (for in Plato the daughters of Necessity sing with the Sirens), and he makes music operate in two opposed ways. By lulling the daughters of Necessity, it releases the actual from transcendental imperatives; by keeping Nature to her law, it asserts transcendental imperatives again. Music both unbinds, and binds. On a subject over which Milton was so deeply torn, we should not expect consistency.

A Bibliography of the Writings of Frederick Sternfeld

Peter Ward Jones

With Fred Sternfeld's scholarly interests so often crossing the disciplinary boundaries, especially those of literature and music, the task of compiling a comprehensive bibliography of his writings would have been almost impossible without the assistance of the author himself, which was invaluable in providing details of many of the less obvious items. It is hoped that the following list of publications is reasonably complete, although the compiler suspects that there may yet be a number of reviews and minor pieces which have escaped attention.

BOOKS

1. *Goethe and Music*, Ph.D. dissertation, Yale University, 1943.
2. *Goethe and Music: A List of Parodies and Goethe's Relationship to Music: A List of References*, New York, New York Public Library, 1954, repr., New York, Da Capo Press, 1979, with a new introduction by S. Levarie. Originally appeared in instalments in *The New York Public Library Bulletin*, liv (1950) and lvi (1952).
3. *Music in Shakespearean Tragedy* (Studies in the History of Music), London, Routledge & Kegan Paul, 1963, 2nd rev. imp. 1967.

BOOKS AND PERIODICALS EDITED

4. *Renaissance News*, i–vii/2 (1948–54). Vol. 1 was preceded by 4 sections of 'Renaissance News', edited by Sternfeld, in *Journal of Renaissance and Baroque Music*, i/1–4 (1946/7), and one further issue distributed separately by Dartmouth College Library.
5. *Proceedings of the Royal Musical Association*, lxxxiv–lxxxviii (1957/8–1961/2).
6. W. Chappell, *The Ballad Literature and Popular Music of the Olden Time* (reprint of the 1859 edn.) with a new introduction by F. W. Sternfeld, 2 vols., New York, Dover Publications, 1965.
7. E. H. Fellowes, *English Madrigal Verse 1588–1632*, rev. and enlarged by F. W. Sternfeld and D. Greer, 3rd edn., Oxford, Clarendon Press, 1967.
8. *The New Oxford History of Music*, vol. 7, *The Age of Enlightenment 1745–1790*, ed. E. Wellesz & F. Sternfeld, London, Oxford University Press, 1973. Sternfeld contributed chapter 11: 'Instrumental Masterworks and Aspects of Formal Design', pp. 611–35. The editors were also

responsible for chapters 6 and 7, 'The Early Symphony' and 'The Concerto', prepared on the basis of material by J. LaRue.

9. *A History of Western Music*, vol. 1, *Music from the Middle Ages to the Renaissance*, and vol. 5, *Music in the Modern Age*, London, Weidenfeld & Nicolson, 1973 (no more published).

10. *Essays on Opera and English Music in Honour of Sir Jack Westrup*, ed. F. W. Sternfeld, N. Fortune, and E. Olleson, Oxford, Basil Blackwell, 1975.

MUSIC EDITED

11. *Songs from Shakespeare's Tragedies: A Collection of Songs for Concert or Domestic Use*, ed. from contemporary sources F. Sternfeld, London, Oxford University Press, 1964; 'Hamlet' material repr. in W. Shakespeare, *Hamlet*, ed. G. R. Hibbard (The Oxford Shakespeare), Oxford, Clarendon Press, 1987, 379–81.

12. W. Shakespeare, *Measure for Measure*, ed. J. W. Lever (The Arden Shakespeare), London, Methuen, 1965: Appendix II, by F. W. Sternfeld, 'Take, o take those lips away' (with transcription), 201–3.

13. *English Lute Songs 1597–1632: A Collection of Facsimile Reprints*, gen. ed. F. W. Sternfeld, 9 vols. (also issued in 36 fascicles), Menston, Scolar Press, 1967–71.

14. W. Shakespeare, *Twelfth Night*, ed. W. W. Mahood (The New Penguin Shakespeare), Harmondsworth, Penguin Books, 1968: 'The Songs' (transcribed and edited with the assistance of F. W. Sternfeld), 193–205.

15. *English Madrigals 1588–1630*, facsimile reprint series, gen. ed. F. W. Sternfeld, assoc. ed. D. Greer, Menston, Scolar Press, 1972; only one volume was issued: J. Wilbye, *The Second Set of Madrigals 1609*.

16. W. Shakespeare, *Twelfth Night*, ed. J. M. Lothian & T. W. Craik (The Arden Shakespeare), London, Methuen, 1975: Appendix II 'The Songs' includes 'There dwelt a man in Babylon' (p. 186) 'transcribed and ed. F. W. Sternfeld'.

17. *An Old English Carol* (Three Magi on the Twelfth Day), Old English ballad tune adapted by F. W. Sternfeld, arranged for mixed voices by C. R. Wilson (Oxford carols = Oxford choral songs X26), Oxford, Oxford University Press, 1978.

CONTRIBUTIONS TO COMPOSITE WORKS

18. 'The Musical and Rhythmical Sources of Poetry' in *English Institute Essays 1951*, ed. A. S. Downer (New York, 1952), 126–45.

19. '*Troilus and Cressida*: Music for the Play' in *English Institute Essays 1952*, ed. A. S. Downer (New York, 1954), 107–37; repr. in *Explication as Criticism: Selected Papers from the English Institute 1941–52*, ed. W. K. Wimsatt (New York, 1963), 53–83.

20. 'Le Symbolisme musicale dans quelques pièces de Shakespeare présentées à la cour d'Angleterre' in *Les Fêtes de la Renaissance*, ed. J. Jacquot (Paris, 1956), 319–33.

21. 'Poetry and Music: Joyce's *Ulysses*' in *Sound and Poetry: English Institute Essays 1956*, ed. N. Frye (New York, 1957), 16–54; repr. in *Literatur und Musik*, ed. S. P. Scher (Berlin, 1984), 357–79, and in French translation (tr. P. Rozenberg) in *Revue des lettres modernes*, vi (1959/60), 391–428.
22. 'Shakespeare's Use of Popular Song' in *Elizabethan and Jacobean Studies*, ed. H. Davis & H. Gardner (Oxford, 1959), 150–66.
23. 'Song in Jonson's Comedy: A Gloss on *Volpone*' in *Studies in the English Renaissance Drama*, ed. J. W. Bennett *et al.* (London, 1959, 2nd edn. 1961), 310–21.
24. 'Music and the Cinema' in *Twentieth Century Music*, ed. R. H. Myers (London, 1960), 95–111.
25. 'La Musique dans les tragédies élisabéthaines inspirées de Sénèque' in *Les Tragédies de Sénèque et le théâtre de la Renaissance*, ed. J. Jacquot (Paris, 1964), 139–51.
26. 'Music' in *The New Cambridge Modern History* (Cambridge, 1957–79), vol. 6 (1970), 101–18 (late 17th and early 18th centuries); vol. 8 (1965), 81–96 (late 18th century); vol. 9 (1965), 228–49 (early 19th century).
27. 'Come live with me and be my love' in *The Hidden Harmony: Essays in Honor of Philip Wheelwright*, ed. O. Johnson *et al.* (New York, 1966), 173–92.
28. 'Expression and Revision in Gluck's *Orfeo* and *Alceste*' in *Essays Presented to Egon Wellesz*, ed. J. Westrup (Oxford, 1966), 114–29; repr. in German (tr. T. M. Marshall) in *Christoph Willibald Gluck und die Opernreform*, ed. K. Hortschansky (Darmstadt, 1989), 172–99.
29. 'Music and Drama' by E. J. Dent, revised, with additional material by F. W. Sternfeld in *The New Oxford History of Music*, vol. 4, *The Age of Humanism 1540–1630* (London, 1968), chapter 14, pp. 784–820.
30. 'Goethe and Beethoven' in *Bericht über den internationalen musikwissenschaftlichen Kongress Bonn 1970 (Gesellschaft für Musikforschung)* (Kassel, 1971), 587–90.
31. 'Shakespeare and Music' in *A New Companion to Shakespeare Studies*, ed. K. Muir & S. Schoenbaum (Cambridge, 1971), 157–67.
32. 'Aspects of Italian Intermedi and Early Operas' in *Convivium Musicorum: Festschrift Wolfgang Boetticher zum sechzigsten Geburtstag*, ed. H. Hüschen & D. R. Moser (Berlin, 1974), 359–66.
33. 'Des intermèdes à l'opéra: la technique du finale' in *Les Fêtes de la Renaissance III*, ed. J. Jacquot & E. Konigson (Paris, 1975), 267–80.
34. 'Intermedi and the Birth of Opera' in *The Florentine Intermedi of 1589*, (BBC broadcast, 17 Sept. 1979), programme book ed. I. Fenlon (London, 1979), 10–16.
35. 'Repetition and Echo in Renaissance Poetry and Music' in *English Renaissance Studies Presented to Dame Helen Gardner in Honour of Her Seventieth Birthday*, ed. J. Carey (Oxford, 1980), 33–43.
36. 'Echo et répétition dans la poésie et la musique' in *La Chanson à la Renaissance*, ed. J.-M. Vaccaro (Tours, 1981), 242–54.
37. 'Poliziano, Isaac, Festa: Rhetorical Repetition' in *Firenze e la Toscana dei Medici nell'Europa del '500*, ed. G. Garfagnini (Firenze, 1983), vol. 2, pp. 549–64.
38. 'The Lament in Poliziano's *Orfeo* and some Musical Settings of the Early 16th

Century' in *Arts du spectacle et histoire des idées: Recueil offert en hommage à Jean Jacquot* (Tours, 1984), 201–4.

39. 'Music in Shakespeare's Work' (with C. R. Wilson) in *Shakespeare: His Work, His Influence*, ed. J. F. Andrews (New York, 1985), vol. 2, pp. 417–24.

40. 'The "Occasional" Element in the Choral Finale from Poliziano to Rinuccini' in *Actes du XIIIe congrès de la Société Internationale de Musique, Strasbourg . . . 1982* (Strasbourg, 1986), vol. 1, pp. 371–6.

41. 'The Orpheus Myth and the Libretto of *Orfeo*' in *Claudio Monteverdi: 'Orfeo'*, ed. J. Whenham (Cambridge, 1986), 20–33.

ARTICLES IN PERIODICALS AND NEWSPAPERS

42. 'Some Russian Folksongs in Stravinsky's *Petrouchka*', *Notes*, ii (1944/5), 95–107; repr., in part, in Boston Symphony Orchestra programme notes, 23 Jan. 1948, and, slightly abridged, in *Stravinsky: Petrushka*, ed. C. Hamm (Norton Critical Score), (New York, 1967), 203–15.

43. 'Renaissance Music in Goethe', *Germanic Review*, xx (1945), 241–60.

44. 'Musical Research in America', *Comparative Literature Newsletter*, iv/3 (1945), 22–4.

45. '*Specter of the Rose*: An Analysis [of George Antheil's Film Score]', *Film Music Notes*, vi (1946), 7–14.

46. 'Bibliography of Periodical Literature', *Journal of Renaissance and Baroque Music*, i (1946/7), 85, 169–71, 247–9, 297–8.

47. 'The Strange Music of Martha Ivers' (an analysis of Miklos Rosza's film score *The Strange Love of Martha Ivers*), *Hollywood Quarterly*, ii (1946/7), 241–51.

48. 'Preliminary Report on Film Music', *Hollywood Quarterly*, ii (1946/7), 299–302.

49. 'Music and the Feature Films', *Musical Quarterly*, xxxiii (1947), 517–32; repr. *Pro Musica Sana*, vii (1978/9), 7–18.

50. 'Cinema Scores', *New York Times*, 10 Oct. 1948, X7.

51. 'Film Music Session at M.T.N.A. in Boston', *Film Music Notes*, vii (1948), 5–6.

52. 'Report of the Audio-Visual Committee: [Section on] Cinema', *Music Teachers National Association Proceedings for 1948* (Pittsburgh, 1950), 329–32.

53. 'Music in the Schools of the Reformation', *Musica Disciplina*, ii (1948), 99–122.

54. '*Louisiana Story*: A Review of Virgil Thomson's Film Score', *Film Music Notes*, viii (1948), 5–14; repr. *Music Journal*, vii (1949), 21 ff.

55. 'The Musical Sources of Goethe's Poetry', *American–German Review*, xv (1949), 16–23.

56. 'Current Chronicle [Virgil Thomson's film score for *Louisiana Story*]', *Musical Quarterly*, xxxv (1949), 115–21; repr., in part, in Philadelphia Orchestra programme notes, 26 Nov. 1948, and Cincinnati Symphony Orchestra programme notes, 25 Nov. 1949.

57. 'The Musical Springs of Goethe's Poetry', *Musical Quarterly*, xxxv (1949), 511–27.

58. 'Music as a Humanistic Study', *Music Teachers National Association Proceedings for 1949* (Pittsburgh, 1951), 85–92.
59. 'Gail Kubik's Score for *C-Man*', *Hollywood Quarterly*, iv (1949/50), 360–9.
60. 'Kubik's *McBoing* Score', *Film Music Notes*, x (1950), 8–16.
61. 'A List of American Graduate Courses in Musicology', *Journal of the American Musicological Society*, iii (1950), 65–8.
62. 'Current Chronicle [Gail Kubik's film score for *C-Man*]', *Musical Quarterly*, xxxvi (1950), 274–6.
63. 'The Teacher–Scholar in the Field of Music', *Association of American Colleges Bulletin*, xxxvi (1950), 300–5.
64. 'Copland as a Film Composer', *Musical Quarterly*, xxxvii (1951), 161–75.
65. 'The Dramatic and Allegorical Function of Music in Shakespeare's Tragedies', *Annales Musicologiques*, iii (1955), 265–82.
66. 'Cadence of Grief [*Don Giovanni*]', *Opera News*, xix/14 (7 Feb. 1955), 6–9.
67. 'The Moor in Speech and Song: *Othello*', *Opera News*, xix/18 (7 Mar. 1955), 3–5, 32.
68. 'A Necrology: [In Memoriam Otto Gombosi]', *Renaissance News*, viii (1955), 121–2.
69. 'The Melodic Sources of Mozart's Most Popular *Lied*', *Musical Quarterly*, xlii (1956), 213–22; repr. in *The Creative World of Mozart*, ed. P. H. Lang (New York, 1963), 127–36.
70. 'Faust before Gounod', *Opera News*, xx/13 (30 Jan. 1956), 6–7, 26–8.
71. 'The Flute: Sacred and Profane: [*Die Zauberflöte*]', *Opera News*, xx/17 (27 Feb. 1956), 4–7, 26, 32–3.
72. 'Mozart after Mardi Gras', *Opera News*, xx/23 (2 Apr. 1956), 4–6, 28–9.
73. 'Mozart of the Champs Elysées: [Offenbach's *Les Contes d'Hoffmann*]', *Opera News*, xxi/6 (17 Dec. 1956), 10–12.
74. 'Necrology: [In memoriam Manfred Bukofzer]', *Renaissance News*, ix (1956), 165–6.
75. 'Vautrollier's Printing of Lasso's *Recueil du Mellange*, London, 1570', *Annales Musicologiques*, v (1957), 199–227.
76. 'A Song from Campion's *Lord's Masque*', *Journal of the Warburg and Courtauld Institutes*, xx (1957), 373–5.
77. 'The Heroine as a Young Man: [Strauss's *Arabella*]', *Opera News*, xxi/13 (4 Feb. 1957), 3–7, 30–1.
78. 'Recent Research on Lute Music', *Music and Letters*, xxxix (1958), 139–42.
79. 'Mozart's Wedding Symphony: [the Act II finale in *Le nozze di Figaro*]', *Opera News*, xxii/10 (6 Jan. 1958), 4–7; repr. in *The Opera News Book of 'Figaro'* (New York, 1967).
80. 'The Sources of Lute Music', *Renaissance News*, xi (1958), 253–7.
81. 'Lasso's Music for Shakespeare's *Samingo*', *Shakespeare Quarterly*, ix (1958), 105–16.
82. 'The Music for the Documentary *The River*', *Film Journal*, no. 12 (1959), 15–20.
83. 'The Use of Song in Shakespeare's Tragedies', *Proceedings of the Royal Musical Association*, lxxxvi (1959/60), 45–59.
84. 'The Role of Music in *Faust*', *Listener*, lxviii (1962), 1065.

85. 'Twentieth-Century Studies in Shakespeare's Songs, Sonnets, and Poems. 1: Songs and Music', *Shakespeare Survey*, xv (1962), 1–10.

86. 'Music in *King Lear* at the Royal Shakespeare Theatre', *Shakespeare Quarterly*, xiv (1963), 486–7.

87. 'Ophelia's Version of the Walsingham Song', *Music and Letters*, xlv (1964), 108–13.

88. 'Music and Ballads', *Shakespeare in His Own Age: Shakespeare Survey*, xvii (1964), 214–22.

89. 'Cavalieri's *Rappresentatione di Anima e di Corpo*', *Salzburger Festspiel Almanach*, 1969.

90. 'Come live with me and be my love' (with Mary Joiner Chan), *Comparative Literature*, xxii (1970), 173–87.

91. 'Les Intermèdes de Florence et la genèse de l'opéra', *Baroque*, v (1972), 25–9.

92. 'Gluck's Operas and Italian Tradition', *Chigiana*, xxix/xxx (1975), 275–81.

93. 'Egon Wellesz (1885–1974)', *Music and Letters*, lvi (1975), 147–9.

94. 'Midwinter Birthday: [Tippett's operas, on the occasion of his 70th birthday]', *Records and Recording*, xviii/4 (Jan. 1975), 14–16 (cf. no. 100).

95. 'Sir Jack Westrup (1904–1975)', *Musikforschung*, xxix (1976), 129–30.

96. 'Mozart's *Idomeneo*', *Salzburger Festspiel Almanach*, 1976.

97. 'The First Printed Opera Libretto', *Music and Letters*, lix (1978), 121–38.

98. 'The Birth of Opera: Ovid, Poliziano, and the *lieto fine*', *Analecta Musicologica*, xix (1979), 30–51.

99. 'Aspects of Echo Music in the Renaissance', *Studi Musicali*, ix (1980), 45–57.

100. 'A Musical Magpie: Words and Music in Michael Tippett's Operas' (with David Harvey), *Parnassus: Poetry in Review*, x/2 (1982), 188–98. Revised and expanded version of no. 94.

101. 'A Note on *Stile Recitativo*', *Proceedings of the Royal Musical Association*, cx (1983/4), 41–4.

102. 'Haydn e la rinascita Shakespeareana nel XVIII secolo', *Chigiana*, xxxvi (1984), 73–7.

103. 'Orpheus, Ovid, and Opera', *Journal of the Royal Musical Association*, cxiii (1988), 172–202.

ARTICLES IN DICTIONARIES

104. *Grove's Dictionary of Music and Musicians*, 4th edn., ed. H. C. Colles, supplementary vol. (London, 1940): 'Guido d'Arezzo' (supplementary information on the Guidonian Hand).

105. P. A. Scholes: *The Oxford Companion to Music*, 6th edn. (London, 1945): 'Misattributed Compositions: Palestrina's *Adoramus Te*' (also in 7th–10th edns.).

106. *Die Musik in Geschichte und Gegenwart*, ed. F. Blume (Kassel, 1949–86): 'Shakespeare'; 'Sternfeld'; 'Wellesz' (supplement, with P. Ward Jones); 'Westrup' (supplement, with P. Ward Jones).

107. *Harvard Dictionary of Music*, 2nd edn., ed. W. Apel (Cambridge, Mass., 1969): 'Film Music'.

108. *Dictionnaire de la musique*, ed. M. Honegger (Paris, 1970–6): 'Goethe'; 'Opéra. B: Italie. 1: Les débuts de l'opéra'; 'Shakespeare'.

109. *The New Grove Dictionary of Music and Musicians*, ed. S. Sadie (London, 1980): 'Goethe'; 'Incidental Music: 2' (with J. Sage); 'Shakespeare: 1'.

SELECTED LETTERS TO THE PRESS

110. 'Schubert's Symphonies', *The Times*, 22 Aug. 1938, 6.
111. 'Tudor Poems', *Times Literary Supplement*, 14 July 1961, 433.
112. 'Poor Tom in *King Lear*', *Times Literary Supplement*, 5 Jan. 1962, 9.
113. 'Hymns and Poetry', *Times Literary Supplement*, 1 Feb. 1963, 77.
114. 'A Lost Poem by Queen Elizabeth I', *Times Literary Supplement*, 4 July 1968, 705.
115. 'The Garcia Sisters', *Times Literary Supplement*, 22 Jan. 1970, 85.
116. 'The Bassoon in *Petrouchka*', *Times Literary Supplement*, 28 Mar. 1980, 367.

NOTES FOR SOUND RECORDINGS

117. *Songs in Shakespeare's Plays*, performed by James Bowman (countertenor) and James Tyler (cittern/lute), Hamburg, Deutsche Grammophon, 1978.

BOOK REVIEWS

Criticism

118. *Studies in the History of Music*, ed. E. Wellesz, vol. 1, F. Ll. Harrison, *Music in Mediaeval Britain*; vol. 2, J. V. Cockshoot, *The Fugue in Beethoven's Piano Music*; vol. 3, M. Lefkowitz, *William Lawes*, iii (1960), 158–61.

Journal of the American Musicological Society

119. B. Pattison, *Music and Poetry of the English Renaissance*, ii (1949), 125–7.

Modern Language Review

120. G. Tomlinson, *Monteverdi and the End of the Renaissance*, lxxxiii (1988), 1009–10.

Music and Letters

121. H. Kirchmeyer, *Igor Stravinsky*, xl (1959), 290–1.
122. L. Conrad, *Musica Panharmonica*, xl (1959), 379–81.
123. J. Künzig, *Ehe sie verklingen: Alte deutsche Volksweisen vom Böhmerwald bis zur Wolga*, xli (1960), 70–1.
124. J. K. Sherman *et al.*, *A History of the Arts in Minnesota*, xli (1960), 73–4.
125. *Le luth et sa musique*, ed. J. Jacquot, xli (1960), 83–4.
126. F. A. Yates, *The Valois Tapestries*, xli (1960), 167–70.
127. *La musique de scène de la troupe de Shakespeare*, ed. J. P. Cutts, xli (1960), 300–3.
128. G. Bandmann, *Melancholie und Musik: Ikonographische Studien*, xlii (1961), 170.

129. *Bericht über den siebenten Internationalen musikwissenschaftlichen Kongress, Köln 1958*, xliii (1962), 71–2.

130. F. Neumann, *Die Zeitgestalt: Eine Lehre vom musikalischen Rhythmus*, xliii (1962), 155.

131. L. Pichierri, *Music in New Hampshire 1623–1800*, xliii (1962), 165.

132. *The Collected Correspondence and Papers of Christoph Willibald Gluck*, ed. H. & E. H. Mueller von Asow, xliii (1962), 259–61.

133. *International Musicological Society: Report of the Eighth Congress, New York, 1961*, xliv (1963), 278–9.

134. B. S. Brook, *La Symphonie française dans la seconde moitié du XVIIIᵉ siècle*, xliv (1963), 388–90.

135. *Mozart: Briefe und Aufzeichnungen*, ed. W. A. Bauer & O. E. Deutsch, vol. 1, xliv (1963), 75–7; vols. 2–3, xlv (1964), 69–71; vol. 4, xlv (1964), 272–3.

136. J. Stevens *et al.*, *Shakespeare in Music*, xlvi (1965), 146–9.

137. M. M. McGowan, *L'Art du ballet de cour en France (1581–1643)*, xlvi (1965), 259–60.

138. *Festschrift Hans Engel zum 70. Geburtstag*, ed. H. Heussner, xlvi (1965), 261–2.

139. B. Huys, *Catalogue des imprimés musicaux des XVᵉ, XVIᵉ et XVIIᵉ siècles*, xlvii (1966), 355.

140. C. McPhee, *Music in Bali*, xlviii (1967), 67–8.

141. M. F. Robinson, *Opera before Mozart*, xlviii (1967), 276–7.

142. S. Sadie, *Mozart*, xlviii (1967), 283–4.

143. P. J. Seng, *The Vocal Songs in the Plays of Shakespeare*, xlix (1968), 171–3.

144. *New Looks at Italian Opera: Essays in Honor of Donald J. Grout*, ed. W. W. Austin, l (1969), 304–6.

145. J.-P. Rameau, *Observations sur notre instinct pour la musique*, facsimile reprint, l (1969), 311–12.

146. H. Kirchmeyer, *Situationsgeschichte der Musikkritik und des musikalischen Pressewesens in Deutschland*, Teil IV, Band III, li (1970), 187–8.

147. F. Blume, *Renaissance and Baroque Music*, li (1970), 191–2.

148. *Musa – Mens – Musici: Im Gedenken an Walther Vetter*, ed. E. H. Meyer, lii (1971), 322.

149. J. H. Long, *Shakespeare's Use of Music: The Histories and Tragedies*, lv (1974), 228–30.

150. H. Vogt, *Neue Musik seit 1945*, lv (1974), 329–31.

151. K. Hortschansky, *Parodie und Entstehung im Schaffen Christoph Willibald Glucks*, lv (1974), 491–4.

152. *Studien zur italienisch-deutschen Musikgeschichte VIII*, ed. F. Lippmann, lvi (1975), 81–3.

153. *Studien zur italienisch-deutschen Musikgeschichte IX*, ed. F. Lippmann, lvi (1975), 395–7.

154. J. W. Kelly, *The Faust Legend in Music*, lviii (1977), 472–3.

155. *Ezra Pound and Music: The Complete Criticism*, ed. R. M. Schafer, lix (1978), 355–7.

156. *Studien zur italienisch-deutschen Musikgeschichte*, vols. 10 & 11, lx (1979), 92–4.

157. E. R. Reilly, *Gustav Mahler und Guido Adler*, lx (1979), 331–2.

158. *Handschriftlich überlieferte Lauten- und Gitarrentabulaturen des 15. bis 18. Jahrhunderts: Beschreibender Katalog*, (RISM B/VII), ed. W. Boetticher, lxi (1980), 107.
159. H. Jung, *Die Pastorale*, lxii (1981), 364–6.
160. J. D. Drummond, *Opera in Perspective*, lxii (1981), 374–6.
161. P. Howard, *C. W. von Gluck: 'Orfeo'*, lxiii (1982), 295–6.
162. R. Donington, *The Rise of Opera*, lxiii (1982), 325–8.
163. E. R. Reilly, *Gustav Mahler and Guido Adler: Records of a Friendship*, lxiv (1983), 95–6.
164. N. Pirrotta & E. Povoledo, *Music and Theatre from Poliziano to Monteverdi*, lxiv (1983), 250–2.
165. J. Rushton, *W. A. Mozart: 'Don Giovanni'*, lxv (1984), 377–8.
166. J. A. Hepokoski, *Giuseppe Verdi: 'Falstaff'*, lxvi (1985), 386–8.
167. N. Pirrotta, *Music and Culture in Italy from the Middle Ages to the Baroque*, lxvi (1985), 397–9.
168. *Early Music History, iv*, lxvii (1986), 166–9.
169. J. A. Hepokoski, *Giuseppe Verdi: 'Otello'*, lxix (1988), 280–3.

Musical Quarterly

170. F. Mendelssohn, *Letters*, ed. G. Selden-Goth, xxxi (1945), 540–3.
171. W. Mellers, *Music and Society*, xxxiii (1947), 267–70.
172. *The Music of Schubert*, ed. G. Abraham, xxxiii (1947), 416–19.
173. A. Einstein, *Music in the Romantic Era*, xxxiii (1947), 570–5.
174. R. H. Schauffler, *Franz Schubert: The Ariel of Music*, xxxvi (1950), 138–41.
175. W. Boetticher, *Orlando di Lasso und seine Zeit*, xlv (1959), 546–9.

New York Times

176. G. Reese, *Music in the Renaissance*, 25 July 1954, book review section p. 17.

Notes

177. C. McCarty, *Film Composers in America*, xi (1953/4), 105.
178. A. Berger, *Aaron Copland*, xi (1953/4), 306–7.
179. A. Boustead, *Music to Shakespeare*, xxii (1965/6), 1038–9.
180. *Shakespeare in Music*, ed. P. Hartwell, xxii (1965/6), 1223–4.
181. W. Braun, *Brittania abundans: Deutsch-englische Musikbeziehungen zur Shakespearezeit*, xxxv (1978/9), 888–9.

Notes and Queries

182. *Lectures on the History and Art of Music: The Louis Charles Elson Memorial Lectures at the Library of Congress, 1946–1963*, ns xix (1972), 307–8.
183. F. Clément & P. Larousse, *Dictionnaire des opéras*, rev. A. Pougin, (reprint), ns xix (1972), 437.
184. J. M. Stein, *Poem and Music in the German Lied from Gluck to Hugo Wolf*, ns xxi (1974), 357–8.

Oxford Magazine

185. J. Stevens, *Music and Poetry in the Early Tudor Court*, ns ii (1961/2), 131–2.
186. *The Autobiography of Thomas Whythorne*, ed. J. M. Osborn, ns ii (1961/2), 152–3.

Renaissance News (Renaissance Quarterly)

187. *Annales musicologiques: moyen âge et renaissance*, viii (1955), 145–7.
188. *La Musique instrumentale de la Renaissance*, ed. J. Jacquot, ix (1956), 211–14.
189. D. P. Walker, *Spiritual and Demonic Music from Ficino to Campanella*, xv (1962), 299–303.
190. *Aspects of Mediaeval and Renaissance Music*, ed. J. LaRue, xxi (1968), 328–31.
191. E. B. Jorgens, *The Well-Tun'd Word: Musical Interpretations of English Poetry 1597–1651*, xxxix (1986), 132–4.

Review of English Studies

192. J. H. Long, *Shakespeare's Use of Music*, ns viii (1957), 64–6.
193. J. Hollander, *The Untuning of the Sky*, ns xv (1964), 307–10.
194. W. Mellers, *Harmonious Meeting*, ns xviii (1967), 462–4.
195. *Music in English Renaissance Drama*, ed. J. H. Long, ns xxi (1970), 111.
196. *Lyrics from English Airs, 1596–1622*, ed. E. Doughtie, ns xxiv (1973), 73–4.
197. J. H. Long, *Shakespeare's Use of Music: The Histories and Tragedies*, ns xxv (1974), 203–5.
198. Z. Bowen, *Musical Allusions in the Work of James Joyce*, ns xxviii (1977), 111–12.
199. *The Singing Tradition of Child's Popular Ballads*, ed. B. H. Bronson, ns xxx (1979), 239–41 (with C. R. Wilson).

Russian Review

200. I. Martynov, *D. Shostakovich; The Mussorgsky Reader*, ed. J. Leyda & S. Bertensson, vii (1948), 100–2.

Shakespeare Quarterly

201. C. Ing, *Elizabethan Lyrics*, iv (1953), 79–83.

Shakespeare Studies

202. F. W. Galpin, *Old English Instruments of Music*, 4th edn., rev. T. Dart, ii (1966), 332–3.
203. C. M. Simpson, *The British Broadside Ballad and its Music*, iv (1968), 434–5.

Times Literary Supplement

204. C. Dahlhaus, *Foundations of Music History*, 7 Oct. 1983, 1074. In addition Sternfeld contributed many anonymous reviews prior to 1974 (when the *TLS* started to print signed reviews).

MUSIC REVIEWS

Modern Language Review

205. *Poèmes de Donne, Herbert et Crashaw mis en musique par leurs contemporains*, ed. A. Souris & J. Jacquot, lviii (1963), 239–40.

Music and Letters

206. *Songs and Dances for the Stuart Masque*, ed. A. J. Sabol, xl (1959), 397–9.
207. W. A. Mozart, *Zaide*, vocal score, ed. W. Oehlmann, xlii (1961), 178–9.
208. A. Le Roy, *Premier livre de tablature de luth*, ed. A. Souris & R. de Morcourt, xliii (1962), 185–6.
209. J. Haydn, *Concerto [for cello and orchestra in] D major*, ed. L. Nowak, xliv (1963), 85–8.
210. R. Johnson, *Ayres, Songs, and Dialogues*, ed. I. Spink, xliv (1963), 188–9.
211. *Music at the Court of Henry VIII*, ed. J. Stevens, xliv (1963), 189–91.
212. *Poèmes de Donne, Herbert et Crashaw mis en musique par leurs contemporains*, ed. A. Souris & J. Jacquot, xliv (1963), 201–2.
213. A. Le Roy, *Psaumes: Tiers livre de tablature de luth, 1552; Instruction, 1574*, ed. R. de Morcourt, xliv (1963), 308–9.
214. W. A. Mozart, *Concerto [for piano and orchestra], K.491*, facsimile edition, xlvi (1965), 285–6.
215. R. Ballard, *Premier livre (1611)* and *Deuxième livre (1614) et pièces diverses*, ed. A. Souris, S. Spycket & J. Veyrier, xlvi (1965), 374–5.
216. *Musica Nova*, ed. H. C. Slim, xlvii (1966), 364–7.
217. T. Morley, *Editions of Italian Canzonets and Madrigals, 1597–1598*, ed. C. A. Murphy; R. Dering, *The Cries of London*, ed. D. Stevens, xlvii (1966), 370–2.
218. F. Cutting, *Selected Works*, ed. M. Long; A. Holborne, *Complete Works*, ed. M. Kanazawa; *Elizabethan Popular Music*, ed. B. Jeffery, l (1969), 539–40.
219. *A Renaissance Entertainment: Festivities for the Marriage of Cosimo I, Duke of Florence, in 1539*, ed. A. C. Minor & B. Mitchell, li (1970), 209–11.
220. F. Cavalli, *L'Ormindo*, ed. R. Leppard, li (1970), 211–14.
221. *The Lute Music of Francesco Canova da Milano*, ed. A. J. Ness, lii (1971), 337–9.
222. J. Peri, *Euridice*, ed. H. M. Brown, lxv (1984), 114–16.

Notes

223. I. Bazelon, *Sonatina for Piano*; G.-C. Menotti, *Ricercare and Toccata*; W. Schuman, *Voyage*; V. Thomson, *Nine Etudes*, xii (1954/5), 329–30.
224. V. Thomson, *Symphony on a Hymn Tune*; *Symphony no. 2*; *Wheat Field at Noon*; *Sea Piece with Birds*, xiii (1955/6), 130–2.

Notes and Queries

225. *Four Hundred Songs and Dances from the Stuart Masque. With a Supplement*, ed. A. J. Sabol, ns xxxii (1985), 526–7.

Renaissance News (Renaissance Quarterly)

226. *The Eton Choirbook I*, ed. F. Ll. Harrison, x (1957), 148–51.
227. *Four Hundred Songs and Dances from the Stuart Masque*, ed. A. J. Sabol, xxxiii (1980), 131–3.

Review of English Studies

228. *Morley's Canzonets for Three Voices*, ed. J. E. Uhler, ns x (1959), 407–9.
229. *Songs and Dances for the Stuart Masque*, ed. A. J. Sabol; *A Score for 'Lovers*

made Men': *A Masque by Ben Johnson*, ed. A. J. Sabol, ns xiv (1963), 409–10.

SOUND RECORDING REVIEW

Musical Quarterly
230. A Copland, *Our Town: Music from the Film Score*; V. Thomson, *The Plough that Broke the Plains: Orchestra Suite from the Film Score*, xxxix (1953), 307–10.

Index of Names

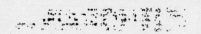